PRAISE FOR

THE PRINCESS SPY

INSTANT *NEW YORK TIMES, WALL STREET JOURNAL,*
AND *USA TODAY* BESTSELLER

"[A] real-life espionage thriller . . . Fast-paced, edgy, and highly engaging."

—*The Wall Street Journal*

"*The Princess Spy* is one of the most glamorous and thrilling espionage tales ever told."

—Vannessa Cronin, *Amazon Book Review*

"Loftis, a historian who's written two previous nonfiction spy thrillers, delivers a rich, deeply researched account of Griffith's espionage escapades."

—*The Washington Post*

"Filled with glamour, glitz, and mysterious characters . . . Sumptuous . . . A lively history of a spirited woman."

—*Kirkus Reviews*

"An entertaining biography [with a] fast-moving narrative . . . Espionage buffs will be enthralled."

—*Publishers Weekly*

"A richly detailed narrative full of twists and turns."

—*Library Journal*

"Spellbinding . . . With splashes of glamour set against dire stakes and covert operations, *The Princess Spy* is a cross between *Code Girls* and *The Only Woman in the Room*."

—BookBub

"[A] thrilling romp across twentieth-century Europe filled with intrigue and unforgettable characters, and will have any reader thinking twice about what they're revealing at their next upper-crust cocktail soiree."

—*Town & Country*

"If you enjoy reading about women doing their bit during World War II, you're going to love this."

—*Woman's Own* magazine (UK)

"[A] meticulously researched, beautifully crafted work of nonfiction that reads like a James Bond thriller."

—*Bookreporter*

"As exciting as any spy novel."

—*Daily News*

THE
PRINCESS
SPY

ALSO BY LARRY LOFTIS

Code Name: Lise
Into the Lion's Mouth

THE
PRINCESS
SPY

THE TRUE STORY OF
WORLD WAR II SPY ALINE GRIFFITH,
COUNTESS OF ROMANONES

LARRY LOFTIS

ATRIA PAPERBACK
New York   London   Toronto   Sydney   New Delhi

ATRIA
PAPERBACK

An Imprint of Simon & Schuster, Inc.
1230 Avenue of the Americas
New York, NY 10020

First Atria Paperback edition March 2022

ATRIA PAPERBACK and colophon are trademarks of Simon & Schuster, Inc.

For information about special discounts for bulk purchases, please contact Simon & Schuster Special Sales at 1-866-506-1949 or business@simonandschuster.com.

The Simon & Schuster Speakers Bureau can bring authors to your live event. For more information or to book an event, contact the Simon & Schuster Speakers Bureau at 1-866-248-3049 or visit our website at www.simonspeakers.com.

Interior design by Jill Putorti

Manufactured in the United States of America

3 5 7 9 10 8 6 4 2

Library of Congress Cataloging-in-Publication Data has been applied for.

ISBN 978-1-9821-4386-2
ISBN 978-1-9821-4387-9 (pbk)
ISBN 978-1-9821-4388-6 (ebook)

For Tom, Ann, and David Blastic
Minha amada familia ersatz

She, who appeared so beautiful a woman,
spoke without hesitating, so readily,
and with so much ease,
and sweetness both of tongue and voice,
that her good sense surprised them
no less than her beauty.

She began the history of her life,
with a clear and sedate voice,
in this manner:
"There is a place in this country
of Andalusia, from which a duke
takes a title, which makes him one
of those they call Grandees of Spain.
This duke has two sons; the elder,
heir to his estate, and in appearance,
to his virtues."

"Scarcely had he seen me,
when (as he afterwards declared)
he fell desperately in love with me,
as the proofs he then gave
of it sufficiently evinced."

—Miguel de Cervantes
Don Quixote de la Mancha (1605)

CONTENTS

Dramatis Personae   xi

Preface   xiii

Prologue   1

CHAPTER 1 Dying to Fight   3

CHAPTER 2 The Farm   11

CHAPTER 3 Close Encounters   23

CHAPTER 4 The Clerk   35

CHAPTER 5 Man of Swords   49

CHAPTER 6 Snatch-22   62

CHAPTER 7 Death by Murder   70

CHAPTER 8 Putting on the Ritz   78

CHAPTER 9 Glorious Gloria   94

CHAPTER 10 Visitors   103

CHAPTER 11 The Body   116

CHAPTER 12 Resurrection   127

CHAPTER 13 The Prisoner   135

CHAPTER 14 The Bohemian   145

CONTENTS

CHAPTER 15 The Lady Vanishes   150

CHAPTER 16 The Count   156

CHAPTER 17 Butch   167

CHAPTER 18 Pay Dirt   175

CHAPTER 19 Intelligence Goes to Ground   183

CHAPTER 20 Paris   190

CHAPTER 21 *La Tienta*   203

CHAPTER 22 The Bookkeeper   212

CHAPTER 23 *Cortando la Coleta*   221

CHAPTER 24 Countess Quintanilla   230

CHAPTER 25 Living the Dream   242

CHAPTER 26 Twin Souls   252

EPILOGUE The Rest of the Story   257

Acknowledgments   269

Notes   271

Bibliography   335

Index   349

DRAMATIS PERSONAE

OFFICE OF STRATEGIC SERVICES

General William Donovan: OSS chief (Washington)

Robert Dunev ("WILLIAMS"): chief code clerk, agent (Madrid)

Aline Griffith ("BUTCH"): code clerk, agent (Madrid)

Edmundo Lassalle ("PELOTA"): Walt Disney Company representative, agent (Barcelona, Madrid)

James MacMillan ("QUERES"): deputy station chief, financial officer (Madrid)

W. Larimer "Larry" Mellon ("LEGION"): agent, French-Spanish chain (Madrid, Barcelona)

Pierre ("PIERRE"): OSS-trained operative (identity unknown)

Frank T. Ryan ("ROYAL"): chief of Iberian Peninsula (Washington)

Whitney Shepardson: head of OSS Secret Intelligence (Washington)

H. Gregory Thomas ("ARGUS"): station chief (Madrid) and operations head, Iberian Peninsula

SPANIARDS

Casilda Arteaga: daughter of the Count of Avila

Cristóbal Balenciaga: couturier, fashion designer (Madrid, Paris, Barcelona)

Juanito Belmonte: bullfighter, son of Juan Belmonte

Álvaro de Figueroa y Torres-Sotomayor: Count of Romanones, grandfather ("*El Abuelo*")

Luis de Figueroa y Alonso-Martinez: Count of Velayos (later, of Romanones), father of Luis de Figueroa y Perez de Guzman

Luis de Figueroa y Perez de Guzman: Count of Quintanilla (later, of Velayos, Romanones)

Manolete: bullfighter

Ana de Pombo: fashion designer

GERMANS

Constantin Canaris: Abwehr agent in Madrid, nephew of Admiral Canaris

Admiral Wilhelm Canaris: head of the Abwehr (Military Intelligence)

Prince Maximilian Egon von Hohenlohe: Austrian royalty

Maria Francesca ("Pimpinela"): daughter of Prince Maximilian Egon

Hans Lazar: German press attaché (Madrid)

Princess Maria Agatha Ratibor and Corvey: German royalty

OTHERS

Barnaby Conrad: American vice-consul and bullfighter

Major William Fairbairn: OSS close-combat instructor

Gloria Rubio von Fürstenberg: Mexican socialite (Berlin, Paris, Madrid, Lisbon)

PREFACE

Hemingway said that nobody ever lives their life "all the way up" except bullfighters. He was wrong.

Spies do as well.

Their existence is an admixture of drama, intrigue, danger, and double-dealing. In most cases, a spy cannot survive without being a consummate liar.

What are we to think, then, about those World War II spies who went on to write memoirs or give interviews for biographies? Were they lying? After all, they had proven during the war that they were skilled at creating an alternate reality. For many war buffs, the testimony of spies is presumed false until proven true. If they really did that, the thinking goes, if that really happened, it would be in the files of the intelligence agency. The problem is that most of the things spies did and saw, and conversations they had, were never recorded. That should be common sense, since the last thing a spy would want is to be caught with something in writing. Even in their post-war debriefings, spies generally did not recount the details of their missions.

The historian's job, then, is essentially one of jurisprudence: applying the rules of evidence to ascertain what is credible, what is inadmissible hearsay, what is circumstantial, and so on. This is done by comparing what the spy claimed with the testimony of other primary sources (i.e., eyewitnesses), and with files found in intelligence archives.

Typically, since former spies are restricted by oaths of secrecy and classification, they don't produce memoirs until thirty or more years after their active service. And over such a stretch, memories—particularly regarding dates and details—fade. In many instances, their recollections are inaccurate, sometimes with evident embellishments.

Accordingly, many of the heroic deeds performed by Allied spies during World War II—agents who risked their lives—have been challenged by historians. And that is certainly the case with Aline Griffith, whose extraordinary experiences working for the OSS I have tried to capture in this book. A few years ago a friend mentioned her name to me and I was intrigued: a thriller-type story about an American woman who had been a spy in Spain. But there was a caveat: he wasn't sure if her story was true. I could dig into her file at the National Archives, of course, but I started with what she had written about her own life.

Aline wrote about her experience as a spy in five books—*The History of Pascualete* (1963), *The Spy Wore Red* (1987), *The Spy Went Dancing* (1990), *The Spy Wore Silk* (1991), and *The End of an Epoch* (2015)—as well as in an article ("The OSS in Spain During World War II") she submitted for inclusion in *The Secrets War: The Office of Strategic Services in World War II*, a book published by the National Archives and Records Administration in 1992.* *The History of Pascualete*, Aline's first memoir, mainly concerned her time refurbishing a historic Spanish estate owned by her husband's family. She began the book, however, with a brief introduction of how she, an American, had ended up in Spain. She had been an OSS spy in Madrid during World War II, she wrote, and it was there that she

---

*She also published a sixth book in 1994, *The Well-Mannered Assassin*, but this was a purely fictional work.

met her husband, Luis Figueroa, a member of one of Spain's most aristocratic families. What is significant about this first book is that Aline accurately stated when she had arrived in Lisbon (the layover stop en route to Madrid)—February 1944—and that her code name was BUTCH.

In 1987, after many documents relating to wartime Allied espionage in Portugal and Spain had been declassified, Aline told another version of her story in *The Spy Wore Red*, albeit with countless alterations, additions, and embellishments. In her preface she wrote that she had changed many names to protect the identities of individuals who remained active in intelligence, to avoid embarrassment of certain persons or their families, or because that person had requested anonymity.

The most important name change was the person who had recruited her, Frank Ryan, whom she refers to as "John Derby." And her boss in Spain, Madrid station chief H. Gregory Thomas, she refers to as "Phillip Harris," changing his code name from ARGUS to MOZART.

One might find it peculiar that she also changed her own code name—from BUTCH to TIGER—even though she had disclosed that it was BUTCH twenty-four years earlier in *Pascualete*. Aline explained the reason for the change in an interview: her editor wasn't crazy about "BUTCH," a less than appealing code name for a beautiful young woman operating in high-society Madrid.

Strangely, Aline also changed the date of her arrival in Europe. Hotel registrations show that she arrived in Lisbon on February 8, 1944, as she had stated in *Pascualete*, but twenty-four years later in *The Spy Wore Red*, she wrote that she arrived in late December 1943. Did she forget? Did she not consult her own prior book to make sure she had the dates correct? Apparently not.

But Aline's mix-up of dates isn't really significant. The bigger question I wanted to answer was whether she fictionalized or embellished all or most of her exploits. If she did, I realized, I'd have to find another spy to write about.

During my initial research I was particularly concerned by the claims of Nigel West, author of scores of books about World War II espionage, that Aline had made everything up. He asserted that Aline had been only an OSS clerk, and not an actual agent.*

West's assertion struck me as odd, though. If Aline had lied about being an agent, wouldn't a number of her OSS colleagues have refuted her story? And why would two of her books have carried endorsements by two former CIA directors? It's unlikely that both William Casey (himself a former OSS agent who had known Aline during the war) and William Colby would have been supportive if they suspected her books were pure fiction.** Casey, in fact, seemed to go out of his way to assure readers of the veracity of Aline's story: on the inside cover of *The Spy Wore Red* he wrote, "Her narrative reflects sensitively and accurately the clandestine intrigue and strategic maneuvers that marked the struggle between the secret services . . . in wartime Spain."

After poring over OSS records—including every word in Aline's files—during a four-day marathon at the National Archives and Records Administration in College Park, Maryland, and reviewing published and unpublished memoirs and letters from Aline's Madrid station colleagues, I came to four conclusions:

1. Aline had in fact trained at The Farm (an OSS school for prospective agents), was a code clerk in the Madrid station from February 1944 until August 15, 1945 (when the OSS office closed), and was a field agent from February 1945 to August 15, 1945.
2. She was a highly productive and valuable agent, producing some fifty-nine field reports, far more than any other Madrid agent, and had more subagents working for her than anyone other than possibly the station chief, Gregory

---

*Nigel West, *Historical Dictionary of Sexpionage*, 326.

**Casey was CIA director from 1981 to 1987. Colby was director from 1973 to 1976.

Thomas, or Larry Mellon, who was supervisor of the French-Spanish escape chains.

3. She imagined numerous events and murders in her three espionage memoirs.

4. Her overall story was quite legitimate, and one killing she mentioned was not only true (I confirmed it with the person who actually handled the corpse), but shocking in its violence.

So there's no question that Aline was an active, highly valued operational agent, but her spy books must be regarded as historical fiction; some parts are true, many others not. What you will find in *The Princess Spy*, then, is what I believe—based upon OSS records and other historical sources—actually happened in wartime Madrid.

And as with all of my books, every word of dialogue found in the text is a direct quote from a primary source, all of which are documented in the endnotes.

Larry Loftis
February 1, 2020

PROLOGUE

It was probably the wind.

Gusts seemed to be blowing all the time in Madrid. Besides, Aline told herself, no one knew where she lived. While her apartment was on the list of safe houses for agents coming through the French-Spanish escape line, no one had yet used it.

She glanced at herself in the mirror, pleased with the way she looked in her red silk dress. Edmundo was picking her up at ten for a cocktail party, and then they were going to La Reboite for dancing. Flamenco would probably start around eleven, and her dress was perfect for all the spinning and turning.

But what about that man who seemed to be following me on the street a few days ago? she asked herself. *He certainly knows where I live.*

She twisted out her lipstick and began to apply it. Yes, that man was disturbing, as were the footsteps she'd heard echoing behind her several times when she'd come home late from the office. Then again, she'd only seen the man's back, and the footsteps the other nights could have been those of the neighborhood night watchman. Besides, it would be impossible for anyone to get on the roof and—

There it is again.

The shutters.

Aline froze for a moment and listened. Everything was still. She was imagining things. Wind blows, shutters creak. She put her lipstick in her purse.

And again.

No doubt this time. Shutters don't creak like that from the wind. Someone was prying them open.

Quietly, she eased back the vanity drawer and removed her pistol. This was precisely the reason for all those endless exercises at The Farm—the shooting in the dark and around corners. She was a good shot, too, although she'd never practiced with this much adrenaline surging through her veins.

The window was in the adjoining salon and she'd have to be careful not to be silhouetted by the moonlight streaming in from her bedroom window. She flipped off the gun's safety and tiptoed into the hallway.

Her breathing was shallow and fast and she prayed her hand would be steady.

Slowly, she began sliding along the wall, edging closer within the shadows.

As she approached the opening to the salon there was another creak and then she saw it.

A man's hand pushing back the curtain.

She raised the gun.

CHAPTER 1

DYING TO FIGHT

May 24, 1941
Estoril, Portugal

The American checked in and surveyed his luxurious surroundings. Estoril's Palacio, Portugal's finest, was everything he had heard: an opulent five-star hotel and resort with a golf course, spa, and Europe's largest casino, all situated alongside the gleaming Tamariz Beach. Royalty often visited here, creating Estoril's reputation as the Portuguese Riviera, and with Portugal's neutrality during the war, many were here now, enjoying the town's safety, beauty, and amenities.

The clerk mumbled in broken English about a form for foreign guests and asked his occupation. Thinking of something generic, he said "businessman" and watched as the clerk wrote *comerciante* on the form.

Stepping away from the registration desk, he could see the pool and terrace tables through the full-length windows. To his right was the Palacio bar, small but handsomely appointed. If the rumors were true, many of its patrons were spies, which meant he'd have to frequent it nightly.

His cover was sound as he had no ostensible reason to be here; America wasn't in the war, after all, and he couldn't be suspected of being a spook since the US had no intelligence agency. He wasn't even in the military. For all practical purposes, he was a ghost.

His name was Frank T. Ryan.

What he was up to was off the record but vitally important to US national interests. And his timing couldn't have been better. British Naval Intelligence officer Ian Fleming had checked in to the Palacio four days earlier. German press attaché Hans Lazar—the most powerful Nazi in Spain—would arrive two weeks later.

Frank Timothy Ryan's Palacio Hotel registration, May 24, 1941. *Cascais Archive*

Meanwhile, an ocean away in rural New York, a tall young woman who had just graduated from the College of Mount Saint Vincent was searching for employment. She had the good looks of a model or actress, but her small town didn't offer those kinds of jobs. Born May 22, 1920, in Pearl River, New York, Marie Aline Griffith was the eldest of six children. Her mother and father also had been born in Pearl River, a hamlet located twenty miles north of midtown Manhattan.

Founded in 1870 by Julius Braunsdorf, a German immigrant who had relocated his Aetna Sewing Machine Company there, the town began to flourish some twenty-two years later when Aline's grandfather, Talbot C. Dexter, moved his Dexter Folder Company into Braunsdorf's building. Dexter had invented and patented a machine that changed the way that books, newspapers, and magazines were assembled.

During Aline's childhood Pearl River was a Norman Rockwell town, with four Main Street attractions: Schumacher's grocery, Rowan's butcher, Sandford's drugstore, and the First National Bank. There was one school—the Pearl River School—and Aline would see no other classrooms until she left for college.

Aline's father managed the Dexter factory and her mother was a homemaker. Their house, situated less than a thousand feet from the Pascack Valley Line, allowed Aline to see and hear the train as it whistled by, twice in the morning and twice in the evening, on its way to and from Manhattan.

Pearl River as Aline knew it during her childhood. The Griffith home was located in the wooded section about where the center of the north-pointing arrow is located. Directly above "Pearl River" the rendering shows the Braunsdorf-Dexter factory where her father worked, and to the right of "Pearl River" the local train can be seen heading into town.

Even in the 1930s and 1940s, Pearl River felt like a town somehow suspended in an earlier time, and some of Aline's schoolteachers had taught her mother. Crime was virtually nonexistent here, but there wasn't much to do other than stroll to the park or hike in the woods. In an effort to promote business and commercial construction, Pearl River branded itself "The Town of Friendly People." Indeed, it *was* a friendly town—a nice, quiet place to raise a family—but when Aline graduated from high school, she couldn't get out fast enough. She was seventeen, yet she knew nothing of the outside world. Life was ticking by, and she was determined to broaden her small-town horizons.

Hoping to attend a university that had football games and dances, Aline was a bit disappointed when her parents chose for her a less exciting alternative: Mount Saint Vincent. It was a Catholic girls' school with the regimen of the Marines: lights out at ten o'clock. It was also in the Bronx, a less than appealing college town.

The adventure Aline had been hoping for seemed far away.

In the summers she found convenient, mundane jobs. After her sophomore year, she worked as a supervisor at Rockland State Hospital, and after her junior year she worked as a secretary for Manny Rooney, a Pearl River attorney. She wasn't quite sure what she wanted to do after graduation, but events soon conspired to create the opportunity she was looking for. During her final semester, the winter of 1941, the Japanese bombed Pearl Harbor, and her younger brothers went off to war almost immediately, Dexter as a fighter pilot in England and Tommy as a submariner in the South Pacific. Aline knew that as a woman she couldn't be a soldier but felt that nothing short of joining the war effort in some manner would fulfill her patriotic longing to do her part. Throughout December she searched for a way to help, but without success.

After the New Year she found employment, but it was a far cry from military service. At five foot nine, slender, and beautiful, Aline was perfectly suited for modeling, so she took a job with Hattie Carnegie in New York City. It was a dream job for any young woman, as Hattie was one of the top fashion designers in the country, but it wasn't Aline's dream.

While Aline wouldn't have known it, Hattie Carnegie was an American success story. When her father died in 1902, thirteen-year-old Henrietta Kanengeiser commenced her business career as a messenger for Macy's. Two years later she began modeling, and in 1909 she launched her own custom clothing business, having changed her last name to Carnegie, a nod to Andrew Carnegie, the wealthiest man in America. Just a few years later Hattie opened her own store just off Park Avenue and was traveling to Paris annually in search of the latest fashions.

From Hattie, Aline would learn not only fashion, but poise, composure, and how to mingle at high-society events—skills that would come in handy later in situations with much higher stakes.

For eighteen months Aline modeled each season's new dresses, parading down runways as if she'd been trained in Paris. But the fittings, makeup, hair styling, and glitz of fashion were the last things she wanted. She was grateful for the work but there was a war going on, and what she was doing on a daily basis seemed almost sinful compared to the sacrifices others were making.

In August 1943 one of her friends, Amy Porter, invited her to a dinner party. Amy was dating a wealthy young man named John whom she hoped to marry, and she wanted to introduce Aline to John's brother Frank, who was coming to town. Frank was in his midthirties, Amy said, and he was flying in from somewhere overseas.

Overseas. Perhaps he'd have firsthand knowledge about the war, Aline thought.

The dinner was at John's apartment in Manhattan, and along with Frank, Amy, and Aline, two of John's colleagues from Standard Oil had been invited. The oilmen sat to Aline's left, Frank to her right. His suit was immaculate and looked hand-tailored, suggesting Wall Street or Madison Avenue. He had light blue eyes, a square, intelligent-looking face, and thin lips. His neck and jaw were thick like a wrestler's, but he had an easy smile. He was handsome, she reckoned, in a college professor sort of way.

As the night wore on the men bantered endlessly about the war, going back and forth about Patton and Rommel, Hitler and

Roosevelt. Aline noticed that Frank was polite but a bit aloof, as if preoccupied with more important matters. He also didn't seem to express any romantic interest in her, which was something of a relief.

When the conversation lulled, Frank turned to her, smiling.

"Are you planning to become a famous model?"

The question caught Aline off guard, but she realized that John must have told Frank that she worked for Hattie Carnegie.

Aline smirked. "Not if I can help it."

"Really? And why is that?"

"I want to get into the war—overseas."

Frank suggested that she could become a nurse, but Aline brushed it off, saying that training to become a nurse would take years. She wanted to get into the war *now*, she said, and in Europe where the real fighting was.

"Now, why on earth would an attractive girl like you, safe and sound here in New York, want to go abroad to become embroiled in a bloody massacre? Someplace where your life could be in danger?"

Aline shrugged. "I love adventure. I like taking risks. All the men I know are eager to get over there. Why should it seem strange that a woman wants to also?"

Frank ignored the rhetorical question and probed about Aline's romantic life. Did she have someone she was in love with? Was she about to get married?

The inquiries were a little personal, Aline thought, but she answered that no, she wasn't in love—not that it should make any difference about what she could or could not do for her country.

"Do you know any foreign languages?"

Aline replied that she had majored in French and minored in Spanish.

Frank flashed his easy smile. "Well, Miss Griffith, if you're really serious about a job overseas, there's a slight possibility I can help. If you should happen to hear from a Mr. Tomlinson, you'll know what it's about."

Aline returned the smile with a glimmer of hope, but at the same time she didn't expect much. Frank hadn't said who Mr. Tomlinson was, or even taken her number, so how serious could he be?

At the very least, though, she felt she'd made a new friend in Frank Ryan.

About two weeks later Aline's father mentioned that their bank had received an inquiry of some sort about them. Her mother thought it probably had to do with their boys now that they were in the service, but her dad worried the investigation might be connected to business.

But when they heard nothing more about it, it slipped from their minds. Then, on the last day of September, Aline received a long-distance call.

"This is Mr. Tomlinson," the man said in a deep voice. "Can you be free for a few minutes tomorrow?"

Aline said she could.

"Then please be in the Biltmore Hotel lobby, at six o'clock. A man with a white carnation in his lapel will be looking for you. Don't mention this meeting to anyone."

At the appointed hour Aline was at the hotel. Soldiers in crisp uniforms were buzzing in and out, a few at the bar having their last drinks before shipping out. After several minutes a distinguished silver-haired man in an expensive suit—duly adorned with a white carnation—greeted her without mentioning his name. He motioned to a quiet alcove where they could talk.

He said he worked for the War Department, and that they might have some work that could interest her. He couldn't tell her exactly what the work would entail, though, until she had passed some tests. He had a calm, soothing demeanor that put Aline at ease, and he seemed to take it for granted that Aline would be interested.

"Would I work overseas?"

The man nodded. "If you succeed in the tests, yes. Can you come to Washington within ten days? It will mean taking leave from your job. You may never go back, if all goes well."

Aline said she could.

He thumbed through a date book and told her she'd need to arrive in Washington on November 1. Handing her a card with a phone number and address to give to her parents, he explained that she would not be at that location, but that calls and messages would be forwarded to her.

"Tell your family you're being interviewed by the War Department for a job. Bring a suitcase of clothes suitable for the country. Remove all labels. Carry nothing with your initials, nor papers or letters with your name. No one must be able to identify anything about you."

He gave her a second card with a different address and told her this was where she was to arrive, no later than noon. "Go directly to the Q Building. Give a false name and home address to the receptionist."

With that he bid her good luck and was gone.

CHAPTER 2

THE FARM

August 17, 1943
Mexico City

Edmundo Lassalle mailed his résumé to Dr. James Hamilton, still mystified over exactly what the Office of Strategic Services did. From his conversation with Hamilton the day before, he understood the position would entail work abroad—perhaps in Latin America or Spain—and Lassalle felt sure his credentials were as good as anyone's.

Born in San Cristóbal, Mexico, in 1914, Edmundo had graduated from the National University of Mexico in 1934—after only two years—at the age of twenty. In addition to his native Spanish, he could read and speak French and Italian, and read Portuguese. So that he might add English to the list, he enrolled at Columbia University in the fall of 1935, but soon thereafter he was offered a scholarship and a part-time teaching position at the University of California. He excelled at Berkeley, graduating Phi Beta Kappa in 1938. Following his path toward a career in academia, he remained at Cal to pursue a doctorate in history.

That path was interrupted in 1940, however, when he was offered a job in Washington at the Pan American Union (forerunner of the Organization of American States, or OAS). He wasn't a US citizen at the time, but the position was open to citizens of Union member countries, which included Mexico, and he was appointed special assistant to the Division of Intellectual Cooperation. The job was something of an academic-diplomatic hybrid, and within his first year he published two white papers: "Higher Education in Argentina" and "The Araucanians."

His work did not go unnoticed. In the fall of 1941 he was offered a position with the Office of the Coordinator of Inter-American Affairs (later to become the Office for Inter-American Affairs, or OIAA). Few had heard of the organization, which was loosely affiliated with the US State Department, but the young man running it was Nelson Rockefeller, grandson of Standard Oil founder John D. Rockefeller.

The agency's principal function was to distribute news, films, advertising, and radio broadcasts in Latin America to counter German propaganda, and Edmundo's job—commencing January 19, 1942—was to advise on implementation regarding Mexico. Since the OIAA had set up a special division for producing radio and motion pictures propaganda, Edmundo consulted often with the main contractor, the Walt Disney Company.*

In March, Edmundo gained US citizenship, and in April he received a promotion and a raise. In spite of the terrific work and high-profile contacts, though, he chafed at what he felt was Rockefeller's top-down, Aristotelian management, believing that the director paid little attention to the counsel of the organization's Latino staffers. After a year Edmundo had had enough and began looking for other employment.

Edmundo's conversation with Dr. Hamilton on August 16 suggested that the position with the Office of Strategic Services had real promise. In his cover letter accompanying his résumé, Edmundo highlighted his credentials:

---

*Walt Disney Productions produced several films for the OIAA, including the highly successful *Saludos Amigos*, released in 1942.

My [OIAA] office has been mainly devoted to research, the ap-praisal and preparation of propaganda material and the handling of confidential projects concerning Latin America. . . . I believe I can satisfactorily perform any assignment which your office may require in any place where Spanish is important; however, I have knowledge of Italian, French and Portuguese.

The references he gave were impressive: Dr. Enrique de Lozado, his OIAA supervisor, and one Henry A. Wallace, vice president of the United States.

For more than a month Edmundo heard nothing. Then in October, while in Hollywood for business, he was summoned back to Washington for an urgent meeting. It wasn't the OIAA calling, though; he was supposed to meet with someone from Dr. Hamilton's office.

Someone named Frank Ryan.

November 1, 1943
Washington, DC

When Aline arrived at the Q Building, 2430 E Street, she was not impressed. Unlike most of Washington's grand structures, the building was single-story and appeared prefabricated. It seemed a most unlikely place from which to launch a top-secret mission.

As she'd been instructed, she gave a false name and the receptionist escorted her to the office where she was to be interviewed. The walls were bare and gray, like a hospital, and from what she could tell the filing cabinets were built into some kind of safe. Military security, perhaps. The man behind the desk, though, gave her a start; sitting there like a seasoned bureaucrat was none other than Frank Ryan, her old dinner date.

Ryan greeted her warmly and asked her to have a seat.

"Your first trip to Washington, isn't it?"

Aline could feel her heart thumping as she nodded. "Almost the farthest I've ever been from home."

"There is nothing I can tell you today about your work," Ryan said, folding his hands. "The most I can do is to warn you to be very careful never to say anything about yourself. You are going to be tested in many ways to see how you adapt to new situations. From now on no one can know anything about you, whether you are American or European, whether you have lived in one country or another. Your success depends entirely on yourself and your ability to learn and to preserve secrecy."

Ryan's voice was low and calm, and with the same deadly serious-ness as the man at the Biltmore. "From this minute on," he added, "you may be followed. And where you will be living, your colleagues may go through your belongings searching for clues to your identity."

He handed her a small slip of yellow paper. "Here are your in-structions. Remember—you may be followed every moment from now on."

Aline glanced at the paper, which revealed an address somewhere in Maryland, outside of Washington, DC. Ryan told her to go to the Hay Adams Hotel and wait at the main entrance for a black Chevrolet sedan—license number TX16248. She was then to ask, "Is this Mr. Tom's car?"

Ryan stood and showed her to the door. "Destroy it afterward," he said, motioning to the paper. "It's a luxury for beginners."

Suitcase in hand, Aline hustled out of the building and then it dawned on her: she had no idea where the Hay Adams Hotel was. Remembering Ryan's warning about being followed, she strolled three blocks, went into a store, called the hotel for directions, and hailed a taxi.

Minutes later the car turned into the circular drive leading to the hotel's portico. The Hay Adams looked just like a government building—a hulking cube built out of the city's ubiquitous gray granite blocks—and was a hive of activity. Bellmen and porters were scurrying about loading and unloading guests' luggage.

Aline got out and scanned the driveway for the black Chevrolet. A bellboy suddenly appeared at her side and tried to take her suitcase. She jerked it back, unsure of what to tell him. She had never stayed at a hotel before and wasn't sure of the protocol. Did bellboys automatically take everyone's luggage?

Brushing him aside, she again searched for the car and found it. As she checked the tag—it was the right one—two men jumped in and the chauffeur started the motor.

"Stop! Stop!" Aline yelled. "I'm supposed to go with you."

"What's your name?"

Aline started to answer but caught herself. "Is this Mr. Tom's car?"

With that the driver took her bag, put it in the trunk and they were off.

The men sitting next to her—a middle-aged man with thinning brown hair and a younger man by the door whose face she couldn't see—didn't say a word, and Aline figured it was best not to greet them or engage in small talk. The car headed east out of the city and after some time she checked her watch. They had been driving for forty minutes and were now on a two-lane country road surrounded by woods. Fleeting thoughts of being kidnapped came and went, but she reminded herself that Frank Ryan was legit, whatever he was up to.

From her seat in the back, Aline noticed that the driver constantly checked the rearview mirror to make sure they weren't being followed.

Some twenty miles south of the capitol they arrived at their destination: Lothian Farm. A 100-acre campus near Clinton, Maryland, it served as an OSS training facility and was officially known as RTU-11. Unofficially, it was just called The Farm.

Aline peered out at a large white house set atop a hill. It was surrounded by woods, and the red, yellow, and brown foliage made the entire estate look like something out of *Town & Country*. A chorus of chirping birds greeted them and she sighed at the tranquil setting, until another noise caught her attention. She cocked her head.

Was that gunfire?

The driver pulled up to the entrance and an army officer met them at the door.

"I'm Captain Williams," he said. "Welcome to The Farm."

As the captain greeted their party, Aline finally got a look at the man who had been blocked from her view in the car. He was simply the most handsome man she had ever seen. He was athletic-looking with thick black hair, skin darkened by the sun, and brooding brown eyes.

Captain Williams seemed to know him, addressing him as "Pierre." It was a name she'd not soon forget.

After the introductions—aliases, Aline presumed—they were led inside. The farmhouse, while spacious, was no country club. Suspended from the ceiling were models of German warplanes and tanks, and along the walls and in every corner were life-size dummies of German, Italian, and Japanese soldiers of various ranks. This was a war college, it seemed, and she wondered if she'd be tested on enemy equipment and uniforms.

Models of German soldiers used at The Farm. *NARA*

Dinner was at six, Williams informed them, and there would be a meeting for new recruits in the library afterward. Turning to a sergeant, he said, "Why don't you take this young lady's suitcase and show her to her room."

The sergeant grabbed Aline's bag and escorted her upstairs. The room was small and spartan, with twin beds, a single bureau, and two small chairs. A young woman with a gaunt face and thick lashes peered up from one of the beds and set a book aside. Aline paused to allow the sergeant to introduce them, but he placed her suitcase on the floor and left.

She glanced at the open bunk.

"Not a word you don't want overheard," the woman said with a distinct French accent. She nodded toward the bed. Below the headrest, Aline saw, was a microphone.

It was a trick the OSS had learned from their big brother, Britain's secret service agency, MI6. Their ally across the pond had had a two-year head start in the intelligence game, and their training schools at Wansborough and Beaulieu served as models for OSS training. A serious danger for any spy, the British had learned, was the proclivity to talk in one's sleep. So MI6 and the Special Operations Executive (SOE), Britain's sabotage-espionage outfit, tested recruits to see if they did, and if so, in what language. The OSS followed suit.

Someone would be listening to Aline throughout the night, every night. If she talked in her sleep, she would be dismissed.

That evening during dinner Aline noticed that she and her roommate were the only women among some dozen male recruits, all of whom looked like seasoned soldiers. How would she compete against *them*? She was the youngest by far and had scarcely seen anything outside of sleepy Pearl River. Even her roommate was years her senior and had a worldly look about her.

When dinner was over, the group made their way into the library. A crackling fire gave the room a warm amber glow, and

Captain Williams was leaning against a desk, apparently sizing them up.

"You're probably wondering where you are," he said when everyone was seated, "and what you are here for." He paused, scanning their faces. "You are in the first school of espionage in the United States, and you are here to be made into spies."

Spies? Aline stirred.

Williams explained that they were being trained for work with an organization called the Office of Strategic Services, or OSS, run by a man named General William Donovan.* There were two main sections, he said, Operations and Intelligence. Operations included sabotage, raids, supply drops, and organization of Resistance groups. The intelligence arm involved secret intelligence (SI)—gathering information about the enemy—and counterintelligence (X-2), operations to thwart enemy intelligence. It seemed clear to Aline that she wasn't being trained to be a commando, so the only question was whether she was being considered for intelligence or counterintelligence.

The course would last several weeks, Williams went on, and some would not make it. "For a few," he said, "your memory won't be sharp enough. Or your responses too slow. Or the fatigue will grind you down—I'd better tell you right now you're going to be put through some pretty rough tests—and you're going to have to follow every order whether you like it or not. You're going to have to be a champ just when you think you're too tired to stay awake another minute—and then you'll have to make split-second decisions."

If anyone didn't like what they had heard, Williams added, they were free to leave. "As long as you sign a paper and swear under oath never to repeat a word you've heard in this room, you can leave now and be driven back to Washington in an hour. And forget you were ever here."

---

*President Franklin D. Roosevelt had established the Coordinator of Information on July 11, 1941, appointing Donovan as its head, which then became the OSS on June 13, 1942.

Aline scanned the room. No one moved.

Williams nodded and told them to turn in early and get a good night's sleep.

"It may be your last."

Class began promptly at eight thirty the next morning and Captain Williams introduced their instructor for the day only as "our friend." His uniform indicated that he, too, was a captain, but his name and background were not mentioned.

"The first thing you'd better get into your heads," the man began, "is that this is a *secret* intelligence agency, not a public information service. The intelligence we provide to the military is *top* secret. Know what that means? It means you can be shot just for knowing it yourself. In other words, one ear doesn't even tell the other."

Now the aliases and mystery with meetings and travel made sense, Aline thought. It also explained the international aspect of her group. In addition to Americans, several of the men in her group were French, one or two were German, one was perhaps Belgian, and two seemed to be from somewhere in Eastern Europe.

The instructor went on: "We're here to save lives. That will be our prime effort. The information our agents obtain of the enemy's forces, their coastal emplacements, their troop movements, road-blocks, antiaircraft guns, their mines—together with knowledge of their intentions—all indispensable."

Over the next two hours Aline learned about security abroad, and how to protect and preserve her cover, followed by two hours in basic cipher. The afternoon brought the first round of weapons training in a field behind the house. There she was introduced to the .45 semiautomatic—the most lethal pistol in existence at the time—which was heavy and bulky and intimidating. She fired at the bull's-eye and missed the target completely, hitting a tree next to it.

The damn thing was too big for her small hand, and it kicked like a mule.

She fired again. And again. And again. Her hand began to ache and it seemed the muscles throughout her body were traumatized, yet she actually enjoyed it. Something about the power, the sound, the concussion, the smell; even the competition with the other recruits was exhilarating.

After dinner the group watched a training film and then had a short class in mapping. Even then, they were not yet finished. Before turning in they had one more class: fighting knife. *Unarmed.*

Stories about their instructor, Major William Fairbairn, had already circulated among the students. He was a legend, something of a celebrity even. Given his reputation, Aline was surprised to see that the man didn't *look* lethal. He was older and quite thin. But Fairbairn's unassuming appearance was deceiving.

At fifty-eight, he was one of the most dangerous men in the world. For thirty years he had served with the Shanghai Municipal Police, founding its riot squad and rising to the rank of assistant commissioner. Shanghai was a city of gangs, thugs, and drug dealers at the time, and Fairbairn was rumored to have been in more than six hundred street fights. The scars on his torso, arms, and hands bore evidence of countless knife fights, and he had even co-developed his own blade, the Fairbairn-Sykes fighting knife.* Between 1927 and 1940, he had trained all US Marines stationed in China. The man was a force.

Aline paid close attention, learning—among other things—how to turn a newspaper into a dagger. Hopefully it would be a skill she'd not need.

Day two brought classes on how to acquire and report secret intelligence, as well as how to recruit and handle subagents. After lunch it was another two hours with Major Fairbairn for close combat training.

The more Aline watched this man, the more intimidating he be-

---

*A double-edged stiletto used by the British SAS and adopted by the OSS. It remains in use today by many commando and special forces units around the world.

came. He had been nicknamed "Dangerous Dan" and "The Shanghai Buster" by British commandos he had trained, and the monikers were apt. He had trained under the founder of judo, Kanō Jigorō, and held a second-degree black belt. He had also trained extensively in jujitsu, boxing, savate, and other styles and had molded them into a ruthless combat system he called "Defendu." When his book by that name came out in 1926, Fairbairn was dubbed the "father of hand-to-hand combat."

The rest of the week brought more cipher and mapping instruction, chain organization, surveillance, and weapons practice. In addition to the .45, they practiced with a .30-caliber carbine and a Thompson submachine gun.

In the late afternoons the recruits were allowed "recreation," but this was hardly the school or YMCA version. Aline and her roommate, together with the men, jumped stone walls, waded through muddy streams, and crawled through weeds and underbrush. On several occasions, just when she thought she couldn't make it, Pierre appeared at her side to encourage her.

"Come on," he said one day, "only two more hurdles to go. Don't get discouraged. You're doing fine."

Often, when she felt she couldn't move another inch, Pierre pushed or pulled her to the finish line.

The second week brought more classes in close combat, weapons, mapping, and coding, and added instruction about German and Japanese intelligence, counterintelligence, searches, reporting, demolition, and booby traps. Another new class Aline found particularly interesting was lockpicking. The rumor was that their instructor, "George," had been released from prison to teach the class, and it was believable because he also taught pickpocketing and safecracking. His real name, appropriately enough, was Lieutenant Compton Crook.

A huge, gangling man, George explained the significance of the training, telling the group: "Before you get your hands on the enemy, you have to break into his house." He grinned and added, "Once you've broken into his house, you can break into his safe."

Intelligence classes were equally compelling. In one session Aline was shown several slides of faces with corresponding biographical data; seconds later the faces would reappear without the text and she'd have to supply the missing details. Then there were slides of maps of various places: towns, landmarks, and rivers would be shown, each with names; then the slides would be flashed again with nothing and Aline would have to recall the names.

One day during close combat practice, Aline and Pierre were paired. Again and again throughout the exercise they were in close physical contact, and when Pierre took her hands to help her up from the ground after a throw, she felt a charge of electricity pass between them.

There was something about this dark, handsome man that Aline found intriguing. And dangerous.

He was the only student who seemed completely at ease with the training, she noticed, as though he'd already been through it before.

CHAPTER 3

CLOSE ENCOUNTERS

On the morning of Saturday, November 13, Aline joined the other recruits in exercises—push-ups, sit-ups, and light jujitsu—and then was back on the shooting range trying to get comfortable with the bulky .45. It had just begun to drizzle when she noticed that Captain Williams was standing a few feet behind her with an umbrella. He motioned for her to follow him and they walked back to the farmhouse.

She needed to change her clothes, he said, because she was once again going to Washington. "You have a meeting this afternoon with Royal."

Royal? Aline waited for him to elaborate, but he said nothing more. When she arrived back at the Q Building in downtown Washington, DC, she discovered that "Royal" was none other than Frank Ryan.

"Well, Butch," he said, "you've fared better than some of us expected."

Aline raised an eyebrow, and Ryan informed her that "Butch" was her new code name, which she would use in the field. And oh, by the way, he added, she would be going to Spain.

"Then I have passed the tests?"

"Yes, but you will need more preparation before we can send you over there. Apart from the normal routine, you will have to study up on your destination. In the library at The Farm there is abundant information on the countries where our agents will be sent. You must become familiar with Spain's geography and history, and be able to recognize the current political personalities."

Ryan explained that she would be assigned to SI—Secret Intelligence—and that her posting was an extremely important one since Spain was critical to Allied success in the war. "On the surface," he said, "the country declares itself neutral. Politically, emotionally, it is aligned with Hitler. Spain is precarious, volatile. Franco won his civil war with German and Italian money [and] troops."

Aline had studied the Spanish Civil War in college and remembered that King Alfonso XIII had abandoned the throne in 1931 because of violent uprisings. Municipal elections on April 12 of that year had brought a fierce competition between the "republicans"—a coalition of communists, socialists, and anarchists—and candidates supporting the monarchy. While the republicans won a majority of votes in Madrid and the large cities, the monarchists dominated the smaller towns and countryside. The monarchists assumed they had won enough seats to control the government, and thus protect the monarchy,* but in Madrid crowds began to gather in the streets. Republican leaders advised the king's ministers that King Alfonso should leave the capital "before sunset" to avoid bloodshed, and he capitulated.

The republican government that assumed power was seen by the monarchists as illegal, and they were further incensed when republican mobs began to burn churches. Incredibly, the scenario seemed to repeat itself in the 1936 elections. The republicans won by the slimmest of margins and their opponents on the right, a "nationalist" coalition of the aristocracy, Catholic Church, military, and the fascist Falangists, believed that the vote tabulation was again improper. Not long after this a nationalist politician was assassinated

---

*On the evening of April 14, 1931, 29,953 monarchists had been elected, while only 8,855 Republican candidates had been elected.

by civil guards and this event seemed to ignite the brewing powder keg.

The nationalists revolted and their movement soon came under the control of General Francisco Franco. Both sides received substantial foreign military aid (republicans from the Russians, nationalists from the Germans), Ryan said, and both sides were guilty of countless atrocities. After a bloody three-year civil war, the nationalists prevailed and Franco was named Spain's Generalissimo and Head of State.

And while Franco held total power as a military dictator, he was nevertheless walking a tightrope. He was, first and foremost, a Spaniard and a Catholic. He wanted no part of the atheism that communism and Nazism brought, nor the destruction of Spanish culture that would surely occur if Spain became a satellite of Russia or Germany. Like most Spaniards, he wanted a truly independent Spain. But he knew that a neutrality without lip service and a few concessions to Germany would provoke Hitler to invade the country to gain control of Gibraltar, and thus the Mediterranean. So Franco apparently felt that he had little choice but to appease Hitler to keep German troops on the French side of the Pyrenees.

His first concession, in August 1941, was the creation of the Blue Division—a contingent of 45,000 Spanish troops—which fought within the German Army on the Eastern Front.

Another concession, Ryan explained, involved shipments of wolframite, the key ingredient in the manufacture of tungsten, an alloy needed for tanks, bullets, and other military assets. Ironically, only Portugal and Spain—both neutral countries—were sources for wolframite, and they supplied both the Allies and the Germans.

"Spain is still a jumble of factions," Ryan went on. He explained that many of those on the losing side of the Spanish Civil War were diehard communists, and yet some of them became close American allies because of their hatred of Germany.

And there was one more thing, he said, that created a bit of intrigue. "Admiral Canaris, the head of German intelligence, the

Abwehr,* is a close friend of Franco and visits him regularly. Himmler** is trying to discredit Canaris with Hitler, claiming Canaris influences Franco not to join the Axis. We are anxious that Himmler not eliminate Canaris from his job because our agents in other countries inform us that Canaris*** is backing plots to assassinate Hitler."

With that, Ryan placed before her something she needed to sign: the OSS oath of office.

Aline's Oath of Office, signed November 13, 1943. *NARA*

---

*The Abwehr was German *military* intelligence. The Nazi party had their own intelligence branch called the Sicherheitsdienst (SD), directed by Ernst Kaltenbrunner. The head of the SD's foreign intelligence arm, whom Aline would later see in Madrid, was Walter Schellenberg.

**Heinrich Himmler, head of the SS, Hitler's private Nazi army.

***Admiral Wilhelm Canaris would later be arrested and executed for his part in the July 20, 1944, attempt to assassinate Hitler.

Aline signed it and Ryan had it notarized.

Meanwhile, Ryan was working to secure the agent who would eventually be teaming up with her in Madrid: Edmundo Lassalle. Edmundo was eager to start, but his cover as the Walt Disney Company's representative on the Iberian Peninsula was still being worked out. First, the OSS would have to hire Edmundo as a civilian, matching his rank and $4,600 annual OIAA salary. Then two contracts would have to be signed: one for Lassalle's employment with Disney, and one between the OSS and Disney whereby the OSS would secretly reimburse Disney for Edmundo's salary and expenses. Once both contracts were signed, Edmundo would be terminated by the OSS and begin his new job. In reality, though, Edmundo would be burning the candle at both ends, since the OSS and Disney both expected real, full-time work.

Messy, but Lassalle's position was critical and it was important that he have an impeccable cover.

Back at The Farm, Aline began week three of her training. She and the other recruits reviewed everything again, but with added pressure. In the weapons class, they now had to disassemble and reassemble—in the dark—Allied and enemy weapons. At the range, they had to stand alongside targets while others practiced so they'd get the "feel" of being fired upon. But the fun was just beginning. Midweek, Captain Williams called her into his office.

"Ready for a couple of trial missions?"

Aline said she was. The prior two weeks had been a blur of Morse code, cipher, surveillance, maps, weapons, and close combat, but she was confident and anxious to test her skills.

"Tomorrow morning at eight," the captain said, "you'll be driven to Union Station, from which you'll catch the twelve o'clock Penn Central to Richmond, Virginia. You have six hours to deliver this message." He handed her an envelope and continued: "Return to Washington on the five o'clock train and you will be met at the station."

He held up a paper. "Memorize this."

Aline saw a name and address for a second and then Williams crumpled it in his hand.

"Your objective," he added, "is to deliver the envelope without its being . . . interrupted, confiscated."

The Penn Central train was crowded, but it took Aline only a few minutes after departure to spot him.

Losing a tag was simple if your timing was good, and she decided to use the oldest trick in the book. When the conductor announced that Fredericksburg was the next stop, Aline slipped into the rest-room. She could feel the train slowing, and then stopping as the conductor announced the arrival.

She waited.

When the train started rolling again, she threw open the lavatory door, bolted for the exit, and jumped onto the platform. Turning back she saw that her tag had not had time to follow. She had lost him, but her exit created a new problem: how was she to get to Rich-mond on time? There wasn't another train until four thirty, and no buses until after that. She was carrying little money—certainly not enough for a taxi—which left only one option.

She hitchhiked.

When she finally arrived in Richmond she found that the ad-dress Williams had given her was a hotel. She went to the front desk and asked the clerk if the man whose name Williams had let her briefly see was in. The clerk said he was not.

Aline checked her watch. She had lost valuable time on the side route and knew she'd have to hustle to make the five o'clock return train.

The clerk asked if she could wait and Aline shook her head. It was already 4:45 and she had to go.

At the station, she called the hotel and asked the operator to ring the guest's room. It was now a few minutes before five o'clock and fortunately the man was in. She gave him a description of the station booth she was calling from and told him he'd find the envelope in the phone book tucked among the *R* pages.

He sounded pleased and she boarded her return train, making it back to The Farm without further incident.

Her next assignment was a bit more complicated. Williams told her she was to go to Pittsburgh and get a job at an aircraft parts factory. Complicating things, she would have no identification, so her ingenuity would be tested. If she managed that, he went on, she was to return to the factory the same night, break in, crack the office safe, and retrieve a conspicuous envelope containing valuable information.

He handed her a set of blueprints showing the location of the factory office and safe. As Aline studied it, he gave her a small card.

"Here's the number to call if you land in jail."

She gave him a sidelong glance and Williams shrugged. It wasn't uncommon, he said, and he assured her that they would spring her if she got caught.

Aline went to Pittsburgh, found the factory, and charmed her way into a job without much trouble, but the criminal mischief was a bit more challenging. She broke in that night and cracked the safe, but there was no envelope. She stared into the empty void for a moment and then it happened.

The alarm went off.

She raced out of the factory, adrenaline surging, and hightailed it back to the station. Boarding the return train in the early-morning light, she mulled what Ryan had said about Spain, its importance, and her role in it. What she was about to do—however large or small—seemed to be an important part of the OSS operation, and of the overall Allied strategy to win the war. But after tonight's fiasco, would she still be chosen for the assignment?

Stepping into the first compartment she placed her small traveling bag on the floor and sat opposite a man looking out the window. Before she could collect her thoughts, the man turned to her.

"Would you like me to put your suitcase on the rack?"

Aline's eyes widened. *Pierre!*

She jumped up and grabbed her bag. "I'll have to go to another coach. You know we're not allowed to speak to colleagues outside The Farm."

Pierre took the bag from her and stowed it. "Don't worry about that. Nobody we know is on this train."

Aline was torn. She didn't want to break protocol, but before she could object, Pierre pulled her down next to him. It was not an unwelcome gesture.

"What are you doing here?" she asked.

Pierre grinned. "And you?"

Aline kicked herself. Of course Pierre wouldn't say what he had been doing, nor would she. It was The Farm's first rule: secrecy. She changed the subject, and they talked about the war for a few minutes as other passengers boarded.

"I wanted to be alone with you for a long time," he finally said, leaning close.

Footsteps sounded by their door and he sat back. It was the conductor, who collected their tickets. Before Pierre could continue, though, a woman with a small child entered their compartment, followed by an army officer.

Aline and Pierre pretended not to know each other for the rest of the trip, and she wondered again what he was doing there. The train arrived at Penn Station and Pierre pulled her bag down from the rack. While the others in the cabin were gathering their things, he whispered: "You will have dinner with me?"

She shook her head. "I can't."

Snatching her bag, she squeezed into the herd of exiting passengers and looked for her connecting train to Washington.

Back at The Farm she told Captain Williams what had happened with the break-in, and he informed her that she had gone to the wrong office and broken into the wrong safe. Still, he said, her partial success had earned her a C+.

She didn't mention seeing Pierre on the train.

*   *   *

Over the next few days she continued with Morse, cipher, and the shooting range during mornings and afternoons, and the study of Spain at night. So that others wouldn't know the specifics of her upcoming assignment, she pulled multiple books for other countries as well. She talked with Pierre several times during the week, still feeling that electric connection to him, but they were never alone for more than a few minutes.

Finally, it was over. From dawn to midnight, November 1 to 21, her training had continued without a break. Aline was a cipher expert now, adept at Morse and coding, and able to handle almost any weapon. The study of Spain had been fascinating, but she knew she needed to brush up on her Spanish to be close to fluent. Williams told her that she had passed the training, and that she'd need to go to Washington the first week of December for final instructions.

On her way to the capital, Aline couldn't help but think of Pierre. She was riding in the same Chevy that had taken them to The Farm a month earlier. They had planned to see each other the following Sunday, but it would be for only a few hours. Still, she couldn't wait.

At the Q Building, Frank Ryan was all smiles.

"I guess this is our last meeting, Butch. You're on your way."

Aline nodded, butterflies swarming.

"You certainly wanted to get into the war badly that night I met you at my brother's house. Well, you're in it and you've earned your way. Here's what you're going to do."

Ryan explained that Aline would be cipher clerk in the OSS Madrid station, which was very small. At the moment, he said, there was only a station chief, a senior coder, and two secretaries. They'd be sending a radio man at some point, along with a financial officer, a Basque expert, and eventually two more cipher clerks. Because the station's coding room was swamped, he was going to do his best to expedite her travel.

"When I met you in New York," he went on, "I had just come back from one and a half years in Spain. I'm the guy who recommended you for this role, and I'm still the guy. You fit into the scenario as if made for the part. But if you fail, it'll be my failure also."

Aline shifted in her chair. She hadn't before considered that Ryan's reputation was on the line in recruiting her.

"You're not having second thoughts?"

She shook her head. "No. I'm scared, excited, but dying to go. I hope you haven't overestimated me."

Ryan reassured Aline that he had confidence in her, and said he was very proud of her. The only thing left now was to meet Whitney Shepardson, chief of OSS's Secret Intelligence branch. At The Farm she'd been told that he was OSS's most powerful man next to Bill Donovan, and he was considered a legend by many. He held degrees from Oxford—where he was a Rhodes Scholar—and Harvard Law School, but he chose international affairs as his occupation. At the close of World War I, the State Department had sent him to the Versailles Peace Conference as an aide to Edward House, President Woodrow Wilson's chief adviser, and later he served as secretary to the commission that drafted the Covenant of the League of Nations.

Aline was shown into Shepardson's office and found its occupant to be a distinguished silver-haired man whose deeply lined face suggested either too much reading or too much pressure. Shepardson rose to greet her and invited her to have a seat.

"I hope you will speak freely to me," he said. "Personal contact with my agents is worth ten of these reports." He held up some papers and set them aside. He then asked her the same question she'd been asked so often lately: Why did she want to join the war effort, particularly in a role that might very well be hazardous?

"Mr. Shepardson, every boy I know is in, including two of my brothers—both younger than I. I love my country as much as they do, and I am just as willing to risk my life. It's not fair that only men should be allowed to fight for this great country."

Shepardson smiled, apparently liking what he heard. "You'll have plenty of opportunity to do something for your country, Miss Griffith. Perhaps more than you realize."

The chief spoke to her about the importance of Madrid, about the enemy's presence there, and about Operation Anvil, the Allied plan to invade southern France. Some of the Madrid station's work would involve that plan, he said, and she would likely come across it in her decoding.

"Your cover will be the American oil mission," he explained, "which is the same for many of our agents there, although we have others using the cover of international companies with offices in Spain. Tell your family and friends to write you through your APO* number. All letters you send will be censored."

Shepardson showed her to the door, letting her know that she would be contacted at the proper time for travel arrangements. "God bless you," he said as they parted.

With OSS's official approval, Aline went home to Pearl River to wait for news of her departure date. The following Sunday, December 5, she met Pierre at the Plaza Hotel. It was a violation of OSS protocol and Aline should have known better, but it was the last chance she'd get to see him before he was off to who-knew-where the following day.

She had carefully planned her attire, wearing her best Hattie Carnegie suit—a blue tweed—with matching cape and hat. Pierre was late, but that didn't matter when their eyes met and he kissed her hand under the glittering chandeliers of the Plaza Hotel lobby. Pulling her close and taking her arm, he suggested they walk across the street to Central Park.

They wandered around the park, peeked inside a museum for a few minutes, talking about everything but the future. Aline won-

---

*Army Post Office.

dered where the OSS was sending Pierre, but she couldn't ask and he couldn't tell her. At one point he alluded to danger ahead and suggested that he might not return. Occupied France, Aline figured.

Pierre then took her to lunch at the most popular place in town: the Stork Club. A favorite haunt of celebrities like Lucille Ball and Frank Sinatra, the Stork Club hosted some twenty-five hundred people on a busy day. It was a marvelous outing and Aline couldn't have been happier.

Pierre ordered champagne, which she had never tasted, and when it arrived he took a small box from his pocket and placed it in front of her. It was from Cartier.

She pulled the ribbon and gasped. Inside was the most stunning ring she had ever seen—a twisting gold band encircling a sparkling sapphire.

She looked at Pierre, swept away. "I don't think I can accept such a valuable gift."

"Of course you can. I want you to remember me."

"I'll remember you no matter what."

Pierre smiled and nodded toward the box.

Aline put the ring on and to her surprise, it fit perfectly.

It all seemed a dream. And like a dream, it had to come to an end.

It was now four o'clock. She had to catch her train, and Pierre had to be on his way to wherever he was going.

They said goodbye and Pierre pulled her close and kissed her.

CHAPTER 4

THE CLERK

While Aline was eager to depart for her assignment, OSS's Secret Intelligence office had a number of administrative matters to address before she could leave. They had ordered her overseas security check when she finished her training at The Farm, but it would take weeks to process.

The OSS also had to work out a compensation plan with the State Department. Since Aline's cover was as a clerk for the American Oil Control Commission, the State Department would issue the check that would be her formal pay. From them she would receive a salary of $1,800 per year (less than the $2,400 salary she made modeling for Hattie Carnegie). Secretly, she would also receive $1,000 per annum from the OSS. And since she would be on call for the code room at any hour, and was likely to have assignments outside normal office hours, the State Department factored into her regular pay an additional $390 per annum for overtime.*

On January 10, 1944, Ryan put in a request for Aline's expedited transport to Spain and was informed that it would take two weeks. The identity and travel schedule of high-ranking military and intelligence

---

*Aline also would receive a monthly living allowance of $128.25, $92 paid by the State Department, $36.25 paid by the OSS.

officers going to Europe was top secret, and passage across the Atlantic was hard to come by. As a result, most OSS agents traveled to their destinations by sea. Because of Madrid's desperate need for Aline's services, however, Ryan wanted something else, something faster.

OFFICE OF STRATEGIC SERVICES
WASHINGTON, D.C.

SECRET

25 January, 1944

TO: Mr. Frank T. Ryan
Col. W. L. Rehm
Mr. R. G. Foster

FROM: Individual Transportation Unit

SUBJECT: Miss Marie Aline Griffith,
"J. H. M." -- Trans. Security No. 5922-C
"W. L. M." -- Trans. Security No. 5832-C

1. This will confirm our telephone conversation to you. This advised you that the Department which was securing transportation for the above party has notified us that they are to report to the Airlines concern on January 27th instead of the previous date given you on January 20th and that they will probably leave on the 28th of January.

Kenneth Mygatt
Chief, Individual Transportation Unit
Transportation Office

cc: Security Officer (Sexton)
Theater Officer (Ryan)

DECLASSIFIED
AUTHORITY

Aline's transportation was so top secret that the means of transport was not mentioned in the OSS scheduling. Traveling with Aline were two men, identified only by their initials: "J. H. M." and "W. L. M." *NARA*

*   *   *

Aline sat in her room at the Biltmore Hotel in midtown Manhattan looking out the frosted window at the softly falling snow. It was January 27 and she had been cooped up here on the fifteenth floor for two days, unable to speak to anyone. This was normal protocol for passengers departing for Lisbon on Pan American's *Yankee Clipper*, the only air service from the US to Europe. The navy feared lurking German U-boats might target the seaplane as it was taking off, or Luftwaffe fighters might cause trouble along the flight path to Lisbon, so passengers never knew until the last minute when they were to depart. They were told to wait in their hotel rooms, perhaps for days, until a call came telling them that it was time to leave.

The *Clipper* was a Boeing 314 long-range flying boat, one of the largest aircraft in the world. It provided luxury transportation that only the wealthy could afford in peacetime, and only high-ranking diplomats and senior military officers could utilize in wartime.* In addition to private sleeping quarters, it had a formal dining room, lounge, bar, and a women's dressing room. It even had a honeymoon suite.

Since only twelve had been built, getting passage on the *Clipper* was rare, even for top-level officials. That Aline had been selected for passage on the *Clipper* spoke volumes about what the OSS thought of her skills and potential. OSS staff working in the Madrid office, including station chief H. Gregory Thomas, all had traveled by sea—a two-week journey just to reach Lisbon.

Finally, late that night the call came, and ten minutes later there was a knock at the door. Two men greeted her without giving their names and said they'd escort her to the Marine Air Terminal at LaGuardia Field. They also said they would be joining her on the flight. Aline's traveling companions were James H. MacMillan and William Larimer Mellon, Jr., one of the heirs to the Mellon banking fortune. MacMillan was to be Madrid's deputy chief and financial officer, and Mellon would be the office's expert on the French-Spanish escape line, a route of safe houses through which downed Allied pilots and blown spies could make their way to safety in Gibraltar, and from there to England.

When the trio arrived at the pier, Aline was struck by how dark it was. Cloud cover masked the moon, and with all the city's millions of windows covered in blackout curtains, the New York skyline had vanished. It was pitch-black and cold. A man in military uniform

---

*A round-trip flight from New York to Southampton or Lisbon exceeded $1,000 (roughly $15,000 in 2020 dollars).

escorted them from the car to a small motorboat. Aline, MacMillan, and Mellon got in and moments later they were bouncing along the waves toward the giant *Clipper*.

Aline had never flown before, or even been near a plane, and the sheer size of this behemoth floating on the waves took her breath away. It was 28 feet high, had a wingspan of 152 feet, and weighed some 82,000 pounds.

She boarded with the others and was surprised to see that the interior was not set up with rows of seats but looked more like a living room; there were armchairs and sofas arranged so that passengers could converse as if sitting in a hotel lobby. She grabbed an open armchair, and moments later the *Clipper*'s engines roared to life and the plane began rumbling across the choppy water.

Pan American's Boeing 314 *Yankee Clipper*.

When they were airborne, a man sitting across from her pointed out that she was the only woman on board, something she had already noticed. He chattered away, describing the dining room upstairs, telling her, "We travel in luxury."

He wasn't exaggerating. The *Clipper* could hold as many as seventy-four passengers and had sleepers for thirty-four. The seating area boasted deeply upholstered chairs and sofas, and the service from the white-coated staff mirrored what one would expect from a fine hotel. The *Clipper*'s chefs, John Salmini and Bruce Candotti, had, in fact, been trained at the Waldorf-Astoria.

When it was time for dinner, Aline was amazed to see that the dining room was like an elegant restaurant: white linen tablecloths, silver and china, and the ever-present steward with a napkin draped over his arm. The meal matched the five-star accommodation, too: shrimp cocktail, turtle soup, salad, filet mignon, mashed potatoes, and asparagus, with peach melba and petit fours for dessert.

From the *Clipper*'s bar, one could order martinis, manhattans, scotch, bourbon, rum, brandy, or wine. This was more than a flying boat; it was a flying hotel.

During the flight, James MacMillan and Larry Mellon formally introduced themselves, telling Aline that they would be working with her in Spain. The *Clipper* would refuel in Bermuda and again in the Azores, the men said, and then they'd land in Lisbon, where they would spend two nights before catching a flight to Madrid.

When they landed in Bermuda, however, there was a surprise. Shortly after refueling the pilot announced that the waves were too large for the plane to take off. It wasn't until several days later that the water runway was smooth enough to allow them to continue on.

February 8, 1944
Lisbon

It was an unforgettable sight. The pilot had invited Aline to watch the landing from the cockpit, and the lights of Lisbon shimmering at dusk were mesmerizing. Paris is known as the City of Lights, but Lisbon is the City of *Light*, and Aline could see why. A yellow tint hovered over the entire area and ancient castles seemed to glow as they rose up from the sea.

Waves of spray splashed across the cockpit windows as the *Clipper* touched water and bounced. Quite a show for Aline's first plane ride.

When everyone had gathered their luggage, MacMillan and Mellon told Aline that they would not be staying in Lisbon, but in Estoril, about half an hour up the coast. Once a quaint fishing village, Estoril was now a world-class resort, they said, something akin to the French Riviera. It had Europe's largest casino and one of the finest hotels in the world—the Palacio. That's where the OSS trio were headed.

When they arrived at the hotel, Aline gazed across the façade. The Palacio was immense, like the Hay Adams, but more elegant. A smartly dressed bellman helped them with their luggage, and Aline noticed that the spacious lobby felt stately but not in the least stodgy. One thing was for sure: it was *expensive*.

They handed over their passports at the front desk, and Aline noticed that the clerk began filling out special forms for her and her colleagues. It was a foreigner's registration that the Polícia de Vigilância e de Defesa do Estado (PVDE)—the secret police—required, she learned later. Portugal had been at this espionage game since 1939—watching over countless "diplomats" from Germany, Italy, Japan, Russia, Britain, France, and other countries—and wanted a paper trail for every potential spy.

Aline's Palacio registration on February 8, 1944. Her departure date of February 10 can be seen at the bottom of the reverse side. *Cascais Archive*

Palacio registration of James MacMillan, Madrid deputy chief and finance officer.
Cascais Archive

Palacio registration of Madrid agent William Larimer Mellon, Jr. *Cascais Archive*

MacMillan headed up to his room, leaving Aline and Larry Mellon to finish their registration. Larry glanced at his watch and asked Aline if she'd like to visit the casino with him. Not only was Casino Estoril Portugal's top attraction, but it was the favored nightspot and meeting place for every spy in Lisbon.* Aside from the gambling areas, it boasted a fine restaurant, a cinema, and the WonderBar—a massive nightclub with a live orchestra and dance floor.

Aline was tired from the trip, but she wasn't about to miss her first night on the job. She quickly unpacked and changed and met Larry in the lobby. They strolled together through the gardens between the Palacio and the casino and, though it was dark, she could see thousands of rose and geranium bushes in beds the length of a football field.

At the entrance she marveled at the bronze-embossed mahogany doors, but the magnificence inside was even more spectacular. Crystal chandeliers hung from cavernous ceilings, and red velvet drapes and carpets gave the place the feel of a royal palace. In the background she could hear the clatter of chips and the whir of roulette wheels.

Left: Casino Estoril and gardens. Right: The WonderBar nightclub. *Cascais Archive*

There was an energy here, a buzz, unlike anything she'd felt before. Throngs of patrons filled every room, and she heard conversations in Portuguese, Spanish, English, German, French, Italian, and Japanese.

---

*Casino Estoril was the inspiration for Ian Fleming's first novel, *Casino Royale*, and what he witnessed there around August 1, 1941 (watching British double agent Dusko Popov) led to his creation of James Bond. See my first book, *Into the Lion's Mouth*, chapter 11.

It made sense. Since Portugal was neutral, Lisbon was a hub of espionage second only to Madrid. Among the diplomats and embassy staffers around her, she realized, there were surely other spies.

Mellon called her attention to a group of Japanese men standing near them. "Aline, watch those fellows. Here in Lisbon they receive information about troop departures from seaports on our west and east coasts, which they relay to Tokyo and Berlin. The Japanese have an excellent worldwide espionage network."

They made their way into the gaming room, where smoke hovered over the players in a hazy gray cloud. As they approached a baccarat table, Mellon leaned close and murmured in her ear that she should never speak above a whisper near a game table. "Gamblers are superstitious, especially when the stakes are high." He nodded toward the table. "There are over ten thousand dollars in escudos and chips on that table right now."

Around midnight they moved on to the WonderBar nightclub, which was bustling. The orchestra was playing a rumba, the dance floor was packed, and every table was taken. Mellon said that the club was famous for its cuisine, and they waited until a table came free to eat a late dinner.

On the way out, Aline saw the cinema's lineup for the week. On tap for the next day was an Errol Flynn swashbuckler, *The Sea Hawk.* It would have been fun to watch, but her life now was more exciting than any film, and it was best to concentrate on her job.

All in all, it was quite a first day for a girl who until quite recently had never been more than a stone's throw beyond her own backyard.

After spending the next day briefing with local OSS agents in Lisbon, Aline, Mellon, and MacMillan checked out of the Palacio the morning of February 10 for their flight to Madrid.

Aline peered out the window of the small Iberia Airlines plane, gazing at the fallow fields of Castile and, beyond that, the outskirts of Madrid. In the distance she could see the snow-capped mountains of the Sierra de Guadarrama. Her eyes followed endless rows of prairies plowed in symmetrical stripes of orange, brown, and red, and the sky was a shade of blue so vivid that it softened the austere landscape.

As they approached Madrid, she started to feel apprehensive. Part of it was that she worried that she might not be up to the assignment, her training notwithstanding. But there was something else, too. "I sensed a mystery," she recalled later, "a sort of magic, not unlike the feelings mentioned by Mérimée or Gautier in their books or any of the other foreigners arriving a century before in stagecoaches or on horseback. Spain during the past century and even before had attracted courageous visitors looking for adventure in this country so unique and unlike the rest of Europe."

Aline's adventure was about to begin.

The plane touched down at Madrid's Barajas Airport, and as it taxied to the terminal, Aline noticed that there was only one other aircraft in sight. As they moved closer, she saw the red-and-black swastika on its tail. It was a Junkers, perhaps a Ju-52.

Her first sighting of the enemy reminded her of the complexity that was Spain. Since the country was neutral in the war, German and British planes could be parked side by side on the tarmac, and Nazi and English propaganda stores could be next-door neighbors in town. And that was where the US Embassy and Aline's job at the Oil Commission came in. While the Germans and British openly courted the Spanish public for support, the Americans operated in more subtle ways. Ambassador Carlton Hayes, when he wasn't meeting privately with General Franco to push him toward Allied-friendly decisions, was hosting cocktail parties and showing Hollywood movies for Spanish diplomats and military officials.

Aline knew that Franco had made countless concessions to Germany to keep Wehrmacht troops out of Spain, but as the war progressed and a German victory seemed more in doubt, he had been slowly drawing closer to the Allies. His decisions on valuable commodities were telling. While he sold wolframite to Germany, he rebuffed Hitler and sold even more to the British and Americans. And he had no problem when the United States said it wanted to open the Oil Commission in Madrid—with its own representatives in place at the docks—to make sure that not one ounce of American petrol made it onto German ships or submarines.

It was a chess match of attrition, really, where Franco quietly slid a German pawn or bishop off the Spanish board each time the Allies progressed on the battlefield.

For Aline and the OSS, though, the difficulty was that Germany's immense presence in Spain was largely invisible; the Junkers and propaganda shops were merely the tip of the iceberg. American and British intelligence knew that below the surface of Madrid lurked hundreds of German operatives from the Abwehr, Gestapo, and SD. Perhaps more sinister was the fact that Germany had untold numbers of fake corporations throughout Spain. Many were likely involved in espionage, and countless others were fronts for laundering Nazi money and loot for delivery to Argentina and Brazil.*

Aline stepped down from the Iberia aircraft into a biting winter

---

*Abwehr agent Johann Jebsen, case officer for British double agent Dusko Popov, told Popov that they had about 520 agents in Madrid, 120 with diplomatic cover, another 400 in various phony firms and jobs. The Germans also had 70 to 100 agents working at a secret shortwave listening and decoding station. The city was literally teeming with Germans, and any porter, bellman, waiter, concierge, or driver could be an informant. If that weren't enough, Nazi secret police (Gestapo) and foreign intelligence (SD) had acquired, with assistance from Spanish authorities, full lists of American and British intelligence officers. Only five months earlier Jebsen had told Kenneth Benton, MI6 Madrid agent, that the Abwehr often had discussions about each member of the British staff. So thorough was their research that Jebsen said he knew, for example, that Benton had previously been posted in Vienna, and had worked under an agent named Kendrick.

chill. The wind was whipping so furiously that she had to hold on to her hat to keep it from being blown off.

The taxi to town was a history lesson in itself, the pitted dirt roads and pockmarked buildings evidence of the country's recent civil war. As they neared the city, the road narrowed and took them through a blighted area where children played in the streets, oblivious to the world around them. There were few cars on the road—automobiles were scarce in Spain—but they passed plenty of bicycles, donkey carts, and carriages hitched to feeble-looking horses.

They came upon a massive redbrick structure, circular in shape, and Aline knew that it was the Plaza de Toros de Las Ventas, Madrid's famous 24,000-seat bullring. It looked like the Colosseum in Rome, with its four stories and arched entryways, and the comparison was not inappropriate: the gladiators here still fought beasts, but they did so in brightly colored silks and slippers. It wasn't exactly the kind of spectacle Aline longed to see, but she knew the popularity of bullfighting would mean she'd have to attend eventually.

After passing through a few more neighborhoods crammed with old, dilapidated buildings, they arrived at a series of impressive plazas, all with fountains and grand statues. Beyond them the street opened onto a wide boulevard lined with stone palaces and manicured gardens behind iron-grilled fences.

The taxi came to a circular drive known as the Plaza de Cánovas del Castillo, and suddenly the Old-World Spain she had expected came alive. The Fuente de Neptuno (Fountain of Neptune)—an eighteenth-century sculpture of the sea god holding a trident atop a carriage being pulled by two creatures, half horse, half fish—stood boldly in the center. On one side of the plaza was the Ritz, and next to it the Prado, one of the greatest museums in the world. On the other side was their destination, the famous Palace Hotel.

Commissioned by King Alfonso XIII in 1911, the Palace had

opened the following year to tremendous fanfare. Not only was the eight-hundred-room Palace the largest hotel in Spain, it was the first in the country to have a bathroom and telephone in each guest suite.

Uniformed bellmen fetched Aline's bags and escorted her inside. In the lobby, Aline peered up at the spectacular glass dome. It was a cylindrical design composed of thousands of small pieces of stained glass, the bottom and top rings of which sparkled in various shades of blue, the others off-white, yellow, and orange. Perhaps by design, the infusion of natural light seemed to evoke a certain felicity from employees and guests alike.

After she checked in Aline saw that a young man was waiting for her with her suitcases at the elevator. It seemed a bit strange, though, as the man wasn't in a bellman's uniform. The elevator opened and in perfect English he asked for her room number. She obliged and discreetly tried to size him up. He was tall, handsome, and well-dressed, with brown hair and green eyes.

He didn't look Spanish.

Something wasn't right. He set her bags inside the door and she tried to tip him, but he refused.

She couldn't close the door fast enough. If the man wasn't Spanish, who was he? It seemed highly unlikely that he was a German agent who just dropped by the hotel to deliver bags for a few hours, but given what she'd heard about the Abwehr's presence in Madrid, it was possible.

That night after dinner Aline walked down the street to the Teatro de la Zarzuela, an opera house built in 1856 and modeled after La Scala in Milan, with a horseshoe design, box seats, and three tiers of balconies. The theater typically offered zarzuela—a traditional Spanish form of musical theater—or opera, but this night it show-cased one of the city's most popular flamenco dancers, Lola Flores.

During her research at The Farm, Aline had learned that Spaniards were united around two particular forms of entertainment: bullfighting and flamenco. Both were weekly rituals and the similarities between them were obvious to even the most casual observer. The brightly colored costumes, the graceful moves, the twisting and turning, and the almost mystical experience felt by spectators made one activity seem like an extension of the other. Flamenco was invented by the Roma, often called Gypsies, and it was no surprise that many great bullfighters—like El Gallo, Cagancho, and Gitanillo de Triana—were of Roma descent.

And since men and women from all levels of Spanish society enjoyed bullfighting and flamenco, Aline knew that her duties for the OSS would require a deep understanding of both. Madrid's upper classes, she had learned—including foreign diplomats and royalty—often hired flamenco dancers to entertain their guests after dinner, so she figured her flamenco education would start tonight.

She found her seat and was immediately enraptured.

Lola Flores was curvaceous and graceful, and when "La Niña de Fuego"—The Girl of Fire—began playing, Aline found the dancer's twisting and gyrating sensual and hypnotic. Snapping her fingers and stamping her feet alongside a singer and two guitarists, Lola mesmerized the audience. This, in fact, was flamenco's intent. "This perhaps is the secret of flamenco's fascination," Aline recalled. "It enables those who partake in it to become intoxicated by its complex musical rhythms. It is an art which opens a magic window to beauty."

The next morning, Aline awoke to a knock at her door. Sitting up in bed, she reminded herself that only Mellon and MacMillan knew she was here. Well, and that strange man who brought up her bags. She threw on a robe and called out: "Who is it?"

"El mozo de espadas."

It was too early in the morning for Spanish, but Aline worked the translation.

Man of swords.

CHAPTER 5

MAN OF SWORDS

Aline cautiously cracked the door.

Three Spaniards in black suits bowed. One was holding the largest bouquet of flowers she'd ever seen—bright red carnations—while the other two held some type of garment that seemed to sparkle.

"Señorita Griffith," one of them said, "I am the man of swords of Don Juan Belmonte, who sends you these gifts."

"Belmonte?"

"Yes, señorita."

"If you please, who is Belmonte?"

The Spaniards looked at each other. What a question. In Spain, Belmonte was a name even more famous than Franco.

Juan Belmonte had invented modern bullfighting and many, if not most, regarded him as the greatest matador ever.* In 1919 he appeared in 109 corridas, killing some 218 bulls in 180 days, a record. On January 5, 1925, Belmonte had appeared on the cover of *Time* and become an international celebrity.

---

*Many considered Joselito, Belmonte's contemporary, the greatest ever, but Joselito readily admitted that Belmonte was the progenitor: "I may be the greatest," he once said, "but Belmonte invented what I do."

In 1932, Hemingway summarized Belmonte's impact on bull-fighting: "He was a genius who could break the rules of bullfighting and could *torear*, that is the only word for all the actions performed by a man with the bull, as it was known to be impossible to *torear*." And what Hemingway had witnessed watching Belmonte was well known to every Spaniard. Unlike the matadors who came before him, Belmonte stood perfectly still, feet together, and kept the bull as close to him as possible. As he performed his magic with the cape, the bull revolved around *him* (rather than vice versa, the custom for four centuries), making Belmonte appear as a graceful ballerina. "The way Belmonte worked was not a heritage," Hemingway explained, "nor a development; it was a revolution." His style was so dangerous, intentionally bringing the bull's horns within inches, that Hemingway called it decadent, impossible . . . even depraved.

But the Spaniards in front of Aline were not speaking on behalf of Juan Belmonte, long since retired, but of his son, Juanito.

"The señorita must have heard of the great Belmonte," the man said. Juanito was nationally famous, not only because of his father but because of his own feats in the ring as well.

Aline was at a loss. "There must be some mistake."

"No mistake," the man said. "Don Juan beheld the señorita last night in the Teatro de la Zarzuela."

Aline nodded. Not wanting to be rude, she accepted the flowers, but what were the other items?

"The *traje de luces*," one of them said, "suit of lights, that Don Juan wore in Toledo when he got two ears."

Aline stood there, puzzled. A pink satin suit covered with sequins? And *ears*?

Before she could respond the other man thrust Juanito's matador cape into her arms. Aline gave it back, telling them she'd accept the flowers but not the clothing and cape.

"Señorita," one of the men said, "do not refuse, *por favor*. Don Juan would never forgive us."

Aline held firm and the men left. She was flattered, of course, but attention was the last thing an OSS operative wanted. In Madrid less than a day and already she had an admirer.

A celebrity, no less.

After breakfast Aline headed to Calle Alcalá Galiano, No. 4, office of the Oil Control Commission. She wouldn't start work until the following Monday, but she wanted to get a feel for the city and see where the office was in relation to everything else. She saw on the map that it was about ten blocks north of the Palace Hotel so she took a trolley.

On the ride up she noticed that a number of people on the car were staring at her. Come to think of it, a few had gawked at her in the hotel lobby as well. Was it so obvious she was an American?

She got off at the Plaza de Colón to catch a glimpse of the statue of Christopher Columbus, and then walked up Alcalá Galiano, a tree-lined street of old, well-preserved buildings. As she passed by a parked black Packard, she noticed the driver watching her.

"Why does such a pretty girl want to wear men's clothes?" the man yelled.

Aline glanced at her outfit: plaid shirt and slacks. *Ah*. Old-World Spain. Dresses from now on, she told herself.

She reached building No. 4 and looked up. It was a grand three-story stone structure with little balconies at each window. It was relatively new, by Spanish standards anyway, but designed to match the centuries-old buildings around it. Now that she'd found her office, she continued on toward the center of downtown. After a few blocks the streets began to narrow and suddenly there were endless rows of shops with a dizzying array of merchandise: top hats, corsets, copper utensils, bric-a-brac of every sort.

At the Plaza de Santa Ana, near the center of town and not far from the hotel, she sat on a bench to drink in Spanish life for a few minutes. The women passing by all seemed to wear black, she noticed, with woolen scarves protecting their faces from the wind.

Men wore long capes—strange but undeniably romantic—or had their coats hung casually about their shoulders. A moment later a horse-drawn carriage went by, followed by mule-drawn carts. Gasoline was hard to come by in Spain, and the few cars she encountered often ran on charcoal.* Everything was old here, but there was a dignity to it. None of the Spaniards around her appeared financially well-off, but they seemed proud.

And happy. Everyone smiled and men tipped their hats in greeting, often complimenting a woman on something she was wearing. Madrid was stuck in the nineteenth century, it seemed, and Aline found it charming. Though it was a large city, it seemed to have some of the same small-town charm as Pearl River.

Back at the hotel, the same three Spaniards who had greeted her that morning were waiting in the lobby. The one from whom she had taken the carnations was now carrying a fresh bouquet. Again, Aline accepted the flowers but reiterated she couldn't accept the cape and suit. The messengers were persistent, though, and she finally relented.

Not long after she returned to her room, the phone rang.

"Señorita Griffith?"

"Yes."

"I am Juan Belmonte, and I would like the privilege of taking you out to buy a box of chocolates."

Aline stifled a laugh. Not every day you get invited on a chocolate date. Between the flowers and the matador clothes, it was clear this bullfighter was accustomed to having his way.

"When would you like to buy these chocolates, Señor Belmonte?"

---

*The energy conversion worked by burning charcoal in a stove in the trunk. It worked, but it was unreliable and greatly diminished the car's power.

Aline wearing Juanito Belmonte's vest from his "suit of lights."

"As soon as possible, señorita. This afternoon would be perfect. I could pick you up around five."

Aline agreed, and said she'd meet him in the lobby. "But how will I know you?"

Juanito paused, and then said, "It is not a problem, señorita, I will know you."

Promptly at five, Aline headed down. The usually quiet and sedate lobby was abuzz. A crowd was gathered around someone signing autographs, but she couldn't make out who it was. Looking around, she didn't see anyone waiting for her and suspected that her date had not yet arrived.

After a few minutes the crowd started moving her way. Scanning the group, she saw that the center of attention—the Spaniard leading the entourage—was a man. Then it dawned on her: this was her bullfighter.

The celebrity.

He didn't *look* like a slayer of beasts. He was short and thin, with dark skin and a jaw that jutted forward like a barracuda's.

"Señorita Griffith," Juanito said, raising her hand to his lips. "May I call you by your first name?"

"Aline."

Juanito took her arm and a doorman shooed away the crowd. Outside, Aline's eyes widened when she saw what Señor Belmonte was driving: a cream-colored Bugatti Royale convertible. She suspected that bullfighters were well paid, but who could afford a Bugatti roadster when few Spaniards even owned a car?

Though young, Juanito was indeed wealthy. At the time, matadors made between $2,000 and $7,500 for an afternoon's work. For the most popular bullfighters, a season would entail eighty to one hundred performances. Adjusting for inflation, top matadors like Juanito were earning several million dollars a year.[*]

They drove to a small village called Villanueva de la Cañada, some twenty miles west of Madrid, and Aline wondered why Juanito had not selected a chocolatier in town. A romantic drive through the countryside, perhaps?

He turned on Calle Peligros and stopped in front of a store called La Mahonesa. Inside, the owner, Don José, greeted Juanito with several bows and then turned to Aline.

"Señorita, it is an honor to have you visit this shop. For one hundred and sixty-six years, my ancestors and I have made Spain's best chocolates. We have served the royal family and the coun-

---

[*]Manolete, the bullfighter who stood alone at the top, had made over $30 million (inflation-adjusted) since 1939.

try's most illustrious citizens. The señorita shall have a box just like the ones we used to prepare for Queen Victoria Eugenia."

Aline watched as Don José began moving down his display, selecting various chocolates and placing them in a box lined with pink silk. When he was almost finished, Juanito said, "Don José, we will be in the car."

Aline looked back. "But what about the chocolates? Shouldn't we wait?"

"Certainly not. In Spain gentlemen do not carry packages."

Juanito opened her door, and moments later Don José came out carrying a silver tray, upon which rested the box of La Mahonesa's finest confections. It was a treat Juanito would often share with Aline in the months ahead.

On Monday, Aline went to the office on Calle Alcalá Galiano and spent most of the day learning the lay of the land. To begin, the American embassy and the Oil Control Commission were located in separate buildings.* The embassy, about twelve blocks away on Calle Miguel Angel, housed only American diplomats and the OSS's X-2 staff.

That morning she met Walter Smith, a career oilman who headed the Oil Commission—a legitimate entity with an important function. In July 1941, as punishment for Franco's appeasement of Germany, the United States had stopped shipments of petroleum to Spain, infuriating the British. Spain needed gasoline so desperately, they had argued, that the lack of it would send the country into civil disorder, thus providing Hitler with an excuse to invade. The US

*On July 5, 1944, Gregory Thomas and Ambassador Carlton Hayes would sign a formal lease, moving the OSS (identified as the "Other Agency") offices into the third floor of the ambassador's residence in the embassy compound (identified as the Montellano property), while Thomas himself would lease space in the adjacent "International Institute" building.

countered that any petroleum shipments to Spain could be resold to Germany, Italy, or Japan.

In early 1942 the parties resolved the issue, but with two contingencies. First, the US would provide Spain with only enough oil to meet its minimum domestic needs, thus negating the possibility of resale. Second, American authorities would be placed in Spain to assure that all shipments would be tracked, and that no oil would find its way to German submarines visiting Spanish ports. To accomplish this, US officials would have to act as internal customs, inspecting incoming shipments and supervising distribution.

The Oil Control Commission was this supervising agency, and it was the perfect cover for Aline and the OSS staff. She would keep normal office hours as an OCC clerk, but behind closed doors she would code and decode incoming and outgoing OSS cables.

The Oil Commission was located on the first floor of the building, Smith explained, with the Secret Intelligence offices on the second floor. He escorted her up a stairway and introduced her to H. Gregory Thomas, the Madrid station chief.

"Miss Griffith," Thomas said, shaking her hand, "I've been expecting you."

Smith excused himself and Aline took a seat. If ever a boss could be intimidating, this was the man. He had a stiff, formal demeanor and his booming voice matched his gigantic, angular physique.

But Aline had no idea just how impressive Thomas really was. He had graduated with first-class honors from Cambridge University, earned a doctorate in law at the University of Paris, and passed the entrance exam for admission to the English Bar. He then went to Spain and studied at the universities of Oviedo, Madrid, and Salamanca, where he earned a second doctorate. When General Donovan became director of the Office of the Coordinator of Information in 1942, he recruited Thomas for his staff in New York. Not long thereafter, since Thomas was fluent in Spanish and French, Donovan sent him to Madrid with oversight of Spain and Portugal. But Thomas was building his organization almost from scratch.

"We've barely twelve US-trained agents in all of Spain," he said by way of introduction. "The Germans have literally hundreds." Everyone in the office had code names, he explained; his was ARGUS, and hers was BUTCH. Jim MacMillan, whom she'd met on the trip over, was the deputy director and the station financial officer. He'd be her immediate supervisor, he said, and Jim's code name was QUERES. Larry Mellon, whom she had also met, was their Basque expert; he would focus primarily on the French-Spanish escape lines and chains. In that capacity, he would spend much of his time in Barcelona and London but would be based initially in Madrid. His code name was LEGION.

The remaining Madrid staff consisted of two secretaries, an administrator, a radioman, and three coders, including Aline. The radio operator, whose name was Robert Turpin, code-named KODAK, would arrive next month. The chief cipher clerk, with whom Aline would work closely, was Robert Dunev, code-named WILLIAMS.

With cover as an Oil Commission clerk, Thomas went on, Aline would be expected to keep normal office hours. But what was considered normal in Madrid was unlike what any American was used to. Business hours were universally recognized as ten or eleven in the morning to one or two in the afternoon, and then six to ten in the evening. The afternoon break was for lunch and a siesta at home with family. The Oil Commission, however, Americanized the Spanish schedule: work began at nine and the lunch-siesta break started at one. Staffers were expected to be back at four and work until eight, sometimes later.

A Spaniard's evening was adjusted accordingly. Dinner reservations were rarely made before ten in Madrid, and drinks and appetizers typically began at half past. The main course followed, sometimes arriving as late as midnight, and conversation continued until the party left for the next stage of the evening. Groups might head to a bar at this point, or visit a theater or opera house, which were open from eleven until two in the morning. After that came flamenco parties, which often lasted until six in the morning. As

Hemingway observed, "Nobody goes to bed in Madrid until they have killed the night."

One reason for the strange hours was that homes did not have air conditioning, and much of the year it would be too hot to sleep until the early morning hours. The other reason was that the Spanish simply loved to live.

And since Aline might overhear valuable intelligence at dinners, receptions, clubs, and parties, Thomas encouraged her to adapt to the local scene and keep her eyes and ears open. He pointed out that Dunev, the chief cypher clerk, had a second identity as a local. His Spanish was so flawless that OSS had created a fake persona for him as "Joaquin Goicoechea," a Madrileño who lived in a studio apartment in a working-class neighborhood. Robert kept a separate wardrobe there, in keeping with Joaquin's status, and would sleep there at least once a week. Aline would have no connection to Dunev's alias, but it was best that she knew he'd often be away from his regular apartment. Aline's role, he said, was less complicated. First and foremost, her priority was the code room, and she would be on call at any hour, day or night, in case an urgent cable arrived. That said, there was one thing he particularly wanted her to keep in the back of her mind when she was out and about.

Heinrich Himmler, Germany's *Reichsführer* and Hitler's second in command, had a top agent in Madrid and the OSS needed to find out who it was. At the moment they had four suspects, all of whom had skeleton files in the X-2 office. First, there was Franco's brother-in-law, Ramón Serrano-Suñer. He was not only the former head of the Falange, Spain's fascist party, but known to be very close to Himmler. He had served in Franco's cabinet as minister of the interior and then as foreign minister, but the general had removed him from his cabinet altogether in September 1942.*

Second, there was Prince Maximilian Egon von Hohenlohe.

---

*As Germany's prospects of winning the war waned, Franco distanced himself from the Falangists, starting with the removal of Serrano-Suñer from his administration.

A fabulously wealthy Austrian, he had married a member of the Spanish royal family and now lived in Madrid. He had at least one castle in Germany, perhaps more, and stood to lose quite a bit of his fortune if Germany wasn't victorious in the war. He had numerous Nazi connections, OSS reports indicated, including Himmler and Hermann Göring, Germany's *Reichsmarschall.** He was also a confidant of Walter Schellenberg, Himmler's foreign intelligence chief, and it was possible that he was rendering political services to the Gestapo.

But Prince Max was an enigma, Thomas said. He had a history of representing Hitler, Himmler, and Göring in secret peace talks, but as early as 1939 Max had presented himself to the Allies as being anti-Nazi. Throughout the war he had maintained close ties with Göring, the Gestapo, and the Nazi minister of the interior, yet also enjoyed good relations with the British. The fourth week of October 1939, he had a highly secret meeting with Richard Austen Butler, Britain's undersecretary of state for foreign affairs, in Lausanne, Switzerland. Prince Max's proposal, made on behalf of Hermann Göring, was for the assassination of Hitler and the substitution of Göring in his place.

Then in mid-July 1940, Prince Max met with Sir David Kelly, British ambassador to the Vatican, in Bern, Switzerland. The meeting had been set up by Spain's minister to Switzerland, and Prince Max quoted Hitler as saying he was "prepared to accept *Einigkeit* [a concord]" with the British Empire, but that time was very short and England must choose "in the next few weeks."

In March 1941 Prince Max approached Sir Samuel Hoare, British ambassador to Spain, requesting a meeting in Madrid. Hoare agreed and in the meeting Max stressed that Germany could never be defeated, but that if peace were made now, Hitler would be reasonable in his terms.

---

*The *Reichsmarschall* was the military's senior field marshal and Germany's highest-ranking soldier.

Finally, in early 1943 Prince Max had his most serious discussions with an old friend, Allen Dulles, OSS station chief in Bern. Max had met Dulles while working as a junior attaché in Vienna in 1916, and had visited him at his home on Long Island several times after World War I. Given their prior relationship, Max was able to orchestrate a secret meeting with Dulles in a car parked on the Liechtenstein-Switzerland border. Working this time on behalf of Himmler, Max asked that if Hitler were deposed, would the Allies recognize Himmler as the legitimate head of the German state and negotiate peace terms with him? Second, what would be the status of Germany and other states in a post-war Europe?

The talks continued for three months, but Dulles never committed to any terms.

All of this wouldn't come out until after the war was over, but even so, Thomas *did* know that Prince Max was slippery. In Lisbon Max declared himself anti-Nazi, yet he seemed to have cozy relationships with many important members of the party. Exactly whose side was he on? No one really knew, but one thing was clear: Prince Max floated in the highest social circles in Berlin, Bern, London, New York, and Madrid, and it was likely that Aline would eventually meet him.

The third name on Thomas's list was Countess Gloria von Fürstenberg. She had recently arrived in Madrid from Berlin and was also staying at the Palace Hotel. She, too, was in contact with Schellenberg, Himmler's foreign intelligence chief, and was rumored to be a favorite of Himmler himself. It was a mystery, though, how she supported herself since she had no job and no visible means of income, unless the Gestapo was secretly paying her.

Like Prince Max, Gloria had a colorful history. Mexican by birth, she was now thirty-one and was considered one of the most beautiful women in the world. In 1931 she had gone to Los Angeles to work with Clarence Brown, the famed MGM director who had helped launch the careers of Joan Crawford and Greta Garbo. Brown, it seemed, had identified Gloria as his next starlet. She returned to Mexico in 1933, however, without having appeared in a film, and then moved on to Paris and The Hague. There she married a Dutchman, Frank Scholtens, only to divorce him shortly thereafter. In 1935 she moved to Berlin, where she met and married Count Franz Egon Graf von Fürstenberg. The couple had two children, and when war broke out her husband joined the Wehrmacht. In 1942 Gloria moved with their children, aged one and four, to Madrid and filed for divorce.

Gloria was a suspect, Thomas said, because of rumored connections to Himmler and her known association with the last suspect, Dr. Hans Lazar.

While Lazar's official title was press attaché of the German embassy in Madrid, he was perhaps the most powerful Nazi in Spain. During the Spanish Civil War he had entrenched himself in the country, working as a correspondent for the pro-Nazi broadcaster Transocean. When World War II broke out, he simply moved his office to the German embassy.

From the beginning, Lazar had pursued a plan to move Spain's public sentiment closer to Germany using propaganda and covert activities. Since Serrano-Suñer and the Falange controlled the Spanish press, Lazar had unmitigated freedom to plant German propaganda in most outlets. With a monthly budget of 200,000 pesetas, he had a bankroll to bribe Spanish journalists and government officials and to hire informants, which he did with abandon. At one point, the OSS estimated, Lazar had as many as four hundred agents reporting to him. Many of those agents, they knew, were informants whose job it was to shadow suspected Allied spies.

Aline would soon know this sensation firsthand.

CHAPTER 6

SNATCH-22

Thomas showed Aline around the office, introduced her to the staff, and left her in the code room with Robert Dunev. Dunev was not much older than she was, Aline figured, with a boyish face and tender eyes, but he came across as older, more seasoned. About six feet tall, he was thin and well-dressed, and his dark complexion suggested he could have been a native Spaniard.

He was also friendly and warm, and she was grateful to have a compatible office mate. Like her, he came from a middle-class New York home and had a small-town, easygoing nature.

Dunev, in turn, was equally impressed with Aline, and relieved to have help. Since his arrival, he had struggled to keep pace with the relentless onslaught of work, much of which could now be shared.

"Life in the code room improved dramatically with the arrival of Aline," he recalled later. "Her looks and her personality, together with her enthusiasm for everything Spanish, boosted the morale in the back rooms of Alcalá Galiano."

The decoding itself, though, was not for the faint of heart. German order-of-battle intelligence was collected daily throughout Eu-

Robert Dunev saving petrol on this day at the office. *Michael Dunev*

rope, and OSS radio operators in places like San Sebastián, Bilbao, and Barcelona would then encrypt and dispatch the information to Madrid's OSS office. These messages, which were top secret and often urgent, would then have to be decoded and radioed to other stations or pouched to Washington.

Messages were always sent in groups of five letters, such as: FSTSD NNCXQ HYEMG. To decode it, Aline would place a "strip," or key, beneath each set of letters, and then apply memorized combinations. Each letter she saw was the result of a combination of two letters: what was in the strip and the actual message. In the above example, Aline's strip would read: BOADS TMISR ATDUC. In the memorized combinations, the letter F could only be formed by applying T + B. Thus, she would know that the first letter of the first word was T. The letter S, in turn, could only be formed by applying H + O. Continuing down the sentence, Aline eventually would have the message:

THREE TANKS DESTR.

But the strips were long, sets of 25 to 30 five-letter units, and they would change every month. Fortunately, the letter combinations never changed so once memorized, the code clerk was halfway home. There was a flaw in the system, though, as a message could be transmitted without being enciphered if the strips were not carefully positioned. Early on Robert had made such a mistake, sending a cable to London about troop movements without the appropriate strip, and thus without the resulting enciphering. His message read:

THEFL OWOFO RDERO FBATT LEINT

If intercepted, the Germans would have understood the message immediately:

THE FLOW OF ORDER OF BATTLE

London had been furious and demanded a court martial for the person responsible. Frank Ryan and Gregory Thomas came to Robert's defense, fortunately, and used the incident to request assistance in the coding room. This mishap, in large part, led to the urgency of recruiting Aline.

One other thing Aline found sobering about her work was that each agent had to have an "escape plan." Since OSS employees did not have diplomatic cover, they would have no immunity if their cover was blown and they were discovered by Spanish authorities to be spies. In fact, espionage was a capital crime in Spain and every OSS agent knew well the burden this added. More frightening, perhaps, was the prospect of a German invasion. In preparation for one of those emergencies, each OSS agent was required to carry 21,900 pesetas—roughly $2,000 in 1944—at all times. This was quite a lot of money, but might be needed for bribes and last-minute transportation.

This contingency plan had already been used once. The summer before Aline arrived, the Madrid OSS office ran out of pesetas. There was no procedure or preestablished plan for acquiring more and the embassy refused to assist. Madrid had cabled Washington on July 3, 1943, stating that they had on hand 827,000 pesetas (roughly $76,000) but had liabilities of 1,300,000 pesetas against this amount. "We hope to increase our peseta balance to five million net this month," the cable said.

Washington didn't respond with a solution, perhaps because the State Department was well aware of Ambassador Hayes's disdain for the OSS and its activities on his "turf." So the only alternative, the Madrid office felt, was to buy the currency on the black market, a crime severely punished by the Spanish government.

Frank Schoonmaker, a Madrid agent who was operating as a wine importer by day, offered to find pesetas and set up a clandestine purchase. Assisting him was a cipher clerk who had recently arrived, an older man code-named TIGER. Unfortunately, they were caught by police while conducting the purchase.

The OSS then had a dilemma: Approaching the Spanish government to rescue the men would have been a tacit admission of illegal espionage. Fortunately, TIGER had just arrived in Spain and the authorities knew nothing about him, so he was summarily deported. Schoonmaker was another matter. The Spanish secret police had for some time known that he was an espionage operative, and the arrest was a golden opportunity to crack the entire American mission. Schoonmaker was thrown in a cell and prevented from seeing visitors.

The OSS consulted the State Department and Ambassador Carlton Hayes initiated discussions with Spain's foreign minister.* From a criminal justice standpoint, the Spanish contended that the American spy had to be punished, and they wanted to use Schoonmaker to set an example. On the other hand, local officials knew very well that their city was teeming with spies from almost every country in the war and had thus far chosen to display neutrality by turning a blind eye to their activities.

---

*Ambassador Hayes was so incensed that he requested OSS's removal from the entire Iberian peninsula. While his request was denied, he did obtain a considerable concession, restricting OSS's SI operations in Spain to "only such intelligence as may be requested or agreed to by the Ambassador and the Military and Naval Attachés, or be requested by the Joint Chiefs of Staff with the concurrence of the State Department."

A compromise was reached between Hayes and the Spanish government. The following night Schoonmaker's cell door was left unlocked, guards were mysteriously absent, and he sprinted out to a waiting car. He was then whisked to the embassy and hidden in the attic. The "escape" made Madrid's headline news, and several days later Schoonmaker, hidden inside an embassy Buick, was driven nonstop to Gibraltar. A Spanish court convicted him in absentia and sentenced him to life in prison.

Meanwhile back in the United States, Edmundo Lassalle was still trying to cut through the bureaucratic red tape preventing him from leaving for assignment. The OSS and the Walt Disney Company continued to wrangle over details for his services, and Roy Disney himself took the lead in negotiations.* The OSS wanted no traceable ties to Lassalle, yet it sought to control every aspect of his time and finances. Disney, on the other hand, wanted a legitimate representative who could provide real services and open doors for producing films on the Iberian peninsula.

After months of deliberations the parties finally agreed to the original terms: Disney would provide Edmundo with a normal salary and expense account, and the OSS would secretly reimburse them. Edmundo would sign an employment agreement with Disney and perform a certain amount of work for the company in Spain, and the reimbursement aspect would be covered by a separate contract between the OSS and the Disney Production Company.

It was the perfect cover: a Trojan horse disguised as Mickey Mouse.

By mid-March, Aline had settled into her new job and decided it was time to discover what Madrid had to offer at night. She had gone to dinner with Juanito the week after arriving, and he had proved to be a perfect gentleman. So when he began inviting her to

*Walt Disney's older brother, and cofounder of the company.

receptions and dinners, she readily agreed. While she had no romantic interest in him, Juanito had access to every level of society and,
as long as she kept any romantic impulses on his part in check, he
seemed to have the makings of a good friend.

Besides, he continued to send flowers.

And chocolates.

While Aline was finding her footing and Edmundo was preparing
to leave for Madrid, the Germans were focused on investigating one
of their own. An Abwehr officer named Johann "Johnny" Jebsen,
they feared, was feeding information to Britain's MI6. Jebsen's territory was Spain and Portugal, and he was the case officer for Germany's best agent, Ivan.* The Gestapo and SD had long suspected
that Jebsen was a traitor, and that Ivan might be a double, but they
never had material proof. They had ordered Jebsen to go to Biarritz,
France, for a meeting where they planned to arrest him and fly him
to Berlin for questioning, but Johnny smelled a trap and made up
an excuse for not leaving Spain. Perhaps under pressure from the
Gestapo, the Abwehr decided to expedite the matter by snatching
Jebsen in Madrid or Lisbon and forcibly taking him back to Berlin.

Kidnapping someone in a foreign country was difficult enough,
but doing so in neutral Portugal or Spain was delicate, to say the
least. If those doing the kidnapping were caught or the plot was
foiled, it would be a diplomatic fiasco and could do serious damage
to German-Spanish relations. But to let Jebsen orchestrate counterintelligence against them was unthinkable.

To handle such matters the Germans had a snatch team, the
Ablege Kommandos, who were experts at making people disappear
quietly. They could either kidnap their victims—drugging them and
sneaking them across the border—or kill them with an odorless,

---

*His name was Dusko Popov, a British double agent who worked for MI6, MI5, and
the FBI.

tasteless, and fast-acting poison that could be added to any food or drink. After twenty minutes the substance left no trace in the body and would clear an autopsy. And the Kommandos were not Germany's only option. Just one year before, in 1943, an Abwehr snatch team had killed a man in Madrid in broad daylight. In that instance, as in most cases involving Germans, the Spanish police looked the other way.

On April 30 Johnny Jebsen disappeared. He was never heard from again.

British intelligence learned later that he had been lured to the German embassy in Lisbon, was knocked out and injected with a sleeping agent, and was then stuffed into the trunk of a car with diplomatic plates. From Lisbon he was driven to Madrid, and from there to Biarritz, where an Abwehr plane was waiting. Jebsen was flown to Berlin and incarcerated in the Gestapo's notorious prison at Prinz-Albrecht-Strasse. Jebsen, the British were sure, was then subjected to "enhanced interrogation"—that is, torture.

The Jebsen kidnapping was evidence that no spy—not even OSS agents operating in neutral Spain—was exempt from danger. But no one could have predicted just how close that danger was. A few days after Jebsen's disappearance, as Aline's office mate Robert Dunev was parking his car in front of the American embassy, he noticed that across the street, hiding behind a Mercedes, there was a man taking his photograph.

Realizing that he had been spotted, the photographer jumped in the Mercedes and sped off. Robert whipped his car around and floored it.

The chase was on.

They raced through the streets of Madrid, but Robert's old car could not keep up with the speedy Mercedes. Somewhere on the Paseo de la Castellana Robert lost him. For several minutes he cruised along the Castellana and then up and down side streets.

Suddenly, he saw it; the Mercedes was parked. He pulled in behind it, but the driver was gone. Robert wrote down the tag number and when he returned to the office he began to dig. As he suspected, the car belonged to the German embassy. He had seen the photographer's face clearly, too, so he began searching for his identity. Combing through OSS and embassy files, he found him.

The man was indeed German and known to be a kidnapper of enemies of the Third Reich. Robert also found out that the man's modus operandi was to drug his victims, bundle them in the trunk of a car with diplomatic plates, and then race across the border into France. From there his victims were transported to Berlin.

CHAPTER 7

DEATH BY MURDER

On May 13, 1944, Edmundo Lassalle finally left the United States en route to Lisbon and Madrid. Sailing aboard the SS *Thome* from Philadelphia, he would not arrive in Lisbon until sixteen days later, on May 29.* Since Portugal was part of his Disney territory, he met with a few media and industry contacts, and two days later he was off for Spain.

He arrived in Madrid on June 1 and wasted no time providing Disney with tangible results. He met with local film industry officials and then gave an interview with one of the city's leading magazines, *Primer Plano*. He was treated almost as a celebrity, the name of Walt Disney being universally known and admired. It was a card that would open any door, Edmundo realized, and one he would begin to use often.

---

*This was the same route, Philadelphia to Lisbon, that Robert Dunev had taken when he sailed for assignment aboard the SS *Serpa Pinto* the year before. The number of days it took the men to reach Lisbon (Dunev, 15; Lassalle, 17) reveals the importance that the OSS placed on getting Aline in position quickly by sending her on the *Yankee Clipper*.

Charla con Edmundo Lassalle,
asesor de Walt Disney, huésped
actual de Madrid

MARLENE DIETRICH

Edmundo Lassalle (on the left in the photo), representative for Walt Disney, in the June 11, 1944, issue of *Primer Plano* (with Paramount Pictures film star Marlene Dietrich on the cover).

After tending to Disney business for a day or so, he received instructions from the OSS that he was to meet his Madrid contact at the Palace Hotel later that week. On the appointed day, he lingered in the lobby and waited for the woman who met the description.

The elevator door opened and Aline scanned the lobby as she slowly made her way to the front desk. Casually, she let her handbag slip from her hands.

Like a poised panther, a dark handsome man darted for it.

"The historical way to meet a lady," the man said, handing it to her.

Aline smiled. He had thick shiny black hair, a mustache trimmed like Clark Gable's, and smoldering dark brown eyes. His caramel skin was smooth and polished, his hands and fingers elegant and graceful.

"Edmundo Lassalle's my name," he said. "Would you do me the honor of joining me for a drink in the bar this evening?"

"How kind of you to invite me," Aline replied, completing the predetermined exchange of passwords.

It was a clumsy rendezvous, but Washington needed to get them together as quickly as possible. Since Edmundo was in deep cover as a representative of Walt Disney Productions, he couldn't be seen going to Aline's hotel room, and certainly not to the American embassy or the Oil Control Commission, as the former was likely watched and the latter might be. The plan Frank Ryan had come up with for Edmundo was that he would be based in Barcelona, liaising discreetly with the OSS station there, but would come often to Madrid. On many occasions, Ryan surmised, Edmundo would carry messages for Gregory Thomas, but he would need a cutout as the go-between.

That cutout was Aline.

Edmundo bowed and kissed her hand, saying he would see her in the evening. His gesture was equal parts theatrical and gentlemanly, and it seemed to Aline as though Washington had paired her with Don Juan.

At nine thirty Aline met Edmundo in the Palace Bar, where he again kissed her hand. They found a table out of earshot of other patrons and Aline asked for details about his cover.

"My cover is that I am Mexican," he said. "The representative of Walt Disney to Spain. This gives me the possibility of appearing neutral and enables me to see people of both sides."

He sipped a gin fizz. "The plan is to take you to a reception given by the Marquesa of Torrejón, where you'll meet Spaniards—foreign ambassadors, a few enemy spies, also many rich, beautiful women from other countries. Only women with influence today can obtain

exit permits from the countries at war. This will be the ideal opportunity to introduce you to the social world of the city."

"Who is the Marquesa of Torrejón?"

"The most popular social leader, and her gatherings are the spici-
est. I hope you have a wardrobe to meet the demands of Madrid's
social life. If not, I recommend a visit to Balenciaga. Darling, as
much as I love the Americans—and work for them—their social
graces don't hold a candle to the Europeans'."

Aline had heard of Cristóbal Balenciaga, the fashion designer
from Getaria, a coastal town just west of the French border. Trained
as a tailor in Madrid, he had started his business in San Sebastian
in 1919 and then opened stores in Madrid and Barcelona. Word
spread that he was one of the few couturiers in the fashion industry
who could actually conceive, pattern, cut, and sew his own designs.
In no time, Spanish high society began wearing his latest creations.
Aline knew that whereas Hattie Carnegie had a remarkable eye for
discovering beautiful clothes, Balenciaga had an unmatched skill in
designing them.

When the Spanish Civil War started, Balenciaga moved his business to Paris, where the influence of the Spanish Renaissance on
his collections enraptured fellow designers and clients alike. His Infanta gown had been inspired by the costumes of Spanish princesses
in Diego Velázquez's paintings, and his "jacket of light" was drawn
from the matador's *traje de luces*, the same type of vest that Aline had
received from Juanito.

After the civil war Balenciaga reopened his Madrid and Barcelona stores, but he remained in Paris. Over the next few years he
became known as the king of fashion, and his reputation lured a
number of talented young designers to apprentice for him, including
Oscar de la Renta and Hubert de Givenchy.*

---

*Balenciaga would go on to dress not only Aline but Grace Kelly, Ava Gardner,
Audrey Hepburn, and Jackie Kennedy. Christian Dior quipped that Balenciaga was
"the master of us all," and Coco Chanel agreed, saying that Balenciaga was "the only
couturier in the truest sense of the word."

Aline made a mental note to visit the Madrid store, and as Edmundo rattled on, she did her best to figure him out. His appearance—immaculate suit with pocket square and polished shoes—suggested diplomat, but his boyish demeanor and irrepressible character suggested otherwise. He was an enigmatic combination of sexy and silly. His chestnut eyes enchanted, right up until he let out a squeaky giggle.

"There will be a smattering of Axis and Spanish personalities at the marquesa's," he told her. "Concentrate on the women, the only way to get invited inside a Spanish home."

He checked his watch. "You must be starved. We have a reservation at Edelweiss."*

"A German restaurant?"

"Yes. To see more of the enemy."

The following evening Edmundo picked up Aline for the reception given by Doña Mimosa, the Marquesa of Torrejón, who lived in a palatial estate on Calle de Ferraz, just north of the Royal Palace. As Aline and Edmundo made their way through the grand salon, Aline noticed that almost all the women were decked out in jewels and elegant black Balenciaga dresses.

They continued strolling and Aline admired her elegant surroundings. The furniture was a mixture of Louis XVI and English baroque, and above the fireplace hung a massive portrait of their hostess.

"El Greco's most famous painting is of this lady's sixteenth-century ancestor's funeral,"** Edmundo said. "Come." He led her to another room, where a Goya hung.

---

*Still in operation today, Edelweiss is located at Calle de Jovellanos, 7, four blocks from the Palace Hotel.

**The ancestor Edmundo is referring to is Don Gonzalo Ruíz, a native of Toledo who had been known for his piety and philanthropy. Posthumously, he became known as the Count of Orgaz. In 1586, Toledo's parish priest commissioned El Greco to paint the burial of Ruíz, and the painting became known as *The Burial of Count of Orgaz*. The piece is used as a classic example of mannerism, and art critics regard it as El Greco's greatest masterpiece.

Aline admired the painting for a moment and then cast her gaze about the room.

Edmundo had been right about the guest list. Within just a few minutes she had recognized Sir Samuel Hoare, the British ambassador to Spain; José Lequerica, Spain's ambassador to France;* the Duke and Duchess of Lerma; the Countess of Yebes; the Duchess of Sueca; and Princess Maria Agatha of Ratibor and Corvey.

Aline and Edmundo followed the current of the party guests and ended up before a woman seated at an antique gilt card table. She was petite and frail-looking, with dyed brown hair and a double portion of rouge on her cheeks. This was their hostess, Doña Mimosa, and she appeared to be explaining to someone the meaning of the tarot cards arranged in front of her.

When Edmundo and Aline were close, introductions were made and Mimosa's face brightened.

"Why, Miss Griffith, do let me give you a reading. I have a strong feeling the cards have something special to tell you."

Aline didn't believe in fortune telling but thought it best to keep her opinion to herself. It wasn't entirely clear if Mimosa believed in it either; it was possible that this was a little performance meant to entertain her guests.

"Come sit by me," Mimosa said.

Aline stepped forward and she heard Princess Agatha murmur: "Mimosa will try anything to make her parties the most amusing."

"Be careful, señorita," Ambassador Lequerica chimed in. "The marquesa is a witch. She reads your mind as if it were her own."

Aline smiled good-naturedly. *Sure she did.*

Mimosa shuffled the cards and began flipping them over. "Now, you all know I have never seen this girl before. All I know about you, Aline, is that you are an acquaintance of Edmundo's and that you are American. Nothing else, is that true?"

Aline nodded.

---

*Who became Franco's foreign minister on August 11, 1944.

Mimosa studied the three cards in front of her: a nine, a five, and a seven. After several moments she looked up. "I see that you are going to be famous in this city. For one reason or another you will be in danger. Ah, and I see you will not return to your home for many years."

She paused and held Aline's eyes. "Shall I go on?"

Aline nodded again and peered over at Edmundo. He was staring at the cards, and Princess Agatha whispered something in his ear.

Mimosa dealt three more cards: a six, a two, and a five. Again she paused, and then said, "The cards show you are going to be embroiled in some kind of international plot." She seemed to wait for a response, but Aline gave no reply. The predictions Mimosa had made thus far, Aline knew, were generic enough to apply to anyone, especially in a room full of diplomats, spies, and wealthy adventurers.

Mimosa turned over three more and said, "There is someone whose well-being you are worried about—and with reason. That person's life is in danger."

Aline's thoughts immediately went to Juanito. Indeed, she worried about him every time he entered the ring.

Another three cards.

Mimosa tapped the middle card. "Adventure and intrigue."

"What kind of intrigue?" Ambassador Hoare asked. "You told me the same thing."

"And me," added the Duchess of Sueca.

The comments reinforced Aline's notion that Mimosa was not really a medium, but was merely entertaining her guests.

Another three cards, and as Mimosa turned over the last one, she said, "There must be some error in the manner in which I have handled the cards tonight. They reveal evil forces are at work around someone you are interested in, Aline."

She tapped the first card several times and then dealt another three.

"I see a bullfight," she said. "Oh, how terrifying, all these black cards—a death by murder."

Mimosa gathered up the cards. "I'm sorry, Aline, I hope I haven't upset you with my little entertainment."

Aline assured her that she had not, and that the reading had been quite enjoyable.

Then it came to her. The numbers and the tapping were a code.

She turned to speak to Edmundo, but he had wandered off. A piano was playing in an adjacent room, and Aline could hear the voices of women singing. She followed the sound and was not surprised to see Edmundo listening to three attractive young girls, one playing the piano and two singing. When the song ended everyone introduced themselves. The performers, Aline learned, were three daughters of the Count of Avila: Casilda, Carmen, and Nena Arteaga. Upon hearing that she was American, they began playing and singing "It Had to Be You." Aline knew the words by heart and joined in.

The sisters were excited to meet an American, and when Aline mentioned that she had brought a small collection of records with her to Spain, they invited her to join them for dinner the following week.

In the taxi on the way home Aline conversed quietly with Edmundo about Mimosa, the cards, and the peculiar tapping. He agreed that it might have been a code used to convey information to someone in the room. It seemed a reach that Mimosa was embroiled in espionage, but there were plenty of communists in Madrid who hated Franco, and a plot to kill him would not have been surprising.

Aline didn't worry about Mimosa's warnings of intrigue and murder, but over the next several days there was something else: she had an unsettling feeling, a prickling on the back of her neck, that she was being followed.

CHAPTER 8

PUTTING ON THE RITZ

It had started several nights earlier. The sound of footsteps. Most of the time when she glanced back there was no one. But one time she was sure she saw him, a man behind her stepping into the shadows.

Her training at The Farm now seemed not only valuable but critical. She mentioned the tags to Gregory Thomas, and he didn't seem surprised. Madrid was a city of intrigue, after all, and both sides were in constant surveillance of the other. How anyone would know that she was an Allied agent, though, was somewhat disturbing. It was time she rented an apartment, they decided, to get her away from any prying eyes. While the Palace and the Ritz across the street were the finest hotels in town, they were undoubtedly teeming with Abwehr and Gestapo agents and informants.

She found a spacious and relatively inexpensive place on Calle Monte Esquina, just a short walk from the office. The rent was only $50 and she was making—salary plus living allowance—$351 a month. Even with a maid, a cook, and a new Balenciaga dress every four weeks, she still had money to spare.

What she learned in her new environment, though, was that each residential building had a *portero*, and each neighborhood a *sereno*. Together, these two individuals provided security: the *por-*

tero acted as a building supervisor by day, the *sereno* its watchman by night. Apartment buildings were locked from 11:00 p.m. to 7:00 a.m., she discovered, and if you arrived home without your keys, you called the *sereno* by clapping. In a matter of seconds he would appear, announcing his approach by banging his stick against the curb. On his belt he carried keys for every house and apartment in his district, and it was customary for residents to call for him even when they had their keys, simply to say hello and let him know they were home.

The *sereno* gave Aline some comfort when she thought she was being followed, but there were times he was down the street opening the door for a neighbor when she needed him.

Meanwhile in the Atlantic, the Allies launched the largest amphibious landing in history on June 6, invading occupied France at the beaches of Normandy. While OSS Madrid received little attention for their contribution, the daily forwarding of messages from Allied intelligence throughout France to Washington no doubt aided American troops storming the beaches and working behind enemy lines. American OSS and British SOE agents operating in southern France had been identifying German troop and tank locations, as well as enemy arms depots, for months preceding the attack. And every message forwarded by Aline or Robert Dunev, however insignificant it may have seemed to them at the time, added to Allied Supreme Commander Dwight D. Eisenhower's overall picture. In many cases, no doubt, the intelligence forwarded led to American bombing runs leading up to the invasion.

But D-Day had little effect on the situation in Spain; Madrid papers carried the news, of course, but daily life didn't change. On June 10, Edmundo moved on to Barcelona and checked in to the Ritz. It was extravagant, particularly on his $7 per diem, but as a Disney representative he felt he needed to play the part of the successful Hollywood executive.

As he had in Madrid, Edmundo wasted no time getting to work. He met with his Barcelona supervisor* and debriefed him on his activities. His boss was impressed and in a report to Gregory Thomas he praised Edmundo's industriousness: "He has made a remarkable number of good contacts in a very short time. I am sure you will agree with me that all in all he has done very well in such a short period of time and that if he continues this good work he will eventually prove to be a most valuable member of our organization."

At the end of June Edmundo returned to Madrid, and the first week of July he and Aline decided to have dinner in the belly of the beast: Horcher's. It was Madrid's finest restaurant but was known to be a regular hangout for Abwehr and SS officers. The German owner, Otto Horcher, had operated a similar restaurant in Berlin—said to be Göring's favorite—and had been given special exemption from military service to open a sister operation in Madrid.

What Aline and Edmundo didn't know was that Horcher's might also provide the enemy some intel about them. Concealed in the flower vase on each table was a hidden microphone.** Not only was Horcher's a letter box—a secret venue to drop off and retrieve messages—it was an active counterintelligence hub.

They arrived at Horcher's at eleven and it was busy but not yet full. The maître d' escorted them to a table and Aline observed the elegant setting: linen tablecloths, high ceilings with elaborate molding, green velvet drapes, and warm ambient lighting. When she took her seat, a waiter placed a pillow under her feet.

---

*Deputy chief "ELTON."

**In a meeting here in 1941, Abwehr agent Johann Jebsen warned his subagent, Dusko Popov—whom he was fairly sure was a double agent for the British—about microphones hidden in the vases.

Horcher's restaurant, Madrid.

As they perused the menu, Aline heard a number of patrons gathering at the entrance and looked up. At the head of the group was a short, stiff-looking man, immaculately dressed. His black suit and the formal starched collar of his striped shirt, together with his pencil-thin mustache and slicked-back hair, gave him the appearance of a film star or a gangster.

Edmundo glanced over. "Hans Lazar. Press attaché of the German embassy."

Aline nodded and tried not to be conspicuous in her watching.

Lazar passed their table and Aline got a closer look at his face. His skin was soft and babylike, but his eyes were sinister—deep and brooding and set in dark circles. A gangster all right, and one of the four suspects Thomas had mentioned as Himmler's possible contact.

"Gives lavish parties in a palace he has rented on the Castellana," Edmundo added as Lazar disappeared into a private room.

There was a murmur again at the entrance, and Aline and Edmundo looked over. A tall, sleek brunette, maybe in her late twenties, was turning heads and conversations. Aline had been a professional model and had worked with many of New York's great beauties, but this woman was exceptional. Her face was like a doll's—perfectly shaped and smooth as porcelain. She was wearing a black satin gown beneath a floor-length sable cape, with long strands of gleaming pearls around her neck. And she was graceful, a swan in a lake of mallards.

"Who is *that?*"

Edmundo smiled. Every Mexican knew the face of Gloria Rubio, the beauty from his home country who had married a wealthy German count. "The one and only," he said, staring and admiring. "The Countess of Fürstenberg."

Gloria sailed smoothly between the tables, disappearing into the room where Lazar had gone.

Aline eyed the closed door. "We now know who Lazar's dinner guest is. Do you know her? She must be fascinating."

"I know her through gossip. The Guatemalan ambassador says he saw her in a casino in Mexico when she was sixteen. Who was it—I can't remember—took her to Hollywood after one look. She was in Los Angeles only long enough to meet some Dutch financier. Frankly, Hollywood was too small for Gloria's ambitions."

German press attaché Hans Lazar and Gloria von Fürstenberg.

Edmundo sipped his wine and told her about Gloria's second husband, Egon von Fürstenberg. "In Berlin she was famous. She palled around with all the bigwigs—Schellenberg, Göring, Himmler. She's clever, too, because when no one could travel anyplace, she managed to go to Paris."

Aline glanced again at the closed door of the private area and pretended to be chilly. Calling the waiter over, she nodded toward a table closer to the room and asked if they could move. When they were reseated, Edmundo complained about the nuisance of changing tables, noting that it was no warmer in their new location. The door to the private room opened and Edmundo followed Aline's gaze.

"Ah. Now I see. Nothing stops you, does it, my dear? I tell you, Aline, you are the woman of my heart. If only you had a title."

The door was open only a second but Aline glimpsed Lazar and Gloria's coat tossed over a chair. A moment later three waiters went in with trays and the door stayed open a second longer, enough time for Aline's eyes to sweep the room.

She drew in her breath. *Couldn't be.*

The door closed again and she told Edmundo she was sure she had seen none other than Heinrich Himmler.

"You're mad, Aline. Himmler hasn't been here since 1941."

When Edmundo dropped her off after dinner Aline returned to the office to call Gregory Thomas. It was after one in the morning but she felt justified making the interruption.

Hearing Aline's assertion that she had seen Himmler at Horcher's, Thomas sighed. "If that were true, I would know he was in the country. There are a hundred squat, bespectacled men in Madrid who might be mistaken for him. Is that all?"

Aline felt like an idiot. Edmundo didn't believe her, and now Thomas. Granted, there were rumors of Himmler sightings all the time in Spain, but she could have sworn that that was him.

Thomas bid her good night and she began walking home. She was dejected but at least she had seen two of the individuals on Thomas's list. It was a start, anyway.

The night was quiet and a few blocks from her apartment she heard them again.

Footsteps.

She increased her pace and the echoing patter quickened behind her. She couldn't tell if the tag was gaining on her, but she lengthened her stride. When she reached her street she didn't see the *sereno*, so she skipped the keys and slipped through the iron bars of the building's exterior door. A minute later she was in her apartment, sliding the security bolt.

The next day Aline had another date with Juanito. They shared a glass of Tio Pepe sherry at a café overlooking the Rio Manzanares and Juanito suggested going across the street to see the Church of San Antonio de la Florida. It was historic, he said, and there was something he wanted to show her.

Inside, they made their way to the inner sanctum, the Chapel of the Royal Seat of La Florida. Aline read a plaque on the wall, which said it had been commissioned by King Carlos IV at the end of the eighteenth century. She gazed up at the towering ceilings glowing with frescoes and gasped. This was indeed Spain's Sistine Chapel.

"Those were painted by Goya," Juanito said. He looked at her and then back to the ceiling. "The eyes in those paintings are like your own, full of smoldering fire."

Aline smiled. Her bullfighter saw everything through the prism of drama and color.

Next they went to the Plaza Mayor, a seventeenth-century square surrounded by ancient buildings with iron-railed balconies.

"That's where the royal family and the court used to watch the bullfights," Juanito said. "When the matador was especially successful, the ladies sometimes threw pearls into the ring."

Juanito then suggested they visit a restaurant with a hidden wine-and-cheese café. They went to the southwest corner of the plaza, and then up and down a series of Roman stone pathways—the Steps of Cuchilleros. The restaurant was Botín, said to be the oldest in the world.

Passing through several domed chambers, they came to what appeared to be a cave. It was Botín's wine café, a long, narrow enclave with a low arched ceiling—like an escape tunnel or dungeon. The entire interior was stone and mortar, but the pieces were cut so precisely that at first it appeared to be brick. In the middle was a black iron grille, apparently for ventilation, and in every alcove there were small lamps. Were it not for the brilliantly white tablecloths and sparkling glasses—reminding patrons they were in a fine dining establishment—claustrophobia would have been difficult to avoid.

Juanito ordered wine and manchego cheese, and then motioned around. "This is where the famous bandit Luis Candelas used to hide, Aline. He stole from the rich and gave to the poor—just like your Robin Hat."

Aline laughed. "Hood. Robin *Hood*."

Afterward they strolled to a restaurant on Calle de Segovia, Madrid's oldest barrio. When they were seated, Aline figured it was time to mix a little business with pleasure and asked Juanito if he knew the Countess von Fürstenberg.

"Of course I know her. Why do you ask?"

"Could you introduce me?"

"Certainly not. She is not the proper friend for you."

Aline smirked. Foiled again by the Old World.

The second week of July, Gregory Thomas informed the staff that the office would be moving. Washington wanted additional security for the OSS operation and files, he said, and most everyone would be moving into Ambassador Carlton Hayes's embassy residence.

The US embassy compound, located alongside the Paseo de

la Castellana,* occupied an entire city block, running from Calle Eduardo Dato to Diego de León. The ambassador's residence was a three-story baroque palace built by the Duke of Montellano, which the United States had leased since 1931. Aside from its central location in the best part of town, the site also contained one of the most beautiful gardens in all of Madrid, full of horse chestnut trees, pine trees, roses, and rhododendrons.

Most of the staff would work from fourteen rooms on the third floor of Hayes's residence, Aline found out, while Thomas and his secretary would set up shop in a small office in the adjacent garage annex. Why Thomas wanted or needed to be in a separate location was anyone's guess.

The coding room was set up in a corner office, and on their first day in the new space Robert Dunev called Aline to the window and pointed across the street to a magnificent building. He told her that it was the home of the Count of Romanones, the highly regarded former prime minister to King Alfonso XIII.

Aline admired the three-story palace, but the Romanones name meant nothing to her. For most Spaniards, though, it was a name that commanded great respect. Álvaro de Figueroa y Torres-Sotomayor, the first Count of Romanones, had served three times as the country's prime minister, seventeen times as a cabinet member, and was one of Spain's wealthiest men. He had been King Alfonso's closest adviser, and the one who had advised him to leave the country and eventually abdicate the throne.

Aline went back to work and decoded an incoming cable from London:

TO ARGUS FROM CHESS STOP HIMMLER PROCEEDING TO AB-
SORB ABWEHR INTELLIGENCE INTO GESTAPO AFTER REMOVAL
OF CANARIS STOP WALTER SCHELLENBERG NOW CONTROLS
ALL GERMAN FOREIGN INTELLIGENCE STOP

*Madrid's equivalent of Paris's Champs Élysées.

The cable's message wasn't surprising. The Allies had suspected that the Abwehr chief, Admiral Wilhelm Canaris, had been working against Hitler and the Nazis for years. What few knew was that senior German military officers had vehemently opposed Hitler and his Nazi Party from the beginning.

In 1933 Colonel General Kurt Freiherr von Hammerstein, Commander in Chief of the Reichswehr* and Germany's top military officer, together with Lieutenant General Erich Freiherr von dem Bussche-Ippenburg, head of the Reichswehr's Personnel Office, met with President Paul Hindenburg on January 26 to dissuade Hindenburg from appointing Hitler as Reich Chancellor, counseling that Hitler was dangerous. During discussions Hindenburg assured them that he would never appoint the "Austrian corporal" as chancellor.** Four days later, however, the ailing Hindenburg did just that, and rumors circulated that the military would launch a putsch to prevent Hitler's installation.

Soon thereafter General Hammerstein met with Dr. Heinrich Brüning, the former Reich Chancellor, to discuss how the Nazi government could be overthrown. The obstacle, they found, was Hitler's appointment of Werner von Blomberg, a naive colonel general, as Reichswehr Minister. Blomberg failed to recognize Hitler's fanaticism, and since Blomberg was now Hammerstein's superior, the general felt that a coup could no longer be successful. He turned in his resignation and retired at the end of the year.

Meanwhile, Hitler brought to power two paramilitary groups, the Sturm Abteilung (SA) and the Schutzstaffel (SS). On paper they were "auxiliary police," but in reality they were Hitler's private army. Unlike the Wehrmacht, the Luftwaffe, and the Kriegsmarine, which were staffed and run by men with formal military training and decades of experience, these were Nazi Party *political* organizations, composed of leaders like Ernst Röhm (SA), a belligerent Bavarian

*German army, later known as the Wehrmacht.

**Referring to Hitler's nationality and top military rank.

crook, and Heinrich Himmler (SS), who had almost no military experience. Tensions between the real German military and the Nazi Party's paramilitary upstarts heightened when Hitler gave the Nazi Party its own intelligence agencies—the SD for foreign intelligence and counterespionage, the Gestapo for domestic intelligence. These agencies, generals knew, would compete with the Abwehr, the military's well-respected and professional intelligence arm.

On February 1, 1934, Hitler chose General Werner Freiherr von Fritsch, a self-professed apolitical officer, to replace the retired Hammerstein. By the spring, however, concerned military leaders were again plotting to overthrow their head of state. Colonel General Gerd von Rundstedt, commander of the Second Army; Major General Erwin von Witzleben, commander of the Third Army; and Colonel General Fedor von Bock, commander of the Eighth Army, were prepared to use their forces against SA troops as part of a plan to force Hitler to resign. Due to the immense planning and secrecy required, though, the putsch never materialized.

Four years later, on February 4, 1938, Hitler began to purge the military, dismissing Blomberg and Fritsch from their posts for failing to support his plan for *Lebensraum* (territorial expansion). At the same time, Hitler declared that the Reichswehr would become known as the *Oberkommando der Wehrmacht* (OKW), and that he would be its supreme commander. Succeeding Fritsch as commander in chief of the Wehrmacht was General Walther von Brauchitsch. Frustrated and appalled, a number of generals approached von Brauchitsch with their resignations. He succeeded in convincing them to remain in their posts, but the plots within the military to remove Hitler and key Nazi leaders continued.

Admiral Canaris, Lieutenant General Ludwig Beck, and Lieutenant Colonel Hans Oster again began conspiring as to how to eliminate Hitler.* General Brauchitsch agreed to go along, so long

---

*Beck was first Fritsch's, and now von Brauchitsch's, chief of staff; Oster was Canaris's chief assistant.

as the coup was supported by a memorandum from the minister of justice. Generals von Rundstedt and von Witzleben remained on board. Generals Wilhelm List, commander of the Fourth Army, and Günther von Kluge, commander of the Sixth Army, were added. Major General Paul von Hase, commander of the No. 50 Infantry Regiment, declared that his troops would fight against the Nazi Gestapo and SS in Berlin. Yet the conspirators were hamstrung by Brauchitsch's passivity and the difficulty of secretly planning such a major event.

In August, upon hearing of Hitler's intention to annex the Sudetenland,* Beck tendered his resignation and declared his retirement. Beck's successor, General Franz Halder, immediately initiated plans for a coup. Halder made no secret among the conspirators of his animosity toward Hitler, describing him as a "bloodsucker and criminal." So once more the generals were lined up: Canaris, Oster, von Witzleben, von Hase, von Bock, von Rundstedt, List, Kluge, Major General Walter Graf von Brockdorff-Ahlefeldt, commander of the 23 (Potsdam) Division, and Lieutenant General Erich Hoepner, commander of the No. 1 Light Division. Lieutenant General Karl-Heinrich von Stülpnagel, Army Deputy Chief of Staff, helped draw up plans and worked on timing. Major Friedrich Wilhelm Heinz, at Canaris's direction and with arms and explosives supplied by Canaris, would direct the troops raiding the Reich Chancellery.**

The president of the Berlin police, Wolf Heinrich Graf von Helldorf, and the vice president, Fritz-Dietlof Graf von der Schulenburg, assured that their men would assist in countering the SS in Berlin.

The conspirators' justification for the coup, they asserted, was Hitler's unlawful intentions regarding territorial expansion, and the

---

*Areas of Czechoslovakia along the German border that were populated primarily by Germans.

**Heinz had already decided, and passed word among his men, that Hitler would be shot during the raid.

inevitable result that it would thrust Germany into another war. So long as they could show the German people and the common soldier that Hitler was taking their country headlong into an illegal war, they held the moral high ground. Since Hitler had agreed to give Halder a forty-eight-hour notice of his intention to invade Czechoslovakia, Halder would use that window to initiate the coup. If successful, the plan would yield two benefits: ousting Hitler and preventing Germany's invasion of another country.

But hurdles to the planned coup were significant. By waiting until Hitler called for the mobilization of the army (thus proving his intention of war), the conspirators would have to countermand the order immediately, all while keeping the plot a secret. They also would have to control the post office and all lines of communication so that provincial leaders could be informed about which Nazi leaders to arrest.

And then there was the matter of governance after the coup. The conspirators agreed that martial law and a state of emergency would be needed for a short while, and then they would usher in new elections under the constitution of the old Weimar Republic. But who would be in charge in the meantime?

In the end, the coup was thwarted by a most unlikely player: the British. Since the Generals' Plot (as it came to be known) all along rested on the charge that Hitler was thrusting Germany into war, any peace agreements with Britain or France would negate their justification for patriotic treason.

And that is precisely what happened. On September 15, British Prime Minister Neville Chamberlain made a surprise visit, meeting Hitler in Berchtesgaden. The German conspirators were outraged. Chamberlain was paying homage to a gangster, they felt, and his visit no doubt led Hitler to believe the British were accepting his territorial aggression. The visit led to the Munich Conference, held September 29–30, and resulted in the Munich Agreement—Britain's acceptance of Hitler's annexation of the Sudetenland in exchange for his relinquishment of other territorial demands.

Upon hearing news of the Munich Agreement, General Halder collapsed over his desk. The one condition to the Generals' Plot had failed, and he never signaled for the putsch. In perhaps the strangest sequence of events, the German military felt betrayed by the British.

There would be other attempts by the military to kill the Führer, all without success. In 1943, for example, Beck and other officers twice tried to kill Hitler, but both plots failed.

And little did Aline or the OSS Madrid office know that only days after they received the cable about Canaris and Schellenberg, Beck and Oster, together with thousands of military officers, would try again on July 20, 1944, setting off a bomb at a meeting Hitler attended at his Wolf's Lair at Rastenburg.* None other than Field Marshal Erwin Rommel had given the putsch his blessing, so long as Beck agreed to serve as head of state after Hitler was gone.** When the July 20 plot failed, the number of military officers implicated in the coup attempt was staggering. After countless plotters were tortured into confessions, and other names extracted, some five

---

*Two other noteworthy events illustrate the direct and ongoing antagonism between the Wehrmacht and the SS. First, when General von Stülpnagel (now serving as the commander of forces in France) received word that the putsch was a go, he had his troops in Paris arrest and jail all 1,200 SS and SD soldiers and agents stationed in the city. A second confrontation between the Wehrmacht and the SS occurred at the end of April 1945. On orders from Heinrich Himmler, a number of SS guards were transporting a group of prisoners near the Italy-Austria border. Along with captured British officers, the prisoners included two Wehrmacht officers who had fallen out of favor with Hitler: General Franz Halder, former chief of the OKW, and Colonel Bogislaw von Bonin, former chief of the operational branch of the army general staff. When the party reached Villabasa, von Bonin made a call to Field Marshal Albert Kesselring's Fourteenth Army headquarters in Italy. The colonel informed the staff officer answering the phone that he, General Halder, and others were being held by Himmler's SS guards, and requested that a company of the Wehrmacht's finest be sent to rescue them. Kesselring's soldiers were promised to arrive by 6:00 p.m. the following evening, and von Bonin suggested to the SS guards that they might want to disappear before the cavalry arrived. In short, there was going to be a shootout between two German groups: the Wehrmacht's seasoned Fourteenth Army soldiers and the Nazi SS guards. The SS guards wisely disappeared before Kesselring's men arrived.

**Rommel's desire, aligned with Beck's, was for Hitler to be arrested and tried for crimes against the German people and occupied lands.

thousand military officers were executed or committed suicide, including sixteen of Germany's top generals and three field marshals.*
Field Marshals Gerd von Rundstedt and Erich von Manstein declined to be involved in the putsch, but nevertheless passively acquiesced by not informing Hitler.

But the message of the Canaris-Schellenberg cable to the OSS Madrid office was clear enough: with Canaris gone, Schellenberg would be moving full force to exert as much pressure on Spain as possible.

That evening Aline prepared for a night out with Edmundo. They were going to drop in on a cocktail party hosted by Ralph Forte, the Associated Press correspondent, and then later swing by the La Reboite nightclub for another party. Edmundo was going to pick her up at ten, and she planned to wear a new red silk dress.

As she was applying her lipstick, she stopped. After a moment, she continued.

It was probably the wind.

Madrid was like Kansas, after all, gusts and swirls coming from nowhere at any hour. Besides, it would be impossible to get on the roof and—

There it was again.

From the other room?

Impossible. How could—

And again. The balcony shutters.

No doubt this time. Shutters don't creak like that from the wind. Someone was prying them open.

Ever so quietly, Aline eased back the top drawer of her vanity and withdrew her pistol. On her tiptoes, she slipped into the shadows in

---

*Generals Ludwig Beck, Karl-Heinrich von Stülpnagel, Henning von Tresckow, Erich Hoepner, Hellmuth Stief, Paul von Hase, Erich Fellgiebel, Hans Oster, Friedrich Fromm, Fritz Lindemann, Friedrich Olbricht, Eduard Wagner, Fritz Thiele, Karl von Thuengen, and Otto Herfurth; Admiral Wilhelm Canaris; and Field Marshals Erwin Rommel, Günther von Kluge, and Erwin von Witzleben.

the hall and flipped off the safety. All of those endless hours at The Farm came down to this. They had practiced in the dark, and inside houses. Two shots to the torso.

Heart pounding, she edged her way to the opening to the salon. *Could she do it?*

There was another creak as moonlight filtered in and then she saw it.

A man's hand pushing back the curtain.

She lifted the gun.

CHAPTER 9

GLORIOUS GLORIA

Aline thought about blindly shooting into the window but decided to wait.

The drapery bulged and she could see a figure stepping inside. She held her aim as the curtain swung.

"Pierre!" she gasped. "What are you doing here?"

"How are you?" Pierre grinned as he came to her, took the gun from her hand, and set it aside. "Didn't expect to see me soon, did you?"

Aline's heart was still racing. "How did you find out where I lived?"

"That's our business, isn't it? Come, let's sit down and talk."

"Pierre, what are you doing here? You know, I almost shot you just now."

"I can't tell you much. Your boss would have my hide if he knew I was visiting you."

Thoughts swept through Aline's mind, none of them good. *Why was he in Madrid? How did he get my address, and why was his visit kept secret?* If he'd gotten her address from Thomas or MacMillan or Mellon, surely one of them would have told her. And why the hell did he have to come in through the balcony like a cat burglar? Why couldn't he just have knocked on the door, or, better yet, *called her* in advance? It was a bit unsettling, but in spite of all that, she was delighted to see him.

They moved to the sofa and Pierre kissed her, gripping her with both arms and pulling her close. Then the doorbell rang.

Edmundo.

Pierre's head jerked toward the door. "Who is that?"

Aline decided to keep it vague. A contact was taking her to a party, she said.

Pierre jumped up and they returned to the balcony. He kissed her quickly.

"I can't be seen. I doubt I'll be able to see you soon. Don't forget me."

The curtain swung and he was gone.

Aline stood there, astonished. *Had that actually just happened?* She reflected a moment and then, trying to look as unflustered as possible, went to the door to greet Edmundo.

Near the end of July, Maria Francesca Hohenlohe, Prince Max's eldest daughter, invited Aline to a weekend party at the family's country residence. Aline had met Maria—whom everyone called Pimpinela—while having dinner with Casilda Arteaga, who was Pimpinela's best friend. Fascinated by the pretty, newly arrived American who was about her own age, Pimpinela determined that they should be great friends.

The Hohenlohe property was near Escorial, about thirty miles northwest of Madrid, and an invitation to the estate, known as El Quexigal, was one of the most coveted in all of Europe. The residence was a sixteenth-century square-shaped castle now used as a finca.* The grounds covered some 4,400 acres, much of which was

---

*Common in Spain and Latin America, fincas are second homes, often luxurious, that are surrounded by farms with full-time workers.

farmed as vineyards by three hundred laborers. Prince Max had bought it in 1927, and Pimpinela's mother, Maria-Piedad de Iturbe, was said to have spent several million pesetas renovating it.

There would be many guests, Pimpinela said, so Aline figured there was a good chance that Gloria von Fürstenberg or Hans Lazar would be attending.

On Saturday afternoon Aline and Casilda left Madrid and headed northwest, toward the Guadarrama Mountains. During the drive Aline asked what Casilda knew about the Hohenlohe family, and there seemed to be little she didn't know.

Pimpinela, she said, was about to turn twenty-two and was the oldest of Max and Maria's six children. Her brothers, Alfonso, Christian, and Max Emanuel, were twenty, eighteen, and twelve, while her sisters, Elizabeth and Beatriz, were sixteen and nine.

Prince Max's full name was Maximilian Egon von Hohenlohe-Langenburg; he was Austrian, but had been born in the family's castle in Rothenhaus, Czechoslovakia. His wife was the daughter of the Spanish Duchess of Parcent, but Pimpinela's great-grandfather on her mother's side was German.

Aline had heard stories of Prince Max's fabulous wealth. In addition to El Quexigal and the Rothenhaus castle, he owned another castle in Santillana, Spain. He also owned a home near San Sebastian, commercial property near Sevilla, a large villa in Biarritz, and two large fincas in Mexico: one near Mexico City, the other by Acapulco.

As they approached Escorial, Casilda pointed out four spires in the distance. "Look, Aline, that's the most important royal palace in Spain, built by Philip the Second in the sixteenth century. The same architect who built the Hohenlohe palace."*

Aline gazed through the window. It was the most enormous structure she'd ever seen.

About twenty minutes later they began descending a hill,

---

*Juan de Herrera.

and Aline saw El Quexigal in its full glory: the castle's dark orange tiles burned brightly against the deep green oaks and pines surrounding it. They passed through gates manned by Guardia Civil—Spain's national guard—and she could see just how old this square-shaped colossus was. It was only two stories tall but seemed to run the length of a football field. The exterior was some kind of sandstone, light orange, with countless small windows on the second floor.

"To me the building appeared impregnable and austere," she remembered later, "reminiscent of knights in armor and children's fairy tales."

El Quexigal, Escorial, Spain

They pulled into the parking area where a chauffeur was unloading luggage from a black Mercedes. Behind the main building were two swimming pools and a tennis court. Not far beyond them was a small chapel and another building for housing servants. Next to that was a smaller building, the estate's school, Casilda said, where the Hohenlohe children were taught alongside the children of the servants, all of whom could read and write and many of whom could speak French.

Aline looked around, admiring. El Quexigal was its own self-contained town.

Inside, a butler invited them to sign the guest book, appropriately placed in a sacerdotal setting between two silver candelabra. As Aline wrote her name, she noticed that the book contained signatures going back several years.

That would come in handy.

While they waited for their bags to be brought in, she and Casilda chatted and ambled about the foyer. Aline had the same sense of awe she had felt when entering the chapel of La Florida with Juanito. There were no Goya frescoes here, but Gobelins tapestries and priceless paintings were everywhere: El Greco, Murillo, Gallego, Berruguete, Tiepolo. Some works dated back to the fourteenth and fifteenth centuries. The furniture was ancient and hand-carved, she noticed, and upon much of it rested countless pieces of Talavera pottery.

Through a set of open double doors they could see the patio courtyard, the interior of the square. It was about the size of two tennis courts and was lined with some fifty stone columns. On the second level a balcony wrapped the entire interior.

The place was a fortress, a finca, a hotel, and a museum all rolled into one. All 150 rooms and 86,000 square feet of it.

Servants appeared with their luggage and two maids escorted them upstairs. They walked down a long corridor and Aline's suitcases were placed in an anteroom with beamed ceilings and a fireplace, beyond which was a bedroom. As she was admiring the red damask canopy over the bed, the maid turned on a lamp and said she would return momentarily to unpack Aline's things.

Casilda met her in the hall and they went downstairs to join the other guests. Going through several salons, they entered a large den where a number of women were having tea and cakes and a tall man in a tweed shooting jacket was bragging to another about the day's hunt.

Pimpinela saw Aline from the other side of the room and rushed over. "How happy I am to have you here, Aline. Come meet my father. My mother will see you later—she never takes tea."

Prince Max was in his early fifties, Aline presumed, and had a thick build. He was about six feet tall, with blond hair and a plump round face.

"Aline, it is a pleasure to meet a friend of Pimpinela's," he said, "and to have you as our guest." Max's English was excellent, but he spoke with a strong German accent.

As she made small talk with Prince Max, Aline observed the guests having tea and noticed Hans Lazar and Gloria von Fürstenberg. This was the second time Aline had seen Gloria, and both times she had been with Lazar. Seated next to them, to Aline's surprise, was the young man who had carried her bags when she had checked in at the Palace, and a gray-haired man whom she had not seen before.

Sitting in another group was the Count and Countess of Yebes, Mimosa Torrejón, and a young man she remembered as Constantin Canaris. Edmundo had pointed him out when they had dinner at Edelweiss one night, and on another evening she had bumped into him while dancing. He was an Abwehr agent, she had learned, the nephew of the former chief, Admiral Wilhelm Canaris.

Out of the corner of her eye she saw Casilda's sister Nena approaching the Lazar-Fürstenberg group, and after a few minutes chatting with Prince Max, Aline excused herself to join them. Nena greeted her and introduced her to the others, starting with the young man she called the Count of Quintanilla.

"I think we have met before," the handsome count said, smiling.

Aline blushed, recalling that she had tried to tip him that first day at the Palace Hotel.

Nena next introduced the older guest, Carlos Beistegui, a distinguished-looking gentleman, and then Countess von Fürstenberg. Aline once again had the notion that the countess was the most ravishing, best-dressed woman she had ever seen. With her height and high cheekbones, Aline thought she could have been a fashion model. And Gloria's outfit was no less stunning: a snug wool checked suit, custom leather shoes with pointed toes, and a matching jacket.

"*Encantada*, Aline."

Hans Lazar then stood and introduced himself. "A pleasure, Miss Griffith."

Lazar was polite, but Aline couldn't get past his appearance; sinister and slick was the only way to describe it. And that was precisely his reputation. The British ambassador, Samuel Hoare, made no bones about his dislike for Lazar. He was "well-dressed, and self-consciously well-mannered," Hoare remembered, "like those operatic Viennese figures created by Straus or Lehar. Those of us who dealt with him came to the conclusion that we were dealing with someone very important. His ambition had no limit."

Aline continued greeting the others, eventually shaking hands with Constantin Canaris. Since he was Abwehr, she figured he'd be useful later.

That evening at nine thirty Aline and Casilda headed downstairs for drinks in the great salon, and at ten thirty everyone moved to the dining room. This area, too, seemed like a museum. Giant tapestries from Cuenca—at least ten meters in length—hung from the walls, and Aubusson rugs covered the wide-planked floor. Silver candelabra adorned antique furniture that had been acquired from French palaces.

Aline peered down the long table and counted eighteen guests. She had been placed between the Count of Quintanilla, whose name was Luis de Figueroa, and Carlos Beistegui. It was like watching a complex choreography, as six uniformed servants scurried in and out to wait on them. She had hoped to engage the handsome young count in conversation, but Beistegui rambled on about living in Paris, bragging that his large house on the Castellana usually sat empty.

After dinner the party moved into the ballroom, where a troupe of dancers was preparing for the flamenco entertainment. Most of the men were drinking cognac now, and Aline figured it was the perfect time to slip away. She excused herself, saying she needed to get something from her room, and made her way through the labyrinth of salons until she came to the front hall.

Checking to make sure the coast was clear, she began inspecting the names in the guest book, turning page after page. Suddenly she heard someone behind her.

"Aline, what on earth are you doing?" asked Pimpinela.

"I was on my way to the ladies' room and then I became fascinated by your guest book. What an interesting life your family has had. And this beautiful house. I've never seen anything like it."

Pimpinela smiled. "I never think about it—to me it's just my family and our home. Wait till tomorrow. It is lovely outdoors."

Aline took a deep breath. Yes, tomorrow.

They chatted for a few minutes and Aline asked if it would be okay to wander around to admire the paintings and tapestries.

"Of course," Pimpinela said. "My house is your house."

Pimpinela returned to the party and Aline bounded up the stairs to the bedrooms. She might have sufficient time, she thought, to snoop around in Gloria and Lazar's rooms—if she could find them. As she made her way down the corridor, though, she saw a figure leaning against the wall. She continued on and saw that it was Constantin Canaris.

"The fräulein is missing the wonderful entertainment," he said. "Or perhaps she is enjoying her own."

Aline smiled but said nothing and went on to her room. So much for snooping around. She could hear that the flamenco party downstairs was going strong, but she decided to turn in. Tomorrow would be a full day, and she was anxious to learn more about Gloria, Lazar, and the Count of Quintanilla.

She fell asleep quickly and began to dream. After some time, perhaps about three in the morning, she stirred in her bed.

There was a sound and she opened her eyes.

It was pitch-dark but she was certain.

Someone was in her room.

CHAPTER 10

VISITORS

The figure moved toward the bed and Aline realized that her gun was across the room in her purse.

The smell came first.

Alcohol. It was Constantin Canaris.

"Don't be afraid," he said, slurring his words. "I know all about you American girls. You give your favors easily." He bent forward to try to kiss her but stumbled.

Aline punched the top of his head. "Get out of here."

Constantin fell to his knees. "I saw the way you looked at him zis afternoon. I've heard all about you American women. You are so easy."

"Get out of here. Before I scream."

Constantin began mumbling and Aline got up and turned on the light. "You're drunk," she said, pushing him into a chair, "and you'll regret your behavior in the morning. But don't worry, I understand. You've got the wrong idea about American girls."

He slumped in the chair, nursing his head. "Vat am I doing?"

Seconds later he passed out and for several minutes Aline tried to revive him. Eventually he staggered to his feet and she watched him meander down the hall to his room.

The next afternoon when she saw him again, it was clear Constantin remembered nothing of the previous night. It wasn't worth telling anyone, and she didn't. But old Major Fairbairn—wherever he was—would have been proud of her right cross. She didn't see Gloria or Hans Lazar, though, and she and most other guests returned to Madrid by early evening.

As days turned into weeks, Aline proved herself to be a fine coder, continuing to alternate with Robert Dunev on night shifts. Some time after her trip to the countryside, Aline was eating breakfast when her doorbell rang. Angustias, one of her two maids, announced that two women were waiting in the salon. Aline had been expecting only one.

These were Resistance operatives coming through the escape line, she knew. One of the principal duties of the Madrid station, in fact, was to supervise and facilitate the flow of information and agents between France and Spain. For years the Allies had worked on establishing chains of local agents, informants, and patriots who could assist in any of four areas: providing information on German troop movements or defenses, particularly around port cities; acting as couriers, delivering information and messages from all parts of France to Madrid; providing safe houses or letter drops; and acting as guides or otherwise assisting agents or downed pilots in crossing the Pyrenees.

A chain organizer could have dozens or hundreds of agents spread across the country, and chain members came from all walks of life—from teenage couriers to dockworkers to widows who offered their homes as safe houses. All told there were thousands of these French agents, and chains rarely crossed lines. Marseille and Toulouse, for example, each had six chains, all working independently.

OSS chains in southern France as of March 7, 1944. *NARA*

OSS Madrid maintained detailed records on every chain, and summary biographies of every agent, often with grades of performance. Typical entries, by code name, included:

From the AKAK chain:

> Brutus - operating out of Marseille. Graded "B." The best AKAK agent and may be the best agent we have in France in all our chains. He has a number of sub-agents.

From the HIHI chain:

> Vichy-2 (BIBI) - operating out of Vichy. This lady is well-placed. Silky told me (706) that if this woman had a microfilm outfit she could send us a number of official documents. A relative is pro-German and editor of "Le-Matin", knows Abetz and many other Germans. Can go to Paris easily and even live there if necessary. Since Feb. 1943 has been working as courier on the Truck Route.

From the ZUZU chain:

Mr. Boua - (in fact a woman) Perpignan letter drop.

Gomez - Spaniard, very high official of the Seguridad. . . . Furnishes all the CE work on foreigners having gone through Barcelona. . . . He has two agents working for him, tailing people, questioning them, etc.

Robert Guy – One of the two chiefs in France. Lives in Paris, recruits the agents, can come to Spain legally. Deals in contraband.

NUMERICAL DESIGNATION OF AGENTS

AGENT NUMBER	CODE NAME	LOCATION
AKAK - 1	Fortress; Castillo	Barcelona
AKAK - 2	Brutus	Marseille
AKAK - 3	Les Trois Mousquetaires	Toulouse
AKAK - 4	Marcellin	Modane
AKAK - 5	Mephisto	Montauban
AKAK - 6	Germain	Lyon
AKAK - 7	Pol d'Eve	Carcassonne
AKAK - 8	Olivier	Montpellier
AKAK - 9	Cassius	Marseille (presumably)
AKAK - 10	Rigaud	Arles or Montauban
AKAK - 11	Charlou	Marseille near
AKAK - 12	Daniel	Prades
AKAK - 13	Jerome	Paris
AKAK - 14	Casset	Modane
AKAK - 15	Tandem	Montpellier
AKAK - 16	Fumse	Beziers
AKAK - 17	Antoine	Frontier
AKAK - 18	Loura	Cerbere
AKAK - 19	Bob	Tarbes
AKAK - 20	Go	Beziers
AKAK - 21	Claude	Cannes, Nice
AKAK - 22	Abbe Constantin	Carcassonne
AKAK - 23	Francois	(Moves around)
AKAK - 24	S.R. des Nur	Avignon-Aix
AKAK - 25		Lourdes
AKAK - 26		Orange
AKAK - 27		Perpignan
AKAK - 28		Port Vendres
AKAK - 29	Rigaud	Marseille
AKAK - 30	Rupoil	Tours
AKAK - 31	Alex	Paris
AKAK - 32	Paquito	Toulouse
AKAK - 33	Cobra	Toulouse
AKAK - 34	Rosette	Nimes
AKAK - 35	Simon	Travels (around Prades)
AKAK - 36		Toulouse
AKAK - 37	L'Ami de Pol; Rigoulot	Carcassonne
AKAK - 38		
AKAK - 39		Lorient
AKAK - 40	Nathanael	Paris
AKAK - 41	Bernard	St. Pierre des Corps
AKAK - 42	De Secretaire	Carcassonne
AKAK - 43	Colmena	
AKAK - 44	Faust	Toulouse
AKAK - 45		Toulon
AKAK - 46		Tarbes
AKAK - 47	Eiffel a Roland	Avignon-Aix
AKAK - 48	Albert	
AKAK - 49	Gerard	Perpignan
AKAK - 50	Rene	Valence

DECLASSIFIED
Authority NND 943005

Page one of the agents in the AKAK chain. *NARA*

The work was highly dangerous, though, as participation on either side of the border was considered a capital offense. In an OSS summary report about the "Truck Route" chain, risk was mentioned as a matter of course: "The chain was partly blown at the end of 1943, some of the members having been jailed or shot and new ones picked up." Another report, sent to ELTON at the Barcelona station, stated: "Although arrests and executions of a number of agents in France within the past month have adversely affected certain of our French Chain operations, I am pleased to report that our activities in this field are expanding rapidly."

Madrid was the information-collecting station and the hub that facilitated passage through Spain. It wasn't enough that an escapee crossed the border; landing in Spain without a Spanish passport and cover meant imprisonment for downed Allied pilots and arrest and possible execution for agents in the Resistance. But if a pilot or agent could make it across the Pyrenees and reach Madrid, the OSS would sneak them to Gibraltar, and from there they would fly to London.

All legs of the journey were perilous, the Pyrenees crossing in particular. Since Germans guarded the French side of the border and Civil Guards the Spanish side, it took a local guide to escort escapees through arduous mountain terrain at night. If caught, all stood to be imprisoned or shot. As such, guides had to be paid and safe houses were scheduled on each side. In many instances an Allied agent might have to wait several days or even a week before a guide could take them.

The experience of Captain Peter Churchill, a British SOE agent who made the journey in 1942, was typical of what agents went through. At a café in Perpignan, some twenty miles north of the Spanish border, he placed a torn postcard on the table. A moment later a young man in his late twenties came over from the bar.

"My name is Pasolé."

The guide.

"A taxi will take us the first kilometers," he said, "then a short walk brings us to the frontier, where we shall spend the night in a barn belonging to a friend of mine. We'll rest there throughout the following day and complete the trip on the next night."

Pasolé's fee was 12,000 francs.

The following evening they met at half past six. Peter had his things in a small hunting bag and noticed that Pasolé had a huge pack that Peter estimated to weigh over fifty pounds.

"Radio parts," the guide said.

Peter asked about Pasolé's family and he said he had a wife and two young girls.

"Where are they now?"

"In hiding."

Peter nodded. Life in the French Resistance.

Pasolé said the road would be clear of any controls until eight, by which time they'd be at the frontier. He knew this, he said, because one of his teammates on the Perpignan football team was a gendarme who would warn him of a patrol.

After a short drive the taxi dropped them off on a deserted country lane. It was pitch-dark so Pasolé tied a white handkerchief to his rucksack so Peter could keep sight of him. And off they went, through fields, hedges, streams, and underbrush. They passed through a small village, crossed another stream, and began their ascent into the mountains. The area was filled with cactus bushes, and even more annoyingly, there was no path.

They got lost.

Pasolé remained undeterred, though, and they trudged around in circles until he regained his bearings. They began climbing mountain peaks, some which seemed to be vertical, only to discover that the route was impassable. Peter began to worry since even a direct route to where they had to walk—Bañolas, on the other side of the Pyrenees—was forty miles. And they weren't traveling anything like a direct route.

After another two hours of steady climbing they reached a tiny village.

"You must keep very quiet going through here," Pasolé whispered, "because of the dogs."

They crept between the houses, silently Peter thought, but apparently not. A dog started barking, then another, and soon there was a canine chorus. Lights snapped on and Pasolé blurted, "Come on!"

They sprinted through the black night into a cluster of trees, and Pasolé jumped into a stream. They splashed onward about three hundred yards but one of the village dogs was still onto them, chasing and barking from the right bank. Pasolé motioned toward a ridge and they kept moving. Suddenly the dog plunged into the water and began closing. The men reached the ridge and clambered out just as the dog arrived. As it tried to come out, Pasolé gave it a swift kick and the animal retreated.

Unfortunately, the rest of the pack were still coming, yelping and barking. Pasolé and Peter bolted for another group of trees and raced through, losing their canine pursuers.

They came to a road, and Pasolé said they would walk with an interval of two hundred yards between them. "If I walk into a trap," he said, "I shall talk loudly enough to warn you to get into the bushes. Should that happen, wait for an hour to allow me time to give anyone the slip and return. If I don't come back, walk straight on to within three hundred yards of the Customs barrier at the top. Turn right up a steep hill, keeping the French and Spanish Customs sheds in view."

About forty minutes later Pasolé pulled up and they took a break. He asked Peter what he had been doing in the war, and Peter lied, telling him he was a downed bomber pilot.

Pasolé said he had taken well over twenty RAF pilots across and Peter nodded, quickly changing the subject.

They took off again up a mountainside, and about an hour later Peter figured they had ascended about a thousand feet. After another hour, they reached the barn safe house and slipped in for the remainder of the night. At nine the next morning a farmer appeared with plates of eggs and coffee. They remained where they were until nightfall and then they set out again. The farmer's son led them some eight hundred yards—to the peak of the Pyrenees—where he said goodbye.

In the distance they could see the lights of Figueras, but Pasolé said the village was too dangerous, that many Allied pilots had been caught and imprisoned there. They'd circle around it, he said, and head to his family's farm just outside of Bañolas, some eight miles or so farther south.

"We shall walk all through the night," he explained. "There will be one stop of a quarter of an hour for a short meal and a smoke." The going would be up and down, he said, and he warned Peter to be careful about steps so as not to sprain an ankle.

For two hours they moved at a brisk pace, scrambling down steep slopes. Pasolé then disappeared over a ledge and Peter heard what sounded like a landslide. He stood where he was and waited. A moment later he heard the guide's voice, some twenty feet below.

"Don't follow me."

Peter circled around the cliff and met Pasolé at the bottom. Fortunately, the guide was uninjured and they carried on until 1:30 a.m., when they had their meal and a cigarette. Minutes later they were back on their feet.

Around 4:00 a.m. they ended up in a maze of terraced vineyards and had to climb over countless walls to get out. They marched on for five straight hours until they reached Pasolé's family's farm, where they were treated to an enormous breakfast. The Civil Guards were expected, however, so they slipped out and hid in a silo until dusk, when they returned for a night in a bed.

In the morning Peter paid Pasolé and they said their farewells. An escape-chain driver took Peter to his home in Bañolas, a safe house. Peter had him deliver a note to the British consul in Barcelona that Monday, and the same afternoon the diplomat arrived to collect him. After a night in the embassy, they were off the next morning for the 400-mile drive to Madrid.

This was the ordeal the two Resistance women in Aline's salon had just endured, and without the aid of a British or American embassy.

Larry Mellon coordinated the Spanish side of the border for OSS escapees, and Aline's apartment was one of the few Madrid safe houses for women. Twice during the prior month she had harbored women passing through, and in both instances they had brought valuable intelligence—maps showing coastal fortifications and roadblocks, and locations of German troops—all critical for Operation Dragoon,* the planned Allied invasion of southern France.

Unsurprisingly, the women in Aline's salon looked like they had been through a battle. One had a bandaged hand, and they both looked and smelled as if they hadn't showered in weeks. Aline welcomed them and the one with the bandaged hand said, "I am Marta. Madeleine, my companion, does not speak Spanish, but she is the one who obtained this information." Marta produced a small packet from her coat pocket. "I guided her across the Pyrenees and on to Madrid. Since we have no identity cards we will have to wait here for a ride back to the frontier. We dare not use the trains or buses. The fish truck that brought us will make another trip back next Monday. Will the señorita allow us to stay until then?"

Aline said that would be fine and motioned to Marta's hand. "Do you want us to get you a doctor?"

Marta shook her head. "We don't want to be seen. We won't go out of the house, and we need a rest. The climb across the mountains was strenuous and dangerous. We have to move like foxes. This will be my last trip. I've already killed two fascist Civil Guards, and if they catch me, I'll be shot without trial."

Aline nodded and looked in their eyes. These women were fearless.

*Previously called Operation Anvil.

She told them she'd be away for the weekend and wouldn't be back until Monday. Her apartment was theirs.

A few hours later, leaving the two exhausted, bedraggled women asleep in her apartment, Aline was off to Toledo. She had been invited to a weekend getaway by Casilda, whose father was hosting an extravagant gala. It was a trip she had been looking forward to, given the city's historic significance.

Few places showcased Spain's past, from Roman ruins to medieval castles and cathedrals, better than Toledo. Situated atop a hill surrounded on three sides by the Tagus River, it had been a center for sword production since 500 BC. Hannibal, in fact, had equipped his Carthaginian troops with its *falcatas* during the Second Punic War.*

Toledo eventually came under control of the Romans, who built the city wall, the Puente de Alcántara—the arched bridge across the Tagus—the Cave of Hercules, and the city's baths and wells. Through the centuries it continued to gain commercial and cultural importance. One landmark, the Primate Cathedral of Saint Mary of Toledo, begun in 1226 and completed in 1493, became recognized as the pinnacle of high Gothic architecture. Charles V, Holy Roman Emperor and King of Spain during the sixteenth century, moved his court to Toledo and made it Spain's capital city.

It was also here where El Greco lived and painted,** and where Miguel de Cervantes set *Don Quioxte*, a work considered to be history's first novel.

Aline's OSS car—driven by one of the agency's chauffeurs—arrived in Toledo while the sun was still bright. The crenellated city walls loomed over them as they bounced along a cobblestone road

---

*The *falcata* is a curved sword common in pre-Roman Iberia.

**El Greco's *View of Toledo* is considered his second greatest masterpiece (after *The Burial of the Count of Orgaz*), and its depiction of sky—with van Gogh's *The Starry Night*—remains one of the most famous in Western art.

and passed under a massive stone arch, at which point the terrain began to incline. At the Plaza de Zocodover a policeman stopped them, saying that the roads were closed for the festivities that evening. From here, he said, they'd have to walk.

The driver grabbed Aline's bags and they continued on up the steep climb. As they walked they passed in front of a succession of grand palaces, and she noticed that each had a different family crest carved into the façade. A moment later they were at the Count of Avila's palace. They entered into a patio area and Aline saw Casilda, her hostess, waiting at the bottom of a wide stone staircase.

"What do you think?" Casilda asked. "You are going to meet General Franco. Papa has invited him here to see the procession tonight."

"I thought you aristocrats were monarchists and didn't like Franco."

Aline had touched on a sensitive and complicated subject. The monarchists were without a political party during Spain's Civil War. As Catholics, they vehemently opposed the communist-led republicans, whom they believed would have abolished the Church and instituted state atheism. Franco's nationalist coalition of Catholics and the military, however, also had no intention of restoring the monarchy. Monarchists, then, had little choice but to support Franco, whom they saw as the lesser of two evils.

"That's more or less true. But when the chief of state makes an official visit to Toledo, he comes to this house, because the kings did also whenever they came to the city."

Casilda introduced Aline to her sisters and they joined a small party for tea, and then all went upstairs to don mantillas for the Franco reception. When they had finished draping and pinning, they heard a commotion in the street and rushed to the balcony.

Three Mercedes-Benz limousines were directly below them and a moment later the Generalissimo appeared. As Franco moved along the greeting line, Aline was intrigued by his appearance. While he wore a red beret and a white military jacket adorned with medals, there was nothing particularly striking or intimidating about him. He was short and plump and had a pleasant expression. Without the military jacket, he could have been a bellman at any hotel.

Aline also noticed that few officers accompanied him and he didn't appear to have any bodyguards. As the party moved inside, she thought about the risk Franco was taking. Throngs of people moved in and out of the house, but there were no incidents.

As she and Casilda watched from the balcony, they could see a procession coming toward them. There were lots of candles, hooded figures in black robes, and then a float with even more candles surrounding a statue. As the illuminated float came closer, Aline noticed that it was not supported by a car, but rested on the shoulders of about twenty men. A woman began singing and when she finished, the men tilted the float toward her—as if the statue were bowing in recognition of the performance—and then tilted it toward the balcony.

Aline wondered why it would bow to the balcony, and then she noticed that behind her was none other than the Generalissimo. She tried to move out of his way but he stopped her.

"I have seen this procession all my life, señorita. You probably have not."

Aline was surprised by Franco's high-pitched voice. "Oh, Your Excellency, I did not know you were there. I would have moved."

Franco smiled. "And I did not know an American girl was hiding under that mantilla."

He was friendly and unassuming and she wanted to talk more, but an aide informed the general that it was time to change balconies.

"Sorry," Franco said. "I would have enjoyed explaining the ceremony to an American."

Aline arrived back in Madrid before dawn on Monday. Everyone was asleep so she opened her bedroom door quietly and set down her bags. As she expected, someone was in her bed and she started to leave when she heard a shutter rocking in the breeze. So as not to awaken Marta or Madeleine, she began tiptoeing across the room to close it.

About halfway she glanced over and froze.

The pillow and sheet were drenched in blood.

CHAPTER 11

THE BODY

Aline trembled.

She inched forward, pulse pounding, fearing the worst. The long black hair was matted and there was a blood streak across the cheek. It was Marta.

She had been shot in the head.

Aline stood there, unable to move, staring at the dead body. Someone had come in through the balcony apparently, but who had known Marta was here? Had the women been followed, the assassin watching and lying in wait? And how could a shot be fired without waking Madeleine, Angustias, or Cecilia?

Unless the pistol had a silencer. Which a snatch or hit team would use.

Then it dawned on her. Marta had been killed in *her* bed. So who was the real target?

She eased the phone off the hook and with a shaking finger dialed Gregory Thomas. She uttered the emergency password and Thomas said, "Do nothing until I arrive."

Aline couldn't bear to stay in the room and went out, closing the door behind her. In the kitchen, Cecilia—the maid who did most of the cooking—was lighting the stove to prepare breakfast.

"Señorita, you look so, so—pale. Is something the matter?"

"No. Please don't disturb the woman in my room."

Aline tried to regain her composure and went down the hall to check the room where Madeleine, the other Basque woman, was staying. She was fine, sleeping soundly.

Thomas arrived minutes later and Aline whispered quickly.

"Who knows about this?" he asked.

"No one."

"What about your maids?"

"I have only spoken to the cook. The other Basque woman is still asleep, and Angustias also."

Aline led him to the room and shuddered again, seeing now the blood that had splattered across the bed.

Thomas inspected the body, his face tightening. He reached for the phone and called Robert Dunev. "Come by Butch's apartment immediately," he whispered, "with a large car. Be quick. Try not to attract attention and don't bring the chauffeur."

Thomas asked Aline for two blankets. Getting a dead body out of the apartment—and out of Madrid—was no simple task. If any neighbor or *portero* caught sight of what was going on, a call to the police would be inevitable—and disastrous. The Spanish would launch an immediate investigation and the entire OSS mission in Madrid would collapse. They had to get Marta out before sunrise, and Dunev would have to find a remote place to dump the corpse.

Aline handed Thomas the blankets and he rolled Marta into one and stuffed the bloody pillow and sheets into the other. While they waited for Robert, he mentioned that he could arrange for other agents to drive Madeleine to the border and sneak her across the mountains. He told her to tell Madeleine and the servants that Marta had become ill and was taken to the hospital.

"But Angustias will miss the pillow, the blanket, and the sheets."

"Let her, but be certain she keeps it to herself."

Aline nodded. Disposing of a body wasn't something taught at The Farm.

Madeleine continued on her journey the following day and the question now was whether Aline should move apartments. The killer, they theorized, was probably a Spaniard seeking revenge for the two Civil Guards Marta had killed. The fact that Madeleine had not also been killed supported that notion. Since Germans had not been involved, and Aline's cover had not been blown, she would remain in her apartment, they decided.

A week or so later Juanito called to invite Aline to see him in action at Las Ventas. Watching the slow death of a bull wasn't exactly what Aline had in mind for her day off, but she knew it would mean the world to Juanito. While she didn't know if she could stomach what appeared to be indefensible barbarism, she understood that she was looking at it from an American perspective. From the Spanish perspective, bullfighting wasn't just a popular pastime, it was a cultural institution that had been around for more than four centuries.

To the Spaniard, bullfighting is not a sport but an art. The results of contests in the bullring never appear in the sports section of newspapers, but in a separate section altogether. And for some, it's more than an art. As one matador explained, "The real *corrida—la corrida formal*—transcends the simple struggle of bull and man. It is in fact a religious ceremony, a reverent blood sacrifice from which still curls the smoke of ancient altars."

As Hemingway observed, "In Spain, honor is a very real thing. Called *pundonor*, it means honor, probity, courage, self-respect, and pride in one word." Spaniards are a proud people, and mere courage is not enough. Courage, if not accompanied with grace and calm, is an ersatz accolade. And bullfighting, Hemingway felt, "is the only art in which the artist is in danger of death and in which the degree of brilliance in the performance is left to the fighter's honor."

One matador with such honor was Juanito Belmonte.

"I hope the fight will be good," he said to Aline, "especially since it's your first. One can never tell how a fight is going to turn out. Success sometimes depends upon the bulls more than on the matador. If the bulls are not brave, if they do not attack, there is no way the bullfighter can do a good *faena*."*

Aline did her best to convey enthusiasm. "I'll be thrilled just to see you in that ring and to learn what goes on."

"You'll see Manolete, too. He's a friend of mine, and it's always a challenge to be in the same ring with him. I hope my bulls are as good as his."

Aline had heard of Manolete, the only matador who could be mentioned in the same breath as Juan Belmonte and Joselito.

"You must go to the bullring at least fifteen minutes ahead," Juanito added. "This is the only occurrence which takes place on time in Spain."

On the appointed Sunday, Aline made her way into Las Ventas with Pimpinela and her sister Elizabeth. On every column, it seemed, there were posters—not unlike for a Broadway play—advertising the show and the stars, Juanito and Manolete.

When they found the seats Juanito had provided, Pimpinela grinned. "*Barreras de sombra*," she said. "Ring seats in the shade—difficult to get and very expensive."

Aline gazed around the stadium. There was an energy here. Some twenty thousand spectators, maybe more, drinking and laughing and cheering.

---

*The series of passes in the final third of a bullfight, just before the kill.

A bullfight poster advertising three of the top matadors
of the day: Juanito Belmonte, Manolete, and Gallito.
Larry Loftis collection

"Look," shouted Elizabeth. She waved at someone and Aline
followed her eyes. A few rows down from them sat Gloria von
Fürstenberg, looking as beautiful as ever. "What a hat. I bet she got
it in Paris."

Aline couldn't disagree. Where else could you find a red wide-brimmed hat to match an elegant navy suit with red pinstripes? "Who are the men with her?"

"One is the German ambassador. The other is Walter Schellenberg. He's an important Nazi. What a pity, he's so handsome."

Schellenberg.

The German who tied everything together. Himmler's intel man in Berlin. He had been head of the Nazi Party's foreign intelligence, but with Hitler's sacking of Canaris, Schellenberg now controlled all of the Abwehr as well. Who would he see in Madrid? Aline wondered. Lazar? Lenz? Himmler's main contact, maybe Prince Max? The fact that he was sitting with Gloria left no doubt about her allegiance.

"Who's that incredible-looking woman in the big hat with the feathers and frizzy orange hair?" Aline asked.

"Ana de Pombo," Pimpinela replied. "She worked with one of the top dress houses in Paris."*

Aline heard a murmur behind her and turned. General Franco and his wife were entering the royal box. Just then trumpets sounded and a gate swung open. Down below, Aline could see a procession coming through—not unlike an American parade, it seemed—led by two men wearing sixteenth-century costumes. These were the *alguacils*, or constables, who would ask the president of the *corrida*—Franco today—for the key to open the bull gate. Following them were Manolete, Juanito, and another matador.

"Look at Juanito!" Pimpinela blurted. "Maybe he will place his cape on our railing." The draping of a matador's cape, she explained, was a high honor that a bullfighter would bestow on a dignitary or lucky young lady at the beginning of a performance.

Aline noticed the green silk slung over Juanito's shoulder. It was embroidered and sparkled in the sun, just like the one he had given

---

*Pombo had also been the costume designer for two recent movies in Spain, *El Hombre Que Las Enamora* in 1944, and *El Camino de Babel* earlier that year.

her. His black hat, the matador's *montera*, looked comical on him but Juanito's face was all business. There was a sternness in his expression, a steely coldness that she'd not seen before.

She knew why and her stomach began to churn. This man, this friend marching proudly in a satin suit, pink stockings, and what looked like ballerina shoes, in minutes would be facing a 1,200-pound beast intent on killing him.

Following the trio were about nine men carrying capes. These were the *banderilleros*, Juanito had explained earlier, the men who would assist him and place the *banderillas*—the pronged colored sticks meant to weaken the bull's neck. Following them came six festooned horses, all with equally decorated riders—*picadors* they were called—carrying lances. A mule team brought up the rear and the procession stopped in front of Franco's box.

Everyone removed their hats and bowed, and then Juanito handed his cape to one of his *banderilleros*. Moments later it was spread out before Aline, Pimpinela, and Elizabeth. The Hohenlohe girls were delirious.

The entire procession exited and Aline heard the rumble of a kettledrum. Another trumpet sounded and an enormous black bull tore into the ring. The thing looked the size of a tractor, but with a foot and a half of horns. It stamped around for several moments, looking for something to ram, and found a target. One of the men carrying capes had draped his over the safety of a board fence and the bull charged. Suddenly other capes appeared and the bull went after them.

This was more than a sport, Aline realized. It was a spectacle—a mélange of parade, circus, theater, and ballet in one open-air venue.

Just then Manolete appeared and the crowd erupted. He was quite skinny, Aline noticed, and seemed haggard. *How could this be the greatest matador in the world?* she wondered.

He didn't look the part. Manolete was so frail that one bullfighter described him as tubercular. But that he was the best was incontrovertible. He would fight more than ninety times during Spain's season, then head to Mexico for their season, followed by Peru for theirs. By the time he finished his tour and returned home, it would be March again and the Spanish season would begin anew in Valencia.

Aline had heard much about this man, some from Juanito, some from others. All bulls were easy for Manolete, everyone said, but like all matadors, Manolete feared his opponents. According to one story, as his costume was being fitted before a fight, he told a visitor, "Excuse me, señorita, if I don't talk too much, but I am very scared." To another bullfighter, he said, "My knees start to quake when I first see my name on the posters and they don't stop until the end of the season."

In the ring, though, he was methodical, serene, and so at ease that he typically appeared bored. In one trademark move—almost suicidal, other fighters felt—Manolete would take his eye off the bull as it charged and look away into the crowd, as if to say, "Just another day at the office; I wonder if it will rain."

Just then the bull charged and Aline's eyes widened as she watched Manolete go to work. Something was apparently wrong with the bull, though, as Manolete killed him quickly, without many passes. She recalled what Juanito had said about the bulls, and how the matadors needed brave ones who would charge in a reliable fashion.

The mule team pulled the carcass out and Aline turned her attention to Gloria and Schellenberg. They seemed to be talking like old friends, laughing and smiling. Aline wondered again why Schellenberg was in town. Was he merely collecting information or was he planning another kidnapping, as he had done in 1940 with the scheme to snatch the Duke of Windsor?*

---

*Operation Willi, as the Germans called it, was the scheme to kidnap the duke in July 1940 by luring him to Madrid from his temporary residence in Lisbon. The plan was eventually aborted.

Trumpets sounded again and a massive black Miura charged in. These breeds were the largest, fiercest, and most cunning type of Spanish fighting bull. Since 1842 they had been carefully bred for muscle, aggression, and intelligence. Spanish fighting bulls, in general, are fearless. They have been known to kill lions and Bengal tigers, and have even charged elephants. Let loose in a city, they will ram cars, trucks, even trains.

Miura bulls, though, were a class beyond. Through centuries of careful breeding at the Miura ranch in Sevilla, they had developed the ability to learn rapidly in the ring, adding significant risk to the matador. Almost all bullfighters wanted to kill them as rapidly as possible, and some matadors refused to even fight them.*

In short, Miura bulls were the most dangerous, and this was the strain of beast that Juanito now faced.

Aline's eyes were glued to the bull as it rushed by, snorting and stamping as it sought a target. She watched it circle the ring and when she turned back, he was there.

Juanito. Alone with the beast.

He lifted his violet cape and swayed it. "*Eh, toro, toro.*"

Aline held her breath, horrified, as the bull charged.

Effortlessly, Juanito worked the cape and the animal lunged after it, narrowly missing him.

Swish.

In an instant, though, the bull turned and attacked again.

Swish.

The crowd roared. "*¡Olé!*"

Aline gripped the rail. She wanted to smile but the tension in her spine stifled any celebration.

---

*After a visit to the Miura ranch and observing these bulls in 1962, Ferruccio Lamborghini began naming his automobiles after them (the Lamborghini Miura in 1966, the Islero in 1968), and changed his logo to a fighting bull.

Juanito, with perfect form—feet together—performing a difficult and dangerous *farol pase* on November 20, 1939, in San Sebastian. *Associated Press*

Time and again Juanito tempted the bull to charge, leading him in consecutive veronicas, or passes. With each successful pass the crowd cheered, and Aline began to understand the popularity of the spectacle. It wasn't just that Juanito tricked the bull, it was how it was done. Like his father before him, Belmonte worked calmly, gracefully, feet together, conducting his orchestra of one. But the danger, Aline knew, was ever-present. The bull was quick and surprisingly agile, his horns often missing Juanito by mere inches.

Aline couldn't believe what she was watching. This little unimposing man who had brought her flowers and chocolates now commanded a newfound respect and admiration. How courageous he was!

As the fight progressed it was difficult for Aline to watch; Juanito kept bringing the bull closer and closer, the horns now grazing his vest with each pass. Effortlessly, he twisted the bull around him, forcing the animal to turn in half its length. It was a terribly dangerous technique invented by Juanito's father, and the crowd roared.

Then it happened.

At the end of a pass the bull hooked his head to the left and Juanito was flung into the air like a smashed piñata. Aline gasped as the *banderilleros* raced to the scene, waving their capes and yelling to draw the bull away from him.

Aline's chest tightened.

Juanito was lying on the ground, motionless.

CHAPTER 12

RESURRECTION

Aline clutched the rail while women around her wailed. She was sure Juanito was dead. As the bull was drawn away and *banderilleros* encircled their fallen matador, she noticed one of Juanito's black slippers lying several yards away from his body. The bull had thrown him with such force that he literally had been launched out of his shoes.

The slipper rested there, black on the yellow clay, a tombstone testament to the Belmonte legacy.

She looked back to the *banderilleros* and gasped again. Juanito was on his feet! She could see that his jacket had been ripped, and a streak of crimson blood was trickling down his pants. But this was madness—Juanito was dismissing the *banderilleros*! Retrieving his cape, he began running after the bull. He wasn't fearful in the slightest, Aline saw; he was angry and indignant.

Again they went at it. Knowing that the bull hooked to the left, Juanito pulled him close on his right. Masterfully, he worked the cape and the bull lunged through. Another trumpet sounded, indicating that it was time for the *picadors*, the two men on horseback who would weaken the massive Miura's neck muscle by "picking" it three times with their lances.

Aline's eyes remained on Juanito as he exited. The man of swords that she had met that day in the hotel appeared at his side to inspect the wound.

Juanito brushed him away and, with the rest of the crowd, watched as the *picadors* went to work. When they were finished several of the men who had been in the original procession returned. These were the *banderilleros* who would place six darts, fastened to the end of sticks, in the same area of the neck and shoulder of the bull. Without these two elements of weakening and lowering the bull's head, Aline was told, the animal would no doubt kill the matador.

The *banderilleros* completed their task and Juanito entered once again, this time with a sword and a *muleta*—a new, smaller red cape. He bowed to Franco's box and then strutted confidently to the adversary who had struck first blood.

At once Juanito engaged the Miura, drawing it closer and closer, wrapping the animal around him. After several passes Juanito turned his back on the bull and began walking away, exposing himself in fearless defiance. The bull charged and Juanito continued the dance, finishing him off with a thrust of the sword.

The crowd roared but Aline dropped to her seat. She was exhausted. To think that Juanito did this more than eighty times a year was mind-numbing. Bullfighters were indeed a different breed.

Juanito moved about to accept the cheers, and fans began throwing flowers, hats, and cigars into the ring. Aline marveled at the spectacle, amazed at how patrons showed their appreciation, but it was not unusual. If a *corrida* crowd was especially pleased by a matador's performance, they'd also throw umbrellas, coats, gloves, and wineskins filled with *manzanilla*.*

But if a fight was beyond accolades, there was no limit to what raving fans would throw. One bullfighter recalled seeing a wooden

---

*An Andalusian sherry. In most cases, the matador would take a ceremonial squirt and throw it back.

leg, women's panties, and even a baby tossed into the ring. The wooden leg, he remembered, went back to the owner, the panties were tucked into the matador's shirt next to his heart, and the baby was lofted atop the *torero's* shoulders and carried for a lap around the ring.

Juanito and his assistants continued to toss back the gifts, and a moment later he was standing beneath Aline and her companions. He threw something up to Aline and she held out her hands.

Pimpinela beamed. "What luck, Aline—to have a famous bull-fighter throw you an ear at your first bullfight."

Aline looked at the ghastly prize and remembered her first morning in Madrid. Juanito's man of swords had boasted about Juanito getting two ears in Toledo. This bloody thing in her hand was an honor, she knew, but Pimpinela had to explain. In every ring in Spain, if a matador performed exceedingly well, the crowd showed its admiration by waving handkerchiefs and shouting "*¡Oreja!*" If the president of the arena saw enough handkerchiefs, he would wave his own, indicating that the *torero* would be honored with an ear of the bull. If the shouting and handkerchiefs continued, the president would award a second ear. And if the crowd persisted still, he'd award the tail. One of the *banderilleros* would then cut the appendages from the dead animal and hand them to the matador, who would circle the ring, holding them aloft, and then toss them to someone special in the crowd.

It seemed a macabre custom but, like everything in Spain, it had a long tradition. In the days when bullfighters made little money, Aline heard, an ear entitled the matador to the meat of the bull.

When the clamor died down Aline glanced again at Schellenberg, who was speaking with the German ambassador's wife. Wondering what Franco had thought of the fight, she turned and looked up. To her surprise she saw Edmundo sitting several rows behind her. He caught her eye and motioned toward Franco's box. The general was gone, but policemen and Civil Guards were rushing all around it. A murmur rumbled through the crowd, and she asked Pimpinela if she could make out what everyone was saying.

"My heavens," she said. "Somebody tried to kill Franco."

That evening Juanito came by Aline's apartment to take her to dinner. As he was opening the car door for her, she tried to think of what to say. In less than one hour that day he had become larger than life.

"I've been trying to think of some completely original compliment," she said, "something you haven't heard. I can't come up with a thing. Juanito, you're extraordinary!"

Juanito smiled. "Thank you, Aline. Coming from an American, that is original. Few of your compatriots understand the art of the bullfight."

Aline made an offhand remark about the bull's chances and Juanito gave her a sidelong smirk.

"Don't you think the bullring a more glorious end than a slaughterhouse in Chicago? Here, the bull has as much chance as the matador—several *toreros* are killed or maimed each season. The bulls are bred for that fight and crave it. They'll attack anything that moves."

Aline nodded and Juanito went on. "This skill was invented by our ancestors to defend themselves against the attack of wild bulls, who always existed here. Today the *corrida* celebrates the courage of man and beast alike. If executed with grace, it is an incomparable experience."

Given what she'd seen that day, Aline couldn't disagree. Still, she had mixed feelings. Watching that fight "overwhelmed me," she remembered later. "I could not look at parts of it, I was shocked and determined never to return." And yet the drama and excitement was undeniable. "Those moments of intense emotion cannot be seen in any other spectacle. What is happening in front of you absorbs your entire being. The intense fear, then the exhilaration that follows when a matador brings the enormous beast swirling around him, the sharp horns barely grazing his body, the magic of man's power to face death with valor and grace."

But bullfighting affected people differently, she understood. American author John Steinbeck, not surprisingly, saw it as a metaphor for life: "I like bullfighting," he wrote to a friend, "because to me it is a lonely, formal, anguished microcosm of what happens to every man, sometimes in an office, strangled by the glue on envelopes."

Aline knew that Juanito would have his own perspective and she asked him for his story—why he was a bullfighter, why he risked his life dozens and dozens of times a year. Was it the exhilaration? The fame? The money?

Juanito paused for several moments, reflecting, and Aline sensed she had touched a nerve.

"My story isn't a happy one," he finally said. "My mother was born in a poor family in Sevilla; my father also. They fell in love, and then he became the world's greatest bullfighter. They intended to marry when he returned from his winter fights in South America. Just after he left Spain, my mother discovered she was pregnant. Her father put her out of his house, and she supported herself by sewing—until my father returned. But my father had married a rich Peruvian girl and when he returned, he refused to see my mother or me. It was only when I was ten years old that he recognized me legally. He had no choice, because I looked so much like him that people stopped me on the street to say, 'You must be the son of the great Belmonte!'

"I became a bullfighter, not because I liked it—to be honest with you, I don't, Aline—but it was the only way I could become rich enough to repay my mother for all she had sacrificed for me. I know I'll never be as great a matador as my father, but at least today I can give my mother any luxury she desires. I've accomplished what I care about most."

Aline looked at Juanito, speechless.

*   *   *

A few days later Gregory Thomas called Aline into his office and said he needed her to go to Málaga that night on the ten o'clock train. It was a simple courier run, but not without a bit of danger. He was hoping to send a more experienced agent, he added—namely Mellon or Dunev—but neither was available.

He handed her a roll of microfilm. "In this strip are the names and addresses of Spaniards ready to hide—and aid—our agents on the underground route from Málaga to the Pyrenees. The culmination of, oh, I'd say about a year and a half of research."

She was to hide the film inside her dress, he said, and deliver it to a man named Blacky at two thirty the next day. They would meet at the Santa Iglesia Cathedral, on the back bench, and Blacky would be wearing a white scarf. She was to sit beside him—not too close—pray, and then pass him the film. No words were to be spoken. If he or she could not make the drop, a second attempt was to be made at the same place at six thirty that evening. If that one failed, the last attempt was to be the following day, again at two thirty.

Aline nodded and Thomas handed her the ticket.

"There may be trouble on the train. A new stipulation requires travelers to carry travel permits. The Germans received theirs a week ago; we're still waiting. You probably will get by without it—your age and all."

Aline was pleased with the assignment. Situated on Spain's southern coast, not far from Marbella, Málaga was said to be one of the most beautiful and interesting places in the world. It had a bullring and cathedrals like Madrid, but with a rugged terrain not unlike southern France; one could lunch at a café downtown and then dine that evening at a mountain overlook. It was known for its almonds, blue grapes, and palm groves, but Aline was thinking more of the alluring beaches.

When she arrived home after work, she smiled at the new delivery: more carnations from Juanito. As if on cue, he called.

"How about dinner tonight?"

Aline hesitated. "I'd love to—but I can't. I'm leaving for a few days."

"Where are you going?"

"Málaga."

"Whom are you going with?"

Aline sighed. Juanito was a gentleman, but a *jealous* gentleman. He had already expressed concern about that dubious man she was spending time with, that Edmundo character, and always wanted to know about any competition.

"I'm going alone."

Juanito tried to invite himself but Aline cut him off, reminding him that he had a fight on Monday in Barcelona.

There was disappointment in Juanito's voice. "Bulls I understand," he said. "Women, never."

The taxi stopped in front of Atocha Station and Aline looked up at the looming reddish façade. The same pillars, the same type of stone, as Las Ventas, only much older. Madrid's train station had been running since 1851 and the flickering gaslights looked original. Since rail was the only form of transportation available to most people, the station was a frenzy of activity. Policemen and porters, soldiers and travelers scurried in different directions.

She weaved her way through the crowd and found her train. Showing the conductor her ticket, she slipped into sleeper number two. It was much nicer than she had expected, with a supple sofa, mahogany table, and burgundy velvet drapes over white lace curtains. It had all the trappings, it seemed, of an Agatha Christie novel.

The whistle blew and the coach began to rock as the train chugged out of the station. Aline put her suitcase away and then jumped at the sound of a knock on her door.

"Who is it?"

"*Policía, señorita.*"

Aline opened the door but left the security chain in place.

"Your passport please, señorita."

Aline released the chain and gave it to him. The officer looked at it a moment and handed it back. "Now your travel permit, please."

"Travel permit? What do you mean?"

The officer was polite but unamused. "Señorita, you should be aware this is a new regulation for foreigners. You cannot leave Madrid without it. Surely you know this."

"No, I did not. I'm terribly sorry."

"In that case, in the morning I will have to take the señorita to the *comisaría* in Málaga."

Aline took a deep breath.

She was under arrest.

CHAPTER 13

THE PRISONER

Aline had never seen a jail before, much less from the inside.

Her police escort nudged a sleeping jailer. "Wake up, Damian. You have a prisoner."

Aline eyed the three empty cells. Aside from the indignity, what if they wanted to search her? She couldn't dispose of the microfilm now even if she wanted to. And how would she make the rendezvous? The situation was getting worse by the minute.

"This young lady is *americana*," the officer said. "Do you hear me?"

The groggy jailer sat up, annoyed at the disturbance. "What can I do, Don Marcelo?"

"She's your prisoner. She cannot leave here or speak to anyone until she has Don José's permission."

Aline followed the back-and-forth. Don José was the *comisario*, she heard, but he was in Ronda attending a bullfight. "Please let me telephone the American consul in Málaga," she interjected. "This matter could be cleared up immediately."

The officer shook his head. "Nothing of the kind, señorita. You are a prisoner of Spain. This is not America. Here it is Spanish law that will determine what is to be done with you."

And nothing would be done until Don José returned.

The iron door clanged shut and Aline sat there, watching the clock. Two thirty came and went and she missed her first appointment. As the afternoon rolled on, she paced her cell. The sun was low now, and every passing minute brought her closer to the thought that she was going to miss the second rendezvous.

At six thirty, the second meeting time, she realized she'd have to escape or risk missing the third and final drop. The jailer had dozed off again, so Aline shook the iron bars and yelled out to him: "This small cell is making me nervous. I need more space."

She opened her mouth to scream and the jailer held up his hand. "No, no. Have patience, señorita." He reached for a ring of keys and ambled over to the cell. "It is against orders, señorita. But I can't stand a woman screaming."

He unlocked her door and then locked the front entrance. Another officer motioned with his arm, indicating that she could mill around the lobby.

Pacing in a small circle, Aline scanned in all directions. Every window was barred. There was a bathroom, she saw, but it had only a small opening in the ceiling. Both jailers were alert and watchful.

Returning to her cell, she wondered what would happen if she missed the third and final drop. How many Resistance agents or escaping pilots would be arrested and executed because they couldn't find safe houses? How many would be asking Larry Mellon why the escape chain had failed?

Today was shot, though, so she sat back and tried to sleep.

In the morning Damian offered a cup of something that resembled coffee, but no food. Aline hadn't eaten since the prior morning, but the gnawing in her gut was from the time. Nine o'clock . . . ten o'clock . . . eleven o'clock. Still no Don José.

At twelve thirty he finally arrived and the jailers jumped to their feet.

"What a fight!" Don José belted out. "Ortega was *una maravilla*."*

---

*Domingo Ortega, with Manolete, Carlos Arruza, Luis Dominguín, and Belmonte, was one of the most popular matadors of the day.

He began to demonstrate Ortega's passes when he saw Aline. "What's this?"

Aline managed a weak smile and Damian explained that she was American.

"But what a way to treat a beautiful señorita," Don José said. Reaching through the bars, he shook Aline's hand. "Do not worry. Whatever your problem is, I will solve it. Damian, unlock this door."

Aline explained that she was unaware of the permit requirement, and Don José began fumbling through his desk. Retrieving a rubber stamp and Aline's passport, he stamped and signed it. Now, he said, they simply needed someone to identify her, and he was friends with the American vice-consul; she'd be out in no time.

Aline glanced at the clock. Finding the consul and getting him here would take a while, and she had only ninety minutes until the final rendezvous. But Don José made the call, and fifteen minutes later a handsome young man limped in.

Don José clapped him on the back. "You won't mind this duty, my boy. You have to identify the passport of a pretty young compatriot." Turning to Aline, he said, "This is Barnaby Conrad, and a damn good bullfighter. That leg was a gift from a Romero bull in Mexico."

Aline looked at the American. He was just a kid, younger than she was. How could he be a bullfighter, much less a diplomat?

She didn't ask, but Conrad's route to both had been most unusual. When he was a nineteen-year-old student at the University of North Carolina, he had enrolled for a semester at the University of Mexico to learn Spanish. Enamored with Hemingway's *Death in the Afternoon*, one day he went to see a bullfight with an American friend, Adrian Spies. After the trumpets sounded a young Spanish bullfighter, Nacho Suárez, began to struggle with a monstrous beast named Pretty Boy. Nacho was scared to death and his passes were skittish and awkward. The crowd booed.

Soon it became ugly. Nacho began stepping back with every pass—cowardly, the audience felt. The boos grew louder. Patrons began throwing cushions into the ring. Some piled cushions together and set them on fire. Others urinated in their wine bottles and flung them at Nacho. Barnaby mentioned the mistakes Nacho was making and Adrian urged him to jump in the ring and prove he could do better. Perhaps it was the tequila, but Barnaby said he'd do it. The only problem was that he had no cape. Another slug of tequila.

Not to worry. He stood, whipped off his Brooks Brothers raincoat and headed down the aisle. Of course it was illegal for a fan to jump into the ring, but on a number of occasions these amateur daredevils—*espontáneos*, the Mexicans called them—showed enough promise that a promoter would sign them. Barnaby jumped the fence and taunted Pretty Boy with his raincoat.

Over the loudspeakers the announcer shouted: "*Madre de Dios! There's a gringo in the ring! A gringo!*"

Just then the bull charged and Conrad waved the animal through with a decent pass. Pretty Boy turned and rushed again, and Barnaby executed a fairly competent *veronica.** The crowd cheered wildly.

Pretty Boy came again, only this time he pulled up short and tossed his head, impaling the raincoat and ripping it from Barnaby's hands. He was defenseless. Fortunately, the coat was covering the bull's eyes, giving Barnaby just enough time to bolt for the fence. As he cleared the barrier, security officers grabbed him and told him he'd spend ten days in jail. Seeing this, another young bullfighter, Felix Guzmán,** removed his hat and held it toward the president of the arena, motioning back to Conrad. The official waved a white handkerchief, calling off the arrest.

Afterward, Felix invited Barnaby to study with him, and two weeks later he fought another bull, but with a real cape. He performed extremely well, but while Felix was giving him comments

*A *veronica* is a type of pass where the matador stands with his left leg slightly forward and entices the bull with the cape held low. As the bull charges he advances the cape and leads the bull through, pivoting on the balls of his feet. The lower the cape and the slower the movement, the better the veronica.

**Guzmán would be killed in the ring in 1943 by a Miura bull named Reventón.

after they were finished, the bull rushed unexpectedly, clipping him at the knee and damaging ligaments.

Barnaby returned to the United States, had surgery on the leg, finished his schooling at Yale, and was off to Sevilla as the youngest vice-consul ever. But the danger and thrill of *la fiesta brava* drew him back to the ring. Little did Aline know, Conrad had been training with Juanito and Manolete, and was being tutored by the legend himself, Juan Belmonte, on his ranch near Sevilla. Don Juan, enamored that an American—a diplomat no less—was trying to emulate his art, was intrigued.

Juan instructed him for hours on end, and Juanito provided the equipment and clothing. As a result, Conrad's progress had been surprisingly fast; while most apprenticed for six to twelve years to become a full matador, he was doing it in two. He fought as *El Niño de California* ("The Kid from California")—a moniker coined by Belmonte—as a *novillero* (junior bullfighter), and was scheduled to take his *alternative* to become a full *matador de toros* (senior bullfighter) in the fall.

But none of that came up and Conrad fulfilled his identification duties and Don José put Aline's suitcase in the backseat of Barnaby's convertible.

"How about lunching with me and going to a bullfight afterward?" Barnaby asked as they got in. "You'll never eat better seafood than in Málaga."

Aline paused, glimpsing her watch. It was 2:15.

"I'm sorry," Barnaby said. "You have plans to meet someone here? A friend, perhaps?"

"Not at all. It's just that I have an important errand." Aline motioned to her suitcase. "I promised Sister Catherine back in New York that I would deliver a box of candles made by her to a priest in the Catedral de Santa María as soon as I arrived in Málaga."

"That's easy, the cathedral's on our way."

Aline smiled and glanced again at her watch as they were leaving. She had ten minutes.

When they arrived at the church it was just past the drop appointment. Telling Barnaby she'd be right back, she pretended to reach for that supposed box of candles in her suitcase and hustled inside. It was dark in the church, light streaming in only through the stained-glass windows, but she could see that the back bench was empty. Had Blacky come and gone, she wondered, or was he also running late?

She slipped into the pew and knelt to pray. Minutes passed and then she heard movement to her right. A man had slipped into her row. A man with a white scarf.

Blacky.

He slid down the pew not far from her and Aline kept her head bowed. When Blacky had settled, she fished the microfilm from her pocket, palming it. Keeping her arm low, she reached out and turned her hand over.

Without moving his head or eyes, Blacky took it.

Moments later Aline was back in Conrad's car and they were off. She sighed and sat back. She had done it. It was a beautiful day and the summer breeze lifted her hair and her spirits. They lunched at a beach restaurant and Conrad introduced her to *chan-quetes*, a tiny fish fried whole and crisp in batter, and *boquerones*— baby sardines.

After the bullfight he gave her a tour, strolling through the marble streets around Calle Larios, the gardens, and ending with a magnificent view from the Nautical Club. So as not to initiate a conversation where he would inquire about *her* job, Aline didn't inquire about his. But how a twenty-one-year-old came to be the youngest vice-consul ever was puzzling.

She should have asked, as they had much in common. Conrad had also been a coder, it turned out, and could have decoded every one of her OSS cables. It all started when he finished at Yale. Looking for any work he could find, he went to the State Department and announced that he'd like to become a diplomat. He was too young and without credentials for that, so they trained him to be a code clerk. In a heavily guarded room in Washington, Barnaby began working with strips just like the ones Aline was using to code and decode secret messages for the State Department.

He thought the system was ridiculously simple, though, and that the average six-year-old could handle it. He was bored and miserable.

One day, having finished his work early, he decided to sketch his attractive coding colleague, Roberta Cameron. He had studied fine arts in college and could pencil remarkably professional profiles in minutes. As he was finishing, he included in the corner two strips that Roberta was holding. In the top one he inserted letters at random. In the second, he penciled: "You are beautiful."

He passed it to her and Roberta smiled and put it in her purse. She invited him to dinner that night and afterward they lounged by a roaring fire. They kissed and Barnaby began to rearrange Roberta's dress when suddenly a light flicked on and a man in a dark suit loomed over them. A second man then appeared behind them, having entered simultaneously through the kitchen door.

"FBI," said the first man. He saw Roberta's purse on the table and opened it. "Where is it?"

Roberta looked at the man and her purse. "Where's what?"

"You know what," chirped the second man. "The diagram."

Roberta said she mailed it to her sister in Texas, and the man turned to Barnaby.

"We know it was a chart of the strip code. Exactly what was written on it?

Barnaby held the G-man's eye and said slowly: "You are beautiful."

The FBI kept them under surveillance until they retrieved the sketch from Texas and sent it to Washington. The two coders weren't German or Japanese agents after all, the FBI concluded. Barnaby had had enough, though, and a week later he stopped by the office of the assistant secretary of state, Adolf Berle. Surprisingly, the secretary invited him in and Barnaby gave it his best shot.

"Mr. Secretary, I'm a code clerk and I think I'm too good for my job."

Berle laughed. "Well, come back tomorrow and I'll tell you whether you are or not."

Barnaby did and Berle said: "Mr. Conrad, I agree with you and so does the code room; you are not made of the stuff great code clerks are. How would you like to be a vice-consul in Spain?"

Barnaby was floored. This was a dream come true.

"'Course, you're too young," Berle said. "At twenty-one you'll probably be the youngest vice-consul we've ever had. But I've checked your background and I think you might be an asset in Spain. We'll get you out on the first boat we can."

Barnaby thanked him and was headed out but then stopped at the door.

"What does a vice-consul do?"

Berle chuckled. "You'll find out."

And so began Barnaby Conrad's foreign service career.

After dinner Aline and Barnaby decided to call it a night, and he escorted her to where she was staying, the Hotel Miramar.

She checked in and was delighted to find that her balcony and room faced the ocean. It was a fitting and welcome respite. She took a long, hot bath and when she came out, she gasped.

While she had been soaking in the bathroom her room had been searched, and the intruder had not been neat about it. As unsettling as that was, she felt a great sense of relief in another way. Since she'd been able to keep her rendezvous with Blacky, there'd been nothing of value in her room for anyone to find.

When Aline arrived back in Madrid, Juanito called to remind her that she had promised him dinner. He picked her up at ten and told her that they had reservations at Lhardy. Founded in 1839, it was another Madrid institution. From the outside, the restaurant's hand-carved, dark wooden façade made the establishment look more like a high-end bookstore than a restaurant.

Juanito said that he'd requested a private dining room, and

they went up a narrow staircase to a small entrance enclosed by a red velvet curtain. Inside there was one candlelit table, neatly arranged with a white damask tablecloth and two gleaming place settings.

Aline stood in the doorway, admiring the intimate setting.

Juanito smiled. "These salons were designed for secret love affairs and confidential conversations. These same walls have witnessed many secrets, even conspiracies against the government."

They ordered and Aline said, "Last weekend in Málaga, I was in jail."

"I know that."

Juanito grinned, amused at seeing Aline's jaw drop. "Do not find that unusual, Aline. I have friends all over Spain."

"But how? How do you know? Who told you?"

Juanito shrugged. "Shall we say, someone who knows I admire you."

Aline shook her head. This man was impossible. She hadn't been tagged going to or from Málaga, at least that she knew of. And the likelihood of Don José calling Juanito out of the blue seemed remote. This was unnerving.

She was supposed to be the trained spy, not him.

Throughout the month Juanito fought almost every day—in Alicante, Mallorca, Valencia, and Guipúzcoa. Aline didn't travel to see any of his fights, but she worried about the constant danger. When he returned to Madrid they had dinner again, and she probed further about his line of work.

"Have you ever been badly gored, Juan?"

He nodded. "Many times."

"How is it you're not afraid?"

Juanito paused and his eyes softened. "I'm scared to death every time I enter the arena, Aline."

*   *   *

One evening when Aline was on call for the night shift of coding, she went in about midnight. After an hour or so of work she left, slipping into the street through the embassy's garden exit.

As she made her way back to her apartment, she heard them again.

Footsteps.

Continuing her pace, she glanced back but saw no one. In the dim glow of the gaslights, she assured herself that a *sereno* was making his rounds.

At the corner of Calle de Fortuny and Marqués del Riscal, though, she heard them again. This time she saw him. The shadow of a man, about fifty meters back.

She quickened her steps and the soft patter behind her kept pace.

Clutching her purse, she broke into a sprint.

So did he.

Racing up the walkway, Aline slid between the iron bars of her building's entrance and bounded up the steps to her apartment. Swinging the door shut, she ran over to the window and peered down.

It was him.

CHAPTER 14

THE BOHEMIAN

On August 8 Gregory Thomas called Aline into his office. He told her that Pierre was in Madrid, at the Palace Hotel. He knew that Aline and Pierre had trained together at The Farm, and he had a message he wanted her to pass along to him.

Aline's heart skipped a beat. She longed to see Pierre but was mystified as to why he would be in Madrid.

Thomas held up a paper. "This cable means that the invasion will take place at Marseille."

Operation Dragoon wouldn't be as big or dramatic as the invasion at Normandy, but it was critical to secure the southern part of the country for the push to Paris. With the D-Day troops pushing in from the northwest, Allied soldiers advancing deep into France from the southeast would create a pincer on the Germans, forcing them to retreat into Germany.

"Contact Pierre," he said. "Tell him his orders are to move his subagents to the Marseille area. They should be in a position to assist our troops when they land. He must act surreptitiously with his own people. Information on the location of the landing is so secret it cannot be leaked, cannot be made known, even to those who have been risking their lives for us these past years."

Aline nodded. She knew full well the importance of secrecy and security.

What she didn't know was that Thomas was lying.

Aline met Pierre that evening in the Palace Hotel bar, thrilled that their rendezvous would be longer and more enjoyable than his previous balcony surprise. When they were seated, he told her he had information she should pass on to Thomas—information he had acquired from Gloria von Fürstenberg.

Aline bristled at the name, wondering how many times Pierre had met with her.

"General Tresckow," Pierre began, "chief of staff of the Second Army now on the Eastern Front, plans to move the Fourteenth Panzer Corps and the Fourth Panzer Division, if their current attack on the Russian front is successful, to southern France. She said her husband is in the Fourth Panzer Division and that's how she knows this."

Aline noted the information and said she, too, had news about Dragoon. Passing along what Thomas had said about Marseille and Pierre's assignment, she added that he was to look for a black Packard, license plate CD406, the next morning at nine in front of the hotel. From there he would be flown to France.

With business completed, Aline could feel the conversation shifting on a dime before Pierre said another word. He looked at her for several moments and the sensual energy she remembered from The Farm was back. She wasn't sure if it was his face, his arms, or his thick lashes, but she was still enraptured.

"You do care for me?" he asked.

Aline didn't know what she felt. Was she smitten? No doubt. In love? No. Intrigued? Unquestionably.

"What about your friendship with Gloria?"

Pierre laughed. He had met her in Paris years before, he said, but that was all. They were just friends. He narrowed his gaze. "You're the one for me."

With that Pierre stood. "I'll be back. And I am going to miss you."

Aline got up and Pierre held her by the shoulders. "I've tried to change—a lot of things. I'll tell you one day."

He held her eyes a moment and then turned and walked away.

"Goodbye, Pierre."

The following day Edmundo passed on intelligence that coincided with Gregory Thomas's instructions. "Max Sciolitti," he reported, "the Brazilian vice-consul, told me this afternoon that he had proof that the Germans are evacuating the Spanish frontier and southern France. He expects an Allied force in Marseille at any moment."

Operation Dragoon was imminent and it seemed everyone on both sides knew an attack would begin soon.

Aline, meanwhile, couldn't get Gloria von Fürstenberg off her mind. She had seen Gloria twice with Hans Lazar, and who but a Nazi sympathizer would be admitted into Horcher's private dining room? Truth be told, Aline was jealous that Pierre seemed to know her well, and she could only wonder if they had been intimate. Aline's interest in Gloria heightened when she heard that Gloria bought her clothes at Ana de Pombo's shop. It was Ana de Pombo, she recalled, who had been sitting next to Walter Schellenberg at Juanito's bullfight.

On her next day off she decided to probe. She had been wanting to buy a new dress for weeks anyway, and what better place to order one than Ana de Pombo's? If Gloria bought her dresses there, surely Ana had the best selection in town.

Without making an appointment, Aline went to Ana's store at 14 Calle de Hermosilla. The storefront, she found, was not unlike Hattie Carnegie's, but the foyer had an eclectic mix of Louis XVI and art deco furniture. A maid greeted her—not a saleswoman, which seemed odd. She would fetch Ana, the woman said, and Aline waited in the empty room. For a successful business, that, too, seemed strange. Where were the other customers?

Moments later a woman with frizzy orange hair appeared. It was the woman Aline had seen at the bullfight, but up close she looked older.

"You want something?" Ana asked in perfect English.

Aline paused. No greeting? No "Hello, I'm Ana de Pombo, welcome to my studio."?

"Yes, I wanted to order some clothes." Aline looked around. "Have I come too late? Or too early?"

"Yes—oh—yes. Of course, just a moment." Ana motioned to a sofa and disappeared to gather some designs.

Aline took a seat and waited. After some time she checked her watch. It had been ten minutes. Since Ana had no other customers, what could she possibly be doing?

Finally, Ana returned with a stack of drawings. "I'm afraid everything from my collection is gone. I have only sketches left. Would you like to see some?"

Aline flipped through the drawings, but this, too, was odd. None of the samples looked remotely like what Gloria wore, and all of them seemed at least two seasons behind the current trends. She gave no response but Ana noticed the lack of interest.

"Maybe you should try Pedro Rodríguez or Flora Villarreal."

"No, I like these designs." Aline motioned to a few sketches. "May I see some fabrics?"

Ana seemed taken aback. "Just a moment, please."

A few minutes later the door opened again, but it was not Ana.

"Why, Aline," Countess Gloria said, "Ana told me you were here. What a wonderful surprise! How did you find this place? I thought I had it all to myself. Ana dresses me and only a few others—how did you hear of her?"

Aline stifled her surprise. "I can't remember offhand."

Gloria joined her on the sofa. "I'm here to be fitted for a dress I intend to wear to the big dinner dance coming up at the Country Club Puerta de Hierro. Are you going?"

"Not that I know of. I'd love to see the dress."

"I'd much rather surprise you. You'll certainly be invited."

Aline nodded, but she was curious why Gloria didn't want to show it. "Well, I'm waiting to see some fabrics."

"Ana is unique, a bohemian. She keeps nothing here. She draws her ideas, discusses them with the customer, and only then orders the materials. Her taste is flawless. And frightfully expensive. Take a tip from me and go somewhere else. She takes ages to finish anything."

Aline paused a moment and then stood. "You're right. I'm a working girl and I have no time to wait."

She left without saying goodbye to Ana. It all made sense now. The woman ran no dress shop.

Her salon was a letter box.

As she made her way back to the apartment, Aline mulled over her discovery. If Ana de Pombo's was a letter box, then Gloria was probably a messenger. Through her, notes or instructions from Hans Lazar or Walter Schellenberg could be dropped off for later pickup by any number of German spies or informants. She decided not to mention it to Gregory Thomas or anyone at the office, though, since it was still conjecture at this point and she wasn't actually a field agent. Instead, she'd have one of her local confidants keep an eye on the place, noting who came and went.

What Aline didn't know was that not only was Ana de Pombo's store a letter box, it was co-owned by Colonel Ernesto Heymann, the Abwehr officer in charge of all of Spain.

Then there was the little problem of who worked there. Ana had recently hired a young woman, Eva, to manage the showroom. Eva was the future sister-in-law of someone Aline knew extremely well.

Robert Dunev.

CHAPTER 15

THE LADY VANISHES

In mid-August Aline learned that what Gregory Thomas had told her about Operation Dragoon's planned landing in Marseille was false; it was a story circulated to mislead the enemy. The real invasion, which had commenced on August 15 and was a tremendous success, occurred farther north along the Côte d'Azur, from Saint-Raphaël to Cavalaire-sur-Mer.

Originally conceived as a feint to draw German troops away from Normandy, Operation Dragoon became an actual invasion plan when the Americans suggested an invasion of southern France at the Cairo conference.* At one point the idea was to invade simultaneously with the Normandy landings, but this notion was rejected when German troops were moved to Italy during the Allied invasion at Anzio.

When Aline asked Thomas about the misinformation he had given her to pass along to Pierre, he was vague, which set off a disturbing chain of thought.

---

*The Cairo Conference, code-named SEXTANT and held to discuss Allied strategy, occurred November 23–26 and December 3–7, 1943. President Roosevelt and Prime Minister Churchill attended both meetings, while China's Chiang Kai-shek attended the former, and President Ismet Inönü of Turkey attended the latter.

She was fully aware of the use of "chicken feed"—false, misleading, or late information given to the enemy—but it made her think about Thomas's use of Pierre to deliver it to Allied personnel. Was a leak expected? Was Pierre used to expose it? She remembered his parting words, that bit about trying to change, and she had a sinking feeling in her stomach.

Couldn't be. A traitor?

She didn't press further and a day or so later she received a call that took her mind off Pierre. It was a call she had feared almost since her arrival in Madrid.

Juanito had been badly gored.

The caller was Juanito's man of swords, and he was calling from La Clinica de los Toreros, the bullfighters' hospital. He was crying and could barely get the words out.

"He was operated on . . . by Dr. Tamananes . . . and is still unconscious."

Aline squeezed the phone. "How serious?"

The man continued to sob, unable to answer.

Aline hung up and raced out. She knew that bullfighting was dangerous, but somehow imagined that experts like Juanito would always be able to avoid serious injury. Reality, though, was quite the opposite: a matador's popularity—and therefore financial success—was proportional to how close he worked to the bull, how many chances he took, how often he allowed the bull's horns to graze his chest or legs.

The odds weren't good: 10 percent of bullfighters were killed in the ring each year, another 13 percent crippled. And over a career, some 40 percent of matadors would be wounded at least twenty times.

The scene at the hospital was chaotic. The entire corridor of Juanito's floor was swarming with reporters, photographers, fans, and friends. Guards, doctors, and nurses had tried to keep people away, but to no avail.

Aline weaved her way through the crowd and saw Juanito's man.

He was still wearing his satin embroidered costume, his eyes blood-shot and weary. Juanito's room was cordoned off, but his chief *ban-derillero* was able to usher her in.

Juanito's mother, Doña Consuelo, stood to greet her. Her face revealed a mother's grief, but amid the tension Aline could see that she was quite beautiful, just as Juanito had said.

"*Gracias* for coming, Aline. Juanito has been asking for you ever since he came out of the operating room. He is still groggy, but *gracias a Dios*, his wound is not as serious as we thought."

Aline glanced at the bed and gasped. Juanito's face was ashen, his complexion bearing evidence of blood loss and shock.

She took his hand and waited until his eyes opened and found hers. He tried to speak but struggled.

"Aline."

He gestured to the counter and then grimaced in pain. "Would you care for some chocolates?"

The unexpected comment kept Aline from weeping. She looked over and saw a box of their favorite chocolates on a table next to his bed. She smiled and shook her head, unable to speak.

"Well, in that case, would you mind feeding me one?"

Aline placed one in his mouth and wondered if it was dangerous for him to eat solid food. Juanito struggled to chew and swallow, and then asked for water. She poured a glass and held it close as he sipped through a straw.

"Chocolates and water," he said. "What else does a man need? Surely not bulls." He turned his eyes to meet hers.

"Will you be my Florence Nightenberg?"

Aline laughed, fighting back tears. "Of course I will."

On the way out she spoke with the doctors. Juanito had been lucky, they said, as the bull's horn had not severed a main artery. He was going to be okay but needed to rest for two weeks. Aline knew better. Juanito would be back in the ring as soon as he could walk.

As she left the hospital, she noticed three men loitering by the entrance. There were others, too, but these looked particularly suspicious. They were smoking and apparently waiting for someone. One of the faces looked familiar, but she couldn't place it. Next to him was a short Spaniard in a baggy suit. She looked at the third man and shivered. It all came back.

The one in the baggy suit she had seen on her train to Málaga. The third man she had seen in front of her apartment one night.

She marched up to Baggy Suit. "Didn't I see you on the train to Málaga?"

He smiled. "Sí, señorita."

Aline's eyes narrowed. "Who are you?"

"But, señorita, you don't know us? We work for Don Juan, and we have seen you often."

Unmoved, she turned to the man she had seen by her apartment. "And I think you have been in front of my house once or twice."

"Not once or twice, señorita," he said kindly. "Almost every night. Well, we changed sometimes, but more often I took that part."

Aline bristled. "But why would you be in front of my house?"

"Don Juan wanted us to protect the señorita and to inform him who the señorita went out with, to make sure the men would bring her to no harm."

Aline didn't know whether to laugh or cold-cock one of them. *They* were the ones who had been following her. One thing was for sure: when Juanito was healthy, he would receive a severe dressing down from Florence Nightenberg.

As August rolled on, Aline discovered something unusual.

Gloria von Fürstenberg had vanished.

She had not been to Ana de Pombo's so-called shop, sources reported, and no one had seen her since August 9. For Gloria to be absent from two weeks of parties and receptions was strange, to say the least. Aline tried not to think about the coincidence that Gloria and Pierre had disappeared at the same time.

Meanwhile, Allied intelligence was catching up on rumored efforts by high-ranking Nazis to sneak themselves and looted art out of Europe.* Argentina and Brazil were the principal destinations, they believed, and Spain seemed to be the conduit.

In May the Foreign Economic Administration—President Roosevelt's organization to engage in economic warfare—had set up a task force to examine what could be done. Dubbing the mission "Project Safehaven," the FEA began contacting OSS X-2 offices, starting with Barcelona, the closest hub to the French border.

To exert pressure on the Spanish to assist in Safehaven, Ambassador Hayes met with Spain's foreign minister, José Félix de Lequerica, in late August. Hayes demanded assurances that Spain would not receive or harbor Axis war criminals, or provide haven for looted property. Lequerica agreed to cooperate. The OSS, though, operated on the assumption that the Spanish would provide little to no assistance in hunting the traffickers or the art.

In France, the Allies continued their push toward Germany, liberating Paris on August 25. It was a major milestone, and Parisians were fortunate and thankful that the German commander in charge of the city, General Dietrich von Choltitz, disobeyed Hitler's order to destroy the city and instead surrendered it intact to the Free French Forces.

Four days later ELTON, Barcelona's deputy station chief, sent Gregory Thomas a cable with the subject heading: **GERMAN PROPERTY IN SPAIN**. In his message, he informed Thomas of FEA's directive, and also advised him of the orders that had been given to Edmundo Lassalle: "PELOTA has been instructed to keep a careful eye on any indication of German property or German interests changing hands."

---

*Field Marshal Erwin Rommel, who was in charge of setting up Germany's defenses along France's northeastern coastline, had always contended that his men had to defeat any Allied invasion by crushing it on the beaches. If the Allies made it onto the mainland, he felt, the war was lost. This setback, combined with defeats on the Eastern Front, led most German officers to conclude that it was just a matter of time before Germany capitulated.

The following week Barcelona updated Thomas on how they intended to use Edmundo: "The question of enemy investments and transfers of capital was thoroughly discussed with PELOTA yesterday, and I expect to see him tomorrow about the same question. I believe that PELOTA is our best approach to the highest banking and industrial circles, and, in accordance with my suggestion, he is proceeding both here and in Madrid to line up persons who will be suitable for our penetration of this society."

In September the FEA formalized Safehaven as an operation and announced four major objectives:

- To restrict German economic penetration outside the borders of the Reich
- To prevent Germany from sequestering assets (including loot) in neutral countries
- To ensure that German assets would be available for post-war rebuilding of Europe
- To prevent the escape of possible war criminals

The State Department would take the lead in overall implementation, but the OSS would act as the investigating and policing arm. To organize the portion of their task to keep looted treasures from leaving Europe, the OSS established the Art Looting Investigation Unit (ALIU), which would be coordinated from the London office.

Gregory Thomas informed Edmundo that, as the station's coordinating Safehaven agent, he would need to go to London for special debriefing. No one would be better suited to crack the German network, Thomas explained, than a harmless Disney executive who had extensive connections in Mexico.

In the meantime, Aline was preoccupied with two disturbing mysteries. Pierre, whom she had not heard a word from or about in more than three months, had disappeared.

And Gloria von Fürstenberg was still missing.

CHAPTER 16

THE COUNT

On December 11 Edmundo left for London, where he would undergo Safehaven training for almost a month. There, he learned that he would have a new priority: discovering German companies and operatives moving Nazi money in and out of Spain and, where possible, the location of any loot. He was encouraged to enlist the aid of any available agents in Madrid or Barcelona, and he decided that Aline would be his perfect sidekick.

The first week of the New Year Gregory Thomas had his hands full keeping tabs on the various scattered cats of the Madrid office, including Lazar, Prince Max, Ana de Pombo, Pierre, Gloria, and now Safehaven. His code name, ARGUS, was apt since, like the king of Greek mythology, he needed to be all-seeing.

And he was. He started the year by informing Robert Dunev that Ana de Pombo's business was a cover operation for the Abwehr. Knowing that Eva, the sister of Dunev's fiancée, Louise Marie, worked at the store, he forbade Dunev from visiting Louise Marie in her home. Dunev had no prior knowledge of Ana de Pombo's connection to the Germans, and it's unclear how Thomas learned it. In all probability, Aline informed Thomas about Ana's relationship with Gloria von Fürstenberg, and the fact that Ana's store wasn't really an active business. It's likely that Thomas learned that Ana's business partner was an Abwehr officer by checking with X-2, OSS's counterintelligence arm, which already had a file on Gloria.

Unable to see Louise Marie at her home, Robert Dunev made the best of it. Here, they're enjoying a romantic lunch date at Madrid's *El Parque del Buen Retiro. Michael Dunev*

On January 9 Edmundo returned to Spain, and Thomas decided that Madrid should be his permanent base. Madrid held more clues in the Safehaven drama than Barcelona, he felt, and he liked the idea of pairing the charismatic Mexican with Aline. It was time, then, to inform Aline that she now *officially* had more duties than just the code room. Like Edmundo and Dunev, she also would be a field agent gathering intelligence and submitting formal reports. But first he had to debrief her on Safehaven itself.

* * *

It was a crisp winter morning and Aline hustled to the office, wondering about the note Gregory Thomas had left on her desk the day before. "Tomorrow morning at nine in my office, urgent," was all it said. The last three months had been relatively quiet and she wondered if she was going to be sent back home. As she passed through the embassy gates, she saw the milkman's donkey cart. "*Vaya usted con Dios, señorita,*" the man called out as he filled a pail. She waved and hurried up the stairway to Thomas's office. He motioned to a side chair and she sat, studying his angular face and expecting him to say her time in Madrid was over. The milkman's donkey began braying and Thomas went to the window and peered out.

Turning back, he said, "I've asked you to come here because we have a new mission for you."

Aline lifted her chin. She wasn't being sent home after all.

"There's a large operation going on now," he began, "in collaboration with the rest of the Allies. It involves uncovering assets that have been looted by the Third Reich and by individual members of the Nazi government. Gold, jewels, art. Assets stolen from governments, private persons, and companies. Often from wealthy Jews whose effects were confiscated or who were tricked into paying a ransom for a freedom they never enjoyed."

Aline could feel her adrenaline spike. This meant more than just keeping her eyes and ears open at parties and occasional freelance work with Edmundo; it was a legitimate assignment as a field agent. A mission.

Thomas took his seat and went on. "Swiss bank accounts are being opened in names we must uncover. The loot is being shipped out of Europe to safe havens in South America. That's why we call it Operation Safehaven. We have many agents working on this—teams in Holland, Belgium, France, and Switzerland. But in Spain, the work will be more delicate.

"The stuff goes by train from Holland and Belgium across France to Bordeaux. From there it is shipped across the Bay of Biscay to

Bilbao. Right now, Madrid is the hub of the wheel for all exports from the war zones. For Nazis trying to escape, too."

Aline's mind began to race, wondering who might be involved. Lazar? Ana de Pombo? Gloria? Was it possible that *Pierre* was involved, even a double agent?

She would be working with Edmundo, Thomas said, and they were to uncover the Nazis' financial network in Spain, particularly the companies the Germans were using as fronts and any individuals who were sending, or trying to send, money abroad. In essence, the goal was to trap the money in Spain. Once accounts were frozen, ill-gotten funds could be confiscated and returned by Allied authorities to the original owners or their descendants. At the top of the list of people to investigate was Prince Max.

Aline would be filing most of her reports with James MacMillan, Thomas said, but she'd also be handling assignments from Larry Mellon. Edmundo, he added, would now be stationed permanently in Madrid, but any information he had should be conveyed through her reports. Since Edmundo didn't have a cover job at the Oil Ministry to give him a reason to visit the embassy, Aline would keep their bosses informed.

A few weeks into their new collaboration, Edmundo was waiting for Aline at a table in the Palace Hotel bar. This peculiar spy, "a delicious confection of warm brown skin, dazzling white teeth, and slick black hair," she remembered later, had become something of a big brother.

Edmundo stood and raised her hand to his lips. "*Divina*, you're ravishing." He stepped back and appraised her chic new Balenciaga outfit.

Aline smiled, reminding herself that this irrepressible flirt had the full trust of Walt Disney and the OSS.

He explained that he had just returned from Lisbon, and that he had gone to Casino Estoril. "My pet, you can't imagine how dowdy the women in the casino in Cascais are these days! Life has been such a monotony since I saw you last."

Aline shook her head and then noticed that Edmundo's attention had been captured by someone entering the bar. She followed his eyes to an attractive auburn-haired woman in a navy silk suit and pillbox hat.

It was Princess Maria Agatha of Ratibor and Corvey, a German heiress who, like Prince Max, had numerous connections to the Third Reich. One of her relatives, in fact, Prince Ernst von Ratibor and Corvey, had found his way onto the US blacklist for dealing with Nazis.* American officials had frozen his assets in the United States, and when Prince Ernst's Peruvian wife, Consuelo Eyre, had sought release of funds held in an American bank, the request was denied.

Aline and Edmundo had discovered only days earlier that Princess Agatha had worked the prior year for Dr. Franz Liesau, a mysterious man who ran a company called Oficina Tecnica. Liesau had countless ties to the Gestapo, sources reported, and Oficina Tecnica was suspected of being a German front for espionage.

Also like Prince Max, Princess Agatha had much to lose if Germany lost the war. Her family owned palaces and estates in Westphalia, Germany, and in Grafenegg, Neuaigen, Asparn, and Corvey, Austria. They also owned considerable land and businesses in and around Ratibor, a town in southern Upper Silesia, Germany. Their wealth stemmed from mining, and their coal deposits in Ratibor were Berlin's principal source of energy.

Incredibly, Edmundo had been playing both sides of the coin. While gaining Princess Agatha's trust by wooing her romantically,

---

*If anyone, or any company, in neutral countries like Spain, Portugal, or Sweden were found to have done business with Germany during the war, they were "blacklisted," which meant that no Allied country would trade or do business with them. In addition, individuals on the blacklist usually would have a counterintelligence file opened on them in X-2's office.

he nevertheless decided that she was a legitimate subject for counterintelligence. As such, he had placed her on the OSS blacklist, which allowed him to socialize with her on the company's dime. It was a violation of everything they had been taught in training, not to mention morally reprehensible, but Edmundo never seemed bothered by contradictions.

Aline remembered him saying to her months earlier that he was sure Agatha was actually anti-Nazi, and Aline could tell that he really was interested in her. Perhaps he was the perfect spy. One minute he was obsessed with gossip about royalty and aristocratic families, the next he was juggling women, Disney, and espionage. But one thing was clear: he was hands down one of the most skilled and productive agents working for the OSS in Europe. And he always made her laugh.

Princess Agatha strolled with her party past their table and Aline caught her subtle wink to Edmundo.

"I'll bet anything you were in Portugal with your favorite princess," Aline said under her breath.

Edmundo flashed a lopsided grin. "What do you expect me to do, my pet? She pursues me, and after all it is part of my work, you know. Agatha gives me the inside track to Gestapo gossip. She may not be a Nazi, but she knows them all. The trouble is, she's getting serious. Can you imagine—she's thinking of marriage! That would certainly improve my seating at these Spanish dinners."

Aline laughed. "Edmundo, you must really be in love. Marrying Agatha won't give you a title. German titles cannot be passed on to husbands. But if you married a Spanish woman with a title, you could become a marquis or a count or a duke."

"You're right. Maybe I'd better reconsider. And I'm getting tired of waiting for a deposed queen to float into town."

Edmundo called for the check, saying he was taking Aline to dinner to meet an important new contact. As they waited outside for a taxi, a convertible Cord pulled into the far end of the circular drive. Aline couldn't see the driver's face as he got out, but she could see that he was young and well built. He was also well dressed, sporting a beige trench coat with a white silk scarf over his shoulders.

A taxi arrived and as she and Edmundo were about to get in, she heard a man's voice: "Aline, hold it a moment."

It was none other than Luis, the Count of Quintanilla, who had pulled up in the Cord. "I'm meeting Casilda. Is she inside?"

Aline nodded. "She's in the rotunda with Pimpinela."

"What a pity you're just leaving. I always seem to miss you. Casilda tells me the Oil Mission keeps you very busy."

Luis invited her and Edmundo to join Casilda and him for dinner at Chipén, but Edmundo chimed in, saying that they had reservations at Horcher's.

Luis bid them good night, and when he had reached the top of the steps, he turned back to look at her.

Aline waved.

"Sorry to have spoiled your evening, *Divina*," Edmundo quipped as they stepped into the taxi.

"What's the matter with you?"

Edmundo shrugged. "I guess I'm worried that you'll marry a grandee before I do."

"Don't be ridiculous. I hardly know Luis Quintanilla. He's practically engaged to Casilda, my best friend. The families are planning the wedding already, and he adores her."

Edmundo cracked a conspiratorial smile. "My pet, the person who should marry the count is yourself."

As January came to a close, Countess von Fürstenberg surfaced again in Madrid after an absence of more than three months. Why she had left and where she had gone, no one knew. The rumors circulating after she disappeared were that she was broke and had left behind large unpaid bills at one of the major Madrid department stores.

The rumors were in fact true, and Gloria's track record was less than stellar. After she disappeared Gregory Thomas had X-2 investigate. Gloria had claimed to have held a Dutch passport, but when OSS agents checked with the Dutch legation, they denied it. Gloria had never presented herself to Dutch authorities in Spain or Portugal, they said. It was also true, X-2 discovered, that Gloria had left town owing 1,500 pesetas to a business known as Julio Laffittee.

They also found out that when Gloria had arrived in Portugal on August 9, she had told customs officials that she was en route to the United States with her two children: Dolores, age six, and Francisco, age three. From there she was supposedly headed to Mexico, where she intended to join her mother, brother, and sister. She emphasized to Portuguese officials that she needed to join these relatives soon as she was "virtually penniless."

What was suspicious about Gloria's story was that, while claiming to be destitute, she nonetheless managed to live in the most expensive hotel in Portugal for more than three months.

Gloria's Palacio Hotel registration. Note that she includes her maiden Mexican name, Rubio, and that the hotel clerk writing in the checkout date used the roman numeral for November. *Cascais Archive*

Portuguese authorities didn't exactly buy her story, and in October they demanded that she provide a written response to various questions, including where she had gained a passport, and on what means she was living. Her responses were complicated.

In 1934 she had married a Dutchman named Frank Scholtens, she wrote, thus gaining Dutch citizenship. She divorced him shortly thereafter, though, and regained her Mexican nationality. The following year she met Count von Fürstenberg in Berlin and married him in London. They lived in Germany until 1942, when she left him and moved to Spain. The German consulate in Madrid, however, confiscated her passport, and she applied for a new one with the Mexican embassy. In 1943 the Mexican consulate in Lisbon issued her a new passport.

Her financial situation, though, remained a mystery. While she had paid off the bill to Laffittee's and continued to live at the Palacio, she reported that she had "no funds" and no account at any Portuguese bank.

Portuguese, Spanish, and American authorities all had unanswered questions about Gloria, but it was clear that she was cagey, crafty, and resourceful.

In late January, Edmundo was spending more and more time with Princess Agatha, and their relationship was becoming increasingly serious.

"Aline," he told her near the end of the month, "I may ask Ratibor to marry me."

Aline's jaw dropped. "Edmundo, how can you do that? *You* put Ratibor on the blacklist. If you married her, you'd have to resign from the service."

Edmundo shrugged. "My dear, I ask you, what else can a man do but obey his heart? And, frankly, what is more important, I ask you: espionage or a title? Didn't a king abdicate his throne for a woman? Well, what can I do? What is a court of law when I,

Edmundo Lassalle, bow as a humble petitioner before the court of love?"

"Are you serious? Are you really in love with her?"

"Aline, think of my future. What does it hold for me after the war ends? Can you see me shuffling papers behind a desk in some American company? Or perhaps you would have me imprisoned in the Pentagon, working for the army. No, my darling, remember: 'Edmundo Lassalle. He danced not in vain.'"

Aline couldn't help giggling at the lines Edmundo had said he wanted on his tombstone.

"As Ratibor's husband," he went on, "consort, if you will—the world of society is mine. We'll live between Mexico City, New York, Paris, Deauville, the Italian Riviera."

Edmundo continued, ranting about how espionage was no longer as exciting as it had been when he started.

Aline found the whole thing disturbing. He was walking a fine line with Princess Agatha. What would Agatha say if she found out he was an OSS agent and had placed her on the blacklist? What would Gregory Thomas say upon hearing of an engagement? Worse, what if Agatha really *was* a Nazi and Edmundo had fallen in love with her? Would he switch sides?

Aline shrugged off the notion and asked him whether Agatha was providing intelligence to pass on to Washington.

Edmundo shrugged. "Every day I trust her less. But I make a valiant effort to keep those old fogies in Washington interested. Why, it makes their day just to receive one of PELOTA's delicious concoctions."

Aline shook her head. "If ARGUS knew!"

Edmundo grew solemn and in a voice fit for theater intoned: "My dearest, as my prized pupil who will one day undoubtedly share my firmament in the galaxy of immortal spies, I tell you from the bottom of my heart—on Judgment Day we will not be accountable to ARGUS. I, for one, intend to be accountable only to Venus."

Aline couldn't help but laugh. Edmundo broke the mold. He was preparing OSS reports detailing his investigation of Princess Agatha—the very woman he had put on the Allied blacklist—and yet he was thinking of marrying her, even though he wasn't *necessarily* in love.

There was just one minor detail Edmundo had failed to disclose.

CHAPTER 17

BUTCH

February 1945
Madrid

Over the ensuing days Aline thought more about Pierre—his strange last comment about wanting to change things, his disappearance, and Thomas's use of him for chicken feed. But that was the chief's business now; after all, Thomas knew far more about Pierre than she did.

Other strange things were happening as well. The first weekend in February, Edmundo went to a society ball with a most unusual date.

Gloria von Fürstenberg.

He told neither Aline nor Gregory Thomas.

On February 5 Aline submitted her first intelligence report as agent BUTCH. It was a memo to QUERES (James MacMillan) about a potential Safehaven suspect. A certain Evarista Murtra, she wrote, the general manager of a firm in Barcelona, had said to a small group two days earlier that he was moving to Cuba with all of his capital. Later that day he cabled a contact in South America, advising the man to deposit all funds in an American bank.

It wasn't earth-shattering news, but it did fall in line with the
Safehaven objective of finding all Axis sources attempting to
transfer funds out of Spain. If X-2 had a file on Murtra as a possible Nazi collaborator, Aline's information might uncover a sur-
reptitious chain.

MADRID, FEBRUARY 5, 1945

To: QUERES
From: BUTCH

SR. DON. EVARISTA MURTRA, LIVING IN BARCELONA AT RONDA SAN
PEDRO 22, GENERAL MANAGER OF COMPANIA ANONIMO A. MURTRA OF
BARCELONA, STATED TO A SMALL GROUP OF INTIMATE FRIENDS ON
FEB. 3rd, THAT HE WAS MOVING TO CUBA WITH ALL POSSIBLE CAPITAL
AS SOON AS POSSIBLE DUE TO THE UNCERTAIN POLITICAL SITUATION
IN SPAIN.

SR. MURTRA ALSO STATED THAT THE UNHIDDEN HATRED OF THE CATALAN
WORKER FOR THE PRESENT GOVERNMENT IS ONLY ANOTHER PROOF THAT
THE CURRENT SPANISH REGIME CANNOT LAST.

ON THE SAME DAY, SR. MURTRA CABLED A SPANISH FRIEND OF HIS IN
SOUTH AMERICA ADVISING THAT FRIEND SHOULD DEPOSIT ALL FUNDS IN
AN AMERICAN BANK IN PREFERENCE TO RETURNING TO SPAIN WITH FUNDS,
SINCE THE FINANCIAL SITUATION HERE IS SO DANGEROUS. HE ALSO
ADVISED FRIEND AGAINST BUYING CERTAIN PROPERTY IN SPAIN, CONTRACT
FOR WHICH SAID FRIEND HAD BEEN AT POINT OF SIGNING.

Aline's first formal field report, submitted to James MacMillan ("QUERES") on February 5,
1945. *NARA*

In March she submitted two more reports. Together she and Edmundo then rooted out a number of Safehaven targets, and in early
April Edmundo discovered a stream of illegal financial transactions
going on in Portugal. Gregory Thomas thought it was significant

enough to notify Washington and that afternoon sent a report to Frank Ryan.

Ryan wasn't surprised, though, as he had just received a cable from the US embassy in Paris stating that the German embassy in Spain was sending 50 to 100 million francs *a day* to Lisbon via diplomatic pouch. These francs were exchanged for Portuguese pesetas, Paris reported, and then transferred back to Madrid, again through the diplomatic bag. The Germans, it was clear, were frantic to liquidate their funds into a safe currency before their country capitulated.

Thomas took off for Lisbon to get details, and on April 17 he sent word to MacMillan and Mellon that "there is a reported flow of material wealth into the German embassy in Madrid and the Consulates in the provincial capitals."

And that flow would only increase.

Three weeks later, on May 7, General Alfred Jodl, Hitler's chief of staff, signed Germany's unconditional surrender at General Dwight Eisenhower's headquarters in Reims, France. The following day Field Marshal Wilhelm Keitel signed the final terms of surrender in Berlin.

It was exhilarating news for Aline and everyone at the American and British embassies, and celebrations and toasts rang in the newfound era of peace.

While the end of the war in Europe might have suggested that the OSS could close its Spanish offices, Aline's and Edmundo's work was now needed more than ever. Millions of dollars and countless works of art had yet to be retrieved, and Safehaven pushed ahead full steam. Four days later, on May 12, Aline submitted no less than six reports, three to MacMillan, three to Larry Mellon, and a fourth memo to Mellon on May 15.

The first memo to MacMillan indicated that Spain's official exchange rate between the peseta and the dollar was about to change: from 10 to 1 to 18 to 1. She had heard this from three reliable sources, she wrote, including a member of the Spanish stock exchange. Not even the State Department had known this was coming. The dollar, Aline's memo suggested, was rapidly becoming the only reliable currency in the world (other than gold).

In a second report to MacMillan, she referenced joint work that she had been doing with Edmundo on Safehaven. For some time, Dr. Francisco Liesau—the man for whom Princess Agatha had worked—had been high on their suspect list, along with his company, Oficina Tecnica. "In May 1943," she reported, "Dr. Liesau carefully put everything he owned including his own apartment to the last piece of furniture under the names of two of his best Spanish friends . . . Manuel de Bofarull y Romana Alfonso XII." She also noted that the Spanish government had just days ago passed a resolution stating that assets of suspected Nazi collaborators could be frozen, even when in the hands of third parties.

Given the information in X-2's files, she wrote, combined with her and Edmundo's findings, the only conclusion was that Liesau "has been a dangerous German agent."

In a sister memo to the Liesau report, she noted that she and Edmundo had a new source with inside information about Liesau's company, Oficina Tecnica, and that she and Edmundo would provide new details soon.

Her first memo to Larry Mellon concerned Marta Film, a company co-owned by a German named Guillermo Linhoff. The company had made Spanish films and imported German and Italian films. Because of the latter, and Germany's well-known production of propaganda films, Marta Film had been blacklisted. Linhoff and his Spanish partner, she reported, were working to reestablish their business in another name to circumvent the blacklist. And one person who seemed to spend a fair amount of time in the Marta Film office was Hans Scheib, a German filmmaker.

Aline's second memo to Mellon was about a German woman he had asked her to investigate, Countess Hexe Podevils. She was married to a German named Herr Schubach, Aline reported, but was separated and living in Madrid under her maiden name. Without question, Podevils had been a liaison officer for the Germans, a "full-fledged Gestapo agent," she wrote, and a war criminal.

Her third report to Mellon was lengthy and a bit off the espionage track. It involved Edmundo, Walt Disney Productions, Roy Disney, and an Italian named Pierre de Beneducci. Aline included excerpts from two February 23, 1944, letters that Edmundo had given her. One was from Roy, the other from Disney's legal counsel, giving Edmundo last-minute information and instructions before leaving for Madrid.

Edmundo was replacing Beneducci, their former Spanish and Italian representative, and it turned out that his predecessor had not been entirely ethical. From what Edmundo and Aline surmised, the man had been licensing Disney's products but keeping all the proceeds for himself. He disappeared during the Spanish Civil War, they said, and Disney had no idea if he was still selling, or attempting to sell, their licensing.

Roy Disney concluded: "We want you to investigate the status of the present activities in Spain of de Beneducci and report to us what he is doing."

It was a delicate situation for the OSS. While they wanted and needed Disney's cover for Edmundo, Disney wasn't paying for his services and agent PELOTA had little time to chase Disney's private business affairs. If de Beneducci had been blacklisted or was a suspect under investigation by X-2, that would be a different matter. Edmundo had not previously said anything about the Disney assignment though, probably because he had no intention of carrying it out. Pursuing de Beneducci would only have distracted him from his real quarry: an aristocratic wife with an impressive title and bank account.

* * *

The State Department, meanwhile, had been doing its own reporting. Two weeks earlier, on May 2, it had taken the unusual step of issuing a formal report stating that Gloria von Fürstenberg was *not* a German operative. At least not at the present time. Though her connections to various Nazis were undeniable, her choice of friends seemed to have been determined on the basis of wealth rather than ideology. In a carefully worded statement, the report announced: "Subject is not actually considered suspect although known to have had various German connections in the German embassy in Madrid (HANS VON STUDNITZ), German agent in the S.D."

The embassy's insertion of "actually," together with a notation that she had ties to a Nazi intelligence agent, suggested that it was something of a surprise that she was not directly fingered as a German informant or agent. The statement had noted that Gloria was planning to divorce her current spouse, Count Franz Egon Graf von Fürstenberg, and marry Prince Ahmed Fakhry, son of the Egyptian minister to France and Spain. And as if to highlight Gloria's motives and establish her reputation as a gold digger, the statement noted that Fakhry was five foot six and twenty-four, while Gloria was five foot nine and thirty-two.*

Aline wasn't convinced that Gloria was innocent. She had too many close ties to ardent Nazis or their collaborators, including Hans Lazar, Prince Max, and Ana de Pombo, for it to be a coincidence. The source of the statement also struck her as peculiar. The report came not from the OSS's X-2 office, which investigated and tracked all potential enemies, but from the State Department's Foreign Service. Ambassador Carlton Hayes had already returned to the United States by this point, but ever since his arrival in Madrid

---

*Fakhry, it turned out, lodged at the Estoril Palacio from August 25 to September 1, 1944—the same time Gloria was there—and appears to be the person who paid for Gloria's fifteen-week stay. Gloria did marry Fakhry in 1946, but divorced him three years later. In 1951, she married Thomas Loel Guinness, a member of the British Parliament and wealthy heir of the Guinness brewery family.

in 1942, the State Department had not masked its animosity toward the OSS.* As far as Hayes had been concerned, the OSS was a threat to cordial relations with the Spanish government. All along he had felt that spying on a "friendly" neutral country was anathema to effective diplomacy. And while the report noted that Gloria had been friendly with Pepe Mamal, the Spanish ambassador to Germany, it drew no connection between that and her numerous other dubious contacts.

The timing, too, was curious. When the report about Gloria was issued, the war in Europe was essentially over and Germany had been expected to capitulate any day. Why issue a report then? Was State saying, "See, we don't need the OSS anymore; these so-called suspects aren't really dangerous to our interests."** It seemed to coincide with recent events back home; President Roosevelt had died on April 12 and his successor, President Harry Truman, had been open from his first days in office about his disdain for American espionage. While FDR, like Churchill, saw the vital importance that intelligence played in the war, Truman, it seemed, couldn't dismantle it fast enough. Aline could only wonder if State was issuing other reports like this one, taking X-2 subjects like Gloria off the table, and reinforcing the notion that the OSS wasn't needed in Spain.

Aline decided she would keep an eye on Gloria, regardless of the State Department's opinion.

Edmundo Lassalle, meanwhile, continued his dance on the front

---

*OSS chief historian Kermit Roosevelt summarized the tension: "Members of the Madrid embassy objected to OSS activities in general, feeling that they themselves were competent to cover developments in Spain. OSS salaries and allowances, often incorrectly understood, caused considerable envy, as did consular ranks of OSS officers."

**The State Department's disdain for the OSS was such that Madrid embassy personnel "made little effort to conceal from Spanish officials the real activities of OSS representatives," wrote OSS chief historian Kermit Roosevelt. "As early as December 1942 an agent leaving Washington was told, 'Good luck, you'll probably have more trouble keeping under cover from Americans than from the Gestapo.'"

lines of romance and espionage. In a memo to Larry Mellon on May 15, he wrote: "I have become quite friendly with Maria Agatha Princess de Ratibor et Corvey and have now seized the opportunity of using her as a possible source of information and contacts, with the pretext of acting as her protector with the American authorities in the dark future."

He did not disclose that he was pursuing marriage with her.

He also neglected to mention one other thing.

He was already married.

Edmundo had wed Emilie Dew Sandsten on April 3, 1936, in New York City while they were students at Columbia University. They had resided originally in Mexico City, where Edmundo planned to take up his career, but moved to Berkeley when he secured a scholarship and part-time teaching position at the University of California. Their daughter, Pepita, was born the following year.

While Edmundo courted Princess Agatha, Aline couldn't help but notice that Luis Quintanilla seemed to be looking for any sign of encouragement from her. He was still dating Casilda Arteaga, but whenever Luis spoke to Aline, he lingered, always extending the conversation.

With the urgency of Safehaven, however, Aline had little time for socializing. At the time of Germany's surrender on May 8, 1945, the OSS's X-2 office had identified in Spain nearly 3,000 agents, 600 suspects, 400 officials, and some 46 commercial firms conducting espionage for the enemy.

Aline kept digging and on May 19 she submitted another report to the Barcelona office. She didn't normally have any contact with the Barcelona station but wanted to let them know that Mariano Calviño, the former Blue Division captain and chief of the Falange in Barcelona, was once again living in their city. He had been in Madrid, she wrote, as she had seen him many times at the Puerta de Hierro club, always cavorting with pro-German Spaniards.

He was also very good friends with Gloria von Fürstenberg.

CHAPTER 18

PAY DIRT

As Germans in Spain frantically pursued their contingency plans—gaining passage to South America—Aline had plenty to do. During the first week of June she submitted five reports, one detailing critical information about two important Nazis. From an informant who had returned from Germany in March, she heard that Heinrich Mueller, the notorious head of the Gestapo, was still alive. Second, a German named Herbert von Bibra—an SS man who in 1944 had become the SD's representative in Spain, was now living in Madrid. Von Bibra was a war criminal, she reported, who had traveled frequently to Czechoslovakia and had ordered many ruthless killings.

On Wednesday, June 13, she made another trip to El Quexigal, the von Hohenlohes' magnificent country estate, this time for Pimpinela's wedding. Prince Max was still high on the Safehaven list of people to watch, and Larry Mellon asked her to find out who the prince was using to transfer money to Mexico. The OSS was certain that Max had been getting money out of Spain, but it was up to Aline to figure out how and through whom.

As on her previous visit, numerous Civil Guards stood watch at the gated entrance. What surprised her, though, was the number of people present. She had been told that the wedding would be "intimate," but by her estimate the affair had drawn some 250 guests. There were a number of Germans, she saw, including Princess Maria Agatha. Several prominent Spaniards, including Miguel Primo de Rivera, Spain's former prime minister, were there also, along with members of many of Spain's wealthiest families. What she didn't find were Mexicans.

Strolling about the house, though, she noticed a number of photos of Max with Bienvenida bullfighters, one of whom she recalled had gone to Mexico in December. Could he have carried Max's money?

Talking to Pimpinela's siblings, Aline learned that Prince Max had gained citizenship from Liechtenstein, and that he and the rest of the family now had Liechtensteinian passports. While Prince Max was fabulously wealthy, it was clear that his most valuable assets were his relationships. He was on close terms, the Hohenlohe children said, with the US ambassador, Carlton Hayes; General Franco; the king of England; and most other European leaders.

Two days later, on June 15, Aline saw Prince Max in Madrid lunching at Chipén with a Spaniard named Paquito Santo Domingo. It was quite possible, she reckoned, that Domingo was Max's conduit to transfer his funds. Back in the office that afternoon, she recommended that Max be followed when he was in Madrid. He usually stayed at El Quexigal, she said, and only came to town for business.

She also worked on building her own network of sources and received MacMillan's approval to begin paying her best informant, FLAMENCO, who would become an official subagent.

During the last two weeks of the month Aline was busy with assignments from MacMillan, and also with a request from the Barcelona station asking for information on two Spanish banks. While chasing leads she stumbled across a surprising nugget. Through Juanito she learned that in 1939 his father had rented a large finca in Andalucia to an entity called HISMA. After some time, Juan noticed that there was a constant stream of Germans in and out of the place. Aline acquired names for several of the visitors and it was clear: the finca had been used by the Abwehr as a safe house. She passed it on to MacMillan.

Meanwhile, her other informant, COLUMN, was collecting information on German front companies. While these companies had been used during the war for espionage, propaganda, and covers for Abwehr and SD agents, there was a great risk now that they'd be used to funnel money and perhaps stolen art to Nazi war criminals who had fled to South America, particularly Argentina. Since this was dangerous work, Aline recommended that COLUMN be paid.

About this time Aline received an engraved invitation to a party hosted by Luis to celebrate his saint's day. Instead of having parties to remember one's birthday, the Spanish recognized the saint for whom one was named; in this case, Saint Luis. Many of Madrid's social and political elite would be there, she was sure, and spending time with the increasingly flirtatious Luis was an alluring bonus.

The count's apartment was on Calle Conde de Aranda, a quiet street across from El Retiro, Madrid's version of Central Park. Aline saw Luis speaking with the Duke of Lerma and Miguel Primo de Rivera when she arrived, so she wandered through the rooms, admiring the count's vast art collection. Two paintings were by Goya, she was certain, and another looked like a Velázquez. Her eyes continued to roam and then came to rest on an impressionist. It looked like a Cézanne.

"I was looking for you," came a voice behind her. "Are you bored, roaming through these rooms alone?"

Aline turned to see her host.

"Not at all. Casilda told me about your collection and I've been admiring your lovely paintings."

Aline wasn't sure why, but something about being alone with Luis made her nervous. She asked where he'd found the Goyas, and he touched her arm as he explained.

"I didn't find them. My great-great-grandfather got them directly from Goya. Most of my collection is inherited, except the one I bought yesterday."

Luis continued touching her arm as he drew her to look at the impressionist and she felt almost dizzy. Then it dawned on her: she was falling in love with him.

"I got that for a song," he said, pointing to another work. "The dealer hadn't the slightest idea of its value. I'm sure it's a Cézanne. You know, Cézanne rarely signed his paintings, only when he was especially requested to do so by a client."

There had been two paintings, he said, that looked like the artist's work.

Aline felt her pulse jump. *Safehaven*. If these were truly Cézannes, there was no doubt they had come through the Nazi line of stolen loot that the OSS had been attempting to uncover. She asked if Luis could take her by the gallery where he had purchased them so that she could examine the collection herself.

They went the next day and Aline was amazed to see that the so-called gallery was located in the Rastro: more of a flea market than an antiques district. Luis found the store and asked the shopkeeper if he would show Aline the rest of the collection that had just arrived.

"I'm afraid a dealer from Barcelona bought that whole shipment yesterday," the man said.

Luis chuckled. "Come on, Don Pedro, don't be lazy. Nobody could have bought all those paintings in such a short time. Why don't you take a look back there?"

The shopkeeper repeated his answer. They were gone.

Luis asked what dealer had bought them and the man said he didn't remember. What about the person who delivered the crates? Luis asked.

Incredibly, the man said he didn't remember that either.

As June turned to July, activity on Operation Safehaven quickened. Aline recruited another subagent, code-named FRANCISCO, who not only would be paid, but who would bring two of his own subagents. Then on July 3, Aline hit pay dirt.

There was a Mexican named Beistegui (the man she had sat next to at Prince Max's dinner party), she reported in a memo to MacMillan, who had just returned to Spain from Paris. From one of Prince Max's sons she had found out that Beistegui was a relative of Max's, and that he stayed at El Quexigal when he was in the country; in fact, he had been there the week before. Most important, she noted, Beistegui had been making frequent trips between Spain and Mexico. It certainly appeared that he was Max's financial courier.

MacMillan was impressed but told her to keep it under her hat until further notice.

Larry Mellon, however, urged Aline to dig up more information on Max. So while everyone in the United States was celebrating the Fourth of July, Aline was in the office working up a memo on the Hohenlohe family tree. Two days later she informed MacMillan that Manuel Ávila Camacho, the president of Mexico, had told Max's sons that if one of them could get to Cuba, he'd send a plane to bring them to Mexico. Then, on July 9, she informed MacMillan that Prince Max had just received a package from Paris, which, curiously, had been sent through the Swiss diplomatic pouch. It was hand-delivered at El Quexigal, she noted, by the Swiss minister in Madrid, Monsieur Brois. And Brois had a second package for Beistegui, who also was staying at El Quexigal.

It was more than strange, Aline concluded, for two civilians to receive packages through diplomatic channels, hand-delivered by a Swiss delegate.

To a finca on the outskirts of Madrid no less.

As the summer wore on, Aline decided to relieve the relentless pace of the Safehaven investigation with a respite: Saturday morning golf at the Puerta de Hierro country club. It would be a nice diversion, she figured, and the fact that Luis was a national golf champion played no small part in the idea.

One morning as she was duffing balls at the practice range, she heard a voice behind her.

"If you don't keep your eye on the ball, you're never going to hit it."

It was Luis. He suggested lessons and for the next several days they met to develop her swing. A week later he asked her to dinner. Casilda was in San Sebastian, he said, and his sister and brother-in-law had invited him to join them at Villa Rosa.

Aline had heard that Villa Rosa had fine cuisine, but she didn't know that it was a flamenco restaurant. So after servings of gazpacho, grilled crayfish, *perdices en escabeche*—partridge in a sour sauce—and a round of sangria, she was surprised when Luis escorted her to the dance floor. The tune the band was playing was a *paso doble*, a sensual dance meant to emulate a bullfight. Just as a matador twisted a bull around him with style and grace, so the *paso doble* dancer would pull and spin his partner around him, often cheek to cheek.

Luis was an excellent dancer and his strong grip, together with the sensual music and constant touching, was undeniably erotic.

"I see you're a real aficionada," he whispered in her ear as he held her close.

The song ended and Aline realized that Luis was holding her

hand, caressing it with his fingers. Then suddenly he let go and looked away.

On the drive back to Madrid neither spoke a word for several minutes. When they reached her street Luis broke the ice, saying that he was leaving in the morning for San Sebastian.

Aline's heart sank. That's where Casilda was staying.

She said nothing and Luis added: "I think it's better that we don't see each other for a while."

There was an awkward silence, and Luis tried to explain: "Casilda and I . . . it's been settled for so long. Almost before I realized it. But now—"

His words broke off but Aline knew. "Casilda's my best friend," she said softly.

"Exactly."

The walk to Aline's apartment was like a funeral march. Neither knew what to say, and when they reached the door they stood there, staring at each other. Aline waited and finally Luis gripped her by the shoulders and kissed her on the lips.

When she opened her eyes he was gone.

While Luis was in San Sebastian, Aline thought of him constantly. The prospect of his marrying Casilda played on her emotions, but there was a serendipitous remedy: Juanito continued to send her flowers and chocolates. Those small distractions, coupled with lunches and dinners with Edmundo, helped to pass the days.

One evening, while she and Edmundo were having a nightcap at La Reboite, he mentioned something she'd never considered. "There are rumors circulating," he said. "President Truman intends to abandon OSS operations abroad."

When FDR had died in April, Aline had known that Truman might have a different agenda, but it had never occurred to her that he'd want to dismantle American foreign intelligence.

"Our jobs are at stake, my pet. What will I do? Spying is the only profession I know."

Aline smiled. If they did lose their jobs, she was going to miss this character.

The orchestra began playing an Argentine tune and Edmundo grabbed her hand.

"Come, *Divina*, let's tango while our ship is sinking."

CHAPTER 19

INTELLIGENCE GOES TO GROUND

Juanito, meanwhile, had recovered from his injuries, and, as Aline expected, he couldn't wait to get back in the bullring. On Sunday he had a fight at Las Ventas and Aline went to watch. As usual, he was spectacular and that evening they had dinner at the Ritz. Afterward, they went across the plaza to El Coto for dancing. While Aline hadn't spelled it out, Juanito seemed to have understood that Aline didn't have romantic feelings for him. He knew that she cared for him, but she never responded to his amorous overtures with anything other than friendly politeness.

During a break from dancing, Juanito told Aline that he had just returned from San Sebastian and that he had seen Luis and Casilda at the Bar Basque. Aline acted uninterested, but in truth Juanito's words sent her spirits tumbling. She began to see less of Juanito and tried to distance herself from Luis, but it was impossible.

"I still thought of him almost every day," she recalled later, "and hated myself for being such a fool. I knew our romance was just a beautiful dream that could never come true."

Life would go on without Luis, of course, and between Safehaven, bullfights, and her flashy partner, she would stay busy. That was her plan, anyway.

When she arrived at work on Monday, Robert Dunev met her at the door of the code room. He looked ill.

"ARGUS wants to see everybody."

Aline, Robert, and the rest of the staff filed into a conference room and Gregory Thomas minced no words.

"I have disagreeable news," he said without preamble or greeting. "The future of the OSS is now being decided in Washington. Now that the war is over, President Truman is not convinced that foreign intelligence is necessary."

Everyone looked around the room. The loss of foreign intelligence would leave the United States woefully insecure.

"You've all done great work," Thomas added, "and maybe one day your country will know of the sacrifices you have made. And I thank each one of you. I, for one, am proud of you."

Everyone had to be out of the country by August 15, he said, as that was the official date for closing the office.

Aline and Robert shuffled back to the code room, unsure of what to do next. They had to close all files, contact and pay subagents, and otherwise drop Safehaven right when the action was heating up.

The next morning Aline asked Thomas if she could finish the Safehaven work she was doing with her subagents and he shook his head.

"Sorry, Aline. It's useless. You must prepare to leave the country. I have received strict orders to terminate all chains, all agents' work, and all espionage."

So that was it. The game was over.

Aline was terribly disappointed, but she had much to be pleased about. She had fulfilled her original goal of serving her country in the war, and she had done so on the front lines of espionage. After Robert Dunev, she had been the top coder in the OSS Madrid office, her original duty, but she also had proved herself as a valuable field agent. With the possible exception of Larry Mellon, who coordinated the escape chain, she had more subagents and filed more field reports than anyone in the Madrid office, including Edmundo. She also had been Madrid's top Safehaven agent, finding, among other things, Prince Max's financial conduit to Mexico. What all of that meant was that she had made a valuable contribution to defeat Hitler and his Nazis. And for that she was proud.

Frank Ryan and James MacMillan, she would soon learn, were extremely proud of her as well.

Back in Washington, Frank Ryan was well aware of the dangers of not only foregoing future intelligence but of jettisoning the contacts and networks they had so diligently acquired over the last three and a half years. While he had already resigned from the OSS, he began working behind the scenes to keep two Madrid staffers in play: Robert Dunev and Aline. This was no small feat, though, since even James MacMillan, Larry Mellon, and Edmundo Lassalle were being sent home.

Dunev was the easier of the two to save, since he had been the first staffer to arrive in Madrid, was the senior coder, and had been Gregory Thomas's personal assistant for special projects. Ryan would have him transferred to X-2, which would be keeping a skeleton staff in Madrid beyond OSS's official termination date. Afterward, Dunev could be employed in the new Allied Mission in Spain—a British-French-American entity created to assist in embassy transitions. He had already supervised the closing of the German embassy in Madrid—an overnight vigil on May 8 to 9—so he would be the logical OSS agent to join them.

Placing Aline would be a little trickier. After making a few phone calls, he found interest from the most logical place: Madrid's Foreign Economic Administration office. The FEA supervised Safehaven—a project that would continue for years—and with Aline's inside knowledge of suspected Nazi collaborators and Madrid front businesses, she was a perfect fit. But it would have to occur in two stages, they said, with Aline being "on loan" from the OSS until the slow wheels of bureaucracy could formally accept the transfer. Until such time, OSS would have to reimburse FEA for Aline's salary. It was possible, Ryan thought, that money could be utilized from OSS's Special Funds account, which was managed in Washington.

Ryan was successful; Aline was accepted into FEA on August 8, effective September 1, and Dunev was accepted into X-2 on August 9, effective August 16. Before Ryan could tell Aline about her transfer, though, the deal between the OSS and FEA fell through. For their part, the FEA decided at the end of August that Aline could be employed only at a government pay scale of CAF-5, rather than the CAF-7 level she had earned with the OSS. And from the OSS standpoint, the account director decided that the organization—which was in the process of dissolution—would not be in a position to reimburse the FEA.

Undeterred, Ryan made alternative plans for her; plans that were unknown to anyone outside the highest ranks of American espionage.

Since Aline had acquired forty days of paid leave, she decided to remain in Madrid after the others left. She had fallen in love with the city—and with all of Spanish culture, really—and the thought of looking for a mundane job in New York was disheartening. No doubt she had been spoiled; after all, she had just spent the last year and a half of her life immersed in a world of espionage, embassy receptions, country club parties, state dinners, bullfights, and flamenco parties. And now she would have all of September—the best time to be in Madrid—to take in the cafés, restaurants, museums, and cathedrals she hadn't had time to frequent during the last eighteen months.

On September 7, the first Friday of the month, she spent a carefree afternoon and early evening at a café on the Castellana, and then headed home at sunset. When she arrived at her apartment, Angustias met her at the door.

"Señorita, a man has been waiting for quite a while." She motioned toward the salon. "He refused to give his name."

Puzzled and a little anxious, Aline went in to find the last man she expected.

Frank Ryan.

He was impeccably dressed, as always, sporting a handsome gray herringbone suit. His hairline had receded a bit since she had last seen him, though—or perhaps it was simply more gray—but his smile was the same and his sapphire eyes were as confident as ever.

"I can't believe that you're really here," she said. "What are you doing in Madrid?"

"My main purpose is to see you. Come, let's sit down and talk. I don't have much time."

Aline asked Angustias to bring in some water and they sat on the sofa.

"It's important I speak to you before you are shipped back to the US." Ryan paused to light a cigarette, exhaling the smoke slowly. "Are you pleased to have received word of returning to Washington?"

"Not at all."

"OSS is being disbanded, but a small organization for the collection of intelligence is being created to preserve a nucleus of trained espionage professionals. Intrepid* and Bill Donovan himself are the driving forces behind this endeavor and—" Ryan paused, formulating his next words carefully, and then said: "You're one of the lucky ones to be included."

Aline wasn't familiar with Intrepid, but *Bill Donovan*? The founder and head of the OSS? She wondered who else was among the lucky ones. Gregory Thomas? MacMillan? Mellon? Dunev? Lassalle?

But there was a catch, Ryan said. Remaining in Spain would require her to renew her visa, which could only be done with the ap-

---

*"Intrepid" was the code name for William Stephenson, head of British Security Coordination, the branch of MI6 operating in the US and Canada and headquartered in New York City.

proval of the American ambassador. "And you must convince him that you won't be doing any espionage in the future."

Aline laughed. "Lie."

Ryan grinned. "Well, after working in this business for almost two years, I take it for granted that you've mastered that."

Aline nodded and Ryan went on.

"We now have a good group of professionals and General Donovan doesn't intend to lose them. At the moment, the State Department wants to control us, but Donovan and the rest of our group believes that intelligence should be a separate entity, so it can operate with total secrecy."

Total secrecy. From her first days at The Farm, Aline learned that this was the unwritten but universally understood motto of the OSS. And Frank Ryan, better than anyone else, knew how to wield it like a conductor's baton.

He told her to send a cable to New York seeking employment and scribbled down an address: 36 Wall Street.

Aline glanced at it. No suite number. Before she could inquire further, Ryan stood and said his time was up. He bid her good luck and left without further details.

Aline sent the cable as directed and two days later she received a response. It was an offer of employment for a job in Madrid. Her eyes fell quickly to the signatory: John J. Ryan & Sons.

She shook her head. *John?* Frank's brother? Well, she wasn't entirely surprised since the selling point of her blind date with Frank in 1943 had been that the family was loaded. That, combined with a landmark address like 36 Wall Street suggested that the family probably owned a giant investment banking business.

Typical Ryan. Operate in the shadows.

That very month an international trade company was quietly formed in Panama, but headquartered in New York City. It was called the British American Canadian Corporation, and its founders read like a who's who of espionage: General William Donovan, head of the OSS; Sir William Stephenson, head of British Security Coordination (BSC); Sir Charles Hambro, head of Special Operations Executive; John Pepper, MI6 agent and Stephenson's deputy; and David Ogilvy, BSC officer. Also included was Edward Stettinius, former US secretary of state.

Oddly, none of the founders had any experience in international trade.

Nor did its president—Frank T. Ryan.

CHAPTER 20

PARIS

Aline wasn't exactly sure what she would be doing for her new employer, John J. Ryan & Sons, a textile importer, but she was thrilled to be able to stay in Spain and conduct whatever business Frank Ryan had in mind. For starters she had to open a company bank account and a "branch office," which she did at No. 11 Calle Marqués de Riscal. Next she had to hire a secretary and conduct bona fide business with Spanish companies, which she soon accomplished with contracts from some of Barcelona's cloth manufacturers. Then one day in the mail she received her first paycheck from Ryan & Sons—in the exact amount she had been receiving from the OSS.

Robert Dunev, meanwhile, had important business to attend to as well. He was staying on at X-2, but he and Louise Marie wanted to get married. The problem, though, was that Spain only recognized Catholic weddings and they weren't Catholic. They decided to resolve the issue by getting married in Gibraltar on September 12. As a favor the British embassy worked out the details, even giving them a nice wedding gift: use of an embassy car for their entire honeymoon.

On the trip back to Madrid they stopped off in Málaga to have lunch with Aline's old buddy, Barnaby Conrad. The vice-consul told them that he would be taking his *alternative*—the test to become a full matador—on September 25 and invited them to come. Robert and Louise Marie said they'd love to see El Niño de California in action, but that their honeymoon called for other plans.

Barnaby Conrad standing before the poster announcing his upcoming *alternative* on September 25, 1945. Juan Belmonte came out of retirement to fight on the card and highlight the event.

*   *   *

Over the ensuing weeks Aline heard rumors of Gestapo agents paying enormous sums to gain passage on ships leaving for Buenos Aires and Colombia. Someone said that Hans Lazar caught a boat to Rio de Janiero disguised as a Franciscan monk. What was most interesting, however, was Edmundo's situation. He had been ordered back to the US and was trying to continue on in the employ of the Walt Disney Company. His plans to marry Princess Agatha, though, continued unabated. How he would work all of that out remained to be seen.

September and October flew by, and on November 5 Aline received another blessing, albeit unwittingly. James MacMillan, who was now back in the US and unaware that Aline was employed by Frank Ryan, recommended her to Whitney Shepardson, OSS's number two, for future espionage. There wouldn't be work with the OSS, he knew, but perhaps a new agency would be formed in the near future and Shepardson would be in a position to hire or recommend new agents.

"She has a special aptitude for intelligence work," he wrote, "and an unusual sense of the importance of security. She has the ability to conduct operations under supervision, as evidenced by her handling of a small number of agents of her own selection. Her judgment of people is basically sound, her perception of situations is quick and her deductions have been accurate in a large number of cases. . . . I suggest that with proper private cover she has great possibilities for further use."

Frank Ryan couldn't have agreed more.

The following day Ryan boarded the *Clipper* to make stops across Europe on behalf of Ryan & Sons and the new firm, British American Canadian Corporation. The goal of the trip was to renew OSS contacts across the continent and seed the soil for future business. Donovan, Stephenson, Ryan, and the others involved with BACC were convinced that without economic aid and US financing, many European cities and all of Germany would fall to the communists. It was a global project that would require financial backing from some of the world's richest families, clearance from some of Europe's highest-ranking diplomats, and counsel from top Allied spymasters.

OFFICE OF STRATEGIC SERVICES

WASHINGTON, D. C.

DECLASSIFIED -
47589
AUTHORITY
BY 23 NARA DATE 5-1-78

November 5, 1945

Memorandum

To: Mr. Whitney H. Shepardson

From: James H. MacMillan

Subject: Marie Aline Griffith

Subject traveled to Spain with the writer, arriving in February 1944. She acted as code clerk till the Spring of 1945, from which time on her evident abilities were used in collecting intelligence.

She rapidly learned to speak fluent Spanish. Her striking looks, personality and intelligence made her a favorite with Spaniards in all social classes, especially in the upper brackets. She kept her poise under circumstances likely to spoil a less well-balanced person, and gained the respect and liking of a large number of people.

She has a natural aptitude for intelligence work, and an unusual sense of the importance of security. She has the ability to conduct operations under supervision, as evidenced by her handling of a small number of agents of her own selection. Her judgment of people is basically sound, her perception of situations is quick and her deductions have been accurate in a large number of cases.

As of this date she is still in Spain. I suggest that with proper private cover she has great possibilities for further use.

James MacMillan's letter of recommendation to Whitney Shepardson.

BACC, in fact, had been stacked for this very purpose; Larry Mellon had persuaded his family to provide financial help, and Ryan would later bring in the Du Pont family. Bache and other New York investment banks were involved. Secretary Stettinius was on board. And BACC boasted an astonishing collection of leaders from the OSS, BSC, SOE, and MI6. Offices would have to be opened in Paris and Zurich, with other important cities to follow. And everyone looked to Ryan to pull it off.

The unavoidable question is whether Ryan and BACC actually conducted espionage, formally or informally, economic or political. On the one hand, there's no proof that they did. On the other, why else would BACC (later, World Commerce Corporation) be packed with top-level espionage leaders from the West, none of whom had experience in international trade? It was clear that BACC would not be acting as a US government agency, and one might ponder how "espionage" is defined. If asked, Ryan surely would have stated that neither he nor BACC would be collecting intelligence about any foreign power, the activity one normally associates with espionage. Rather, the group's intended goal, as stated, was to foster trade. Granted, the purpose of facilitating capitalism in European countries was to prevent them from falling to communism, and he would have said that there was nothing untoward in that aim.

And Ryan's personal openness about his activity reinforces the point. While secrecy was his general rule, this trip was different. Because his profile with the OSS had been low, it was important for him to establish personal public credibility for the overall mission, yet keep BACC's name out of it.

That very day the *New York Times* announced his trip, identifying him as a partner in the Wall Street firm Bache & Co., and vice president of John J. Ryan & Sons. The newly formed BACC went unmentioned. If he were going to be conducting espionage, he'd established the perfect cover.

And just when Aline couldn't have been busier, Luis reappeared. He invited her to dinner one evening, mentioning that Casilda was in Portugal. They went to Jockey, a trendy new restaurant, and then to La Reboite for dancing. Luis's cool green eyes enchanted as always, as did his embrace. "When we danced," she remembered, "the touch of his arm around me, his body next to mine put me in a spell like before."

Flies to Europe Today For Business Survey

Frank T. Ryan

Frank T. Ryan, partner in the New York Stock Exchange firm of Bache & Co., is leaving today by Clipper on a survey trip to England and the Continent and plans to explore the possibilities of resuming the firm's former activities in the international security and commodity markets. Mr. Ryan, a vice president of the textile firm of John J. Ryan & Sons, Inc., will also visit textile interests abroad in connection with the recently announced program of the Export-Import Bank to finance up to 85 per cent of the value of American cotton exported to certain European countries.

Ryan's trip announced in the *New York Times*, November 6, 1945.

It was three in the morning when he dropped her off, and for two agonizing days she waited for his call. Finally it came, and he invited her to golf at Puerta de Hierro. It was a wonderful club—twenty-five holes, a swimming pool, a bar at the nineteenth hole—and she had fond memories of the swing lessons Luis had given her there.

After several minutes on the drive over, Luis turned to her.

"You seem lost in thought."

Aline shrugged. She was thinking about Casilda.

"The war's ended," she replied. "I realize that things can change. So much of the time one spends planning and worrying about the future turns out to be useless. I'm not going to do that anymore."

Luis eased off the gas, cruising slower. "You're perfectly right. I've gone through some changes too." He drove for a while and then asked, "So from now on you'll live for the moment?"

"Who knows." Aline paused, and then grinned. "Yes, on second thought, perhaps I will."

Luis nodded and held her eye. "We agree on that. I'm ready to live for many more moments like this."

For two weeks they golfed by day and dined by night, never mentioning Casilda or the cares of the world. To keep up with work and play, Aline sacrificed sleep, often catching no more than a few hours. Yet, she didn't mind.

One evening she met Luis for dinner at El Pulpito, a quaint restaurant on the Plaza Mayor. Taking her by the hand, he explained that he had broken up with Casilda, and that one day he'd explain why.

Aline said it wasn't necessary, but her heart wanted to say more. She wanted to tell him that nothing could make her stop seeing him, not even Casilda, whom she still considered her best friend. She wanted to tell him that he was the only thing she thought of, night and day.

When Luis dropped her off that evening, he said he wanted her to meet his father and stepmother. At the door, he kissed her and said he'd be in Toledo for the next two days visiting his grandfather.

Aline went inside, thoughts racing. Why would Luis want her to meet his parents, and in the next sentence say he needed to speak to his grandfather, who was out of town? Why couldn't Luis just wait until his grandfather returned to Madrid?

Could it be?

The next morning when Aline arrived at the new John J. Ryan & Sons office, her secretary handed her a cable. Her expression suggested it was less than pleasant news.

It was from Frank Ryan.

CLOSE MADRID OFFICE IMMEDIATELY STOP PROCEED TO PARIS STOP ROOM RESERVED AT HOTEL SAN REGIS STOP NEW OFFICE IS IN THE HOTEL PLAZA ATHENEE STOP OUR PARIS REPRESEN-TATIVE IS AWAITING YOU WITH INSTRUCTIONS THERE.

Aline closed her eyes.

No.

The odds. Between the job and Luis, everything had been working out perfectly until now. Ryan had moved her seamlessly to Ryan & Sons, and she hadn't missed a paycheck. Luis had broken up with Casilda and his actions suggested he was thinking about asking her to marry him.

How could she now move to Paris?

But she couldn't disobey her boss's orders, and she couldn't tell Luis a word about the work she actually did, either.

Over the next two days she wrapped things up. She let her secretary go, terminated the office lease, and informed clients in Barcelona that the office was moving to Paris. But she wasn't giving up on Luis. She decided to keep her apartment and the two maids. The expense was minimal compared to her salary, and the presence in Madrid would give her hope—no, an *intention*—of returning to Spain. And to Luis.

The following morning she ran some errands and when she arrived back, her apartment was filled with flowers. Not a bouquet like Juanito always sent—a truckload.

Luis was back from Toledo.

He called moments later with excitement in his voice. "When can I see you? How about lunch?"

Aline still had errands to finish so she told him they'd have to meet for dinner. Luis agreed, but there was a hesitation in his voice. He suspected something was wrong.

The minute she got in his car that evening, he expressed his concern.

"Tell me, what's up? Even your voice on the phone was different this morning."

Aline couldn't put it off any longer, so she came out with it. "I have to go to Paris two days from now. It's a new job, opening another office there for my company."

"For how long?"

"I have no idea."

"That's impossible. I thought you liked Madrid."

"I love Madrid, Luis. But I'm a working girl, and there's no way I can avoid fulfilling my obligations to the company I work for."

Luis was speechless. She explained that she would be keeping her Madrid apartment, small consolation though it was, and told him that she was miserable, too. She asked that he not make it worse.

"If you were so miserable, you wouldn't leave."

Luis's voice was cold and he was hurt. In his aristocratic world, one could do whatever one wanted, each day, every day. He didn't understand that working stiffs had no such freedom. She had no trust fund to fall back on. She also had no ring.

Remaining in Madrid wasn't an option.

Luis stewed for several moments and then said he'd visit her in Paris. But to do so, he explained, would be exceedingly difficult. Acquiring an exit permit was rare, and on top of that, Spaniards were not allowed to take money out of the country.

Aline nodded but realized it was precisely this kind of impediment—distance—that ruined many relationships. She struggled to find a way to express her feelings but couldn't think of the right words. Luis hadn't proposed; he hadn't even said "I love you." What was she supposed to do?

It was a silent pact between them: they would both be miserable.

And they weren't the only ones. Emilie Lassalle, Edmundo's wife of ten years, had it worse. When Edmundo was reunited with her in Washington the second week of November, he informed her that he would be divorcing her in order to marry Princess Agatha.

No remorse. No apology. A better opportunity just came along. No hard feelings.

On November 21 Frank Ryan checked in to the Estoril Palacio, his last stop before heading home. It had been a whirlwind trip, with stops in Madrid, Paris, Zurich, Prague, Lisbon, and countless other cities. But the groundwork was set. Aline would open the Paris office, and he'd have other former OSS agents open shop almost simultaneously in several other countries. BACC was a force to be reckoned with, even without the help of Washington. Europe would begin rebuilding, and BACC would be at the head of it, directing needed commodities across the continent. And as post-war Europe's old alliances began to shift and former friends became enemies, having a network of experienced American intelligence operatives already in place across the continent might turn out to be a very useful thing—even if nobody but Frank and his fellow board members knew anything about it.

Paris

Aline marveled at the Hôtel San Régis. It was what everyone thought of when they imagined the City of Lights: elegant nineteenth-century French architecture, iron-railed balconies with covered awnings, Old Master paintings, and impeccable service. It was a block from the Seine, a block from the Champs-Elyseés, four blocks from the Eiffel Tower, and a short stroll from the Arc de Triomphe.

That was one more thing she admired about Frank Ryan: he did everything first-class. The *Yankee Clipper*. The Estoril Palacio.

The Madrid Palace. Now the San Régis. Truly he was a dream employer.

She checked into the hotel and looked on the map for the Hôtel Plaza Athénée. It was just a short walk from the San Régis, she saw, not even four blocks.

On Monday she met her local boss, John B. "Jack" Okie. He had been an OSS agent in Lisbon during the war, and she had met him briefly once in Madrid. At thirty, he was only a little older than she was, but he had impressed the brass in Lisbon, and Ryan apparently had heard. And since Jack had arrived in Paris first, most of the administrative matters—office, bank account, secretary—were already in place.

Together, she and Jack began calling the business contacts that Frank Ryan had supplied. At first they dealt with French companies, but before long they were establishing contacts and bartering deals in Czechoslovakia, Switzerland, Sweden, and East and West Germany.

The city was almost a full-time assignment in and of itself. With pent-up energy from four years of occupation, Paris was an around-the-clock party. Parisians, it seemed, had long awaited a time when they could enjoy getting dressed to the nines, and it was not uncommon for women to wear long gowns and chic hats to restaurants and nightclubs. Since Aline had stocked up on Balenciaga dresses in Madrid, the formal attire was not a problem, although she couldn't resist adding two new dresses from the flagship store.

When she arrived for a second fitting, none other than Monsieur Balenciaga attended her. When he was finished, he asked if she would be willing to be photographed for *Vogue* in the dresses she had purchased. Aline hesitated at first, but then realized that to reject his offer would come across as something of an insult and possibly deprive him of some good publicity. She agreed.

And Balenciaga, in turn, was grateful. When Aline next visited the store to order another dress, the vendeuse told her that Monsieur

Balenciaga had said he would lend her any of his evening gowns. She took him up on it.

Dates were not hard to come by in Paris and she went out almost every night, often with businessmen Ryan wanted her to meet. When Ryan was in town, he'd take her along to meet a certain contact or group, telling her in advance the information he wanted to extract.

December 25, 1945

Christmas in Paris. *Alone.*

The city was beautiful, Aline thought, and Christmas decorations everywhere proclaimed "Joy to the World," but there was no joy in her heart. She missed Luis. Indeed, the sights were wonderful—it was her first time in Paris—but the Seine and the Eiffel Tower were nothing if not elixirs of romance.

Luis had been calling every few days, but the long-distance connection usually was so bad that neither could make out much of what the other was saying. When she called him, sometimes she'd have to wait hours before the call would go through, and even then the call would often drop as soon as he was on the line. What encouraged her, though, was that Luis was working on his exit permit to come visit her.

They switched to letter writing after the New Year, which was more romantic anyway, but Luis's letters were short and, more disconcerting, he never said he loved her. But he was determined to see her—she knew that—and it was enough.

She continued wining and dining BACC contacts, and one day Luis surprised her by calling her at the office. This time the line was crystal clear.

"I've been reading the Paris newspapers," he said. "What were you doing at Maxim's with the king of Yugoslavia?"

Aline smiled. King Peter II was only three years her senior and was quite handsome. Before she could answer, Luis added: "I played golf with him and he's not only a bad golfer, but he's also a big bore."

Aline mumbled an answer, pleased that Luis was jealous.

January 1946

After the New Year Aline returned to New York to visit her family. She hadn't seen her parents or brothers in two years, and she knew this might be her only chance for a year or more. Ryan allowed her to stay until the end of March, by which time she was eager to get back to work, to Europe, and to Luis.

She returned to Paris at the beginning of April and Luis cabled to say that he had finally finagled his exit permit. He would be in Paris the following Tuesday, the telegram said. She immediately called him in Madrid but couldn't get a connection until late that evening. She was "delirious with joy," she told him, and couldn't wait. Luis said he was bringing his father, and that they would pick her up at the San Régis. They would have dinner, he added, at Le Grand Véfour.

Luis's words were pearls. If he was bringing his father to Paris, would the trip not include a proposal?

Tuesday, April 9, 1946

Luis stood at the San Régis front desk with his father. There must be a mistake.

What do you mean she has checked out?

Luis scanned the lobby, but Aline was nowhere to be found.

CHAPTER 21

LA TIENTA

Washington

Like Oz pulling the strings behind the curtain, Frank Ryan considered his players across Europe. Robert Dunev was in Madrid and could be called upon if needed. Jack Okie had the Paris office running smoothly. Hans Czernin was taking care of Prague. Aline Griffith would open Zurich. Eric Erickson could help with Stockholm. Everything according to plan.

Switzerland

The train rocked along, but Aline didn't feel like sleeping or reading. Or talking to anyone. She was sick.

Frank Ryan had struck again, and at the most inopportune time. Why did Jack Okie have to hand her the overnight ticket to Zurich *just hours* before she was to meet Luis and his father? Why couldn't she meet the Eastern European agent on Thursday, or even Friday? Why was it so urgent?

With the short notice, she had no time to plead with Ryan or warn Luis. He and his father were on a train to meet her just as she was leaving the city. She left him a note at the front desk, but who knew if he'd even receive it? And even if he did, she knew he'd be livid. She couldn't blame him.

Her dream job with her dream boss was looking more like a mistake every day. First the departure from Madrid, now the disappearance from Paris. Luis wouldn't put up with that. Not twice, anyway.

She tried to sleep but it wouldn't come.

When she arrived in Zurich she checked in to the hotel where Ryan had made a reservation, the Hôtel Baur au Lac, and asked if there were any messages. In the note she had left at San Régis, she instructed Luis to send a telegram here with a number where she could reach him.

No messages.

She met with the BACC contact later that day and then checked again with the front desk. Nothing. And she had no idea where Luis and his father were staying.

Several days passed and Luis didn't call. Aline was beside herself. A week went by and she began calling Madrid but couldn't reach him. A second week. A third week.

Perhaps it was over, she thought. Luis had had enough. She kept calling, though, and finally she reached him. As she had feared, he never received her note at San Régis, and his voice was frigid and indifferent.

"It's obvious to me now, Aline, that I will never understand you. And I would like to add that it was most embarrassing for me to have you stand up my father as well. He'd made a great effort to accompany me on the trip."

Aline had no defense. She stumbled through her mea culpas, but Luis was having none of it.

She waited a few days and sent him a long letter of apology. There was no reply. She sent another letter. Again, no reply.

It was over.

She opened the Zurich office and followed the procedure she had formulated in Madrid: establish contacts, attend cocktail parties and dinners, and meet whomever Ryan thought was important.

At one party a friend of Aline's, Helga Nehring, introduced her to Argentina's ambassador to Switzerland, Benito Llambí. Llambí had been a military officer and a close associate of Argentina's president, Juan Perón. Everyone knew that the Perón government had been closely aligned with Hitler during the war, and countless Nazis—including war criminal Adolf Eichmann—had slipped quietly into the country as the Third Reich crumbled. And from what she and Helga had heard, the Argentine embassy in Switzerland had bank account information for many Nazi fugitives.

Given her previous work on Safehaven, Aline couldn't resist the opportunity to get to know Llambí. It was possible, just possible, that he knew details about the art looting or money transfers she'd been investigating before the OSS was dissolved. In any event, all diplomatic contacts were useful in her new work and she handled him accordingly.

Llambí, who at thirty-nine was thirteen years Aline's senior, was smitten. Aline had not the slightest romantic interest in him but kept on friendly terms. Some weeks later Aline received a call from Pearl River. It was her father.

Benito Llambí had asked permission to marry her, her father said.

Aline was floored. *What?* Benito was crazy, she replied. Absolutely deranged. She had *zero* interest in the Argentine and had no idea how he could have thought otherwise. Her father said he understood and Aline hoped that was the end of it.

Back to Spain

A few weeks went by and Aline asked Frank Ryan if she could schedule a month's vacation to return to Madrid. Ryan approved, but said they'd need to wait until he could get someone to cover for her while she was away.

They decided she could go in June, and Aline was hoping that she could repair things with Luis. It was a long shot—she had not heard a word from him since the call in April. But aside from Luis, she also missed Madrid. She missed her apartment and her cheerful maids, Angustias and Cecilia. She missed the bullfights and flamenco, the midnight dinners on the Castellana. Spain was home, with or without Luis.

She took the train from Zurich to Paris, where she changed for one headed to the border. It terminated at Hendaye, France, the famous border site where in 1940 Franco had deceived Hitler about joining the Axis and allowing German troops onto Spanish soil to attack Gibraltar.

Franco's actions, she remembered, had proved that this seemingly unimpressive man was actually quite savvy. All along he had been coy, leading Hitler to believe that Spain would eventually join the Axis, but always mentioning conditions that had to be met before Franco could commit. Hitler negotiated with Franco for seven hours, but the Generalissimo's conditions—such as Spain acquiring Gibraltar and French Cameroon, along with significant shipments of food, oil, and arms from Germany to Spain—were so onerous that Hitler became frustrated. He would later say that he'd rather have had three or four teeth extracted than to suffer another meeting with Franco.*

After everyone disembarked from the train, Aline and the other passengers were informed that they'd need to walk across the Bidasoa Bridge to Irun on the Spanish side for the next train. It was yet another Franco move that had been subtle but brilliant: to make Hitler's invasion of his country more difficult, Franco had Spanish train tracks narrowed, thus eliminating the possibility of locomotives full of German troops and equipment steaming across the border.

When she was halfway across the bridge spanning the Bidasoa River, she stopped and scanned the horizon. The sun was setting and history seemed to open before her. How many Spanish and French

---

*Two months later, on December 31, Hitler wrote to Italy's Mussolini of his disappointment: "Spain has refused to collaborate with the Axis Powers. . . . We had completed our preparations for crossing the Spanish frontier on January 10th and to attack Gibraltar at the beginning of February."

kings had met on this very spot over the centuries? she wondered. In the first century Irun had been a Basque Roman town called Oiasso, and before that, it was the home of the Vascones.* It was a hub of civilization.

Along the banks, fishermen were casting their lines, and she couldn't help but wonder if Luis was doing the same. Was he dating Casilda again or had he found someone new? Even if he wasn't, would he want to see her again?

She strolled along, catching up with the other passengers, and wondered if she really loved Luis as much as she thought. It would certainly be easier if she could just forget him.

She boarded the Madrid express, fixed up her bed, and fell fast asleep.

When she awoke the train was pulling into El Escorial station. She was only an hour away from Madrid now, and she could feel the butterflies stirring. Sliding back the velvet and lace drapes, she gazed at Castile as the train moved out. The parties at Hohenlohe's El Quexigal seemed only yesterday, and the orange tiled roofs and ancient structures flashing by brought everything back.

All of it reminded her of Luis.

As the train rolled into Madrid, Angustias and Cecelia were waiting, waving and calling to her from the platform. On the drive to the apartment neither of her maids disclosed their little secret, and Aline opened the door to find flowers everywhere: red roses, lilies, forsythia, and narcissi. Their guilty grins confirmed it—they had told Luis when she was arriving—and her heart began to race once again. Luis had called them multiple times, they said, asking for news of her.

Just then the phone rang. It was Luis, who said he'd pick her up for dinner at nine thirty. It couldn't come fast enough. When he knocked, she rushed to the door before Angustias or Cecelia could get there.

Luis was all smiles. "I was wondering all day if you were going to stand me up again."

---

*The Vascones were a pre-Roman tribe believed to be the ancestors of the Basques.

Aline flushed. Embarrassed. Lovesick. Luis looking as handsome as ever—tan, fit, and composed.

"Are you going to invite me in?"

She grinned and stepped aside. Luis walked directly to her bar and, as if nothing had ever happened, poured himself a whiskey and soda. Raising it, he said, "In the future, my beauty, you're not going to fool me so easily."

It was like a normal date before she had left for Paris, except for one thing: they had chaperones. With Luis's sisters and brothers-in-law, they went to the Palace bar for drinks, Chipén for dinner, and the Villa Rosa for flamenco. They had dinner again three times that week, always with relatives, and Aline began to wonder why. Why the formality? Why didn't he want to be alone with her?

The following week they finally had a date by themselves, and Luis took her to a new nightclub, La Barca. On the dance floor he whispered in her ear: "This time you're not going to escape, *guapa*."

She could hardly bear to say it, but she told him she had to return to Zurich in a month.

Luis flashed his magnetic smile. "That's what you think."

Overnight, life became just as before: golf at Puerta de Hierro in the morning, dinner at Madrid's finest in the evening. Life, it seemed, had reset itself.

Aline cabled Ryan to ask for more time and he agreed.

One day Luis invited her to a *tienta* at the Avila ranch owned by his uncle, the Count of Mayalde. A *tienta*, she had learned from Juanito, was a testing of young bulls. Spanish fighting bulls had been bred for four centuries to create the most lethal animal on the planet, and the *tienta* was a vital part of the process.

Only the bravest, most aggressive bulls made it to the ring, and not until they were four years old. When bulls turned two, they were tested to determine which ones would qualify.

"The bravery of the bull is the primal root of the whole Spanish bullfight," Hemingway wrote in *Death in the Afternoon.* "The best of all fighting bulls have a quality, called nobility by the Spanish. The bull is a wild animal whose greatest pleasure is combat and which will accept combat offered to it in any form, or will take up anything it believes to be an offer of combat." Seeing that quality displayed in the bullring, he concluded, was "something unearthly and unbelievable."

While only bulls would ever see the ring, male *and* female calves were tested because, as breeders learned through the years, a fighting bull acquired his size from the father but his heart—his fighting spirit—from his mother. And to prevent a bull from ever coming into contact with a man on foot, male calves were tested in various ways by *picadors* on horseback.* If the bull charged aggressively and repeatedly, it was bound for the ring; if not, it was marked for veal.

The test for female calves—which also had horns and were quite dangerous—occurred in a corral about half the size of a bullring. There, apprentice matadors, or *novilleros*, would practice their passes with the cape, and the breeder would watch carefully to evaluate the tenaciousness of the heifers. If they were especially brave, they'd be earmarked for motherhood. The irony was that while the heifers were smaller than the bulls, they were trickier to fight. Being lighter than their male counterparts, they were faster and more agile, allowing them to turn more abruptly and sharply.

Like most formal events in Spain, a *tienta* was a fiesta, and was always preceded by a banquet. By Aline's count, there must have been some eighty guests at the Mayalde ranch, all drinking red wine and milling about a giant buffet table. She glanced around and was relieved to see that Juanito wasn't there, but Spain's finest matador— the incomparable Manolete—was. It was the first time she had seen

---

*Bulls have tremendous memories, fighters and breeders have learned over the centuries, and if a bull had previously experienced a man on foot, particularly with a cape, it would mean certain death for matadors in the bullring.

him out of his matador's costume. Instead he was wearing the traditional Spanish riding outfit: brown wool jacket, tight gray pants, embroidered leather chaps, and a wide *cordobés* hat. She was a few yards away, but she could see that it was true what the papers said—he *did* look like an undriven nail.

And as she moved closer, the testimony of Manolete's years of fighting was hard to miss. His face was long and gaunt, like the ones painted by El Greco, and his eyes were sunken, melancholy. She also caught a glimpse of two facial scars she'd never seen from the stands: a deep angled track above his left brow, and a long comma-like gash running from the corner of his mouth to the side of his jaw. He was twenty-eight but looked forty.

Yet there was a calmness and gentleness about him that defied his immense celebrity.

After a few minutes people began drinking from a wine pigskin that was passed around, and everyone watched as two *novilleros* tested several heifers. After that, amateurs were invited to have a go. Two men took up the challenge; both executed nervous and clumsy passes but managed to complete their turns uninjured.

Another heifer was brought in and Manolete, who was sitting close by, turned to her.

"Would you like to try this one, Aline?"

It would have been next to impossible to turn down one of the three greatest matadors who ever lived, but Aline realized she actually *wanted* to give it a try. Part of it was that she was an American girl, and so was expected to know nothing about bullfighting, and part of it was to impress Luis.

But she didn't look his way before accepting. Though her heart pounded, she felt a degree of confidence because Juanito had shown her basic passes a year earlier, and working with a cape was much like dancing, or perhaps ballet. As Barnaby Conrad had put it: "A bullfighter is a dancer, but a dancer on a tightrope. The passes he does are as formalized and laboriously practiced as the *entrechat* and *tour jeté*, but whereas if the ballet dancer makes a mistake on the stage he merely loses face, the matador can lose a leg or his life."

While Aline wouldn't be trying any pirouettes—those fancy spinning moves she had seen Juanito do—she could at least show she was as good as the two men who had just tried.

Manolete offered to take the other half of the *capote*—the large cape used in the first part of a bullfight—but she declined. She wanted the excitement of doing it alone. He handed her a bright pink cape and she made her way down. The heifer was on the other side of the corral and she visualized what she had seen Juanito, Manolete, and other bullfighters do.

She swung the cape from side to side.

In an instant the beast charged. It was racing toward her at an alarming speed and the thought flashed before her: *Aline, what are you doing?*

She held out the cape and the heifer rushed through.

Swish.

The exhilaration and adrenaline came next. *This* was why the bullfighters did it. The danger. The rush.

The calf turned quickly though and came at her again.

She held the cape low and again the heifer stormed through, tossing its head up as it passed. The crowd cheered and Aline glanced at them, accepting the praise.

When she turned back, it was too late.

A horn ripped through her jacket and she was airborne.

CHAPTER 22

THE BOOKKEEPER

There was a sensation of timelessness and then a sudden jolt as Aline's body crashed to the ground. Everything was a blur and there was a lot of commotion, but she felt someone pulling her leg. She spit up sand and heard men shouting. Then a flurry of capes.

"What a silly thing to do," came a friendly voice near her ear.

It was Luis.

Aline tried to find him through the cloud of sand, but she distinctly heard his next words: "You'd better stop these wild American pranks and marry me."

Aline's eyes widened as Luis picked her up and examined her. "Are you all right?"

The heifer's horns had caught her jacket but missed her body, fortunately. There was no blood, but her leg hurt and her head was pounding. She nodded.

Wait. *Did Luis just propose?*

On the drive back to Madrid, Luis said nothing about his remark. He talked about bulls, *tientas*, and how foolish it was for her to jump in the ring. Not a word about marriage.

When he said good night at the door, it was business as usual. Aline trudged to her bedroom, perplexed. Was Luis merely toying with the idea of marriage? Was his remark a sort of romantic Freudian slip?

A week went by and he didn't call. There, it seemed, was her answer.

Finally, he asked her to join him again for morning golf and evening dinners, but there was never talk about anything permanent. As her date to return to Zurich grew closer, she received a cable from Ryan indicating that her next post would be Prague. Luis would have to make a decision.

When he next picked her up for golf, she announced that she would be leaving soon. "This time my work is going to take me far away and I don't think I'll be able to return for years."

Luis seemed unphased. "You know we're going to get married one day. You should give up your job and stay in Spain with me."

"Luis, I cannot quit my job."

"Why not?"

"Because I work for a living." Aline realized this was a foreign concept to Luis; none of the girls he knew worked for a living. In any case, it was time to call his bluff.

"If we're going to get married," she said, "you will have to name a date now."

Luis beat around the bush and then said, "Well, we'll get married."

Aline did her best to hide her frustration. Why was it so hard for Luis simply to say, "I love you. Will you marry me?" Did the Spanish do it some other way?

She dropped the subject and the golf and dinners carried on as before. She ordered her train tickets and let Angustias and Cecelia know that she would be leaving, this time for good; she was terminating the lease on the apartment.

On the last day of her vacation, Luis came by in the early afternoon.

"Why is Angustias crying?" he asked when he and Aline were alone in her bedroom.

"Because I am leaving tonight. I'm sorry, Luis, but I will not be able to lunch with you today. Since I'm leaving for good, I am having my last lunch in Madrid with a friend."

"What?"

"All this time I haven't seen anyone but you. None of my other friends. I have a lunch engagement at Jockey."

Aline could see Luis's temperature rising, but there was no avoiding it.

"How can you have a lunch engagement at Jockey?" he asked. "You always have lunch with me."

She explained that she was having lunch with Raimundo Lanza, a handsome Italian prince whom Luis knew, and she was leaving momentarily.

Luis stood there, astonished. "You're really leaving Spain?"

"Tonight. Here are my tickets."

Luis stared at them and then at the suitcases. Angustias, who had been eavesdropping in the hall, suddenly burst into tears and Luis looked at her and then back at Aline.

"Now if you'll excuse me," Aline said, "I don't want to be late."

"But I thought we were going to get married?"

"What an incredible coincidence. So did I."

"Aline, be reasonable. You never told me you had made these preparations. Until right now I've been unaware that you really intended to leave."

Aline pressed her lips, her emotions dancing along the edges of anger, righteous indignation, sadness, and composure. "But the man is supposed to ask the girl to marry, not vice versa. It embarrasses me to keep mentioning the subject."

"Keep mentioning! You have imagined all of this. I've been asking you to marry me since I first met you. I will talk to my father right now."

"No, Luis, I think you would like to marry me, but I also believe, if you were decided to do so, you would have made it definite before now. I understand your family would not be pleased to have you marry an unknown American. . . . Forget it. I don't want to put you through any disagreeable situations for my sake. And I really have to go. Goodbye."

She grabbed her purse and headed for the stairs, tears welling.

"Wait," Luis said, following. "At least let me take you there."

"No. I prefer to go alone."

Aline rushed out the door just as a taxi was driving by. She hailed it and jumped in.

About the time she and Raimundo were having dessert, Luis appeared at their table.

"Aline, I would like to speak with you. Alone."

Aline excused herself and she and Luis went to a quiet corner. His voice was urgent.

"My father is waiting for you right now, our priest is with him. Everything is set."

"What do you mean everything is set?"

"Naturally my father has to talk to you. And since you didn't believe that I was going to marry you, how else can I prove to you that I'm serious?"

Aline paused. For all that she'd wanted Luis to propose, this was happening too fast, and not in the sequence she had expected.

"Are you telling me that you asked your father if you could marry me?"

"No, I *told* him that I was going to marry you. But in this country one's parents must be properly informed and the family priest must make the preparations."

Aline was dizzy. What happened to the old-fashioned romantic evening with the presentation of a ring and proposal on one knee?

"My father and the priest are waiting," Luis said again. "We'll be married one month from today. That's the quickest I can arrange the papers, I'm told."

Before she could respond, he added: "Now you can send a cable to your company and say that you will not be returning. Ever."

Forgetting to say goodbye to Raimundo, Aline swept out of the restaurant with Luis and they hurried to the meeting with Luis's father and the priest.

She had met Luis's father, the Count of Velayos, several times, mostly at horse races. He was president of horse racing in Spain, and they would sit in his father's box at the track with generals and other dignitaries. However, they never had much opportunity to talk, and Aline didn't really know him.

When they arrived at Luis's father's home, he greeted her with a handshake. He was polite but formal, and not particularly warm. It seemed clear to Aline that the family had expected Luis to marry a Spaniard, preferably someone with a noble pedigree.

"My son says he wants to marry you," he began. "For us, in Spain, this is a serious decision. As you may be aware, we cannot dissolve a marriage in this country. It is for better or for worse and for always. I suggest you think this matter over for a while."

"I have already thought it over, and I am aware of your customs and laws, and I am also a Catholic. Even if I were not, please don't think that everyone in the United States gets divorced!"

The count nodded and his eyes softened. "Is it necessary that the wedding take place within a month? Why do you set this ultimatum?"

Aline blushed. That was not exactly a correct summary of the situation.

"I cannot afford to live in Madrid without working, and my parents would not approve. I would like to get married to Luis in the United States, but since foreign exchange is restricted, he says it is difficult to get visas and leave the country."

"In that, Luis is correct." He turned to the priest. "One month is not much time to prepare a proper wedding, but I suppose it can be done."

The priest nodded and explained the papers that would have to be signed in the United States.

Luis's father seemed annoyed at the rush but suggested they proceed along to see Luis's grandfather, who was waiting.

As their car approached the home on the Castellana, it all came to her. *This* was the palace across from the embassy that Robert Dunev had pointed out in the office that day. Luis's grandfather was none other than the Count of Romanones, the former prime minister and principal adviser to the king. Since Luis's last name was Figueroa and his title was Count of Quintanilla, and his father was the Count of Velayos, she had never connected the Romanones name. But titles, Luis explained, were inherited. When Luis's grandfather died, Luis's father would become the Count of Romanones, and then upon his father's death, Luis would.

A uniformed guard opened the palace gates and Luis pulled up to a side door. Aline snuck a glance at him as they hurried inside; he seemed more nervous than she.

"Do not be frightened by *El Abuelo*," Luis said. "He is overpowering, but if he doesn't like you at first, he will eventually. He can be affectionate and his sense of humor is famous."

Aline was getting the picture. The family had to approve the marriage, and Luis's grandfather was the most important person to win over. This explained Luis's nervousness. Whether there would be a wedding ceremony depended upon her performance in the next hour.

They went through a foyer with thirty-foot ceilings and came to a wide curving staircase. On either side were suits of armor.

How appropriate, Aline thought. *I'm going into battle.*

As they ascended, Luis said: "My grandfather is accustomed to getting his way. Everyone in the family is frightened of him."

Aline slowed her pace. "Are you afraid of your own grandfather?"

Luis nodded. "Absolutely."

Great. Just great. She was thirty seconds from meeting the former prime minister, the most famous man in Spain, and even his own family was afraid of him. This was worse than the *tienta*.

Luis caught her eye. "Don't worry. I am going to marry you, no matter what he says."

They reached the top of the stairs and Luis escorted her through several rooms. The Count of Romanones, eighty-four years old, was resting in an armchair with a blanket over his legs. His bright blue eyes, Aline noticed, were vibrant and alert, defying his age. They were also evaluating.

"*Quien es?*" the count inquired.

Luis nudged Aline forward. "*Abuelo*, this is my *novia*."

"*Quien es?*"

Luis stepped closer. Louder: "*Abuelo*, it's my *novia*. I would like to present my *novia*."

Grandfather nodded and asked Aline to come closer, inspecting. He began rubbing his hands, thinking, or perhaps still evaluating. There was warmth in his eyes, though, and suddenly he grinned.

"*Bueno*, so you want to marry my *nieto*, my *primogenito*? Tell me, what do you see in him?"

He motioned to a chair and Aline took a seat, pondering her answer.

"Frankly," he added, "I don't see anything."

Before she could respond, the count chuckled. "Bring the chair closer," he said.

Aline scooted forward.

"Closer."

She pulled it so that their knees were almost touching.

"Now give me your hand."

Aline did and he began to speak softly, but with a sparkle in his eye. "Whenever I have the good fortune to be with a beautiful woman, it has always been my custom to hold her hand. I can think better this way. Now tell me, what sort of fellow is the president of your country? They tell me that Truman is doing very well, and I can bet that you're going to have him for another term."

Relieved at the softball question, Aline answered and the count went on, inquiring about politics and the United States in general.

They talked for an hour but *El Abuelo* never brought up Luis, her family, or the marriage. Aline couldn't believe it, that business about him being intimidating; he was the kindest old man she'd ever met.

Soft steps echoed behind them. It was Luis, approaching slowly, unsure if *El Abuelo* had completed his examination.

Grandfather waved him in. "Luis, your marriage has my blessings. What this family needs is some new blood, and Aline is just the one."

That evening Aline called her parents. She had kept them in the dark about Luis since the notion of marriage had been so remote. It was best, she figured, to be direct.

"I'm getting married, Mother."

"Oh, Aline, I'm so happy. To whom, dear? Some boy in your office?"

"No, Mother. He's a Spanish boy who lives right here in Madrid."

"Spanish? Oh, no, Aline, you're not thinking about marrying a Spaniard?"

Aline sighed. Here we go. "Well, I'm more than thinking about it. I'm going to marry him."

"Oh, Aline, I hope you're not doing anything rash. Can he speak any English?"

"Better than I can. He also speaks French and German and Italian and . . . look, Mother, have faith in me. You're going to adore Luis."

"What's his name?"

"Luis. Looo-eees."

"You must get married here in Pearl River. When are you coming back?"

"No, Mother, you will have to come here. It's difficult for Spaniards to leave the country."

"But you will live here in America, won't you?"

"We will live in Spain."

"But what kind of living can he make over there?"

"Don't worry about that, Mother."

"I have to worry about you, dear. Now what does Luis do?"

"Well . . . I don't know exactly, but it's not important. He's the champion golfer of Spain."

"Oh, no, Aline. A golf bum. Don't tell me—"

"Mother, he's no kind of bum. He's a count."

"A count? You mean a bookkeeper? I think you had better give this a lot of thought. You should come right home. In a little while, you'll forget all about it."

Aline sighed again. This wasn't going quite as planned. She let her mother know that she *was*, in fact, getting married.

In Spain.

To the bookkeeper.

The next day Aline cabled Frank Ryan in New York to let him know that she was resigning from the company, effective immediately, to get married.

Forty-eight hours later he was at her door.

CHAPTER 23

CORTANDO LA COLETA

Frank Ryan, always composed and confident, seemed agitated and nervous.

Aline showed him into the salon and he came quickly to the point.

"I have come here to discuss this idea of your impending marriage. I want to make you understand there are important reasons for you to postpone this marriage for the good of your country. This is not the time for a patriotic girl such as yourself to leave the company."

Ryan paused to see if Aline would give a reaction, but she remained silent.

"We need you," he went on. "We have great plans for you. We have planned a 'fresh-up' course for you in Washington." From there, he said, she would open the Prague office.

Aline was touched by Ryan's confidence in her and understood that there were few former OSS agents who didn't have families and could move about as she could. She admired Frank immensely and didn't want to let him down, but her mind was made up.

Frank slipped an envelope from his jacket and held it out. "Here is your ticket back on the *France*, the best ocean liner crossing the Atlantic nowadays. It leaves in six days. Do not abandon us now. You can postpone your wedding for a year at least."

Aline held the envelope, saying nothing, and they looked at each other. She remembered an expression she had learned from Juanito: *cortando la coleta*. Literally, it meant "cutting the ponytail," but it was used to say that a matador was giving up the fight. Throughout the history of bullfighting matadors had worn ponytails, which they fastened up in a bun at the base of their neck. If a bullfighter was retiring, he would cut his *coleta*. Juanito's father, revolutionary that he was, decided one day to cut his, even though he wasn't retiring. But the phrase carried on.

As gently as she could, she explained to Ryan that, for her, it was time to move on. To get married and start a family.

Undeterred, Ryan gave it one more shot. He explained that the company's new name was World Commerce Corporation, and that things were moving quickly. "You are unaware of the plans we have for World Commerce. We considered it prudent that you and others not be informed of the current changes. But I can assure you that you will miss a very exciting adventure. You are perfect for the role we had chosen for you."

Aline said nothing and Ryan wiped his brow.

"Think this over. Do you realize you are giving up a great career? An exciting career? No other young woman today holds such a unique opportunity. And you are still so young."

Aline knew why Ryan was pressing. He wanted someone who had not only professional training in espionage, but also front-line experience with security protocols and the ability to fit in at cocktail parties, dinners, and receptions. Someone who had the ability to dig in such a way that the other person would not be put on their guard. It was very possible she was the only person who had all of the qualities Ryan was looking for.

She was moved, but Ryan's plea didn't change her resolve. She was in love with Luis and nothing could stop her from marrying him.

Cortando la coleta.

*　　*　　*

Days later she received a call from an unexpected source.

Edmundo.

He and Princess Agatha were getting married in Madrid in August, he said. Would she attend? She would, and she did.

Aline was a guest at their wedding at the San Jerónimo el Real Church on August 1, which was covered in the *New York Times* two days later.

Disney Iberian Agent Marries Princess of Ratibor and Corvey

By Wireless to THE NEW YORK TIMES.

MADRID, Aug. 1—Princess Maria Agatha of Ratibor and Corvey and Edmundo Lasalle, Iberian representative for Walt Disney Productions, were married in San Jeronimo Real Church here this evening.

The bride is the daughter of the late Duke of Ratibor, Prince of Corvey, and Princess Oettingen-Metternich. Her husband, son of the late José Maria Lasalle, former Foreign Minister of Mexico, attended Columbia University and the University of California. At the latter he was elected to Phi Beta Kappa Society, received a doctorate in history and was associate professor of history.

Announcement of Edmundo's marriage to Princess Agatha in the *New York Times*, August 3, 1946.

Edmundo wouldn't be carrying on in espionage, Aline knew, but his marriage to Princess Agatha fulfilled his real dream: high society. That, and avoiding a nine-to-five job.

To his delight, some would now address him as "Prince Edmundo."

Luis Quintanilla, meanwhile, was working on details of *their* marriage, starting with Aline's dress. Spanish custom, he told her, was that the groom selects and pays for the wedding dress.

Aline couldn't argue with that.

Luis showed her an old photograph of his mother in her wedding dress. It was beautiful. With a princess line silhouette and a chain of orange blossoms from waist to floor, it had a long train of white satin damask. She wore a tiara and a white lace mantilla extending the length of the train. His mother had died in an automobile accident when he was eight, and he said it would be an honor to her if Aline wore a dress modeled on the same design.

He motioned to the tiara. "That, you will have to wear. Every bride in my mother's family has worn it for two hundred years."

He added that it was also a Spanish tradition for the groom to give the bride a diamond bracelet.

"But Luis, I'd like a ring. In America, the custom is a ring."

"Well, maybe I'll give you a ring, too, but you must have a diamond bracelet because that is the custom."

Aline didn't protest further. There was something delightful about these Spanish traditions.

"Luis, what about the woman's gift to the groom? What am I expected to give?"

"You must buy me a gold cigarette case. I've already chosen the one I want at my family's jeweler, Paco Sanz. When you go there, he will show it to you."

That night they went to Jockey for dinner and Luis set a box before her. Aline opened it and was awestruck. It was a ring with the largest ruby she'd ever seen—probably the largest in Spain—set between two equally impressive diamonds.

"This was a present from my grandfather to my grandmother, then from my father to my mother."

As Aline gawked Luis brought forth a gleaming pearl necklace, its clasp set with diamonds. This had been his mother's as well, he said. He asked Aline to put it on and he produced another box, this one with matching pearl and diamond earrings. Days later he gave her the diamond engagement bracelet.

Aline was flabbergasted. She had never desired expensive things, and here she was, not even thirty, with priceless jewelry and heirlooms. She realized that the one gift she was to give Luis—the cigarette case—had to be extraordinary.

She went to Paco Sanz's the next afternoon and introduced herself to the owner.

Paco beamed. "Ahhh, si, señorita, I recognized you. El Señor Conde has selected the loveliest cigarette case that we have."

He set it before her and Aline tried not to gasp upon seeing the price. It was clearly the most expensive case Paco carried, but it paled in comparison to the jewels Luis had already given her. To buy it, she'd have to forgo the two new Balenciagas she had planned to have made.

She smiled. "It's perfect."

With her resignation from World Commerce and Luis's commitment to marriage acknowledged by both families, there was now no need to rush the ceremony, and she and Luis planned the wedding for late spring or early summer at San Fermín de los Navarros, the nineteenth-century church where Luis's parents and most of his family had been married.

They announced the engagement on December 12 and the following day the *New York Times* made it known to the public at large: "Aline Griffith Engaged."*

After the New Year, with wedding preparations well under way, Aline had one important thing to share with Luis that she had been putting off for months: her OSS work. Connecting an aristocratic family with espionage—even on behalf of America—was not something that would go over well with most Spaniards, Luis's family in particular.

---

*While the *New York Times*'s "outing" of Aline as a former OSS agent might have been startling to her, the *Times* had already done this previously, and in far more dramatic fashion. Before the war had even ended, the *Times* revealed the OSS association of Reginald C. Foster, a staffer at the Washington office, on April 6, 1945.

ALINE GRIFFITH ENGAGED

Former OSS Madrid Aide Fiancee of Ex-Premier's Grandson ·

MADRID, Dec. 12 (U.P.)—The engagement of Miss Aline Griffith, daughter of Mr. and Mrs. William F. Griffith of Pearl River, N. Y., to Luis Figueroa y Perez de Guzman el Bueno, Count Quintanille, grandson of Count Romanones, who was Premier of Spain during the reign of the late King Alfonso XIII, has been announced. ·

The wedding will take place here in the early spring.

Miss Griffith met her fiancé during the war, when she was on the staff of the OSS unit at the embassy here. She has remained in Madrid as the representative of an importing and exporting firm.

Aline's engagement announced in the *New York Times* on December 13, 1946.

It was unlikely that Luis, in Madrid, would have seen the *New York Times* announcement—which mentioned Aline's work for the OSS—and even if he had, he wouldn't have known what it was. So one night after dinner, Aline decided to come clean.

She told him she had been an American spy during the war, operating out of the US embassy in Madrid.

Luis chuckled. "Preposterous."

No, it was true, she said. But before she could explain the American Oil Mission, Luis began working himself up, enjoying the moment.

"You, a spy!" he roared. "Really, Aline, you do have a great imagination."

Aline wondered whether to let it go or press it. Luis made the decision for her, continuing: "And you better not tell your fantasies to anyone. It wouldn't improve their opinion of you."

Luis looked at Aline a moment and then burst out laughing. "You a spy! Bah!"

January 1947
Madrid

At Balenciaga's salon Luis produced the photo of his mother and the vendeuse took Aline's measurements. Luis and Aline selected the material, noted the length of the train they desired, and rose to leave. As they gathered their things, the vendeuse told them that she had spoken on the phone with Señor Balenciaga from Paris, who said he was impressed that Aline was marrying the *primogénito* of the Count of Romanones, and that he had known all along that the American girl was destined to become somebody.

On the drive back Luis announced that he had rented a place in Capri for their honeymoon. They would spend the summer there, he said, and then tour Europe and America.

"We will decide later how long we stay in each place."

Aline didn't know what to say. This was another world.

Over the next few months she and Luis worked on details of the wedding. They would have a dinner and dance following the ceremony, Luis decided, at the home of his eldest sister, Isabel, the Duchess of Tamames. She was staying at her finca in Cordoba at the moment, however, so Luis suggested a trip there to formalize plans.

Cordoba was an ancient city, he explained, rich in Arabic architecture from centuries of Moorish control. "My great-grandfather was from Cordoba and I inherited his famous palace in the middle of the city. But Isabel inherited his large finca." Unfortunately, he added, he had sold the palace a few months earlier. "It was very ancient but I never passed even one night in the place. Evidently my great-grandfather, Perez de Guzman el Bueno, was a very important person in Cordoba. The palace is unusual—it was built so the owner could go up to the second floor on horseback. I would have liked that."

Aline was getting to know her fiancé better each day, and how dramatically different their perspectives were. What she considered the marvels and mysteries of Spain—the old palaces and monuments and castles—were run-of-the-mill artifacts for Luis. What excited him was golf and hunting.

After the Cordoba trip, they began to pin down a wedding date. They originally set a date for the beginning of June, only to change it because Manolete was fighting in Madrid later in the month. It would be the last time they would be able to see him in the ring before leaving for their honeymoon, so they settled on June 26.

As the wedding date approached, however, calamity struck. Days before Aline's parents were scheduled to leave New York, her brother Tom was seriously injured in an automobile accident. Not wishing to leave him, they sent Aline's nineteen-year-old brother Bill in their stead.

June 26, 1947
Church of San Fermín de los Navarros, Madrid

As the ancient bells chimed in the tower above her, Aline stood in awe at the back of the church with her brother Bill at her side. It was surreal that she was wearing what Luis's mother had worn—dress, train, and tiara—in *that* very church at *her* wedding. The guests numbered in the hundreds, almost none of whom Aline knew. In front of her were Luis's relatives and all the grandees of Spain. *El Abuelo*, she knew, was sitting in the first pew.

The organ bellowed out the first chords of the processional and Aline's heart began to race. There were no wedding rehearsals in Spain so you had to do it right the first time. Fortunately, she had played the part of the bride in countless fashion shows for Hattie Carnegie, so there was comfort in knowing she wouldn't trip over her dress.

She slipped her hand inside her brother's arm and noticed for the first time she was trembling. "Bill," she whispered, "we must walk very, very slowly. Just keep in step with me."

As they proceeded down the aisle, Aline prayed that she looked like the bride Luis wanted his family to see. Up ahead she could see Luis and the priest, and ten men surrounding the altar who would be the formal witnesses. Two of the men—Paul Culbertson, US embassy chargé d'affaires, and Edward Maffitt, second secretary—were her representatives.

One person she didn't spot was Benito Llambí, her erstwhile Argentinian suitor, who was seated in the crowd.

He was fingering a revolver.

CHAPTER 24

COUNTESS QUINTANILLA

Sitting in the pew beside Benito Llambí were two of Luis's friends, who noticed the Argentine nervously sliding the pistol in and out of his pocket. Not wanting to disrupt the proceedings, they moved quickly and quietly, disarming Benito and whisking him outside, where they shoved him into a car and drove away.*

Aline and Luis, unaware of the drama occurring behind them, came together in front of the altar with Luis's sister Isabel and Aline's brother Bill standing at their sides, alternates for Luis's mother and Aline's father. With the glow of seven chandeliers upon them, Aline and Luis placed rings on right hands—the Spanish custom—and the priest introduced the groom and bride: the Count and Countess of Quintanilla.

After they signed the marriage documents, Luis whispered to her: "Before we go to the big party at my sister's house, let's slip out and make a visit to see *El Abuelo*. He will not be able to come to the party and we'll never have time before we leave for Rome tomorrow morning."

Aline understood that Luis's grandfather wouldn't be able to handle a dinner with several hundred guests, and she was glad to visit him at his home, still wearing her wedding dress.

*After the wedding Aline heard details about the Benito Llambí incident. "When they spoke to him," she recalled later, "he told them he was not going to allow Luis to marry me, that he was the man Aline should marry."

El Abuelo seemed surprised to see them, but his eyes sparkled with joy. Once again he had Aline sit next to him and took her hands.

"Aline, I have attended many weddings in my life. I have seen many people of different stations joined in matrimony, but I want you to know that today I was very proud of you. You walked down the aisle . . . like a queen."

Aline fought back tears, as did Luis.

The wedding was announced the following day in the *New York Times*.

At 36 Wall Street, Frank Ryan set down the paper and smiled.

U. S. GIRL WEDS COUNT

War Department Employe Bride of Wealthy Spanish Nobleman

MADRID, June 26 (AP)—Miss Mary Aline Griffith of Pearl River, N. Y., a wartime employe of the United States Embassy, was married here today to Luis de Figueroa, Count of Quintanilla, a grandson and heir of the Count of Romanones, holder of one of the largest fortunes in Spain.

Count Romanones, last Foreign Minister under the deposed monarchy, commented that he was "happy over the uniting of my family with a family of the United States, a nation for which I always have had the greatest affection and admiration."

The Count of Quintanilla already is one of Spain's wealthiest young men through an inheritance from his mother.

The marriage, which took place in the Church of San Fermin de Los Navorras, was attended by many members of the Spanish nobility. Paul Culbertson, United States chargé d'affaires, and Edward P. Maffitt, second secretary of the United States Embassy, were witnesses for the bride.

The couple departed for Lisbon on their wedding trip.

Aline's wedding announced in the *New York Times*, June 27, 1947.
Note that the *Times* erred not only with Aline's first name, writing that it was Mary rather than Marie, but also with the honeymoon destination, declaring that they were off to Lisbon, rather than the correct city, Rome.

Aline in her wedding dress, posing with Luis's nieces and nephews.

On the flight to Rome, Aline and Luis recognized another passenger in the first-class Iberian cabin: Eva Perón, wife of the Argentine president, Juan Perón. She was hard to miss as she was wearing a pink straw hat, with feathers, and a veil covering her eyes. Despite the late June weather, a mink stole rested over the arm of her seat.

Eva had sent them a priceless Ming vase as a wedding gift, and Aline had had mixed feelings about thanking her. While it was rude not to thank someone for a wedding gift, especially someone married to a head of state, Juan and Eva were universally considered Nazi collaborators.

Not long after takeoff Luis went to the rear of the first-class compartment to talk to some men—apparently Eva's bodyguards—and Eva came over and took Luis's seat. In her hand she carried a copy of *ABC*, Madrid's newspaper, which had a photo of the wedding on the front page.

Eva asked who had made the dress, and Aline told her it was a Balenciaga. Eva carried on for some time about the difference between Balenciaga's Madrid store and the salons in Rome. It was important for her, she said—as the president's wife and as a state figure—to pay attention to such matters because she was expected to create a sensation each time she appeared in public.

Aline nodded, thanked her for the vase, and then asked Eva about the Nazi money which had been sent to Argentina.

Eva glared at her. "*Querida*, take my advice. If you want to live long enough to enjoy your honeymoon and the life of a grandee countess, do not ever talk about such things. It can be very dangerous. *Comprendes?*"

With that, Eva returned to her seat.

When they arrived in Rome, Aline learned that Luis had made reservations to stay an entire week because of a series of receptions set up by *El Abuelo* and Luis's father. First was the formal dinner in their honor hosted by the Spanish ambassador to Italy, Señor Sangroniz. Aline had met him in Paris during her stint with World Commerce and was delighted when the ambassador provided her with a new Spanish passport reflecting her new name: the Countess of Quintanilla.

The next day the Prince and Princess of Torlonia (sister of Spain's exiled King Juan) hosted a dinner for them, followed by another at the French embassy the next night. Luis was surprised by the ambassador's greeting: "What a pleasure to have my beautiful friend Aline in this embassy," the Frenchman said.

Unbeknownst to Luis, Aline had met him in Madrid when the ambassador was head of the Free French intelligence service.

Luis didn't probe, though, and Aline had no desire to bring up her wartime work as a spy, which had been the source of such amusement for him in the past.

From Rome they took the train to Naples, and from there the ferry to Capri. Their mutual friend Italian prince Raimundo Lanza—the very man Aline had abandoned at lunch during the drama with Luis over his marriage intentions—had rented for them the entire second floor of a palazzo overlooking the beach. Below them lived Princess Caraciollo, a Spaniard whom Luis knew from Madrid, and Princess Manona Pignatelli.

At night Luis and Aline would take a horse-drawn carriage—cars were not allowed in Capri—into town for drinks and dinner. To Aline's pleasant surprise, it was customary to shop in the quaint stores before *and* after supper.

Each morning they would head down to the rocky beach where a boat—or boats—with friends and acquaintances would arrive to take them to swim in clear water. Aline was amazed at the number of dignitaries whom Luis knew. One of the boat guests was Eva Mussolini, daughter of the ill-fated Il Duce. Aline knew that Eva had married Count Ciano, but she didn't know that Mussolini had had Ciano executed for objecting to Italy's alignment with Hitler. Also in the group was Pamela Churchill, the British prime minister's daughter-in-law, and Gianni Agnelli, who would soon become the president of Fiat.

One day the boat party decided to lunch at a restaurant on the other side of the island. When they were close to the shore, everyone dove into the water to swim ashore. Aline began swimming and a few dozen yards past the boat she looked back for Luis. She stopped, treading water.

Luis was floundering, going under and then bobbing up, gasping for air.

He was drowning.

Aline swam back and assisted him to shore.

When they caught their breath, she asked how it was that such a great athlete couldn't swim.

Luis shrugged. "When we were children during our summers in Biarritz our governesses never allowed us in the water for more than a few moments and even then just far enough to get our legs wet. I never had the chance to learn how to swim."

Aline was stunned. Luis *knew* he couldn't swim, yet rather than lose face by admitting it to the others, his Spanish pride compelled him to plunge in, drowning be damned. There was much, she realized, she still had to learn about her husband.

While Luis had received a privileged, protected upbringing—governesses, butlers, tutors, and tailors—she had always sensed that he was extremely brave and the swimming incident confirmed it. She inquired about his arm, the one that had been injured during the civil war and had a large chunk of muscle missing. Before their marriage, Luis had always shrugged it off as a souvenir of the fighting.

But fighting for whom? Where? How?

She pressed Luis to tell her, once and for all, about his arm, about the war, about what had happened to him and his family.

Luis gathered his thoughts, as if remembering a nightmare, and started from the top.

"The day the war began, July 17, 1936, I was playing golf in Puerto de Hierro. My sister, Isabel, had played golf earlier and was waiting for me to finish my game so we could go home together. For some time there had been demonstrations in the streets by communists, people in the club referred to them as *rojos*. I was seventeen and didn't know much about politics. But I knew that a week before the police had difficulty preventing a mob from burning a church. But despite the lack of safety, my family had remained in the city because my stepmother's father was seriously ill in the hospital.

"When I came in the clubhouse, Isabel was very upset. 'Papa has telephoned,' she said. 'Blanca's father's operation is over but papa says we must not go home. The house is being watched by a group of dangerous-looking people. He insists we meet him at the hospital instead. There is too much unrest in the streets.'"

Luis paused, reacting to the memory, and then said that when he arrived at the hospital, two nurses were struggling to remove a large body from a stretcher to an emergency table.

"I stepped closer to help. The sight was horrible. A man's bloodied body covered with black scorched flesh, his face was almost unrecognizable, his hair was singed, he was delirious and groaning with pain. As I helped to move the body, one of the nurses told me that the *rojos* had hung the bodies of three monks by the feet over the altar and set them on fire. 'This one is still alive,' she said."

Luis went on, explaining that his father arrived at the hospital and one of the doctors he knew said it wasn't safe for any of them to go home. "There are dozens of gangs of *rojos* attacking homes, arresting the owners, and beating up anyone who appears privileged."

Luis's paternal grandparents were in Biarritz at the time, Luis explained, but his maternal grandparents, the Ariases, were in Madrid. He called their home, and the butler told them that his grandfather had gone for a walk that morning on the Castellana but never returned. Panicked, his grandmother, Torre, had fled to the Palace Hotel.

That evening Luis went to the Palace to see Torre. Around midnight the concierge told them that he had just heard what had happened to Arias. He had been shot and killed, the concierge said, by a group of reds shooting randomly at people who appeared well-dressed. Luis's grandfather was one of the first.

"My grandmother of course was desperate and determined to go out herself to look for his body and give him a proper burial. But the concierge told us they would kill her too."

The bodies had been dumped in the city's public cemetery, the concierge added.

Luis slouched in his seat and lit a cigarette, reluctant to continue the story. "The place was horrible," he finally said. "Stinking bodies all around. It must have been about two o'clock in the morning and I had to use a flashlight. Finally I found him, my poor grandfather, just thrown in a heap, blood all over his face and clothes."

Luis paused again, remembering. "I loved my grandfather, who was gentle and kind to us, and to everyone. That night was an experience I'll never forget."

Aline could see it was painful for Luis to relive the scene, so she waited until later to ask again about his arm. He agreed to continue his story, albeit only briefly. He was seventeen, he said, but had joined to fight with the Nationalists, whom his entire family supported. His injury had happened during fighting in Victoria: "I was left for dead among others in the field. It must have been late at night or early in the morning when a doctor and two nurses were looking through the bodies scattered all over the battlefield. By a miracle a good friend of my sister, Isabel, was among the nurses and she recognized me. I was unconscious. I was taken into the operating room and that doctor was able to remove entirely the gangrenous part of my arm."

She shook her head, stunned, not knowing what to say.

Luis was stoic, frozen in the past. "Exactly nineteen of the boys and men in my family were killed in that war. I was the only male left of that generation in our family.

"We were too young to know anything about politics," he went on. "However, I can tell you there were plenty of foreigners in our war; most favored the other side. At the very beginning, masses of Russians piled into Madrid. They draped a three-story picture of Lenin over the façade of the great post office building in the Plaza de Cibeles. They also created torture centers called *chekas*. The Russians did much to incite the civil war and to divide us Spaniards."

Aline took his hand, absorbing Luis's pain and memories. The more she learned about her husband, the more she loved and admired him.

Meanwhile in Spain, on August 28, Manolete was fighting in the nearly forgotten town of Linares. Small venues like this were not really worth his while, and the ring administrators certainly couldn't afford the fee for Spain's greatest matador, but when a bullfighter was on tour, the small towns were convenient layovers on their travels between Málaga, Seville, Cordoba, Valencia, Madrid, and Barcelona, and the parties found ways to make it work.

It was important for Manolete to be spectacular this day because Linares was close to his hometown of Cordoba, and because Luis Miguel Dominguín—his closest rival—was also on the card. Only twenty years of age, Dominguín was heir apparent to Manolete's throne as *Numero Uno*. When the trumpet blew, both fighters were determined to give their best.

Manolete killed the first bull with a workmanlike effort but the crowd was unimpressed; he was the top bullfighter to enter a ring in decades and they demanded perfection. Dominguín followed and he was remarkable. The crowd cheered as if they had witnessed history's greatest performance.

Manolete was now even more resolute. His second bull—Islero— like the one that had killed the incomparable Joselito a generation earlier, was a Miura. Manolete's manager, Camará, watched the bull coming down the tunnel and shivered. "Malo—bad, bad," he said to Manolete. "It hooks terribly to the right. Stay away from this one, *chico!*"

But Manolete could do no such thing. He had to give the performance of his life. He had to show the crowd that he was still the best.

Immediately he began working Islero close, ignoring Camará's shouts to stay away from him. As the fight progressed, Manolete brought the bull closer and closer, executing the Pass of Death, his own highly dangerous *manoletina*, and fifteen suicidal "natural" passes. It was the show of a lifetime.

Camará knew that the time to kill was drawing near and remained nervous, notwithstanding Manolete's flawless performance. "Stay away from him, man!" he shouted. "Off to the side and get away quick!"

Manolete, though, was determined. He would kill the most dangerous bull in the most dangerous position: from the front. As the animal charged, he lunged over the right horn and plunged the sword deep into the withers. Islero, at the same time, wrenched his head up, goring Manolete in the groin. Manolete flew through the air and slammed hard in a heap. Islero spiked at him twice and then keeled over.

British critic John Marks once wrote: "The bullfight is sometimes condemned as the particularly depraved combination of a spectator-sport and a blood-sport, in which the gloating witness runs no personal risk. The accusation is unjust. The bullfight audience takes neither part nor pleasure in causing pain to the victims of the fiesta, whose sacrifice is not contrived as an end in itself, to provide selfish amusement, but solely as a means to conjure up visions of movement and color, and to excite the sublime tragic emotion which Aristotle defined as pity mixed with fear."

As Barnaby Conrad put it, bullfight fans go for one reason: to see the near death of the matadors. Thus, the fighters who most gracefully maximize their chance of death within the aesthetic ritual are recognized as the best.

On this day, the best bullfighter in the world gave the audience what it wanted. And more. He gave them everything.

Manolete was dead.

When Aline and Luis heard the news at their next stop, Venice, they were heartbroken. Their Italian hosts, not understanding, were surprised at their grief. But Manolete was not just a national treasure and international star; he was their friend. It was only yesterday, it seemed, that he had offered to help Aline at the *tienta*. Now he was gone.

*   *   *

In Venice the parties and receptions for Luis and Aline continued, and at one event they met Elsa Maxwell, the American gossip columnist and radio personality. What she was best known for, though, was hosting elaborate parties for royalty.

During the evening, Luis heard Elsa ranting about the Spanish Civil War, and he couldn't help himself. "What you are saying is absolutely incorrect," he told her. "You had better ask me since I was in that war."

Aline grimaced, thinking the two might quarrel. She left them at it and circled back a half hour later to find that Luis and Elsa were bosom buddies. A week later they saw Elsa again, just before she was to leave for New York. When Luis mentioned that he and Aline would be arriving in New York on November 11, she said: "I will make a reservation in the hotel Carlyle for you. Luis, you can't stay anyplace else, and you will have a party in your honor the next day." She gave Luis her card and said to call.

In early September Aline and Luis returned to Madrid for a short rest and then began preparing for the third leg of their honeymoon. Luis wanted to spend October in Paris and London, and then all of November in the US, starting in New York and then perhaps driving cross-country to California.

Meanwhile, two of Aline's former colleagues, Robert Dunev and Frank Ryan, were busy picking up where the OSS had left off. On September 18, Congress passed the National Security Act of 1947. The act established the Air Force Department and merged the War and Navy departments into the National Military Establishment. It also created a new espionage organization—one that would employ Dunev.

The Central Intelligence Agency.

Six days later, on September 24, the *New York Times* quietly introduced a company on page 35 of the financial section: the World Commerce Corporation, formerly known as the British American Canadian Corporation.

BUSINESS WEDNESDAY, SEPTEMBER 24, 1947. The New York Times WEDNESDAY, SEPTEMBER 24, 1947. FINANCIA

WORLD TRADE BODY READY TO FUNCTION

American - Canadian - British Group Will Seek Solution to Exchange Problem

PLANS WIDE INTERCHANGE

Stettinius, Grew, Donovan Are Among Directors—F. T. Ryan, Textile Man, President

Expansion and activation of the World Commerce Corporation, an organization of American, Canadian and British financial and business interests created to promote international trade through private means, was announced here yesterday.

Frank T. Ryan, president of the corporation, in making the announcement at a meeting in the Bankers Club, disclosed that the interests represented by his family company, John J. Ryan & Sons, Inc., textile exporters and partners in the New York Stock Exchange firm of Bache & Co., had joined the venture originally formed in September, 1945. There will be no public financing.

Others financially interested in the enterprise, it was explained, are the following: Atlas Corporation; Robert Benson & Co., of London; Glore, Forgan & Co. of New York and Chicago; Hambros Bank of London; Ladenburg, Thalmann & Co. of New York; the Mellon interests of Pittsburgh, and Transamerica Corporation. Also identified with the corporation are former Secretary of State Edward R. Stettinius; Maj. Gen. William J. Donovan; former Ambassador to Japan, Joseph C. Grew, Sir William Stephenson and E. W. Bickle, J. H. Gundy, James Y. Murdoch and E. P. Taylor, of Canada.

Seeks to Bridge Exchange Gap

"The corporation is designed to build a bridge between the existing shortages of exchange and the world's needs," Mr. Ryan explained. "As a matter of principle the World Commerce Corporation refuses to believe that when a country is without dollars we must cease trading operations."

"The firm has world-wide coverage, being presently represented in forty-seven countries of the globe and through six partially owned subsidiaries in Canada, Brazil, Mexico, Egypt, Panama and the Philippines, the latter in course of organization," he continued.

"The firm also has controlling and management interest in Biddle-Sawyer Corporation, an international firm dealing in bulk chemicals and drugs with affiliates in England, India and the Argentine. World Commerce Corporation currently is conducting operations in industrial and manufactured products of United States and foreign origin as well as international commodities, Mr. Ryan explained. These activities, he said, are designed to create foreign exchange in sufficient sums to permit "the continuous and uninterrupted flow of products despite the current difficulties in foreign exchange payment facilities."

Acts as Distributor

The corporation also serves as distributor and agent for a number of well-known American manufacturers in foreign territories. In addition, Mr. Ryan said, it seeks to help promote industrial development in backward areas and in those areas suffering from wartime destruction by making available services of technicians and through introducing modern production methods.

"The time is at hand for American commercial alertness and ingenuity to assume world leadership in devising ways and means for maintaining and broadening international trade," he declared. "Business, financial and political leaders must be brought to the realization that the United States must buy as well as sell if we are

omy. Across-the-board tariff modification should be high on the agenda of Congress when it reconvenes."

World Commerce Corporation was originally formed in September, 1945, as the British American Canadian Corporation. At present the group has a paid-in capital of $1,000,000 and has access to additional funds to achieve its objectives, according to Mr. Ryan.

The board of directors of World Commerce Corporation follows: [roster partially illegible]

The World Commerce Corporation goes public in the *New York Times*, September 24, 1947.

Frank Ryan, World Commerce's president, was interviewed for the article and explained that the company was an international trade group with "world-wide coverage, being presently represented in forty-seven countries of the globe and through six partially owned subsidiaries in Canada, Brazil, Mexico, Egypt, Panama, and the Philippines, the latter in course of organization."

Coincidentally, Robert Dunev had just landed in the Philippines. He was to be the CIA's first representative in Manila.

CHAPTER 25

LIVING THE DREAM

Few would have noticed the fine print of the *New York Times* article, but the list of the board of directors for World Commerce included the top echelons of Allied intelligence during the war: OSS chief General William Donovan; British Security Coordination chief Sir William Stephenson; MI6 agent and Stephenson aide John Pepper; OSS director of Europe Russell Forgan; and OSS Iberian peninsula head Frank Ryan. In the "others financially interested" section of the article, even fewer would have connected the dots between Hambros Bank of London and Sir Charles Hambro, head of Special Operations Executive, or between "the Mellon interests of Pittsburgh" and OSS's Larry Mellon.

This, apparently, was by design. And former OSS agents brought in to open WCC offices would be completely under the radar. Yet the question remains: Did WCC conduct any type of espionage, or was it merely facilitating trade, as it had announced? Did Ryan recruit former OSS agents because they were seasoned spies or simply because he knew them, knew of their skills, and knew that they were reliable? Was it a coincidence that WCC had an office in the Philippines that was in the "course of development" at the same time that Robert Dunev had started work there for the CIA?

These are questions that perhaps only Frank Ryan, William Stephenson, or William Donovan could answer.

Whatever the case, with assistance from Stephenson, Ryan went to work. In another extended trip to Europe he met with bankers, financiers, manufacturers, industrialists, stockbrokers, and commodities merchants who could assist with international trade. He also met with a coterie of British military intelligence leaders, including: General Colin Gubbins, SOE chief following Hambro; Lord Selborne, minister of economic warfare; Brigadier W. T. Keswick, SOE chief of Asia; Colonel Douglas Dodds-Parker, SOE chief of North Africa; and one Ian Fleming, assistant to Admiral John Godfrey, director of Naval Intelligence.

How Ryan balanced actual trade with foreign intelligence (if actually conducted) is unclear, but his overall goal was to thwart Stalin's drive to expand communism throughout Europe. With most of the continent economically devastated, particularly Germany, Ryan knew that Russian agents would advance the communist agenda in each country, eventually making them Soviet satellites if it took root.

Post-war control of Germany, historically an economic power, was critical. On October 16, with an introduction from Donovan, Ryan sent a letter to General Lucius Clay, commander in chief of US forces in Europe and military governor of the American zone in Germany, writing: "In our view the restoration of economic balance in Europe is fundamentally a problem of industrial and agricultural production. The purposes to be served by such production are the maintenance of populations and the creation of internationally exchangeable values which are essential in supporting the continuance of the productive operations."

And World Commerce, he explained—created to address this need—was prepared to work with private or public entities. "The financial resources available to W.C.C.," he noted, "are substantial."

*　　*　　*

In November the US leg of Aline and Luis's honeymoon began. The couple boarded the stately RMS *Queen Elizabeth* at Southampton for the trip across the Atlantic, arriving in New York on November 11. As previously planned, they checked in to the Carlyle. Awaiting them at the front desk was an invitation: Elsa Maxwell was throwing a party in their honor the following night. Among the guests was Jack Warner, head of Warner Bros. Studios. Luis and Jack hit it off that night and Jack invited Luis and Aline to visit him and his wife, Ann, in Hollywood.

At Elsa's other parties they met the Duke and Duchess of Windsor, who became fast friends, and countless other celebrities. They also hit Manhattan's famous nightclubs, and Luis was particularly enthralled by all of the shops along Fifth Avenue. But one thing he couldn't understand.

"Americans are always running as if they were going to a fire," he said to her one day. "What are they hurrying for? Nobody walks fast like that in Madrid."

Pearl River was their next stop and Aline worried that Luis might be bored with the small town, but as it turned out he loved it. The slow pace and friendly people were what he had imagined of America. Luis also got along swimmingly with her parents, spending a surprising amount of time in the kitchen showing Aline's mother how to prepare a traditional Spanish dinner.

One day Aline took Luis to see the building where she had spent elementary, junior, and high school. It was an unimpressive red-brick building facing the football field. She pointed at the rooms and explained that, starting with kindergarten, she had spent a year in each one.

Luis looked at the building the way Aline had gawked at the ancient treasures of Spain.

"You really spent a year in each of those rooms?"

Aline nodded.

"How lucky you have been. All my life I wanted to go to a school, a real school. But my father and grandfather would not permit it. Instead, the professors came to us. Never was I able to know what it was like to go to school to play games with other boys. And just when I was about to go abroad to begin the university, the civil war broke out."

Luis gazed admiringly at the football field. "You are so lucky to have had all those years in such a perfectly marvelous school. This is all like seeing a movie for me."

Aline looked at her husband. Luis spoke five languages, was an expert in art, antiques, and music, yet he had never played a football game, never attended a pep rally, never had a newspaper route. Outwardly, growing up in a palace with sixty servants, he was extremely privileged; but inwardly—in so many aspects of life that mattered—he was impoverished. And he knew it.

One day Luis went for a stroll by himself down Pearl River's Main Street. When he returned, he had the excitement of a child who had been to the circus.

He had seen a barber shop, he told Aline's mother. "I saw the sign and would really like to go. How does one make an appointment?"

Aline's mother glanced at his hair. "You don't need a haircut, Luis, and you don't need an appointment."

"No, but I want a haircut anyhow because I've never been in a barber shop in my life. In Spain the barber comes to the house. That's no fun."

In no time Luis was pals with Mr. Preziosso, Pearl River's only barber.

The scenery would change once again when they took up Jack Warner's offer to visit him in California. Luis bought a car so they could drive across the country and see more of real America. Once they were in Hollywood, it was more parties and celebrities. Jack introduced them to Humphrey Bogart, Lauren Bacall, Frank Sinatra, Ava Gardner, Audrey Hepburn, and Deborah Kerr. In the years to come, Hepburn, Kerr, and the Duchess of Windsor would become Aline's best friends.

By the time Luis and Aline returned to Spain it was June 21, 1948. They had been on their honeymoon exactly one year. It was good to be home—and Madrid was now truly home—but Aline had another reason to settle down.

She was pregnant.

On February 21, 1949, she gave birth to a baby boy and *El Abuelo* created quite a stir when he came to visit them at the hospital. Nurses and doctors alike were catching glimpses of the great Count of Romanones, and one of them placed a comfortable chair for him next to Aline's bed. As he admired the newborn in Aline's arms, he nodded.

"*Bueno, bueno.* He looks strong. What name are you giving the child?"

"Oh, naturally Luis, like his father."

El Abuelo bristled and rapped his walking stick on the floor. "Bosh! That's impossible. This child is my *primogenito* and will carry my title one day. He must be called Álvaro like me."

Aline and Luis knew there was no point in arguing. Upon Luis's death, this boy would become the fourth Count of Romanones. Fortunately, Aline's next child was also a boy, born a year later, February 5, 1950, and Luis had his namesake. This child would become the eleventh Count of Quintanilla. And the year after that, they had a third son, Miguel.

Interestingly, Álvaro inherited Aline's brown eyes and dark brown hair, while Luis and Miguel had their father's green eyes and light brown hair. And since Luis wanted the boys to receive the same benefits that Aline had had in Pearl River, they went to schools like other children. However, so that they would be multilingual, Luis and Aline spoke English at home, but gave the boys a French governess. They also had lessons in tennis, horseback riding, golf, shooting, piano, guitar, and, of course, flamenco. And since Luis had taken up painting—his other passion besides hunting and golf—he introduced the boys to that, too.

Aline and the boys in Madrid, 1964. *Getty Images*

One thing Luis wanted to guard against, though, was spoiling the boys. One summer when Álvaro was eight, Luis and Aline sent him to stay in Pearl River with her parents. Álvaro would have to work and learn how to make money, Luis had told him, and Aline's mother came up with the perfect chore: Álvaro would pick vegetables in the garden and sell them door-to-door to the neighbors. Whatever money he made was his to keep.

When Álvaro arrived and was told of his duty, he went about the work with such zeal that after a week, Mrs. Griffith told him he'd have to sell fewer vegetables because she needed some for her own use.

The budding entrepreneur shook his head. She would have to buy his vegetables like everyone else, he told her.

*　　*　　*

In 1956 Aline received a call from Archibald Roosevelt, the CIA's station chief in Madrid. He told her that the organization needed assistance from former OSS agents living in foreign countries for small assignments. They were quite aware of her frequent international travels with Luis, he said, and of her extensive contacts with political leaders throughout Europe. Her job would be simple enough: if she would kindly tell him when she and Luis were about to depart for a foreign country, he would give her the name of a person they'd like her to talk to or suggest a bit of information they'd like her to uncover. When she returned from the trip, she would simply turn in a short report as she had done for the OSS. In essence, she was on call for "odd jobs." Aline couldn't and didn't tell Luis about any of this, of course, but she gladly obliged. The work she did for the CIA during this period, however, remains classified.

In 1962 the assets of her former employer, World Commerce Corporation, were sold and it ceased operations. Under Frank Ryan's leadership WCC had been highly successful. In its last financial statement, WCC showed $16.1 million in assets, $6.5 million in liabilities, and $9.6 million in total capital.* The stated reason for its sale—"tax purposes"—is as mystifying as the cold trail left behind by Ryan himself. Whether he joined the CIA at this point is uncertain.

That same year, just as Aline was named to *Vanity Fair's* International Best-Dressed Hall of Fame, she was able to gather her best friends close: she and Luis; Audrey Hepburn and her husband, Mel Ferrer; the Rothschilds; and the Duke and Duchess of Windsor all bought homes in the new Marbella Club resort. Almost overnight Marbella had become the Monte Carlo of Spain. International media dubbed it the summer home of the "jet-setting" crowd, which attracted even more celebrities and socialites.

---

*Adjusting for inflation, these figures would be $137 million, $55.7 million, and $82 million in 2020 dollars.

American media couldn't get enough of her. In a 1963 article spanning almost half a page, the *New York Times* interviewed Aline about her role as a fashion icon and included three large photos. The following year *Life* magazine did the same, with full-page spreads. This sleek American-Spanish countess who traveled the world, made the best-dressed lists, went on partridge shoots, and was married to a now-popular painter, was simply too alluring to pass up.

She was also renovating and decorating Pascualete, a seven-hundred-year-old estate Luis had inherited. Located between the Spanish towns of Trujillo and Cáceres, not far from the Portuguese border, the site had stone carvings dating back to the Romans. When Aline began the work the site had no electricity, no running water, and no plumbing. While living there to supervise renovation, she ran a generator at night to provide light. Upon completion of the work she published *The Story of Pascualete* in London in 1963, and republished it in the United States the following year under the title *The History of Pascualete: The Earth Rests Lightly.**

During these years Aline encouraged her friends to visit Spain, and the most popular attraction was the Seville Festival, held every April. Dating back to 1847, the Feria de Abril is a weeklong event and includes horseback parades in traditional costumes, bullfights, flamenco dancing, fireworks, and drinking and eating in more than a thousand *casetas* (private tent parties). In 1966 Aline and Luis hosted not only Audrey and Mel for this event, but also Jacqueline Kennedy and the Duchess of Alba.

One weekend that same year, Guy de Rothschild and his wife, Marie-Hélène, hosted an extravagant ball. Among the guests for the event were Elizabeth Taylor, Richard Burton, Brigitte Bardot, and Salvador Dalí. The evening before, during a buffet dinner in the salon, Aline was thrilled to see that Audrey Hepburn was also there.

"I'm so excited," Audrey said as she greeted Aline. "Do you know I've never been to a ball before?"

---

*The subtitle came from a Roman engraving found in the house.

Aline raised an eyebrow. "How's that possible? You of all people. Why, I've seen you in so many balls—in *War and Peace*, and *My Fair Lady*, and—"

"That was only in the movies, and that doesn't count—that's not like a real ball—it's just work. I've never been to a real ball in my life."

Aline smiled. "Well, Audrey, you are lucky. Your first ball tomorrow will be the most glamorous ball in the world."

Audrey was so unlike her Hollywood persona, though; she was actually shy and not particularly outgoing. "But she had such kindness and love for everyone," Aline explained later, "such truthfulness in her friendships, plus a bewitching sense of humor."

Luis's grandfather died in 1950, followed by Luis's father in the late 1960s, and Luis became the Count of Romanones. By this time Aline had perfected the art of gathering and keeping friends, weaving them together in a tapestry that spanned from Madrid to Paris to New York to Hollywood. And while she was in high demand as a socialite and fashion icon, Luis's reputation as an exceptional painter drew interest from galleries in New York and Palm Beach.

This photo of Aline and Luis with one of his paintings appeared in *Vogue* in 1964. *Getty Images.*

On a Thursday evening in May 1970 in New York City, Aline and Luis attended an exhibition by a talented local artist, Marsha Gayle. It was important for Luis to attend high-profile gallery showings because of his own collections, and Aline loved running into old friends, many of whom patronized the arts. The *New York Times* ran a story about the event three days later, on May 10, with photos of Gayle, Aline, and Luis. Missing from the photos was Gayle's husband, who apparently was camera-shy. His name was Ryan.

Frank T. Ryan.

CHAPTER 26

TWIN SOULS

Over the next ten years Aline and Luis continued on the celebrity circuit, at an even faster pace it seemed. In 1981 President Ronald Reagan appointed Aline's former OSS colleague William Casey CIA director, and Aline and Luis decided to take apartments in Washington and New York. She could meet with Casey periodically in DC, and Luis could frequent the gallery exhibitions in Manhattan.

In 1984 Aline was given an honorary doctorate by her alma mater, the College of Mount Saint Vincent, and two years later Miguel, Aline and Luis's youngest son, married the beautiful Magdalena Carral in her family's seventeenth-century home in Mexico City.

But as life was beginning on many fronts, so it would wane on others. In April 1986 Aline received news that her dear friend of almost forty years, the Duchess of Windsor, had died at her home in Paris. After the funeral and burial in the Royal Mausoleum at Frogmore, Aline was touched to learn that the duchess had bequeathed her a very special gift. In the car on her return to the London airport, Aline opened the small box. Inside was one of the duchess's favorite pieces of jewelry: a diamond bracelet and wristwatch. Wallis had once told Aline that it contained one of her and the duke's well-kept secrets. Aline turned it over to read an endearing engraving the duke had written.*

The real blow, though, came the following summer. Aline had just released *The Spy Wore Red*, her account of her time in Madrid during the war, and was on a book tour in the United States when she received a call from Luis. He was staying with the Rothschilds in Paris and had not been feeling well, he said. Originally thinking it might be the rich French food, Luis visited a doctor who told him he had a "liver problem." Luis flew to New York to see specialists, who advised that with a strict diet he would eventually get better. Aline and Luis returned to Madrid and carefully adhered to the physicians' guidelines. Luis's condition didn't get better, however, and in mid-October he fell into a coma and died.

Aline was despondent. As long as she'd known him, Luis had been a model of energy, vibrancy, and strength. "I felt destroyed and miserable," she wrote later, "so I went to Pascualete—alone. Even there I felt lost. The house seemed to have lost its warmth; I missed him still more. . . . It was cold—all I could do was sit in front of the burning fireplace and think of Luis who had been the heart and soul of my life. I had no interest in anything. Not even my children could help me adapt to the terrible void. He had been my love, my friend, my teacher. He had taken me to new worlds—even the world of art, antiques, and paintings. And added to that Luis's character had been the most admirable I had known."

Theirs was that special, often elusive love that Dostoyevsky had envisioned more than a century before. "If it is for love that a man and a woman have married each other," the Russian wrote in *Notes from the Underground*, "why should that love ever pass? Cannot it be fostered? Why should love ever pass if the husband be kind and honorable? Of course, the fervid passion of the first few weeks cannot last eternally; but to that love there sometimes succeeds another

---

*Aline preserved their secret by keeping the words confidential.

and a better love. When that has come about, husband and wife are twin souls who have everything in common."

Aline and Luis indeed had become twin souls, and she didn't know how to live without him. "The great sadness that overtook me was like a sickness," she remembered. "For a long time in Pascualete, I did not improve—but I remained there alone for one month. But eventually Pascualete was where I found some peace and gradually I returned to my normal life."

Aline's life changed after Luis's passing. She began to split her time among Madrid, Pascualete, and New York over the next thirty years, spending much of it with her children and grandchildren. When in the US, she would give lectures about her OSS days and sign books. But Pascualete, the place Luis had so loved, was her haven.

After *The History of Pascualete* and *The Spy Wore Red*, Aline continued to write, publishing four more books: *The Spy Went Dancing* (1990), *The Spy Wore Silk* (1991), *The Well-Mannered Assassin* (1994), and *The End of an Epoch* (2015). *The History of Pascualete* and *The End of an Epoch* were nonfiction books, while *The Well-Mannered Assassin* was a novel. Her three memoirs about her espionage career—*The Spy Wore Red*, *The Spy Went Dancing*, and *The Spy Wore Silk*—were published as nonfiction, but all were highly fictionalized.*

Like Edmundo Lassalle, Aline was a unique and remarkable character. While she was not a war heroine (impossible while operating in a neutral country), she nonetheless gave her country valuable service in Spain, work that was sometimes dangerous. Her employment with Ryan after the war remains mysterious, as does World Commerce Corporation itself.

That she had a storybook romance and marriage with Luis is unquestionable, and she appears to have been a splendid mother.

---

*Discrepancies regarding Aline's activities while with the OSS (imagined murders, for example) are detailed in the endnotes accompanying the dates of events.

Why she felt the need to embellish her exploits as a spy in the books she passed off as memoirs is puzzling, but she always had a flair for the dramatic. Interestingly, in a 1992 article she contributed to *The Secrets War: The Office of Strategic Services in World War II*—a book published by the National Archives and Records Administration and likely read by most living OSS agents—Aline was forthright, excluding from her essay the murders and wild events she had imagined in her books.

Perhaps she simply couldn't see that her true story needed no embellishment. She'd lived an extraordinarily multifaceted life as a small-town girl, a model, a spy, a wife, a mother, a socialite, a fashion icon, and a celebrity. She'd left the safety of home and put herself in danger in order to help defeat the Nazi threat, then found the love of her life in a fairytale romance. Aline was smart, resourceful, determined, and fearless. Perhaps most remarkably, she also had a spirit that allowed her to adapt to almost any situation in which she found herself.

Like Hemingway's bullfighters—some of whom became her lifelong friends—she lived her life "all the way up."

Aline, Countess of Romanones, died on December 11, 2017, at the age of ninety-four. She was survived by three children, thirteen grandchildren, and twelve great grandchildren. Her eldest son, Álvaro, is the current Count of Romanones and upon his death his oldest child, Cristina, will become the Countess of Romanones.

THE REST OF THE STORY

JUANITO BELMONTE

Like his famous father, Juanito was not killed in the bullring. He retired as a wealthy matador in the mid-1950s, but he had been deeply affected by the death of his matador friend, Manolete, in 1947. Not long after that, Juanito married a beautiful Spanish girl with whom he had three children. He died of a sudden heart attack before his fiftieth birthday.

"It was a sad shock for me," Aline recalled after hearing the news on the radio. "Juanito had been one of my first real friends in Spain and had introduced me to many of the country's pleasures. He had not only been extremely brave in the ring—but he was also kind to everyone and generous. With his sense of honor and dignity he represented those characteristics I admire in Spaniards."

BARNABY CONRAD

Barnaby Conrad lived the life Ernest Hemingway had fantasized. He was a boxer (captain of the freshman team at the University of North Carolina), diplomat, bullfighter, bon vivant, novelist, nonfiction writer, pianist, portrait painter, teacher, and nightclub owner. After the war he left the diplomatic corps and moved to Lima, Peru, where he worked as a cocktail pianist, portrait painter, and bullfighter.

Two years later he returned to the United States and began a writing career. He published his first novel, *The Innocent Villa*, in 1948, and then multiple books about bullfighting: *La Fiesta Brava: The Art of the Bull Ring* (1950), *Matador* (1952), *My Life as a Matador: The Autobiography of Carlos Arruza* (1956), *The Death of Manolete* (1958), and *Barnaby Conrad's Encyclopedia of Bullfighting* (1961). American media were spellbound.

"It's rather difficult to tell the reader right off about Barnaby Conrad," Harvey Breit wrote in his July 6, 1952, *New York Times* article. "For a young chap—he's just turned 30—he's done, and is doing, too much. Of course, he is a novelist, having with his second novel ('Matador') hit the jackpot." As Breit noted, Conrad at thirty had already accomplished more than most do in a lifetime.

Matador went on to sell more than three million copies. No less an authority than John Steinbeck said it was his favorite novel of the year, and William Faulkner sent a copy to his niece, writing, "I'm sending you a wonderful book called *Matador*. . ."

But Conrad was only just beginning. In 1953 he opened a San Francisco nightclub, El Matador, but couldn't let go of the exhilaration found only in *la fiesta brava*. He returned to Spain and continued to fight bulls. In 1958, however, the odds caught up with him.

In a fight in El Escorial, Conrad was badly gored. The bull's horn plunged nine inches into his left leg and he was rushed to the hospital. After surgery he remained in critical condition. News of the incident traveled fast, and New York cafés buzzed with talk about the famous author-matador's plight.

At Sardi's restaurant, actress Eva Gabor saw British playwright Noël Coward and blurted, "Noël dahling, have you heard the news about poor Bahnaby? He vass terribly gored in Spain!"

"He was *what*?"

"He vass gored!"

Noël sighed. "Thank heavens—I thought you said bored."

When the exchange (recorded by columnist Leonard Lyons)

made its way to Spain, Conrad thought it would make a splendid epitaph: "Gored but never bored."

He eventually recovered, retired from bullfighting, and returned to the US, where he resumed drawing, painting, and writing. In 1969 he published a memoir, *Fun While It Lasted*, about his adventures bullfighting in Mexico, Peru, and Spain. He then founded the Santa Barbara Writers Conference and began teaching creative writing, and in 1990 he published *The Complete Guide to Writing Fiction*. Four years after that he published a book with stories he had collected from running his nightclub, El Matador, titled *Name Dropping: Tales from My Barbary Coast Saloon*. He would eventually write eleven nonfiction books and seven novels.

His artwork was equally compelling. Two of Conrad's charcoal drawings, of Truman Capote and James Michener, hang in the National Portrait Gallery (part of the Smithsonian Institution) in Washington, DC.

On February 12, 2013, Conrad died at his home in Carpinteria, California. He was ninety years old.

ROBERT DUNEV

Robert Dunev, Aline's colleague in the Madrid code room, went on from the OSS to the CIA. As the sole CIA agent in Manila, he established an office and information network from scratch.

In the fall of 1949 the CIA sent a senior officer—a major—to Manila to study the plan and assist in the new agency's creation. Soon thereafter, however, Washington notified Dunev that an associate of the major's had been identified as a double agent, thus compromising not only the major but Robert as well. The CIA recalled both to Washington and Dunev's employment with the agency was terminated.

Robert, his wife, Louise Marie (who went by the nickname "Ninus"), and their newborn son, Peter, moved back to Madrid in March 1950, where Robert took a job working for his father-in-law. The couple had another son, Michael, in 1952, and a daughter, Christine, the following year.

Robert moved on to posts with the Haute Couture Cooperative of Spain, Revlon, and Hilton, before becoming the marketing director for Sterling Drug, an international pharmaceutical company, in 1964. At this time the CIA Madrid office asked him to perform some jobs "on the side," which he did, and then continued on with small tasks while posted with Sterling in Lima, Peru, and then in Buenos Aires, Argentina. It was there in 1971 that he asked for full termination from the CIA so as not to jeopardize his career in marketing, and continued on with Sterling, taking up posts in São Paulo, Brazil; Kingston, Jamaica; and San Juan, Puerto Rico. Louise Marie died in 1981 and Robert retired. He married Ofelia González Tolezano the following year, and they relocated to Miami.

Robert Dunev died in 2006. His sons, Michael and Peter, kindly provided invaluable assistance about their father for this work, including access to their father's unpublished memoir, *A Spy Reminisces*.

GLORIA VON FÜRSTENBERG

Gloria's post-war activities really began when she disappeared from Madrid in 1944 and stayed at the Estoril Palacio Hotel, just west of Lisbon. Though she had told Portuguese officials she was "penniless," she managed to stay at the most luxurious hotel in Portugal for more than three months, from August 9 to November 20. The answer to how she could afford to stay in this hotel with her two children lies with the arrival of another guest, Egyptian Prince Ahmed Fakhry, grandson of King Faud I, who checked in to the hotel on August 25 and remained until September 1.

After the war, there was never any evidence that she had been a German spy or informant.

In 1946 Gloria married Prince Fakhry, her third husband, but the marriage would end in divorce in 1949. Two years later, on April 7, 1951, Gloria married Captain Thomas Loel Guinness, a British member of Parliament and heir to the Guinness beer fortune. Loel's wealth, which came largely from banking and real estate, was almost beyond measure, and the couple had residences in Paris, Normandy, New York City, Acapulco, and Manalapan, Florida. The Florida home, called the Gemini and located at 2000 Ocean Boulevard on a 15-acre compound on Palm Beach's peninsula, is a 62,000-square-foot mansion with thirty-three bedrooms, forty-seven bathrooms, a pool, spa, tennis court, botanical gardens, and a PGA-style four-bunker golf hole. With over 1,200 feet of shoreline on the Atlantic and Intracoastal Waterway, it is one of the most impressive homes in the United States. In 2016 the Gemini was put on the market for $195 million. It remains for sale as of this writing and is listed by Sotheby's with a price tag of $115 million.

From 1963 to 1971, Gloria was a contributing editor to *Harper's Bazaar*. Considered to be one of the most elegant women of all time, she was dressed by Balenciaga, Christian Dior, Chanel, Yves Saint Laurent, Givenchy, and Halston, and appeared in *Vogue*, *Harper's Bazaar*, and *Women's Wear Daily*. She appeared on Eleanor Lambert's International Best-Dressed list from 1959 through 1963 and was inducted into its Hall of Fame in 1964.

Gloria died of a heart attack in 1980 at the Guinness estate in Epalinges, Switzerland, just north of Lausanne. She was sixty-seven.

PRINCE MAX VON HOHENLOHE

In *The Spy Wore Red* and *The Spy Went Dancing*, Aline disguises Prince Max von Hohenlohe's identity, calling him "Prince Niki Lilienthal." In *The Spy Went Dancing*, she has him being murdered on a hunting trip in Toledo in 1945. In reality, Prince Max died of natural causes in 1968 in Marbella, the resort town developed by his son, Alfonso. As Prince Max had feared, the Hohenlohe-Langenburg family lost much, if not most, of its wealth in Germany and Czechoslovakia after the war. Alfonso restored much of it in 1955 by marrying the Austrian-Italian princess Ira zu Fürstenberg, a Fiat heiress, but they divorced five years later, in 1960. After that, Alfonso dated one of Aline's Hollywood friends, Ava Gardner, and then another star, Kim Novak, before marrying Austrian actress Jocelyn Lane in 1973.

Marbella's success, unfortunately, attracted unseemly residents—members of the Russian mafia and Arab arms dealers. Alfonso sold his shares in the Marbella Club in the 1990s and moved to Ronda, Spain, to commence a wine business, which became successful.

The family's palatial finca, El Quexigal, caught fire in 1956, and the house and many priceless paintings were destroyed. In 1979 the Hohenlohe family hired Sotheby's to sell the remaining paintings, with the proviso that the artwork remain in Spain. To assure that this request was honored, Spain's Ministry of Culture designated El Quexigal a historical-artistic monument. The collection was valued at over 100 million pesetas.

The family would later sell the Quexigal estate to Grupo Eulen, a Madrid-based company with operations around the world.

EDMUNDO LASSALLE

In *The Spy Went Dancing*, Aline has Edmundo dying in London in 1966. In a death made to appear as a suicide, she has him working for the CIA and being bumped off by the KGB. The real story is less dramatic and more disheartening. Edmundo did die in London, but on August 1, 1974, rather than in 1966. He never worked for the CIA, and did, in fact, commit suicide.

His was a life filled with promise, but with devastating ends. Edmundo had been chasing windmills of royalty and high society during the war, and he finally seemed to have arrived after marrying Princess Maria Agatha. Sadly, his dreams never materialized.

As noted in the text, he divorced his first wife, Emilie, in order to marry Maria Agatha, notwithstanding that he and Emilie had a young daughter, Pepita. Soon after his second marriage, he had a professional disappointment. He had traveled from Madrid to New York in the spring of 1947 to discuss his future with the Walt Disney Company, a two-week stay that was paid for by the company. But while Roy Disney had encouraging words, the company—apparently experiencing financial difficulties—decided not to continue his employment. So he and Agatha moved to Mexico City, but the marriage soured and they divorced four years later, in 1951.

Three years after that Edmundo would try again, this time marrying Nancy Norman, an heiress of Sears, Roebuck & Co. They lived on Fifth Avenue, overlooking Central Park, and Nancy and Edmundo had three children. But that marriage failed, too, and they divorced in 1966. He married again promptly thereafter, to Patricia Rinehart, who had two children of her own. Edmundo adopted them, and they had a child together as well. At this point Edmundo had seven children (including the two adopted) by three of his four wives.

Though he had a good job working for the International Fund for Monuments, it required constant travel. In 1971 his health, as well as his fourth marriage, began to unravel. He had a heart condition, he wrote to his daughter Pepita from Rabat, Morocco, adding that "doctors say my condition is serious and I have but a few years to live." He and Patricia divorced the following year, with a settlement that offered Edmundo a trust allowance valued at over $1 million, provided that he lived in London.

And so in 1974, in failing health and with a string of broken relationships, Edmundo took his own life at age fifty-nine.

WILLIAM LARIMER "LARRY" MELLON, JR.

As an heir to the Mellon banking and oil fortune, Larry Mellon did not need to work—but he did, and hard. After the war he owned and operated a cattle ranch near Rimrock, Arizona, but in 1947 he had a life-changing experience. He read about the life and work of Dr. Albert Schweitzer, the Alsatian medical missionary who had founded a hospital in Gabon, Africa, and decided to do the same. He wrote to Dr. Schweitzer and asked how he might go about it and Schweitzer responded with details about the medical training needed and how to set up a clinic.

At the age of thirty-seven, Mellon enrolled at Tulane University to pursue a medical degree, and his wife, Gwen, enrolled to become a laboratory technician. Seven years later, in 1954, Mellon received his degree. Now age forty-four, he decided to build and operate a mission in the Artibonite Valley of Haiti, a poor and disease-ridden area with a population of 150,000. The Albert Schweitzer Hospital opened two years later, in 1956. Mellon personally financed the building and equipment, which cost $2 million at the time.

While he worked on the medical staff, he also spearheaded community efforts to install wells, water systems, and roads. For the next thirty years, ministering to the people of Haiti became his life's work. In 1951 Mellon sent Aline more than ten million units of penicillin to distribute to the poor of Madrid.

On August 3, 1989, Larry Mellon died of cancer and Parkinson's disease at his home in Deschapelles, Haiti. He was seventy-nine.

PIERRE

The identity of Pierre remains a mystery. In *The Spy Wore Red*, Aline indicates that his real name was François Ferronière, code-named PIERRE, OSS agent number 333. But OSS records show no agent by that name, code name, or number, and only include names of The Farm trainees from two classes, neither of which was Aline's.

In her Author's Note at the beginning of the book, Aline admits she changed the names of some in her story, but the true identities of most of the players are easily identifiable through the OSS files at the National Archives and Records Administration. Aline's character John Derby, for example, code-named JUPITER, was in fact Frank T. Ryan, code-named ROYAL. Similarly, her character Jeff Walters was Robert Dunev, code-named WILLIAMS, and Prince Niki Lilienthal was Prince Max von Hohenlohe. She did not disguise Edmundo Lassalle's name, however, perhaps because by the time of her writing he had already died (although she changed his code name from PELOTA to TOP HAT).

But Aline's PIERRE was not assigned to the Madrid station, so without a cross-reference to his real name or code name, it's impossible to identify him among the OSS's more than fourteen hundred employees.

Aline writes in the note: "The man I call 'Pierre' has been disguised, I hope, as has been the man code-named Mozart. But there was a Pierre, and there was a Mozart."

The latter is readily identifiable. Mozart, whom Aline calls Phillip Harris, was really Madrid's station chief, Gregory Thomas, code-named ARGUS.

In Aline's Prologue and Epilogue she writes of running into Pierre in 1984, but again without revealing his true identity. A possible reason for the secrecy is that Aline's books reveal Pierre to be a traitor and serial murderer. I believe these murders to be fictional embellishments (see the Notes for details), and thus I have not included them in my work. While there's no way to know for sure, my guess is that Pierre—like Aline's John Derby, Phillip Harris, and Jeff Walters—really existed. If so, he would have trained with her at The Farm and quite likely have pursued her and visited her in Madrid. Was he a traitor, as Aline suggests? Any evidence to prove that has yet to be found.

GREGORY THOMAS

Immediately after the war, in 1945, Gregory Thomas returned to his prior employer, Chanel, and was named president of company's US division. He married in 1950 and would run Chanel for twenty-seven years, retiring in 1972. Without children, he and his wife moved to Masarkytown, a small village about sixteen miles inland from Florida's west coast.

He died at the Lakeland Regional Medical Center on October 9, 1990, at the age of eighty-two.

FRANK T. RYAN

Frank Ryan is one of the most fascinating characters I've come across in many years of World War II research. He was in charge of OSS's Iberian peninsula—Spain and Portugal, the two hotbeds of espionage—but always managed to stay behind the scenes. He was thorough in his work and left few trails. His OSS files are sparse, and he resigned almost immediately after the war in Europe ended, on May 31, 1945. It appears he knew that President Truman intended to disband the OSS, and he began his own venture.

What is most striking about Ryan is the level of confidence others placed in him. When perhaps the two most influential espionage bosses of World War II—William Donovan and William Stephenson—decided to form the British American Canadian Corporation (later World Commerce Corporation), neither wanted to run it. They could have chosen Whitney Shepardson, Donovan's number two, or Charles Hambro, SOE's chief. But instead they chose Ryan, someone several rungs down the food chain. And for good reason: Ryan was a consummate professional, dedicated, experienced, and well-versed in applying the need-to-know doctrine. His tours of Europe before and after the war revealed wisdom in seeking firsthand knowledge of the lay of the land.

Like Aline, he was also adept at acquiring and keeping contacts. There is little doubt that the financial involvement of the Mellon family in funding the World Commerce Corporation is due to the influence of Larry Mellon, one of Ryan's agents. And when former secretary of state Edward Stettinius retired from WCC's board of directors in 1950, Ryan replaced him with an even bigger gun, Alfred V. Du Pont.

What espionage Ryan conducted through World Commerce may never be known. Perhaps the company simply used Western intelligence—including contacts and information—that had been developed during the war to thwart the spread of communism throughout Europe. At the beginning of 1945 Ryan, Donovan, and Stephenson already understood that if no effort was made on the part of the West to assist in the economic redevelopment of Europe, Stalin would push his iron curtain farther and farther west.

Ryan's admiration of Aline was genuine, too, and he and Aline remained lifelong friends. In her 1990 release, *The Spy Went Danc-*

ing, she includes a photo of herself with him from 1966. From that point on we don't see much of Ryan.

True to fashion as one of World War II's greatest spymasters, Ryan simply faded away quietly into the background. Unlike the agents he ran—Thomas, Mellon, Lassalle, and Aline—his passing received no obituary in the *New York Times*.

As Frank T. Ryan would have wanted it.

ACKNOWLEDGMENTS

I owe a huge debt of gratitude to many who assisted in this work.

First, to my all-wise, all-seeing friend and beta-reader, Susannah Hurt. As she did with *Into the Lion's Mouth* and *CODE NAME: LISE*, Susannah provided stellar initial comments, my favorite of which was "This can be better." She was always right, of course, and you the reader are the beneficiary. To her, my heartfelt thanks.

I am also deeply grateful for the encouragement and assistance provided by the children and grandchildren of individuals in this story. I could not have provided the depth and details about Robert Dunev and the OSS Madrid coding room without access to Dunev's unpublished memoir, *The Spy Reminisces*, kindly provided by his sons, Michael and Peter (who also provided the excellent photos of Robert).

And once again I am indebted to Cristina Neves of the Arquivo Histórico Municipal de Cascais (Portugal) who, as she did with *Into the Lion's Mouth*, provided all of the Palacio Hotel registrations that you see in the book. She was also kind enough to check newspaper records on the dates that Aline was in Estoril in 1944, and provided the actual Casino Estoril theater schedule during that week.

Likewise, many thanks to Suzanne Zoumbaris at the National

Archives and Records Administration for her invaluable assistance with the OSS files during my marathon sessions there.

And to Peter Borland, Sean Delone, and everyone at Atria Books and Simon & Schuster for their endless efforts, especially Atria's art director, Jimmy Iacobelli, for this magnificent cover.

Finally to my agent, Keith Urbahn, who is simply the best in the business.

NOTES

Preface

xiii *all the way up*: Ernest Hemingway, *The Sun Also Rises*, 9.

xv *February 1944 . . . BUTCH*: Aline, Countess of Romanones, *The History of Pascualete*, 3, 8.

xv *John Derby . . . Phillip Harris . . . MOZART . . . TIGER*: Aline, Countess of Romanones, *The Spy Wore Red*, 16, 83, 87.

Prologue

1 *shutters . . . gun*: For details on this scene, see Chapter 8 and accompanying notes.

Chapter: Dying to Fight

3 *May 24, 1941 . . . The American . . . Frank Timothy Ryan*: See Ryan's Palacio registration in the main text, courtesy of Cascais Archives. See also Cristina Pacheco, ed., *Hotel Palácio, Estoril-Portugal: Boletins de Alojamento de Estrangeiros: Boletins Individuais, 1939–1944*, 164–65. This volume contains all Palacio registrations that survived the war (only two registrations during 1943 survived). Ryan's registration reveals that he checked in on May 24, but the hotel ledger does not indicate when he checked out. While he did not yet work for the OSS (which hadn't been created), his passport was issued from Washington.

3 *Estoril's Palacio*: For background on Estoril and the Palacio, see Larry Loftis, *Into the Lion's Mouth: The True Story of Dusko Popov—World*

War II Spy, Patriot, and the Real-Life Inspiration for James Bond, 35–36, 64, 80–85.

3 *many of its patrons were spies*: The Palacio now refers to its bar as the Spy Bar, and its drink menu includes images of the hotel registrations of Ian Fleming and Dusko Popov. On my visit to the Spy Bar, I was given one of these menus, the pertinent pages of which can be seen on my blog at LarryLoftis.com.

4 *Ian Fleming had checked in to*: A copy of Ian Fleming's Palacio registration on May 20, 1941, can be seen at Loftis, *Into the Lion's Mouth*, 81. Fleming's stay is also recorded in Pacheco, ed., *Hotel Palácio*, 176–77.

4 *German press attaché Hans Lazar*: Pacheco, ed., *Hotel Palácio*, 186–81.

4 *graduated from the college of Mount Saint Vincent*: Office of Strategic Services personnel card (OSS Form 1517e) for Aline Griffith, RG 226, Entry A1 224, OSS Personnel Files 1941–1945, Box 294, File "Griffith, Marie Aline," National Archives and Records Administration (NARA).

4 *Born May 22, 1920 . . . Pearl River School*: Ibid.

4 *Founded in 1870 . . . Julius Braunsdorf*: Orangetown Historical Museum and Archives, https://www.orangetownmuseum.com/pearl-river.

4 *Aetna Sewing Machine . . . Talbot C. Dexter . . . Dexter Folder Company*: Ibid. See also Romanones, *History of Pascualete*, 3–4; *Spy Wore Red*, 13; Aline, Countess of Romanones, *The End of an Epoch*, 83. In Aline's descriptions of Pearl River's founding, her details are slightly off, most likely because she is repeating what she had been told by her mother. In *The History of Pascualete*, Aline writes: "Pearl River began when my mother's father, Grandfather Dexter, decided to build his new factory there, some time at the end of the last century." In *The Spy Wore Red*, she writes: "My father, who managed a factory which manufactured folding machines for print plants (founded by my grandfather) . . ." And in *The End of an Epoch*: "The town had been started by my grandfather." As noted in the text, however, the town was founded by Julius Braunsdorf, and Aline's grandfather moved his operation into Braunsdorf's factory (rather than building his own).

4 *Her mother and father*: See E. W. Andrews's "Aline Marie Griffith" memo dated September 13, 1943, in Aline's OSS personnel file at RG 226, Entry A1 224, OSS Personnel Files 1941–1945, Box 294, NARA.

5 *Schumacher's . . . Rowan's . . . Sandford's*: Romanones, *History of Pascualete*, 3–4.

5 *First National Bank*: While Aline's *The History of Pascualete* mentions

"National Bank" (p. 4), her OSS file reveals that the bank's full name was First National Bank & Trust Co. See Aline's March 29, 1946, correspondence to R. C. Read at the Office of the Assistant Secretary of War in her OSS personnel file at RG 226, Entry A1 224, OSS Personnel Files 1941–1945, Box 294, NARA.

5 *Aline's father managed*: Romanones, *Spy Wore Red*, 13. See also *Aetna Sewing Machine* note above regarding the accurate history of this factory.

5 *Their house*: Romanones, *History of Pascualete*, 4.

5 *The Town of Friendly People*: Orangetown Historical Museum and Archives, https://www.orangetownmuseum.com/pearl-river.

6 *Catholic girls school*: Romanones, *History of Pascualete*, 5.

6 *Rockland State Hospital . . . Manny Rooney*: Aline's OSS personnel card, RG 226, Entry A1 224, OSS Personnel Files 1941–1945, Box 294, NARA.

6 *Dexter as a fighter pilot . . . Tommy*: Romanones, *Spy Wore Red*, 9–10; *History of Pascualete*, 5.

6 *Hattie Carnegie*: Aline's OSS personnel card, RG 226, Entry A1 224, OSS Personnel Files 1941–1945, Box 294, NARA. See also Romanones, *Spy Wore Red*, 8.

7 *August . . . Amy Porter . . . dinner party*: Aline, Countess of Romanones, "The OSS in Spain During World War II," *The Secrets War: The Office of Strategic Services in World War II*, 123; *Spy Wore Red*, 9–10; *History of Pascualete*, 6. In her article for *The Secrets War*, Aline places the date of the dinner in August. In *The Spy Wore Red*, however, she puts it in September, while in *The History of Pascualete*, she writes that it occurred in July. Given that the OSS requested a security check for her on September 13 (see Aline's OSS personnel card, *op. cit.*), the August date is most probable.

7 *John . . . Frank*: In all of her espionage books, Aline disguises Frank Ryan as "John Derby." Not until 1992, in her article for *The Secrets War*, does she reveal his true identity. She again uses his real name in her last book, *The End of an Epoch* (p. 45), published in 2015. In *The Spy Wore Red*, she refers to his brother as "Mike." Frank Ryan had three brothers, and "Mike" in Aline's story is in all likelihood Frank's brother John, founder of John J. Ryan & Sons, a company for which Aline would later work.

7 *blue eyes . . . thin lips . . . neck and jaw*: See photos of Frank Ryan in the

New York Times ("Flies to Europe Today for Business Survey," November 6, 1945), and Aline, Countess of Romanones, *The Spy Went Dancing*, photo section.

8 *Are you planning . . . Now why*: Romanones, *Spy Wore Red*, 11–12.

8 *Do you know . . . majored in French and minored in Spanish*: Ibid., 12. Interestingly, Aline's OSS personnel card indicates that she was fluent in Spanish, but had a "slight" or working knowledge of French. RG 226, Entry A1 224, OSS Personnel Files 1941–1945, Box 294, NARA.

8 *If you should happen to hear from a Mr. Tomlinson*: Romanes, *Spy Wore Red*, 12. In *The History of Pascualete* (p. 6), Aline states that she was given the next level of instruction via a letter from the War Department, which said that its representative would contact her. In all likelihood, the letter was a formal confirmation of Ryan's disclosure.

9 *inquiry of some sort*: In correspondence to Mrs. Marjory Hutcheson, E. Wyllys Andrews (OSS Washington) requested the background check for Aline on September 13, 1943. Aline Griffith personnel file, RG 226, Entry A1 224, OSS Personnel Files 1941–1945, Box 294, NARA. See also Romanones, *Spy Wore Red*, 13.

  OSS background checks were conducted by the FBI, and Robert Dunev (Aline's office mate in the Madrid code room) noted that it had inquired about him with his friends, neighbors, and former teachers. Robert Dunev, *The Spy Reminisces*, 6.

9 *This is Mr. Tomlinson . . . Would I work*: Romanones, *Spy Wore Red*, 13–14. See also *History of Pascualete*, 6.

9 *"the Biltmore Hotel lobby"*: The palatial Biltmore Hotel, now known simply as 335 Madison Avenue, opened in 1913. Situated adjacent to Grand Central Terminal, it was one of three hotels constructed as part of the Terminal City development (the other two being the Commodore—now the Hyatt Regency—and the Roosevelt).

10 *November 1*: By Aline's account, her meeting with Tomlinson was on September 30, 1943, and her meeting with Frank Ryan in Washington was on October 8. However, Aline's OSS personnel file indicates that her security clearance was not issued until October 6, two days before her all-important meeting. In addition, her file indicates that she did not enter The Farm until November 1. See "Marie Aline Griffith" undated memo indicating her security clearance date, as well as her time at The Farm (November 1–29, 1943), and correspondence from Robert Wauchope to Weston Howland on November 22, 1943, indicating

that Aline had finished her training. [Wauchope has her finishing at The Farm a week before the summary memo.] See also William Larimer Mellon, Jr.'s memo to Reginald C. Foster on October 26, 1943, indicating that Aline "has been entered at The Farm for November 1," RG 226, Entry A1 224, OSS Personnel Files 1941–1945, Box 294, NARA. Accordingly, Aline's date for the Ryan meeting appears to be about three weeks off.

10 *Tell your family... Go directly*: Romanones, *Spy Wore Red*, 14; *History of Pascualete*, 6. This clandestine procedure comports with the instructions given to Robert Dunev, Aline's office mate in the Madrid coding room. Dunev, *Spy Reminisces*, 7–8.

Chapter 2: The Farm

11 *résumé to Dr. James Hamilton*: Robert Huddleston, *Edmundo: From Chipas, Mexico to Park Avenue*, 17–18. Note that Huddleston is Edmundo's son-in-law; his wife, Pepita Lassalle Huddleston, is Edmundo's daughter.

11 *San Cristobal... National University... Columbia University... Berkeley*: Ibid., 1–5.

11 *Pan American Union... Division of Intellectual Cooperation*: Ibid., 5, 10–11.

11 *Higher Education in Argentina... The Araucanians*: Edmundo's "Argentina," included within *Higher Education in Latin America*, and "The Araucanians" were both published by the Pan American Union and can be found today on Amazon.

12 *fall of 1941, he was offered*: Huddleston, *Edmundo*, 14.

12 *Office of the Coordinator of Inter-American Affairs... Office for Inter-American Affairs*: President Franklin D. Roosevelt created the OCIAA by Executive Order 8840 on July 30, 1941, naming Nelson Rockefeller as its coordinator. The entire order can be seen in the archive collection of the University of California at Santa Barbara, or online at https://www.presidency.ucsb.edu/documents/executive-order-8840-establishing-the-office-coordinator-inter-american-affairs. On March 23, 1945, Roosevelt changed the name of the organization to Office for Inter-American Affairs (OIAA) by Executive Order 9532. For details of the history and activities of the OCIAA and the OIAA, see generally, Edwin D. Anthony, ed., *Records of the Office of Inter-American Affairs*.

12 *January 19, 1942*: Huddleston, *Edmundo*, 14.

12 *motion pictures propaganda*: Anthony, *Records of the Office of Inter-American Affairs*, 24–25.

13 My [OIAA] office: Correspondence from Edmundo to his wife, Emile, on August 27, 1943; Huddleston, *Edmundo*, 17.

13 *My (OIAA) office*: Ibid., 18.

13 *The references . . . October . . . Frank Ryan*: Ibid., 34. Edmundo didn't record meeting with Ryan that day, but since Ryan was the head of OSS's Iberian Desk (where Edmundo was ultimately assigned) and would have had to sign off on Edmundo's employment, it would be logical to assume that this is who he met with.

13 *November 1, 1943*: As mentioned in the note for Chapter 1, Aline's recollection of the date of her meeting with Frank Ryan (October 8, and from there directly to The Farm) appears to be inaccurate as her OSS personnel file indicates that her security clearance was not issued until October 6. In addition, she did not enter The Farm on October 8 as two entries in her file state that she arrived there on November 1. RG 226, Entry A1 224, OSS Personnel Files 1941–1945, Box 294, NARA.

13 *Q Building*: Romanones, *Spy Wore Red*, 14, 16 (noting that the building was single-story and prefabricated); Dunev, *Spy Reminisces*, 6 (noting that the building was two-story and "temporary"). By 1943 the OSS occupied four large buildings at 2430 E Street, NW, Washington, DC, and the Q Building was apparently adjacent to this quad.

13 *walls . . . filing cabinets . . . Ryan*: Romanones, *Spy Wore Red*, 16; *History of Pascualete*, 7. In both accounts Aline hides the identity of Frank Ryan, referring to him as "John Derby" in *The Spy Wore Red*, and as "the man I had met at the dinner party in New York" in *The History of Pascualete*. She later identifies him in her 1992 article, "The OSS in Spain" (p. 127), and again in 2015 in *The End of an Epoch* (p. 45). Contrary to Aline's account in *The Spy Wore Red*, she did not receive the code name "TIGER," and would not have received her field code name here. She would later receive the code name "BUTCH" (see ensuing text and accompanying note), and her alias for training at The Farm would have been her own name, or a close variation (i.e., "Ally" from Aline, or "Mary" from Marie). Example aliases at The Farm include "Bobby" for Robert Dunev, "Barbara" for Barbara Cagiati, "Herman" for Henry Harjes, "Phil" for Philip Stearns, "Hub" for Boroslav Hruby, "Matt" for Andrew Mathews, "George" for George Bally, "Charley" for Rene Charpentier, "Vic" for Victor Cordovi, "Ed" for Edward Begliomini, "Ramon" for Romolo Al-

NOTES

cini, and "Roland" for Roland Papucci, NARA. In a few instances students were given aliases unrelated to their real names, such as "Frenchy" for Robert Spauer or "Hugo" for Mario Volpe. See Students for RTU-11, October 11, 1943, RG 226, Entry UD 161, Box 11, NARA.

13 *Your first trip . . . heart thumping*: Romanones, *Spy Wore Red*, 16.

13 *There is nothing*: Romanones, *History of Pascualete*, 7.

14 *folding his hands*: Romanones, *Spy Wore Red*, 16.

14 *The most I can do*: Romanones, *History of Pascualete*, 7.

14 *voice was low . . . From this minute on*: Romanones, *Spy Wore Red*, 17.

14 *yellow paper . . . Here are your instructions*: Romanones, *History of Pascualete*, 7.

14 *Hay Adams Hotel . . . license number TX16248*: Romanones, *Spy Wore Red*, 17; *History of Pascualete*, 7. Aline provides the instructions in both accounts, although the details differ slightly. In *The History of Pascualete*, the hotel is the "Hotel Adams," and the tag number is transposed: 24168 rather than 16248. The correct name of the hotel, which operates today, is the Hay Adams Hotel. The veracity of the clandestine procedure is verified by the virtually identical instructions given to Robert Dunev by Ryan's predecessor, Lieutenant Commander William Vanderbilt, a year earlier. In his memoir, Dunev writes (*Spy Reminisces*, 9):

He then told me to be at the East entrance of the Mayflower Hotel that afternoon, before five, that afternoon, and that when a black Ford, license plate #___arrived, I was to introduce myself to the driver as "Bobby." When I arrived at the Mayflower . . . I found three other civilians . . . awaiting the arrival of the same black Ford.

14 *Destroy it afterward*: Romanones, *Spy Wore Red*, 17.

15 *Stop! Stop! . . . thoughts of being kidnapped*: Ibid., 18.

15 *the driver constantly checked*: Dunev, *Spy Reminisces*, 9.

15 *Lothian Farm . . . RTU-11 . . . The Farm*: John Whiteclay Chambers II, "Office of Strategic Services Training During World War II," 3, 8. See also, John Whiteclay Chambers II, *OSS Training in the National Parks and and Service Abroad in World War II*, 59, 61, 63. For Aline's brief summary of her training here, see Romanones, "The OSS in Spain," 123. Her detailed account, perhaps embellished in places, is found at *The Spy Wore Red*, 19, *et seq.*

15 *gunfire*: Romanones, *Spy Wore Red*, 19.

16 *I'm Captain Williams*: Dunev, *Spy Reminisces*, 10. In *The Spy Wore Red* (p. 19), Aline uses an alias for this Army officer, referring to him as "Whiskey."

16 *Captain Williams seemed to know . . . Pierre*: Romanones, *Spy Wore Red*, 19. The OSS had seven training areas and two assessment stations, and often recruits would train at more than one area, thus meeting staff and other recruits. Aside from RTU-11, the training areas were Area A (advanced special and morale operations, and operational groups) in Prince William Forest Park, Virginia; Area B (basic special operations and advanced operational groups) in Catoctin Mountain Park, Maryland: Area C (communications) in Prince William Forest Park, Virginia: Area D (maritime and special operations) in Smith's Point, Maryland: Area E (basic secret intelligence, counter-intelligence, and morale operations) in Towson, Maryland: and Area F (basic operational groups and assessment) in the Congressional Country Club, Bethesda, Maryland. The assessment areas were Area S, in Country Estate Fairfax, Virginia, and Area W, in Townhouse, Washington, DC. See Chambers, "Office of Strategic Services Training," 3.

16 *suspended from the ceiling . . . life-size dummies*: Dunev, *Spy Reminisces*, 10. The photo of four of The Farm's life-size dummies is located at RG 226, Entry UD 161, Box 10, NARA.

17 *a sergeant*: Dunev, *Spy Reminisces*, 10. Dunev has a sergeant assisting Captain Williams, and it appears that Aline gave him the alias "Sphinx." His true identity may have been Mr. Melas, the Welfare Officer at The Farm. See "Schedule of Instructors-RTU-11, Class B-17, 11 Dec.–23 Dec. 1944," RG 226, Entry UD 161, Box 12, NARA.

17 *Why don't you*: Romanones, *Spy Wore Red*, 20.

17 *Wansborough and Beaulieu . . . proclivity to talk*: See Larry Loftis, *CODE NAME: LISE—The True Story of the Woman Who Became WWII's Most Highly Decorated Spy*, 16–20. See also M. R. D. Foot, *S.O.E.: The Special Operations Executive, 1940–46*, 79–86; M. R. D. Foot, *SOE in France*, 53, 55.

17 *from one of the beds*: Dunev, *Spy Reminisces*, 10.

17 *Not a word*: Romanones, *Spy Wore Red*, 21. Aline gives this roommate the code name "Magic," which was not the case; The Farm used first-name aliases, rather than code names. See note accompanying *walls . . . filing cabinets* on page 276.

17 *Someone would be listening . . . dismissed*: Ibid., 12.

17 *the only women among*: Romanones, "The OSS in Spain," 123.

17 *How would she compete*: Romanones, *Spy Wore Red*, 24.

18 *You're probably wondering*: Romanones, *History of Pascualete*, 8. See also *Spy Wore Red*, 23. In *The History of Pascualete*, Aline has this meeting occurring immediately after arrival, in the officer's office; in *The Spy Wore Red*, she places it after dinner in the library.

18 *Operations and Intelligence*: Romanones, *Spy Wore Red*, 23. Aline's remembrance of the OSS sections is slightly confused (for example, referring to the MO division as Mobile Operations, rather than the correct title, Morale Operations), but she writes that it was after dinner at this meeting when the recruits were given an overview of OSS work and why they were being considered. For a complete chart of the OSS sections, see Lawrence H. McDonald, "The OSS and Its Records," *The Secrets War: The Office of Strategic Services in World War II*, 92.

18 *President Franklin D. Roosevelt had*: See McDonald, "The OSS and Its Records," 81.

18 *The course would last several weeks*: For most students, the course lasted three or four weeks. See Chambers, "Office of Strategic Services Training," 8 (indicating a four-week term). For Aline's coding room colleague, Robert Dunev, the course lasted three weeks; Dunev, *Spy Reminisces*, 14. Aline's OSS personnel file is a bit contradictory. On her summary personnel card, it shows: "School: 11/1/43–11/29/43." However, Robert Wauchope's correspondence to Weston Howland on November 22, 1943, indicates that Aline had finished her training and was expected to be sent to Spain. RG 226, Entry A1 224, OSS Personnel Files 1941–1945, Box 294, NARA. Note also that some students received additional training at other OSS facilities.

18 *For a few*: Romanones, *Spy Wore Red*, 24.

19 *Class began*: Robert Dunev remembered that classes began at 7:00 a.m. (*Spy Reminisces*, 12), while Aline recalled that classes began at 8:00 a.m. (*Spy Wore Red*, 25), but The Farm schedules for 1944 and 1945 reveal that they began at 8:30 a.m. and 8:00 a.m., respectively. See, e.g., class schedules for Class No. B-17 (commencing December 11, 1944) and Class No. B-28 (commencing May 14, 1945) at RG 226, Entry UD 161, Boxes 12 and 11, respectively, NARA.

19 *our friend . . . The first thing*: Romanones, *Spy Wore Red*, 26. OSS records at NARA contain only a list of Farm instructors during December 1944. At this time the officer conducting the Tuesday-morning security class was a Lieutenant Dickens. "Schedule of Instructors-RTU-11,

Class B-17, 11 Dec.–23 Dec. 1944," RG 226, Entry UD 161, Box 12, NARA. Since Aline attended The Farm more than a year earlier, however, the instructor may well have been a captain, as Aline remembered.

19 *French . . . German . . . Belgian . . . Eastern Europe*: Romanones, "The OSS in Spain," 123.

19 *We're here to save*: Romanones, *Spy Wore Red*, 26.

19 *next two hours . . . security . . . cover . . . cipher*: See the class schedules for Class No. B-17 (commencing December 11, 1944) and Class No. B-28 (commencing May 14, 1945) at RG 226, Entry UD 161, Boxes 12 and 11, respectively, NARA. See generally, Chambers, "Office of Strategic Services Training," 8. See also Romanones, "The OSS in Spain," 123.

19 *weapons training*: See the class schedules for Class No. B-17 (commencing December 11, 1944) and Class No. B-28 (commencing May 14, 1945) at RG 226, Entry UD 161, Boxes 12 and 11, respectively, NARA.

19 *.45 semi-automatic . . . hitting a tree . . . hand began to ache*: Romanones, *Spy Wore Red*, 40. See also Dunev, *Spy Reminisces*, 13.

20 *training film . . . mapping . . . fighting knife:* See the class schedule for Class No. B-17 (commencing December 11, 1944) at RG 226, Entry UD 161, Boxes 12 and 11, respectively, NARA.

20 *instructor, Major William Fairbairn*: See "Schedule of Instructors-RTU-11, Class B-17, 11 Dec.–23 Dec. 1944," RG 226, Entry UD 161, Box 12 and the class schedule for Class No. B-17 (commencing December 11, 1944) at RG 226, Entry UD 161, Boxes 12 and 11, respectively, NARA.

20 *thirty years . . . Shanghai Municipal Police*: W. E. Fairbairn, *Get Tough! How to Win in Hand-to-Hand Fighting, as Taught to the British Commandos, and U.S. Armed Forces*, v, back cover. See also correspondence from K. J. McEuen, Shanghai Police Commissioner, March 4, 1925, in the introduction to W. E. Fairbairn's *Defendu: Scientific Self-Defense*.

20 *trained all US Marines*: Fairbairn, *Get Tough!*, v.

20 *newspaper into a dagger*: Romanones, "The OSS in Spain," 123.

20 *Day Two . . . recruit . . . handle . . . close combat*: See the class schedules for Class No. B-17 (commencing December 11, 1944) and Class No. B-28 (commencing May 14, 1945) at RG 226, Entry UD 161, Boxes 12 and 11, respectively, NARA.

21 *Dangerous Dan . . . The Shanghai Buster . . . six hundred fights . . . black belt . . . Defendu:* George Langelaan, *Knights of the Floating Silk*, 65–74; Tank Todd and James Webb, *Military Combat Masters of the 20th*

Century, 58; Loftis, *Into the Lion's Mouth,* 161–65; I. C. B. Dear and M. R. D. Foot, eds., *Oxford Companion to World War II,* 1019; Denis Rigden, *How to Be a Spy: The World War II SOE Training Manual,* 15–17; Fairbairn, *Defendu.*

21 *.45. . . . .30-caliber carbine . . . Thompson submachine gun*: See the "Master Outline of Two Weeks Basic O.S.S. Course at RTU-11, December 29, 1944" at RG 226, Entry UD 161, Box 12, NARA.

21 *recreation*: See the class schedules for Class No. B-17 (commencing December 11, 1944) and Class No. B-28 (commencing May 14, 1945) at RG 226, Entry UD 161, Boxes 12 and 11, respectively, NARA.

21 *jumped stone walls . . . Come on*: Romanones, *Spy Wore Red,* 29.

21 *second week . . . close combat . . . weapons . . . lockpicking*: Ibid.

21 *George . . . gangling man*: Ibid., 28.

21 *Lieutenant Compton Crook*: See "Schedule of Instructors-RTU-11, Class B-17, 11 Dec.–23 Dec. 1944," RG 226, Entry UD 161, Box 12; see also Compton Crook's March 13, 1945, correspondence to H. B. Cannon, RG 226, Entry UD 161, Box 11, NARA.

21 *Before you get your hands*: Romanones, *Spy Wore Red,* 28.

22 *Intelligence classes . . . slides of faces . . . maps*: Ibid., 34.

22 *close combat practice . . . sensual*: Ibid., 33–34.

Chapter 3: Close Encounters

23 *November 13*: November 13, 1943, was the day that Aline signed her OSS Oath of Office, and it was most likely signed and notarized while she was in Washington visiting Ryan to hear about her post in Madrid. These two events would have coincided with her completion of the first two weeks of training at The Farm, which covered the RTU-11 Basic Course outline. See "Master Outline of Two Weeks Basic O.S.S. Course at RTU-11" at RG 226, Entry UD 161, Box 12, NARA.

23 *push-ups . . . sit-ups . . . jujitsu . . . .45*: Romanones, *Spy Wore Red,* 40.

23 *You have a meeting, Royal*: Ibid. In addition to disguising Frank Ryan's real name (calling him "John Derby"), Aline also changed his code name from ROYAL to JUPITER. Where she does so, as here, I have used the correct name, ROYAL. Ryan's four OSS files are listed under ROYAL and can be found at RG 226, Entry 139, Box 81, Stack 190, Row 8, Compartment 6, Shelf 6, and RG 226, Entry 127, Box 19, Stack 190, Row 7, Compartment 20, Shelf 7, NARA. Documents containing his code name include: correspondence with agent 527 on May 24 and

June 16, 1943; letter to Colonel Rehm on August 2, 1943; and memo from E. M. Lucas to F. G. Dyas on June 21, 1943.

23 *Well, Butch*: Romanones, *Spy Wore Red*, 41 (replacing Tiger with Butch). Aline places the date when she first acquired a code name before she even enters The Farm, but this wasn't the case; at The Farm she would have been given a normal first-name alias. Her acquisition of a field code name—BUTCH—appears to have occurred in this meeting with Ryan when he disclosed her assignment to Spain.

23 *her new code name*: Aline has five files in the OSS records at the National Archives and Records Administration (NARA), one under her real name for the personnel file, and four under her code name, BUTCH. The personnel file is located at RG 226, Entry A1 224, OSS Personnel Files 1941–1945, Box 294, Stack 230, Row 86, Compartment 26, Shelf 3 (File "Griffith, Marie Aline"). The BUTCH files are located at RG 226, Entry 127, Box 22, Stack 190, Row 7, Compartment 20, Shelf 7 (three files under "BUTCH") and at RG 226, Entry 197A, Box 76, Stack 190, Row 38, Compartment 24, Shelf 5 (filed under "BUTCH [Agent]").

While Aline discloses her true code name in *The History of Pascualete* (p. 8), published in 1963, she changes it to TIGER in her three espionage books: *The Spy Wore Red* (1987) (p. 16), *The Spy Went Dancing* (1990) (p. 24), and *The Spy Wore Silk* (1991) (p. 33). The change, not surprisingly, came from her publisher. Sam Vaughan, Aline's editor at Random House, stated that her submitted title for *The Spy Wore Red* was *CODE NAME: BUTCH*. Since the name Butch "had other implications," Random House felt a change was in order (quoted in Barbara Kantrowitz, "Cloak and Daggers," *Newsweek*, March 24, 1991). Ironically, since my 2019 release about female spy Odette Sansom is entitled *CODE NAME: LISE*, my book proposal for *The Princess Spy* carried the proposed title *CODE NAME: BUTCH*. Without knowing anything about Aline's story with Random House, my literary agent said, "Um, no. That name conveys . . . um . . . You'll need a different title."

In the *Newsweek* article, Aline states that she had multiple code names—Butch, Tiger, and Sugarlump, among others—but the only name appearing in her OSS files is BUTCH. In all likelihood, Aline borrowed the code name TIGER from the OSS cipher clerk with that code name who briefly worked in the Madrid office. See the January 17, 1944, Madrid station memo stating: "Attached are expenses incurred by 'TIGER.' Are not to be charged to his personal account but are to be absorbed by Madrid acct. Authority—Argus." RG 226, Entry 197A, Box 76, NARA. Aline's code-room colleague Robert Dunev writes in his memoir that this agent, TIGER, was subsequently deported from Spain after being caught trying to acquire pesetas (for the OSS Madrid office, which was running low on local currency) on the black market. Dunev, *A Spy Reminisces*, 50.

In *The History of Pascualete* (p. 8) and *The Spy Wore Red* (p. 16), Aline also states that her agent code number was 527. This is inaccurate, as agent 527 was the chief of the Barcelona station. See the diagram of Spain personnel as of April 11, 1944, at RG 226, Entry 139, Box 81, NARA. Note also that Frank Ryan sent a detailed letter to agent 527 on May 24, 1943, months before he had even met Aline. RG 226, Entry 224, Box 669, NARA. Unfortunately, none of the documents in Aline's files records her code number (all identifying her with only her real name or BUTCH).

23 *Then I have passed . . . On the surface . . . King Alfonso*: Romanones, *Spy Wore Red*, 42–43.

24 *"before sunset"*: Hugh Thomas, *The Spanish Civil War*, 32.

25 *Franco*: The most accurate assessment of Franco's political predicament and position is from a man who knew him fairly well, the US ambassador to Spain, Carlton J. H. Hayes, who published his memoir, *Wartime Mission in Spain, 1942–1945*, immediately after leaving his post in 1945. See generally, Stanley G. Payne, *Franco and Hitler: Spain, Germany, and World War II*, and Thomas, *Spanish Civil War*. Note in particular the role played by Conde de Romanones, Àlvaro Figueroa y Torres, Aline's future grandfather-in-law, who was three times the president of King Alfonso XIII's Council of Ministers, in *The Spanish Civil War* (p. 21).

25 *wolframite . . . tungsten*: For a review of the importance of wolframite, particularly to Portugal, see Loftis, *Into the Lion's Mouth*, 31, and Donald G. Stevens, "World War II Economic Warfare: The United States, Britain, and Portuguese Wolfram," 539–55.

25 *Spain is still*: Romanones, *Spy Wore Red*, 43.

25 *Admiral Canaris*: Ibid., 43–44. For a short synopsis of Canaris vis-à-vis Franco and Spain, see Paul Leverkuehn, *German Military Intelligence*, 129–32. For a full treatment of Admiral Canaris, see John H. Waller, *The Unseen War in Europe: Espionage and Conspiracy in the Sec-*

ond World War; William L. Shirer, *The Rise and Fall of the Third Reich*; and Anthony Cave Brown, *Bodyguard of Lies*.

26 *Oath of Office*: RG 226, Entry A1 224, OSS Personnel Files 1941–1945, Box 294, NARA.

27 *Edmundo Lassalle . . . Walt Disney Company . . . $4,600*: Huddleston, *Edmundo*, 35–36. The financial structure proved troublesome for Edmundo's entire time in Spain. As Disney's high-profile representative who would be actually performing real and valuable services for them, the company gave him a large ($5,000) expense account with which to entertain prospective clients. Notwithstanding Edmundo's corporate cover, however, the OSS blocked this and held him to the same $7 per diem that other OSS agents received. The OSS's PELOTA (Edmundo's code name) Special Accounts file is replete with memo after memo dealing with this issue. RG 223, Entry 197A, Box 78, NARA.

27 *disassemble and reassemble in the dark*: Romanones, *Spy Wore Red*, 47; Dunev, *Spy Reminisces*, 13.

27 *stand alongside targets . . . feel of being fired upon*: Dunev, *Spy Reminisces*, 13–14.

27 *Ready for a couple of . . . Your objective*: Romanones, *Spy Wore Red*, 37. As part of The Farm's final exams, students were sent on clandestine missions into nearby cities with a specific task, sometimes to place dummy explosives, sometimes to get a job without identification, sometimes to display lock-picking skills. See Robert Dunev's mission at the *Here's the number* note below.

28 *hitchhiked*: Ibid., 38.

29 *Here's the number . . . safe . . . C+*: Ibid., 39–40. Robert Dunev received a similar assignment. He was dropped off one morning at a Baltimore hotel with $200 and told to land a job at a local defense plant without any identification. He would be retrieved that evening, The Farm instructor said. Dunev, *Spy Reminisces*, 20–22.

29 *Would you like . . . What are you doing*: Romanones, *Spy Wore Red*, 45–46.

30 *I wanted to be alone . . . I can't*: Ibid., 46.

31 *dawn to midnight, November 1 to 21*: In *The Spy Wore Red* (p. 34) Aline mentions that her training went "twenty-one days straight," and her OSS file suggests that she was at The Farm from November 1 to 21, 1943. Her date of employment, which commenced her first day at The Farm, is recorded in her personnel card (OSS Form 1193), located at

RG 226, Entry Entry A1 224, OSS Personnel Files 1941–1945, Box 294, NARA. See also Robert Wauchope's correspondence to Weston Howland on November 22, 1943 (indicating that Aline had finished her training at The Farm), at the same NARA location. Her file is somewhat contradictory, however, as her summary of initial dates card (also at Box 294) indicates that she was at "School" (i.e., The Farm) from November 1 to November 29. While Aline might have returned to The Farm for a fourth week, Wauchope's letter suggests otherwise.

31 *same Chevy . . . I guess this is*: Romanones, *Spy Wore Red*, 54–55.

31 *cipher clerk*: In *The Spy Wore Red* (pp. 55–57) Aline states that she was being sent to Madrid as an agent to work on Operation Anvil (later Dragoon) and Operation Bullfight (an operation that does not appear in OSS records). This was not the case. As her OSS personnel card indicates, she was sent to Madrid as a cipher clerk. RG 226, Entry Entry A1 224, OSS Personnel Files 1941–1945, Box 294, NARA. That said, she *was* a member of OSS's Secret Intelligence group, and she *had* been trained in all aspects of espionage. Like all other Madrid staffers (other than secretaries), in addition to her day job, she would have been expected to be available to assist with any secret intelligence matters the office encountered. Robert Dunev, for example, had the exact same training as Aline, and was the station's senior cipher clerk, but was given secret intelligence assignments as well. Dunev's cover was so complete that SI gave him two identities. His main OSS cover was as an embassy clerk (where he would do his OSS coding). For this job he had a furnished apartment near the embassy on Miguel Angel Street. However, for special assignments he was also "Joaquin Goecoechea," a local Spaniard. For this identity he rented a one-room studio in a poor section of town. He kept a separate wardrobe at this apartment and slept there at least once a week. Dunev, *Spy Reminisces*, 31.

31 *station chief . . . senior coder . . . radio man . . . financial officer . . . Basque expert*: The Madrid station chief at the time was H. Gregory Thomas ("ARGUS"), and Robert Dunev ("WILLIAMS") was the coder. The financial officer (James MacMillan, "QUERES," or 857) and Basque expert (William Larimer Mellon Jr., "LEGION") would fly with Aline to Lisbon and Madrid, and the radio man, Robert Turpin ("KODAK," or 617), would arrive in March. As late as April 11, 1944, the Madrid office had added only five more staff members: three for Analysis and Procedure ("QUEEN," "TICK," and 706), one for coding

("OMAHA"), and one for the radio room ("PANCHO"). See the diagram of personnel at RG 226, Entry 139, Box 81, NARA.

31 *When I met you*: Romanones, *Spy Wore Red*, 55.

31 *one and a half years in Spain*: Aline's memory of what Ryan said, and Ryan's assertion about this time in Spain, is confirmed by archive records. Lisbon was the first stop on any trip from the US to Spain, and Palacio Estoril hotel records reveal that he checked in there on May 24, 1941. Pacheco, ed., *Hotel Palácio*, 164–65. In addition, in correspondence to Col. Lane Rehm on February 3, 1943, Ferdinand Meyer writes: "It is necessary for the Subject [Frank T. Ryan] to make a survey trip to Spain in connection with certain phases of our operation there. He expects to be away several months." RG 226, Entry 127, Box 19, NARA.

32 *Shepardson . . . Oxford . . . Harvard . . . aide to Edward House . . . secretary*: "Whitney Shepardson, 75, Dies; International Relations Expert," *New York Times*, June 1, 1966, 47.

32 *I hope you will . . . You'll have plenty*: Romanones, *Spy Wore Red*, 56. In Aline's dialogue here she states that Shepardson gave her an important mission he called "Operation Bullfight" (p. 57). This scenario is highly unlikely since Aline's role at the time of her departure for Spain was simply that of code clerk. See W. L. Mellon's October 26, 1943, letter to Reginald C. Foster, wherein he states: "Miss Griffith has been entered at The Farm for November 1, 1943 to receive basic training with special emphasis on cipher. She is one of three girls whom we intend to send to Madrid as code clerks, in response to urgent requests from our office there." RG 226, Entry A1 224, OSS Personnel Files 1941–1945, Box 294, NARA. In addition, "Operation Bullfight" does not appear in OSS archives or in historical military sources. Accordingly, I have not included that portion of Aline's story.

33 *Your cover will be . . . American Oil Mission*: Romanones, *Spy Wore Red*, 58. See also "The OSS in Spain," 122, and *The End of an Epoch*, 29. Robert Dunev identified it as the "U.S. Petroleum Mission." Dunev, *Spy Reminisces*, 15. The proper name, as identified in OSS correspondence at the time, was the American Oil Control Commission. See correspondence from E. W. Andrews (OSS's SI office) to William A. Kimbel (State Department) on September 13, 1943, at RG 226, Entry A1 224, OSS Personnel Files 1941–1945, Box 294, NARA. For details on this correspondence, see the *American Oil Control Commission* note in Chapter 4.

For background on how the mission was founded and what it did, see Ambassador Carlton Hayes's memoir, *Wartime Mission in Spain, 1942–1945,* 80–82 (Hayes identifies it as the "American control commission").

33 *"many of our agents there"*: In April 1942 OSS Secret Intelligence sent its first two agents to Madrid and Lisbon, both operating as oil attachés in this State Department oil mission cover. They were to split their time equally, supervising oil sent to Spain and collecting information for SI. By October 1944, the OSS had sent fifty-two agents to these two stations under State Department cover, and twenty under private cover.

33 *Sunday, December 5*: In *The Spy Wore Red* Aline has her meeting with Pierre before her meeting with Shepardson (pp. 51–53). Given that she and Pierre would still have been at The Farm, such a meeting would have been extraordinarily difficult, especially since neither had a car. She mentions that her meeting with Shepardson was in early December (p. 56), in all likelihood either Thursday, December 2, or Friday, December 3. Aline mentions meeting Pierre on a Sunday (p. 51), so December 5 would be the most probable date of their rendezvous.

33 *Plaza Hotel . . . Carnegie suit . . . Stork Club*: Romanones, *Spy Wore Red,* 51–52.

34 *the Stork Club . . . 2,500 people*: Russell Whelan, "Inside the Stork Club," *American Mercury,* September 1944, 357–65.

34 *ring . . . I don't think*: Romanones, *Spy Wore Red,* 52–53.

Chapter 4: The Clerk

35 *overseas security check*: See Aline's OSS card with clearance dates, which states:

Overseas Security: requested 11/22/43 Issued 12/22/43
School: 11/1/43–11/29/43
Request for transportation: 1/10/44
Departed: 1/28/44

35 *American Oil Control Commission*: This was the correct name of the cover organization. See correspondence from E. W. Andrews to William A. Kimbel on September 13, 1943, stating: "It would be greatly appreciated if you could arrange with State Department to have Miss

Marie Aline Griffith appointed a clerk at the Madrid Embassy, attached to the Oil Control Commission.... [A]s she will work entirely for O.S.S., any part of her salary paid by the State Department should be charged to the fund held with them for that purpose. Mr. Walter Smith, the head of the Oil Control Commission, is aware of our need for added code clerks, and has expressed his entire approval." RG 226, Entry A1 224, OSS Personnel Files 1941–1945, Box 294, NARA.

35 *salary of $1,800 ... $1,000 ... $390 ... living allowance*: See Aline's salary and deductions cards, as well as the Madrid staff compensation ledger, contained in her personnel file at RG 226, Entry A1 224, OSS Personnel Files 1941–1945, Box 294, NARA.

35 *$2,400 ... Hattie Carnegie*: See Aline's "Personal History Statement" (Form SA-1) in her personnel file at RG 226, Entry A1 224, OSS Personnel Files 1941–1945, Box 294, NARA.

35 *January 10 ... transport*: See Aline's OSS card with clearance dates at RG 226, Entry A1 224, OSS Personnel Files 1941–1945, Box 294, NARA.

36 *Aline's transportation was so top secret*: This document (correspondence from Kenneth Mygatt to Frank T. Ryan, et al., January 25, 1944) is from Aline's personnel file at RG 226, Entry A1 224, OSS Personnel Files 1941–1945, Box 294, NARA.

36 *Biltmore ... snow*: Romanones, *Spy Wore Red*, 58.

36 *January 27*: Aline's recollection of dates and of her own age are highly confused. In her first book, *The History of Pascualete* (p. 3), she correctly records that she arrived in Spain in February 1944. In her second book, *The Spy Wore Red* (p. 58), she states that she left for Spain on Christmas Eve, 1943 (before the OSS had even requested her transport), and arrived in Madrid on December 31 (p. 69). In "The OSS in Spain" (p. 122), Aline writes that she began her service in Madrid in January 1944. In her final book, *The End of an Epoch* (p. 9), she again declares that she left for Spain in 1943 (p. 9), but later in the book (p. 187) she declares that she arrived in January 1944 and went to watch a flamenco star, Lola Fores, with Edmundo Lassalle on her first night there. Lassalle did not arrive in Madrid, however, until June 1944.

Equally perplexing is Aline's recollection of her age when leaving on assignment. In *The History of Pascualete*, she declares that she was "barely twenty-two." In *The End of an Epoch*, she states that she was "barely twenty-one." Aline was born on May 22, 1920, so she was almost twenty-four when she departed for assignment.

The date when Aline *actually* left for Spain is January 27, 1944. The date when she arrived in Madrid is February 10, 1944. See Exhibit A of April 11, 1946, memorandum from C. G. MacMillan to E. Caswell Jones:

> Entrance on Duty Date: November 1, 1943
> Departure for Post: January 27, 1944
> Arrival at Post Date: February 10, 1944
> Termination date: August 15, 1945

[Note that her card for summary dates has her leaving on January 28.] RG 226, Entry A1 224, OSS Personnel Files 1941–1945, Box 294, NARA. See also Aline's reimbursement file, at RG 226, Entry 197A, Box 76, Folder 431. The first entry ("BUTCH"), dated February 15, 1944, shows Aline's reimbursements for her travel to Madrid, including her per diem. The dates mirror the MacMillan memorandum noted above (i.e., departure from New York on January 27, 1943, passing through Lisbon, and arriving in Madrid on February 10, 1944).

As shown in the main text with her Estoril Palacio Hotel registration, Aline arrived in Lisbon on February 8, stayed two nights at the Palacio, and flew to Madrid on February 10.

36 *cooped up here on the fifteenth floor for two days*: Romanones, *Spy Wore Red*, 58; *End of an Epoch*, 9. Note that Aline confuses the length of time at the hotel: in *The Spy Wore Red*, she's at the Biltmore "three days and three nights," while in *The End of an Epoch*, she's there for two days, departing on the second night.

36 Yankee Clipper . . . *sleeping quarters . . . dining room . . . lounge . . . honeymoon suite*: Roy Allen, *The Pan Am Clipper: The History of America's Flying Boats, 1931 to 1946*, 90–93; James Trautman, *Pan American Clippers: The Golden Age of Flying*, 226–27.

37 *passengers never knew until the last minute*: Romanones, *Spy Wore Red*, 58; *End of an Epoch*, 9.

37 *a round-trip flight . . . $1,000*: Allen, *Pan Am Clipper*, 89.

37 *including station chief H. Gregory Thomas*: Romanones, "The OSS in Spain," 123–24.

37 *traveled by sea*: For example, Aline's partner in the coding room, Robert Dunev, traveled to Lisbon aboard Portugal's *Serpa Pinto* (Dunev, *Spy Reminisces*, 23), and her sidekick, Edmundo Lassalle, traveled aboard the Portuguese freighter, the SS *Thome* (Huddleston, *Edmundo*, 48).

37 *call . . . ten minutes . . . Two men*: Romanones, *End of an Epoch*, 9.

37 *James MacMillan and William Larimer Mellon Jr.*: Romanones, "The OSS in Spain," 124; *End of an Epoch*, 11. Most of Aline's reports in her BUTCH file are to "QUERES" (MacMillan), although one or two were prepared for "LEGION" (Mellon). The NARA QUERES files are located at RG 226, Entry 127, Box 19, and RG 226, Entry 197A, Box 76. The LEGION SI files are located at RG 226, Entry 127, Box 1, while his X-2 files are located at RG 226, Entry 127, Box 24.

37 *Marine Air Terminal at LaGuardia*: Aline mentions taking off from Long Island Sound ("The OSS in Spain," 123), but the specific location was Pan Am's marine terminal at LaGuardia airfield. See Trautman, *Pan American Clippers*, 134–35, 242, 260, 268.

37 *dark . . . pitch black . . . cold . . . military uniform*: Romanones, *End of an Epoch*, 9, *Spy Wore Red*, 59.

38 *28 feet high . . . 152 feet . . . 82,000 pounds*: Trautman, *Pan American Clippers*, 246; Allen, *Pan Am Clipper*, 109.

38 *We travel in luxury*: Romanones, *End of an Epoch*, 11.

38 *seventy-four passengers . . . sleepers for*: Trautman, *Pan American Clippers*, 246.

39 *chefs . . . Salmini . . . Candotti . . . Waldorf*: Allen, *Pan Am Clipper*, 90.

39 *white linen tablecloths . . . silver and china . . . napkin draped over his arm*: Trautman, *Pan American Clippers*, 226.

39 *shrimp cocktail . . . turtle soup . . . filet mignon . . . petit fours*: Allen, *Pan Am Clipper*, 90, Trautman, *Pan American Clippers*, 226.

39 Clipper's *bar . . . martini . . . manhattan . . . scotch*: Pan Am Clipper Bar Menu, 1951.

39 *Bermuda . . . waves were too large*: Romanones, *End of an Epoch*, 11. This delay resolves the issue of why the plane left on January 27, but the party didn't arrive in Lisbon until February 8. OSS records confirm the departure date, and Palacio records confirm the arrival date, but Aline's account in *The End of an Epoch* is the only source revealing the cause of the delay.

39 *pilot had invited her to watch*: Romanones, *History of Pascualete*, 8; *End of an Epoch*, 11.

41 *visit the casino . . . bronze-embossed mahogany doors*: Romanones, *End of an Epoch*, 12.

41 *Crystal chandeliers . . . red velvet drapes*: Ibid., 13 (Aline describing the curtains as "burgundy"). Photos of the crystal chandeliers can be seen in Estoril's archives housed at *Archivo Municipal de Cascais*, Portugal, and virtually every spy who wrote about visiting the casino mentioned the chandeliers and red velvet curtains. See, e.g., Desmond Bristow, *A Game of Moles: The Deceptions of an MI6 Officer*, 151.

42 *clatter of chips and whir of roulette wheels*: Romanones, *End of an Epoch*, 13.

43 *Aline, watch those*: Ibid. In the next line after this dialogue, Aline quotes MacMillan as saying that Japanese agents were in the casino, picking up messages, "including dates and hours transmitted by the numbers played at the roulette table—right under our noses." In all probability, she borrowed this from Dusko Popov, the British double agent who in 1974 had revealed this very method used by the German Abwehr to provide him with a place and time for one of his meetings in 1941. See Dusko Popov, *Spy Counter-Spy*, 91; Loftis, *Into the Lion's Mouth*, 49. That the Japanese would be using the precise communication system used by the Germans three years earlier is unlikely. Accordingly, I have omitted this part of Aline's quote.

43 *baccarat*: Aline recalled that the game was *chemin de fer* (*Spy Wore Red*, 63; *End of an Epoch*, 13), a European version of baccarat where the players have an option to "stand" with their cards or take a "hit" (another card), but Dusko Popov, who played the game at this casino in 1941, described it as baccarat. Popov, *Spy Counter-Spy*, 151.

43 *Gamblers are superstitious*: Romanones, *Spy Wore Red*, 63; *End of an Epoch*, 13.

43 *Errol Flynn . . . The Sea Hawk*: Casino Estoril Cinema program, February 7–13, 1944 (courtesy of Cascais Archive).

43 *quite a first day*: According to Aline, much more happened that night, but at least half, and perhaps all, of what she declared was untrue. In *The Spy Wore Red* (pp. 64–65) and *The End of an Epoch* (p. 15), she writes that Mellon pointed out that on the dance floor was one of their fellow OSS agents, "TOP HAT." This agent's real code name was "PELOTA," and his real name was Edmundo Lassalle. Lassalle was, in fact, the agent with whom Aline would work in Madrid. However, Lassalle could not possibly have been in Lisbon in February 1944

because he was still in the US; Edmundo did not even sail for Europe until May 13, 1944, when he left from Philadelphia aboard the SS *Thome*. When Edmundo arrived in Lisbon on May 30, he wrote to his wife, complaining that the conditions on the ship were "atrocious" (Huddleston, *Edmundo*, 48, 54).

Why Aline would fabricate Lassalle's presence that night is unclear, but it highlights what she claimed happened next. When Aline and Mellon were making their way out of the casino after dinner, she wrote in *The Spy Wore Red* (p. 65) and *The End of an Epoch* (p. 15), she witnessed a murder. She and Mellon heard a woman shriek, she claimed, and then she turned to see a man lying facedown with a knife protruding from his back.

This supposed murder has several problems. First, it is not mentioned in any OSS file. Since the man supposedly murdered was, according to Aline (*Spy Wore Red*, 101), an OSS informant, this would be highly unusual. Second, the murder does not appear in any Lisbon or Estoril newspaper reports on February 9 or 10, 1944. Third, and most important, the man whom Aline claims to have committed the murder was none other than Edmundo Lassalle (*Spy Wore Red*, 102), who was still in the US at the time.

Accordingly, I have omitted from the story Aline's embellishment of Lassalle's presence and the alleged murder.

43 *Aline, Mellon, and MacMillan checked out . . . flight to Madrid*: The Palacio registrations shown in the main text reveal that all three checked out on February 10, 1944. In her 1992 article "The OSS in Spain" (p. 124), Aline confirms that Mellon and MacMillan were with her on the flight to Madrid. Strangely, in her last book, *The End of an Epoch* (p. 19), she has the men remaining in Lisbon, contending that she flew to Madrid alone.

43 *Iberia*: Romanones, *Spy Wore Red*, 68; *End of an Epoch*, 19.

43 *fields of Castile . . . snow-capped Guadarrama . . . orange . . . brown . . . red, blue*: Aline covers this view from the plane in three of her books: *The History of Pascualete* (p. 3), *The Spy Wore Red* (p. 68), and *The End of an Epoch* (p. 19).

44 *apprehensive*: Ibid.

44 *I sensed a mystery*: Romanones, *End of an Epoch*, 19.

44 *Barajas Airport . . . swastika . . . Junkers*: Romanones, *Spy Wore Red*, 68; "The OSS in Spain," 124; *End of an Epoch*, 19–20.

44 *Ambassador Carlton Hayes*: See generally, Hayes, *Wartime Mission in Spain*. See also David Eccles, *By Safe Hand: The Letters of Sybil & David Eccles, 1939–42*. Eccles was Britain's principal economic adviser for the Iberian peninsula, and in his memoir, he assesses Franco's position and intentions, coming to the same conclusion as Ambassador Hayes. Eccles writes: "To what conclusion will the reader of this book have come about Franco's real intentions? In the twelve months following the collapse of France, when half of Europe thought we had no chance of winning, did Franco want to enter the war or stay out? . . . Whatever he may have said in public to please the Germans and their friends his instincts and his behavior during and after the war point to a deep preference for neutrality. . . . I had friends who were very close to Franco. Once or twice they said the pressures on him were so great that he might have to surrender to the war party but they never said that he wanted to join the Axis. Quite the contrary." *By Safe Hand*, 417.

45 *German operatives . . . Johann Jebsen . . . 520 agents*: Popov, *Spy Counter-Spy*, 103. See also David Kahn, *Hitler's Spies: German Military Intelligence in World War II*, 248.

45 *70 to 100 agents working at a secret*: Walter Schellenberg, *The Memoirs of Hitler's Spymaster*, 133.

45 *full lists . . . Jebsen . . . Kenneth Benton . . . each member of the British staff*: Kenneth Benton, "The ISOS Years: Madrid 1941–3," 395, *et seq*. See also Schellenberg, *Memoirs of Hitler's Spymaster*, 133. Jebsen's meeting with Benton is confirmed in MI5 files at KV 2/854 (p. 8) and KV 2/856 (p. 759B), UK National Archives.

45 *winter chill . . . wind, hat*: Romanones, *History of Pascualete*, 3; *Spy Wore Red*, 68; *End of an Epoch*, 19.

46 *dirt roads . . . children . . . cars . . . bicycles . . . donkey cart . . . Plaza de Toros*: Ibid.; Hayes, *Wartime Mission in Spain*, 22; Romanones, *Spy Wore Red*, 68–69.

46 *Palace Hotel*: Aline records her stay at the Palace with some detail in *The Spy Wore Red* (pp. 69–70) and *The End of an Epoch* (p. 21). Unfortunately, her imagination seemed to be her guide. In *The Spy Wore Red*, she arrives at the hotel at 4:40 p.m., December 31, 1943. In *The End of an Epoch*, she arrives precisely at 11:00 a.m. in January 1944. In reality, Aline arrived at the Palace Hotel on February 10, 1944. See Exhibit A of April 11, 1946, memorandum from C. G. MacMillan to E. Caswell Jones indicating "Arrival at Post Date: February 10, 1944." RG 226,

NOTES

Entry A1 224, OSS Personnel Files 1941–1945, Box 294, NARA. See also Aline's departure from Lisbon on February 10 in the Palacio Hotel registration in the main text.

In both accounts, Aline writes that she was met in the Palace lobby—per Washington instructions—by Edmundo Lassalle (whom she gave the code name "TOP HAT"). Such a meeting was impossible, of course, since Lassalle was still in the US and would not arrive in Madrid until June 1.

47 *young man . . . perfect English . . . tall, handsome, and well-dressed*: Romanones, *Spy Wore Red*, 69–70; *End of an Epoch*, 21–23.

47 *a German agent*: Romanones, *End of an Epoch*, 22.

47 *Teatro de la Zarzuela . . . Lola Flores . . . La Niña de Fuego*: Romanones, *Spy Wore Red*, 74–75; *End of an Epoch*, 187. Who Aline had dinner with and attended the theater with is a mystery. She writes in *The Spy Wore Red* and *The End of an Epoch* that Edmundo Lassalle was her date, but he would not arrive in Madrid until June. Logic would suggest that she went with either Larry Mellon (with whom she had visited Casino Estoril) or James MacMillan, both of whom had joined her on the flight to Madrid. In *The Spy Wore Red* Aline places the date of this night as New Year's Eve, 1943, and in *The End of an Epoch* she puts it as January 1944. The correct date is February, however, since Aline arrived in Madrid on February 10, 1944.

48 *Flamenco was invented*: Romanones, *End of an Epoch*, 189.

48 *El Gallo . . . Cagancho*: Barnaby Conrad, *La Fiesta Brava: The Art of the Bull Ring*, 159; Ernest Hemingway, *Death in the Afternoon*, 212–14, 216. Their real names were Rafael El Gallo and Joaquin Rodriguez, respectively.

48 *Gitanillo de Triana*: Romanones, *End of an Epoch*, 190; Barnaby Conrad, *Matador*, 237.

48 *the secret of flamenco's . . . flamenco dancers to entertain groups*: Romanones, *End of an Epoch*, 188.

48 *Who is it . . . El mozo de espadas*: Romanones, *Spy Wore Red*, 77; *End of an Epoch*, 34.

Chapter 5: Man of Swords

49 *Three Spaniards . . . carnations . . . Señorita Griffith*: Romanones, *Spy Wore Red*, 77; *End of an Epoch*, 34.

49 *If you please*: Ibid.

49 *I may be the greatest*: Conrad, *La Fiesta Brava*, 129.

49 *In 1919 he appeared in 109 corridas*: Ibid., 25.

49 *He was a genius . . . The way Belmonte*: Hemingway, *Death in the Afternoon*, 68–69.

49 *The señorita must . . . The* traje de luces: Romanones, *Spy Wore Red*, 77–78; *End of an Epoch*, 35.

51 *Calle Alcalá Galiano, No. 4*: Romanones, *Spy Wore Red*, 78; "The OSS in Spain," 124; *End of an Epoch*, 31. See also Dunev, *Spy Reminisces*, 27.

51 *Why does such a pretty girl*: Romanones, *Spy Wore Red*, 78.

51 *three-story . . . relatively new*: Dunev, *Spy Reminisces*, 27.

51 *Plaza Santa Ana . . . Señorita Griffith . . . When would you like*: Romanones, *Spy Wore Red*, 79; *End of an Epoch*, 34.

54 *Bugatti Royale . . . roadster . . . type 41*: Romanones, *Spy Went Dancing*, 49; *Spy Wore Red*, 80.

54 *matadors made between $2,000 and $7,500*: Walter Smith, who headed the Oil Control Commission, expressed in 1952 that a matador's fee at the time was $2,000 to $10,000 per afternoon, and that a season was one hundred performances. Walter Smith, *Glimpses of Spain*, 50. Given that the year is 1944, I have adjusted the fee downward.

54 *Manolete . . . $30 million*: In 1950 American matador Barnaby Conrad wrote that in Manolete's eight years as as senior matador, he had made approximately $4 million. Conrad, *La Fiesta Brava*, 3. But that was between 1939 and 1947; adjusted for inflation to today's dollars, Manolete had made some $56 million. By 1944, he would have cleared at least $30 million.

54 *Calle Peligros . . . La Mahonesa*: Romanones, *Spy Wore Red*, 80.

54 *Señorita, it is an honor*: Ibid.

55 *separate buildings . . . July 5, 1944 . . . Gregory Thomas and Ambassador Carlton Hayes*: The lease between Thomas, representing the OSS, and Hayes, representing the State Department, is found at RG 226, Entry 197A, Box 76, NARA. Since Thomas was a lawyer, it is likely that he drafted the agreement.

55 *Walter Smith . . . July 1941 . . . early 1942 . . . U.S. and Spain reached an agreement*: Hayes, *Wartime Mission in Spain*, 80–81.

56 *Miss Griffith . . . gigantic, angular physique*: Romanones, *Spy Wore Red*, 83.

56 *Thomas . . . Cambridge . . . Paris . . . Salamanca . . . Spain and Portugal*: OSS internal memo dated July 21, 1943, included in the file: "OSS Ac-

tivities in Italy; Hitler's Correspondence with Mussolini; Plans for the Invasion," https://www.cia.gov/library/readingroom/docs/CIA-RDP 13X00001R000100160005–2.pdf.

56 *station chief . . . ARGUS*: Gregory Thomas's OSS files, listed under "ARGUS," are all located in Record Group 226 of the NARA. His Madrid SI files are located at Entry 211, Box 12; Entry 210, Box 303; and Entry 127, Boxes 23 and 24. His Madrid X-2 files are located at Entry 127, Box 24. His Madrid OSS files are located at Entry 168, Box 34 and Entry 127, Box 13. His Lisbon SI files are located at Entry 148, Box 68. His Bern file is located at Entry 210, Box 542. His London file is located at Entry 190, Box 262. His Washington files (which include general OSS, SI, X-2, Spain, and a Lisbon/Barcelona file) are located at Entry 196, Box 83; Entry 210, Boxes 72, 91, 303, 313, 465, 515, and 526; and Entry 214, Box 2.

57 *We've barely twelve*: Romanones, *Spy Wore Red*, 84.

57 *MacMillan . . . QUERES*: James H. MacMillan's Madrid SI files, listed under "QUERES," are located at RG 226, Entry 127, Box 19, NARA. He has another file pertaining to finances at RG 226, Entry 197A, Box 76. For confirmation of his role as finance officer and deputy chief, see, e.g., MacMillan's correspondence to Douglas Dimond (OSS chief of Special Funds) dated December 19, 1945, in this file.

57 *her immediate supervisor*: The vast majority of Aline's OSS reports are addressed to QUERES.

57 *Larry Mellon . . . LEGION*: William Larimer Mellon Jr.'s Madrid files, listed under "LEGION," are located at RG 226, Entry 127, NARA. Within that entry, his OSS-designated files are located in Box 1, while his X-2 files are in Box 24. He also has a Paris X-2 file located at Entry 190B, Box 17.

57 *an administrator*: Margaret Kasley, code named KATHY, to whom Aline directed one or two reports, has only one NARA file, located in the financial reports section at RG 226, Entry 197A, Box 76.

57 *Robert Turpin . . . KODAK*: Robert G. Turpin's Madrid SI files, listed under "KODAK," are located at RG 226, Entry 139, Box 81, NARA. His Madrid financial records are located at Entry 197A, Box 76. He also has two Washington files, listed under his last name, located at Entry 190, Box 710 and Entry 92A, Box 23.

57 *would arrive next month*: Turpin arrived in Madrid on March 16, 1944, according to his hotel records in Lisbon (he checked in to the Estoril

Atlantico, next door to the Palacio, on March 10, 1944, and departed on March 16). Cristina Pacheco, ed., *Grande Hotel e Hotel Atlântico, Boletins de Alojamento de Estrangeiros: Boletins Individuais, 1939–1944,* 270–71.

57 *Robert Dunev . . . WILLIAMS*: Robert Dunev's Madrid files, listed under "WILLIAMS," are located at RG 226, Entry 127, Box 19, and at Entry 197A, Box 76, NARA.

57 *Business hours . . . siesta . . . flamenco*: See Hayes, *Wartime Mission in Spain,* 41; Walter Smith, *Glimpses of Spain,* 190; Dunev, *Spy Reminisces,* 37.

58 *Nobody goes to bed*: Hemingway, *Death in the Afternoon,* 48.

58 *Dunev . . . second identity*: Dunev, *Spy Reminisces,* 31.

58 *Heinrich Himmler . . . had a top agent*: Romanones, *Spy Wore Red,* 84.

58 *four suspects . . . Suñer . . . Hohenlohe . . . Furstenberg . . . Lazar*: Ibid., 85.

58 *Ramón Serrano-Suñer . . . head of the Falange . . . interior . . . foreign minister . . . September 1942*: Hayes, *Wartime Mission in Spain,* 25, 57–58; Winston Churchill, *The Second World War,* vol. 2, *Their Finest Hour,* 522, 528; Payne, *Franco and Hitler,* 15, 81–82, 87–88, 135–48.

58 *Prince Maximilian Egon von Hohenlohe*: Aline disguises the identity of Prince Max, referring to him as "Prince Nikolaus Lilienthal." Prince Max's file in OSS's X-2 section is located at RG 226, Entry 119A, Box 55, NARA.

59 *Himmler and Hermann Göring . . . services to the Gestapo*: Romanones, *Spy Wore Red,* 85.

59 *confidant . . . Schellenberg*: Ibid., p. 3.

59 *1939 Max*: Klemens von Klemperer, *German Resistance Against Hitler: The Search for Allies Abroad, 1938–1945,* 92.

59 *fourth week of October 1939*: John Costello, *Ten Days to Destiny,* 59; Waller, *Unseen War in Europe,* 111–12, 165.

59 *mid-July 1940 . . . Sir David Kelly . . . Bern*: Costello, *Ten Days to Destiny,* 345; Waller, *Unseen War in Europe,* 165.

59 *prepared to accept*: Costello, *Ten Days to Destiny,* 345; Waller, *Unseen War in Europe,* 165.

59 *March 1941 . . . Sir Samuel Hoare*: Costello, *Ten Days to Destiny,* 456; Peter Padfield, *Hess: Flight for the Führer,* 166.

60 *1943 . . . Max had met Dulles . . . Long Island . . . secret meeting*: Leonard Mosley, *Dulles: A Biography of Eleanor, Allen, and John Foster and Their Family Network,* 144–45.

60 *The talks continued for three months*: James Srodes, *Allen Dulles: Master of Spies*, 261. The conversations between Prince Max and Dulles were recorded in various German memos discovered by the Russians after the war. The discussions have been labeled the "Bull-Pauls" discussions because Dulles is referred to as "Mr. Bull," and Prince Max is referred to as "Herr Pauls." The extent to which the Russians redacted the documents is a matter of debate among World War II scholars.

60 *Gloria von Fürstenberg*: Gloria's file in OSS records, listed under "Fürstenberg," is an X-2 file located at RG 226, Entry 124, Box 14, Stack 190, Row 7, Compartment 17, Shelf 4, NARA.

60 *Mexican . . . thirty-one . . . Los Angeles . . . Clarence Brown . . . Paris . . . Frank Scholtens . . . von Fürstenberg . . . children*: See Gloria's X-2 card, with information collected by Portugal's PVDE (secret police), at RG 226, Entry 124, Box 14, NARA. See also OSS correspondence of October 13, 1944, from Charles Gray to Van Brink. Ibid.

61 *Dr. Hans Lazar*: Lazar's file in OSS records, listed under "Lazar," is an X-2 file located at RG 226, Entry 210, Box 350, Stack 250, Row 64, Compartment 21, Shelf 1, NARA.

61 *Transocean*: Jimmy Burns, *Papa Spy: Love, Faith, and Betrayal in Wartime Spain*, 354, citing "Los espias Nazis que salvo Franco," *El País*, January 26, 2003.

61 *monthly budget of 200,000 pesetas*: Payne, *Franco and Hitler*, 122.

61 *four hundred agents*: Burns, *Papa Spy*, 98.

Chapter 6: Snatch-22

62 *Life in the code room*: Dunev, *Spy Reminisces*, 56–57.

62 *German order-of-battle . . . Messages were always sent*: Ibid., 44–45.

64 *escape plan . . . 21,900 pesetas . . . roughly $2,000*: Ibid., 31.

64 *ran out of pesetas . . . July 3 . . . 827,000 . . . We hope to*: Correspondence from E. W. Andrews to Col. W. Lane Rehm dated July 7, 1944, RG 226, Entry A1 224, Box 17, NARA.

65 *Schoonmaker . . . TIGER . . . arrest . . . escape*: Dunev, *Spy Reminisces*, 49–53. Frank Schoonmaker's OSS file is located at RG 226, Entry A1 224, OSS Personnel Files 1941–1945, Box 687, NARA. Agent TIGER's files are located at RG 226, Entry 110, Box 3, Folder 27 and RG 226, Entry 190, Box 238, File 534, NARA.

65 *Ambassador Hayes . . . only such intelligence*: Kermit Roosevelt, *Overseas Targets*, 34.

66 *Edmundo Lassalle . . . Walt Disney Company . . . contract*: Huddleston, *Edmundo*, 39–43.

66 *Juanito . . . receptions . . . dinners . . . chocolates*: Romanones, *Spy Wore Red*, 104, 116.

67 *Johann Jebsen . . . Ablege Kommandos . . . killed a man*: Loftis, *Into the Lion's Mouth*, 193.

68 *April 30 . . . Jebsen disappeared . . . Lisbon . . . injected . . . Biarritz*: Ibid., 222–24, 227; Heinig Report, January 6, 1947, KV 2/3568 (6b), UK National Archives.

68 *Robert Dunev . . . Mercedes . . . Paseo de la Castellana . . . kidnapper*: Dunev, *Spy Reminisces*, 57.

Chapter 7: Death by Murder

70 *May 13 . . . SS Thome . . . Philadelphia . . . May 29*: Huddleston, *Edmundo*, 52–54 (citing Edmundo's correspondence from the ship, from Lisbon, and from Madrid). The dates of Edmundo's departure from the US and arrival in Lisbon and Madrid are significant insofar as Aline claims to have met him in Madrid's Palace Hotel on December 31, 1943 (*Spy Wore Red*, 69), and to have seen him days before at Casino Estoril in Lisbon (*Spy Wore Red*, 64). These connections were impossible, of course, since Aline and Edmundo were both in the US at the time; Aline did not arrive in Madrid until February 10, and Edmundo did not arrive until June 1.

70 *Robert Dunev . . . SS Serpa Pinto*: Dunev, *Spy Reminisces*, 23.

70 *interview . . .* Primer Plano: "Hollywood, al habla: Así era, hace 2 meses la Meca del cine," *Primer Plano*, June 11, 1944 (unpaginated).

71 *The historical way . . . Edmundo Lassalle's my name*: Romanones, *Spy Wore Red*, 69. Aline's date regarding her first meeting is clearly inaccurate. Since Edmundo left for Barcelona on June 9 (per his correspondence on June 10), I believe this is the approximate date (June 2 or 3) that he and Aline met at the Palace.

72 *That cutout was Aline*: That Aline was Lassalle's cutout is clear from the number of reports where she passes along information with the preamble, "from PELOTA" (see, e.g., BUTCH memo to LEGION on July 13, 1945, RG 226, Entry 127, Box 22, NARA), and from the lack of reports from Lassalle to any Madrid staffer.

72 *My cover is that . . . Who is the Marquesa*: Romanones, *Spy Wore Red*, 71–73.

73 *Cristóbal Balenciaga... tailor... Paris... Infanta*: Beth Duncuff Charleston, "Cristobal Balenciaga (1895–1972)," *Heilbrunn Timeline of Art History*.

74 *There will be a smattering*: Romanones, *Spy Wore Red*, 74.

74 *Doña Mimosa... Calle de Ferraz... Balenciaga*: Ibid., 92–93. The date Aline gives for this reception, January 1944 (p. 103), is impossible since Aline and Edmundo were both still in the US at that time. The more likely date, when both were in Madrid, is the first week of June.

74 *El Greco's most famous*: Ibid., 93.

75 *Samuel Hoare... Lequerica... Duke and Duchess of Lerma*: Ibid., 94–95.

75 *Why, Miss Griffith... The cards show... I see a bullfight*: Ibid., 94–97.

77 *piano... Casilda... Carmen... Nena*: Ibid., 97–98, 121.

77 *followed*: Ibid., 104, 107.

77 *Franco... a plot to kill him*: Ibid., 98–99. In Aline's details she states that Mimosa was a subagent of Edmundo's, and that she was passing the code to him. As noted above, Aline's date of January 1944 for this event is impossible since Edmundo did not arrive in Madrid until the beginning of June. It's unlikely that he would have acquired subagents in just a week, although the card reading and rumor of an assassination plot may well have been accurate.

Chapter 8 :Putting on the Ritz

78 *Calle Monte Esquina... Balenciaga*: Romanones, *Spy Wore Red*, 105.

78 *$351 a month*: This amount was the aggregate of compensation (salary and overtime plus living expense) provided by the OSS and the State Department. See Aline's compensation card and the Madrid staff compensation budget at RG 226, Entry 197A, Box 76, NARA.

78 *portero... sereno*: Romanones, *Spy Wore Red*, 92; *End of an Epoch*, 33.

79 *watchman... clapping... stick*: Walter Smith, *Glimpses of Spain*, 185–86; Romanones, *End of an Epoch*, 33.

79 *June 10... Edmundo... Barcelona*: While Edmundo's personal correspondence of June 10, 1944, suggests that he arrived on the ninth (Huddleston, *Edmundo*, 56), the deputy chief of the Barcelona station (code named ELTON) stated in a memo to ARGUS (Gregory Thomas) on July 24, 1944, that Edmundo had arrived on the tenth. RG 226, Entry 127, Box 18, NARA.

79 *Ritz*: Edmundo's June 10 correspondence states that he was staying at the Barcelona Ritz. Huddleston, *Edmundo*, 56.

79 *$7 per diem*: All Madrid staff, including Gregory Thomas, were limited to a $7 per diem, and Edmundo's file is replete with memos that, notwithstanding Disney's effort to provide him with a reasonable expense account, the OSS wanted him held to no more than the $7 amount given to others. See, e.g., June 16, 1944, correspondence to ARGUS (signature somewhat illegible, but appears to be "Jim"; in all likelihood this was James MacMillian, the financial officer for the Madrid station) at RG 226, Entry 197A, Box 76, NARA.

80 *ELTON . . . He has made a remarkable*: ELTON memo to ARGUS (Gregory Thomas) on July 24, 1944, RG 226, Entry 127, Box 18, NARA.

80 *Horcher's . . . hidden microphone . . . Johann Jebsen . . . Dusko Popov*: Popov, *Spy Counter-Spy*, 102.

81 *Hans Lazar . . . Gives lavish parties*: Romanones, *Spy Wore Red*, 110–11.

82 *Who is that . . . Gloria von Fürstenberg . . . I know her . . . In Berlin*: Ibid., 111–12.

83 *Ah . . . You're mad*: Ibid., 113–14.

83 *If that were true*: Ibid., 115. Given that there were no sightings of Himmler in Madrid at this time, it appears that Aline's assertion was mistaken.

83 *rumors of Himmler sightings*: Hayes, *Wartime Mission in Spain*, 263.

84 *Tio Pepe . . . San Antonio . . . Those were painted*: Romanones, *Spy Wore Red*, 117–18.

84 *That's where . . . Steps of Cuchilleros . . . This is where . . . Of course I know*: Ibid., 118–19.

85 *second week of July . . . Gregory Thomas informed . . . additional security . . . embassy*: Aline places this announcement on March 27, 1944 (Ibid., 126), but that date is off by more than three months. The lease between Ambassador Hayes and Thomas was signed on July 5, 1944, so the move could not have occurred beforehand. The executed lease agreement is located at RG 226, Entry 197A, Box 76, Folder 429, NARA.

85 *Paseo de la Castellana . . . Calle Eduardo Dato*: Dunev, *Spy Reminisces*, 26; Romanones, "The OSS in Spain," 124.

86 *entire city block . . . Duke of Montellano . . . horse chestnut . . . roses*: Hayes, *Wartime Mission in Spain*, 22–23.

86 *Thomas . . . secretary . . . garage annex*: Dunev, *Spy Reminisces*, 27.

86 *the three-story baroque palace*: The property appears to have been around Calle Rafael Calvo, 39, which faces the Castellana and is directly across

from the American embassy. Both Àlvaro Figueroa (Aline's grandson) and Michael Dunev (Robert Dunev's son) have suggested that the original structure, like most in the Castellana, was torn down to make room for a modern commercial building.

86 *one of Spain's wealthiest men*: See "Palace in Spain Burns: Count Romanones and Family Are Routed in Night Clothes," *New York Times*, January 14, 1935, 2; "Even in May, There's Just No Rest for the Partygoer," *New York Times*, May 10, 1970, 76 ("He owns something like a fourth of Spain," referring to Luis, Àlvaro's grandson, the 3rd Count of Romanones).

86 TO ARGUS FROM CHESS: Romanones, *Spy Wore Red*, 129 (Aline's quote changing Thomas's code name to MOZART).

87 *Canaris, had been working against Hitler . . . Abwehr officers had*: Countless books have been written about the efforts of Canaris, senior German military leaders, and members of the *Schwarze Kapelle* to oust or assassinate Hitler. See Agostino von Hassell and Sigrid MacRae, *Alliance of Enemies: The Untold Story of the Secret American and German Collaboration to End World War II*, 253–58 (regarding the Canaris diaries); Charles Burdick and Hans-Adolf Jacobsen, eds., *The Halder War Diary, 1939–1942*; Michael Balfour, *Withstanding Hitler in Germany, 1933–45*; Peter Hoffman, *The History of the German Resistance, 1933–1945*; Klemperer, *German Resistance Against Hitler*; Ger van Roon, *German Resistance to Hitler: Count von Moltke and the Kreisau Circle*; André Brissaud, *Canaris: The Biography of Admiral Canaris, Chief of German Military Intelligence*; Heinz Höhne, *Canaris: Hitler's Master Spy*; Michael Mueller, *Nazi Spymaster: The Life and Death of Admiral Wilhelm Canaris*; and Shirer, *Rise and Fall of the Third Reich*. See also the entries for Beck, Canaris, Halder, Oster, and the *Schwarze Kapelle* in Dear and Foot, eds., *Oxford Companion to World War II*, and Marcel Baudot, et al., eds, *The Historical Encyclopedia of World War II*.

87 *Hammerstein . . . Bussche-Ippenburg . . . Hindenburg . . . January 26 . . . Austrian corporal*: Peter Hoffman, *The History of the German Resistance, 1933–1945*, 24.

87 *Brüning . . . turned in his resignation*: Ibid., 25.

87 *SA . . . SS . . . auxiliary police . . . Röhm . . . Himmler*: For an excellent background on both organizations, Röhm, and Himmler, see Heinz Höhne, *The Order of the Death's Head: The Story of Hitler's SS*.

88 *Fritsch . . . Rundstedt . . . Witzleben . . . Bock*: Hoffman, *History of the German Resistance*, 25.

88 *Blomberg . . . Fritsch . . . Lebensraum . . . Brauchitsch*: Ibid., 36–40. See also Klemperer, *German Resistance Against Hitler*, 66.

88 *Canaris . . . Beck . . . Oster . . . Brauchitsch . . . Rundstedt . . . Witzleben . . . List . . . Kluge . . . Hase*: Hoffman, *History of the German Resistance*, 42–44; Klemperer, *German Resistance Against Hitler*, 105–7; Shirer, *Rise and Fall of the Third Reich*, 372–75; Roon, *German Resistance to Hitler*, 167–68; Hassell and MacRae, *Alliance of Enemies*, 41, 46, 59; and Dear and Foot, eds., *Oxford Companion to World War II*, 117 (Beck entry), 189–90 (Canaris entry), 848 (Oster entry), 982–83 (*Schwarze Kapelle* entry).

89 *Beck tendered his resignation*: Hoffman, *History of the German Resistance*, 62; Roon, *German Resistance to Hitler*, 168; Shirer, *Rise and Fall of the Third Reich*, 374.

89 *Halder . . . bloodsucker and criminal*: Hoffman, *History of the German Resistance*, 83.

89 *Canaris . . . Oster . . . Witzleben . . . Brockdorff-Ahlefeldt . . . Hoepner . . . Stülpnagel*: Ibid., 84–89; Klemperer, *German Resistance Against Hitler*, 105–9; Roon, *German Resistance to Hitler*, 168–71; Shirer, *Rise and Fall of the Third Reich*, 374–75; Hassell and MacRae, *Alliance of Enemies*, 77–79.

89 *Heinz . . . Helldorf . . . Schulenburg*: Hoffman, *History of the German Resistance*, 90–91.

89 *Heinz had already decided . . . Hitler would be shot*: Ibid., 93.

90 *Halder . . . forty-eight-hour notice*: Ibid., 85.

90 *Neville Chamberlain made a surprise visit*: Ibid., 93; Klemperer, *German Resistance Against Hitler*, 108; Shirer, *Rise and Fall of the Third Reich*, 384–91.

90 *Munich Conference . . . September 29–30*: Shirer, *Rise and Fall of the Third Reich*, 414–21. See also the entry under "Munich Pact" in Baudot, et al., eds., *Historical Encyclopedia of World War II*, 337.

91 *Halder collapsed over his desk*: Hoffman, *History of the German Resistance*, 109.

91 *Beck and other officers*: Schlabrendorff had tried to kill Hitler twice: on March 13, 1943, he put a bomb on Hitler's plane (which failed to ignite), and on another occasion he conspired with an assassin to plant a second bomb but at the last minute the man got cold feet. After

NOTES

the July 20, 1944, putsch, Schlabrendorff was arrested and subjected to such torture that he passed out. The next day he suffered a heart attack. When he sufficiently recovered, the Gestapo repeated the procedures and again Schlabrendorff passed out. For details of the tortures, see fn. 49 in Loftis, *CODE NAME: LISE*, 226–27.

91 *Beck and Oster . . . July 20, 1944 . . . Wolf's Lair*: The putsch, codenamed Valkyrie, has been written about at length. For excellent summaries, see Hoffman, *History of the German Resistance*, 412–60; Shirer, *Rise and Fall of the Third Reich*, 1033–69; Klemperer, *German Resistance Against Hitler*, 375–85; Dear and Foot, eds., *Oxford Companion to World War II*, 982–83 (*Schwarze Kapelle* entry).

91 *Rommel had given the putsch his blessing*: Shirer, *Rise and Fall of the Third Reich*, 1031–32; Hoffman, *History of the German Resistance*, 351–54.

91 *five thousand military officers . . . sixteen . . . three field marshals*: Shirer, *Rise and Fall of the Third Reich*, 1069–79; Hoffman, *History of the German Resistance*, 507–34.

91 *General von Stülpnagel . . . arrest and jail all 1,200 SS*: Ibid., 475; Shirer, *Rise and Fall of the Third Reich*, 1060.

91 *second confrontation . . . Halder . . . von Bonin . . . Villabassa . . . Kesselring*: Peter Churchill, *Spirit in the Cage*, 220–22; Loftis, *CODE NAME: LISE*, 228–29, 232.

91 *Rommel's desire . . . Hitler to be arrested*: Hoffman, *History of the German Resistance*, 352–54; Shirer, *Rise and Fall of the Third Reich*, 1031.

92 *von Rundstedt . . . von Manstein . . . acquiesced*: Hoffman, *History of the German Resistance*, 290, 351–52.

92 *Generals Ludwig Beck . . . Heinrich von Stülpnagel . . . Field marshals Erwin Rommel . . . Günther von Kluge*: Shirer, *Rise and Fall of the Third Reich*, 1069–79; Hoffman, *History of the German Resistance*, 507–34.

92 *Ralph Forte . . . La Reboite . . . shutters . . . pistol . . . man's hand*: Romanones, *The Spy Wore Red*, 130. In this passage Aline states that her gun was a revolver, while the pistol she says she was given by Thomas earlier (*Spy Wore Red*, 87) was a Beretta .25, which would have been impossible since Beretta did not manufacture the .25 caliber (model 950) until 1952. He could have given her a Belgian Melior .25, however. On page 145 of *The Spy Wore Red*, Aline again refers to a Beretta as a revolver. It appears, then, that Aline referred to any pistol as a "revolver," which is odd since she trained with many types of guns at The Farm.

Chapter 9: Glorious Gloria

94 *Pierre!... Who is that*: Romanones, *Spy Wore Red*, 130–31.

95 *Maria Francesca ... Pimpinela*: Aline disguises Hohenlohe daughter's name in *The Spy Wore Red* (p. 21), identifying her as Carola Lilienthal. Interestingly, Aline never knew that "Pimpinela" was only Maria Francesca's nickname. In a memo to James MacMillan, Aline gives Maria's name as Pimpinela. See BUTCH memo to QUERES, June 19, 1945, RG 226, Entry 127, Box 22, Folder 150, NARA. Maria Francesca's full name can be seen in photographs marked by her mother, Doña Maria Piedad de Iturbe, in the blog by royal archivist, Marlene Eilers Koenig. Royal Musings, September 23, 2008, Royalmusingsblogspot com.blogspot.com.

95 *El Quexigal ... Prince Max had bought*: Jorge Piedrahita, "El Quexigal: Finca de Reyes y Nobles Desde Inmemorial," July 30, 2010, https:// jorgepiedrahita.blogia.com/2010/073001-el-quexigal-finca-de-reyes -y-nobles-desde-inmemorial.php. See also, "El Quexigal," nuestroin condecebreros.es/pagina/6.html.

96 *On Saturday afternoon*: Romanones, *Spy Wore Red*, 132. This Saturday appears to be July 22, 1944.

96 *Maximilian Egon von Hohenlohe–Langenburg ... Rothenhaus castle ... Santillana ... Biarritz*: See "Memorandum for the Officer in Charge," September 27, 1945, from Special Agent George G. Charig, 307th Counter Intelligence Corps Detachment, Seventh Army, at RG 226, Entry 119A, Box 55, NARA.

96 *Look, Aline*: Romanones, *Spy Wore Red*, 132–33.

97 *To me the building*: Ibid., 133.

98 *Gobelins tapestries ... El Greco ... Murillo ... Talavera pottery*: Piedrahita, "El Quexigal." See also, "El Quexigal," nuestroincondecebreros.es /pagina/6.html.

98 *150 rooms ... 86,000 square feet*: Ibid.

99 *How happy I am ... Nena*: Romanones, *Spy Wore Red*, 135–36.

99 *Prince Max ... early fifties ... thick build ... six foot ... blond hair ... round face*: See "Memorandum for the Officer in Charge," September 27, 1945, from Special Agent George G. Charig, 307th Counter Intelligence Corps Detachment, Seventh Army, at RG 226, Entry 119A, Box 55, NARA.

99 *I think we have met ... Encantada*: Romanones, *Spy Wore Red*, 136–37.

99 *had dinner at Edelweiss . . . bumped into him*: Romanones, *Spy Wore Red*, 75, 90 (Aline referring to him as the admiral's godson).

99 *Abwehr agent . . . nephew of Admiral Wilhelm Canaris*: Kahn, *Hitler's Spies*, 246. See also Popov, *Spy Counter-Spy*, 85.

100 *Samuel Hoare . . . sinister eastern Jew*: Burns, *Papa Spy*, 353, citing Samuel J. G. Hoare, *Ambassador on Special Mission*.

100 *Lazar . . . well-dressed*: Burns, *Papa Spy*, 353.

100 *Constantin Canaris*: Aline's identity of this man, whom she refers to as "Constantin Weiderstock," has been confused by one author writing in the World War II genre. Nigel West (pseudonym of Rupert Allason) in *Counterfeit Spies* suggests that Aline is mistakenly referring to Gustav Leisner, head of the Abwehr's Madrid station. On page 56, West writes: "Constantin von Weiderstock, who is referred to as controlling the Abwehr in Madrid . . . is described as 'a young fellow' and 'a favourite [sic] disciple of Admiral Canaris', [sic] who also happens to be his godfather. This is odd because the senior Abwehr officer in Madrid at that time was a naval contemporary of Admiral Canaris during the First World War, whose real name was Commander Gustav Leisner."

West, however, is the one who is confused, succumbing to both a citation error and a grammatical error. On page 75 of *The Spy Wore Red*, Aline writes: "Constantin von Weiderstock, a favorite disciple of Admiral Wilhelm Canaris, who controls the Abwehr." West's citation error is that he adds "*in Madrid*," to the sentence, thus allowing the jump from Canaris, who headed the Abwehr, to Leisner, who was the Abwehr's chief of station in Madrid.

West's grammatical error is the classic misplaced or dangling modifier. In Aline's sentence, "who controls the Abwehr" modifies "Admiral Wilhelm Canaris," not "Constantin von Weiderstock." Aline has correctly placed the modifier next to the noun it modifies. West's rendering of the sentence would have "who controls the Abwehr" modifying "Weiderstock" at the far end of the sentence. If Aline had been trying to connect the modifier to Constantin, she would have written: "Constantin von Weiderstock, who controls the Abwehr, is a favorite disciple of Admiral Wilhelm Canaris." A second, less appealing way she could have written it would have been simply to omit "who" in the sentence, rendering it: "Constantin von Weiderstock, a favorite disciple . . . , *controls* the Abwehr."

Aside from the citation and grammatical errors, it appears that West is unaware that Admiral Canaris's nephew, whose name was Constantin, worked for the Abwehr in Madrid during World War II. In his excellent work *Hitler's Spies* (pp. 246, 248), David Kahn sets forth the Abwehr personnel in Madrid in June 1944, which included: "Specialist-Captain Constantin Canaris [a nephew of the admiral]" (brackets in the original). Similarly, in Dusko Popov's memoir, *Spy Counter-Spy* (p. 85), Popov notes that Johnny Jebsen (his German friend and Abwehr case officer) informed him that Admiral Canaris's nephew was with the Abwehr in Madrid.

100 *tapestries from Cuenca . . . silver candelabra*: Piedrahita, "El Quexigal." See also, "El Quexigal," nuestroincondecebreros.es/pagina/6.html.

101 *names in the guest book*: Aline appears to have gone to weekend parties at El Quexigal on several occasions. On one outing, which she detailed in a June 19, 1945, memo to QUERES (James MacMillan), she reports that she looked at this guest book. RG 226, Entry 127, Box 22, Folder 150, NARA. The question, then, is whether she looked at it once or twice. It appears that she tried to examine it on her first visit to El Quexigal, in July 1944, but was thwarted in her attempt to see much when she was interrupted by Prince Max's daughter. On the visit the following summer, Aline was able to record several names of interest (Liesau, Kiechle, Spitsky); she also saw several German names but was unable to get them down.

101 *Aline, what on earth*: Romanones, *Spy Wore Red*, 143. Here Aline provides dialogue with Pimpinela von Hohenlohe, whom she refers to as Carola. Aline states that at this, her first visit to El Quexigal, she begins to photograph pages of the guest book with the "spy camera" contained in her "slender cigarette lighter." This is highly unlikely since, at this point in 1944, she has not been engaged as a reporting agent and there is no record of her receiving a camera of any kind. In addition, there are no images or photos supposedly taken by her in the OSS files. Finally, in her June 19, 1945, report noted above, she does not mention having a camera when she looks at the guest book. Equally compelling is the fact that the OSS used Eastman Kodak cameras disguised as matchboxes, not lighters (see the CIA's article, "Weapons & Spy Gear," at https://www.cia.gov/library/publications/intelligence-history/oss/art08.htm, and "CIA Museum Provides Glimpse into Intelligence History," at https://www.cia.gov/news-information/featured-story-archive/2007

-featured-story-archive/cia-museum.html), and that cigarette lighter spy cameras were not invented until 1951 (one of which is showcased in the Vintage Cameras Museum in Kampong Glam, Singapore), some seven years after Aline claims to have used one.

101 *The fräulein*: Romanones, *Spy Wore Red*, 145.

Chapter 10: Visitors

103 *Don't be afraid . . . Get out of here*: Romanones, *Spy Wore Red*, 146–47. According to Aline, she happened to have a capsule of sodium amobarbital ("truth serum") in her makeup case, and she also happened to have a pitcher of water and glass on her night table. Pouring the contents of the capsule into the glass and adding water, she states that she then had Constantin drink it, telling him it was bicarbonate of soda. She then interrogates him and he confirms that Himmler had been in Madrid.

I have not included this part of Aline's story as it seems far-fetched. Aline wasn't a field agent at this point, so she wouldn't have been given capsules of truth serum. In fact, it would be a rare occasion that an *active* agent would have been supplied the drug, if the OSS even had it. On April 1, 1945, a team of medical experts at Cornell University Medical College *began* a study for General Donovan on whether there was "any agent that would be useful in extracting information from persons who are reluctant to yield it." An initial report completed on September 21 revealed that a substance the team identified as "TD" had some value, but was approximately equal to alcohol in effect. The overall study, Donovan was told, would not be completed until June 30, 1946. Correspondence from Dr. H. G. Wolff, associate professor of medicine, Cornell University, to General William Donovan, September 21, 1945, RG 226, Entry A1 92, Box 81, NARA.

In addition, given that OSS and British postwar records make no mention of Himmler traveling to Spain in 1944, the Himmler sighting itself seems highly unlikely, thus negating Constantin's confirmation of it.

In Aline's story of the weekend, she also wrote that Mimosa had spoken to her about the Germans being "on to her," that she had taken ill soon thereafter, and that she had died the next day. This series of events is not found in any OSS records, or in Robert Dunev's memoirs, and I therefore have not included it. Likewise, I did not include Aline's assertion that Gregory Thomas had given her a radio detector to search for a radio on the premises, or that he had instructed her to crack and rifle Prince Max's safe.

104 *chains . . . map*: Everything about chains—organizations, agent and informant names, safe houses, and routes—was detailed and highly classified. NARA has collected all of the OSS chain information and placed it in one box, which is located at RG 226, Entry 210, Box 7, NARA. This box is marked "OSS Classified Sources and Methods Files—WITHDRAWN RECORDS."

105 *From the AKAK chain . . . Page one of the agents in the AKAK chain*: "The AKAK Chain" memorandum, January 21, 1944, RG 226, Entry 210, Box 7, NARA.

107 *Truck Route . . . The chain was partly blown*: "French Chains Operated from Spain: 1943–1944" memorandum, RG 226, Entry 210, Box 7, NARA.

107 *My name is Pasolé . . . 12,000 francs . . . Radio parts*: Peter Churchill, *Of Their Own Choice*, 175–78.

109 *You must keep . . . If I walk into . . . We shall walk*: Ibid., 182, 184, 189.

111 *Dragoon*: In *The Spy Wore Red* (p. 164), Aline suggested that the women also carried information regarding Operation Overlord. However, the date of this meeting with the two women appears to have been in July 1944, after the D-Day invasion on June 6.

111 *I am Marta . . . What do you think*: Romanones, *Spy Wore Red*, 165–66.

114 *I have seen . . . Sorry*: Ibid., 168.

115 *blood*: Ibid., 169.

Chapter 11: The Body

116 *shot in the head*: This murder is confirmed by Robert Dunev, who removed the body. Aline contends, however, that a revolver was found beside Marta's hand, suggesting that it was either the murder weapon or that Marta had committed suicide with it (*Spy Wore Red*, 169). This notion, however, seems implausible, since the gun she alleges to have seen did not have a silencer affixed, and without one the shot would have awakened the entire household and countless neighbors.

116 *Do nothing until . . . Señorita . . . Who knows about*: Romanones, *Spy Wore Red*, 169.

117 *Come by Butch's apartment . . . But Angustias*: Ibid., 170–71. Marta's murder, and Robert Dunev's assignment to remove the body, is confirmed in Dunev's memoir. "She [Aline] refers to me as 'Jeff Walters,'"

he wrote in *A Spy Reminisces* (p. 57), "and, in several instances, refreshed my memory, including the night I was summoned to remove a body from her apartment."

In this passage Aline has Thomas saying, "The assassin was not after Marta. He was after you." This seems most unlikely since Marta had already stated that she had killed two Civil Guards (p. 165), and there was no evidence of Aline's cover being broken, and no reason the Germans would have had the slightest interest in her then. While she was being followed, she points out later that it was Juanito's men who were tagging her. Equally important, Aline would have no reason to be on a hit list. She wasn't even an active agent. Dunev, who was shadowed by the Germans and perhaps targeted for kidnapping, had been an active agent for more than a year by this time. At most (if Aline's cover had actually been broken), Aline would have been targeted for surveillance, not assassination. Marta, on the other hand, would have been on the Spanish "arrest or shoot" list for killing two Civil Guards.

118 *Juanito*: As explained in earlier notes, the dates for events given by Aline in her books (and article) are almost always wrong. As such, we don't know the exact date of her first bullfight, but I believe it was about the time in the text (July 1944, whereas Aline has it occurring in May). Juanito no doubt invited her to watch him on many occasions, and the photo of Aline wearing the vest from his "suit of lights" confirms his affection for her.

118 *The real* corrida: Conrad, *La Fiesta Brava*, 172.

118 *Hemingway . . . In Spain*: Hemingway, *Death in the Afternoon*, 91.

119 *I hope the fight . . .* Barreras de sombra: Romanones, *Spy Wore Red*, 180–81. See also Aline's *The End of an Epoch* (p. 36) (referring to the "barrera seats").

121 *One is . . . Who's that*: Romanones, *Spy Wore Red*, 181–82.

121 El Hombre Que Las Enamora . . . El Camino de Babel: Ana de Pombo entry, imdb.com.

121 *alguaciles*: Conrad, *La Fiesta Brava*, 36.

121 *Look at Juanito*: Romanones, *Spy Wore Red*, 181–82; *End of an Epoch*, 37.

121 *trumpets . . . nine men . . . procession . . . veronicas*: Romanones, *End of an Epoch*, 37–38; Conrad, *La Fiesta Brava*, 36–44; Walter Smith, *Glimpses of Spain*, 45–46. Smith, who as head of the Oil Control Com-

mission was Aline's cover boss, continued to live in Madrid after the war and witnessed countless bullfights. See also Hemingway, *Death in the Afternoon*, 26–34, 58–62.

121 *green silk . . . black hat . . . montera . . . pink stockings*: Romanones, *Spy Went Dancing*, 50; *Spy Wore Red*, 182; *End of an Epoch*, 37.

122 *kettledrum . . . trumpet*: Conrad, *La Fiesta Brava*, 38.

122 *Manolete . . . skinny . . . haggard*: Romanones, *Spy Wore Red*, 183; *End of an Epoch*, 38.

122 *appearing tubercular*: Conrad, *La Fiesta Brava*, 3.

123 *Excuse me, señorita . . . My knees start*: Ibid.

123 *scheme to kidnap the Duke . . . Operation Willi*: See Schellenberg, *Memoirs of Hitler's Spymaster*, 127–43.

124 *black Miura bull*: Romanones, *Spy Went Dancing*, 50. In *The Spy Wore Red* (p. 183) and *The End of an Epoch* (p. 39), Aline describes the bull as black and white, without indicating that it was a Miura bull.

124 *Since 1842*: See the Miura website at: ganaderiamiura.com.

124 *kill lions . . . Bengal tigers . . . charged elephants . . . cars . . . train*: Hemingway, *Death in the Afternoon*, 109, 111.

124 *Miura bulls . . . ability to learn*: Ibid., 129.

124 *Islero . . . Manolete . . . Lamborghini*: See "The bulls that inspired Lamborghini model names," *Motorworld*, September 30, 2013.

124 *Eh, toro . . . Olé*: Romanones, *Spy Wore Red*, 183; *End of an Epoch*, 39–40.

126 *Juanito was flung . . . dead . . . jacket ripped . . . blood*: Romanones, *Spy Wore Red*, 184; *End of an Epoch*, 40.

Chapter 12: Ressurection

127 *one of Juanito's black slippers . . . Juanito brushed him aside*: Romanones, *Spy Wore Red*, 184.

128 *flowers . . . hats*: Ibid., 185; *End of an Epoch*, 41.

128 *umbrellas . . . gloves . . . coats*: Walter Smith, *Glimpses of Spain*, 48.

128 manzanilla . . . *wooden leg . . . women's panties . . . baby*: Conrad, *La Fiesta Brava*, 146.

129 *What luck*: Romanones, *Spy Wore Red*, 185; *End of an Epoch*, 41.

129 Oreja . . . *handkerchiefs . . . an ear entitled*: Conrad, *La Fiesta Brava*, 146.

130 *My heavens*: Romanones, *Spy Wore Red*, 185; *End of an Epoch*, 41.

130 *I've been trying . . . Don't you think*: Romanones, *Spy Wore Red*, 186–87.

130 *overwhelmed me . . . Those moments*: Romanones, *End of an Epoch*, 42.

131 *I like bullfighting*: John Steinbeck letter to Barnaby Conrad in 1952, cited in Conrad's *Matador* (p. 223).

131 *My story isn't*: Romanones, *Spy Wore Red*, 187–88.

132 *Málaga . . . microfilm*: Romanones, "The OSS in Spain," 126. This article, written for and published by the NARA, is by far the most reliable of Aline's remembrances of her time with the OSS. In this 1992 piece, she correctly identifies Frank Ryan, Gregory Thomas, William Mellon, James MacMillan, Robert Dunev, "Ben" Turpin (whose first name was Robert), John J. Ryan and Sons, and World Commerce. See also Aline's *The History of Pascualete* (p. 9), and *The Spy Wore Red* (p. 199).

132 *In this strip . . . There may be trouble*: Romanones, *Spy Wore Red*, 192–94.

132 *known for its almonds, blue grapes, and palm groves*: Walter Smith, *Glimpses of Spain*, 111.

133 *How about dinner*: Romanones, *Spy Wore Red*, 196.

133 *sleeper number two . . . Who is it . . . In that case*: Ibid., 198–99.

134 Arrest: Romanones, "The OSS in Spain," 126; *History of Pascualete*, 9; *Spy Wore Red*, 199. Aline also mentions her Málaga arrest in *The Spy Wore Red* (pp. 200–1), *The History of Pascualete* (p. 9), and *The End of an Epoch* (p. 373).

Chapter 13: The Prisoner

135 *Wake up . . . Please let me . . . This small cell*: Romanones, *Spy Wore Red*, 201–2.

136 *What a fight*: Ibid., 203–4. In *The History of Pascualete* (p. 9) Aline writes that she spent two nights in the jail, and that on the second morning the police chief presented her with a bouquet of red carnations. In *The Spy Wore Red* version of the story, she is there only one night. The discrepancy may be explained by what she wrote in *The End of an Epoch* (p. 373): "My orders had been to deliver microfilm to an agent who had come from Algiers. . . . I took the night train from Madrid to Malaga, but since I did not have the necessary 'travel permit,' I was taken to the police station and put in jail. . . . But thanks to Barnaby Conrad . . . I was released the next day and able to make delivery. . . . During that visit charming Barnaby Conrad drove me along the coast and we stopped to take a swim at a lovely beach in a small village called Torremolinos not far from Malaga."

Since her detailed account in *The Spy Wore Red* includes a bullfight, dinner, and a tour after her release from jail, the swim could not have occurred this day. It appears that Conrad took her for a swim *the following day*, thus accounting for two nights in Málaga, but consistent with one night in jail.

137 *You won't mind*: Romanones, *Spy Wore Red*, 205.

137 *University of North Carolina... Mexico City*: Barnaby Conrad, *Fun While It Lasted*, flap copy, 76. See also Harvey Breit, "Talk with Barnaby Conrad," *New York Times*, July 6, 1952.

137 *Adrian Spies... Nacho Suárez... Pretty Boy*: Conrad, *Fun While It Lasted*, 6–7.

138 Madre de Dios... *Felix Guzmán... ligaments... surgery*: Ibid., 12, 56–57, 76, 126.

139 *Juanito... Manolete... Juan Belmonte... El Niño de California*: Ibid., 122–39, 163, 196. See also Harvey Breit, "Talk with Barnaby Conrad," *New York Times*, July 6, 1952; David Dempsey, "Fun While It Lasted," *New York Times*, August 24, 1969; Dunev, *Spy Reminisces*, 63.

139 *most apprenticed for six to twelve years*: Hemingway, *Death in the Afternoon*, 68.

139 *How about lunching*: Romanones, *Spy Wore Red*, 205.

140 *Blacky... fished the microfilm... chanquetes*: Ibid., 206. According to Aline's version of the story in *The Spy Wore Red*, she transferred not only microfilm to Blacky, but a gun and radio transmitter as well. First, while it is possible that she could have transferred these, I have not included them because it seems unlikely that Gregory Thomas would have given her such large and difficult items to conceal, particularly since she was not yet a field agent. Second, Aline mentions only the microfilm in her most reliable writing, "The OSS in Spain" (p. 126), and also in *The End of an Epoch* (p. 373). Had she truly delivered a gun or radio, I believe she would have mentioned it in these nonfiction accounts.

140 *twenty-one... youngest vice-consul ever*: Conrad, *Fun While It Lasted*, 91; See also Harvey Breit, "Talk with Barnaby Conrad," *New York Times*, July 6, 1952; David Dempsey, "Fun While It Lasted," *New York Times*, August 24, 1969.

140 *finished at Yale*: Conrad, *Fun While It Lasted*, 76, 79, 86; David Dempsey, "Fun While It Lasted," *New York Times*, August 24, 1969.

140 *State Department... code clerk*: Conrad, *Fun While it Lasted*, 87.

141 *Roberta Cameron... You are beautiful*: Ibid., 87, 89.

141 *FBI . . . You are beautiful . . . Mr. Secretary*: Ibid., 89–91.

142 *Hotel Miramar . . . room had been searched*: Romanones, *Spy Wore Red*, 206–7. That Aline's room had been searched wasn't unusual, even in a neutral country. MI6 agent Dusko Popov stated after the war that in every hotel, regardless of locale, his belongings had been searched, and that those investigating included German, American, British, Russian, Italian, and Japanese operatives. See Frederick Bear, "Dusko [007] Popov: Exclusive Interview," *Genesis*, November 1974, 68.

142 *Lhardy . . . These salons*: Ibid., 212.

143 *Have you ever been*: Ibid., 216. Juanito's comment confirmed what Hemingway had said more than a decade earlier: "Nearly all bullfighters are frightened at some moment *before* the fight begins." Hemingway, *Death in the Afternoon*, 58. In *Matador*, Barnaby Conrad wrote in 1950 that bullfighters always wanted people in the dressing room before the fight "to distract them from the sinking fear-feeling that they all get," and even the great Juan Belmonte said, "We all have mouths as dry as Sahara." Conrad, *La Fiesta Brava*, 26, 34.

144 *Calle Fortuny and Marqués de Riscal*: Romanones, *Spy Wore Red*, 223.

Chapter 14: The Bohemian

145 *This cable means . . . Contact Pierre*: Romanones, *Spy Wore Red*, 260.

146 *General Tresckow . . . You do care*: Ibid., 263.

147 *Max Sciolitti*: Huddleston, *Edmundo*, 59.

147 *14 Calle de Hermosilla . . . You want something*: Romanones, *Spy Wore Red*, 228.

148 *Why, Aline . . . Ana is unique*: Ibid., 229.

149 *Colonel Ernesto Heymann*: Dunev, *Spy Reminisces*, 58–59.

149 *Eva, to manage*: Ibid., 55, 58.

Chapter 15: The Lady Vanishes

150 *Operation Dragoon*: For an overview of Operation Dragoon (formerly Anvil), see Dear and Foot, eds., *Oxford Companion to World War II*, 418–22.

151 *La Clinica de los Toreros . . . He was operated*: Romanones, *Spy Wore Red*, 280.

151 *10 percent . . . 13 percent . . . 40 percent*: Conrad, *La Fiesta Brava*, 25.

152 *Gracias . . . Aline . . . Florence Nightenberg*: Romanones, *Spy Wore Red*, 280–81.

153 *Didn't I see . . . Don Juan wanted us*: Ibid., 282.

154 *Safehaven*: For a comprehensive summary of Safehaven, see G. Edward Buxton's memo of April 16, 1945, to all OSS officers and chiefs at RG 226, Entry 127, Box 23, NARA. See also Kermit Roosevelt, *Overseas Targets*, 37.

154 *Lequerica . . . demanded assurances*: Hayes, *Wartime Mission in Spain*, 255. The Spanish did, in fact, assist in the Safehaven effort, stiffening customs inspections at the border and seizing a shipment of looted goods at Irun in September 1944. Ibid., 264.

154 *August 25 . . . ELTON . . . PELOTA has been instructed*: Huddleston, *Edmundo*, 63.

155 *The question of enemy*: Ibid., 63–64.

155 *four major objectives . . . ALIU . . . London*: Ibid., 62, 64. For details of an OSS ALIU team operating in Germany, see Lynn Nicholas, *The Rape of Europa: The Fate of Europe's Treasures in the Third Reich and the Second World War*, 378–82.

Chapter 16: The Count

156 *December 11 Edmundo left for London*: Huddleston, *Edmundo*, 65.

156 *informing Robert Dunev . . . Ana de Pombo's*: Dunev, *Spy Reminisces*, 59.

157 *January 9 . . . Edmundo . . . Madrid*: Huddleston, *Edmundo*, 66, 77.

158 *Tomorrow morning . . . Vaya usted . . . Miss Griffith*: Romanones, *Spy Went Dancing*, 23–24.

158 *There's a large . . . The stuff goes*: Ibid., 25–26.

158 *work with Edmundo*: Ibid., 27. Aline refers to him as TOP HAT, rather than by his true code name, PELOTA. She also gives the impression that she, not he, was the lead in the investigation, which was not the case.

159 *reports with James MacMillan*: Aline filed a total of fifty-nine reports, thirty-one of which were to "QUERES" (James MacMillan). See Aline's BUTCH files at RG 226, Entry 127, Box 22, and her reports in the Madrid X-2 and SI files at RG 226, Entry 127, Box 26, NARA.

159 *a delicious confection . . . Divina . . . My pet*: Romanones, *Spy Went Dancing*, 30.

160 *Princess Maria Agatha von Ratibor*: Princess Maria's name appears in several OSS memos produced by Edmundo and Aline, and both used

her as a confidential source. In *The Spy Went Dancing* (pp. 31, 112, page 2 of photo section), Aline disguises her name as "Princess Renata von Walperg," which is ironic since she correctly identified her three years earlier in *The Spy Wore Red* (pp. 94–95, 101, 284). In the dialogue here I have rendered Aline's "Renata" to her correct name, Princess Maria Agatha, who typically went by her middle name alone, Agatha.

160 *Prince Ernst von Ratibor . . . blacklist . . . Consuelo Eyre*: Huddleston, *Edmundo*, 77.

160 *Dr. Franz Liesau . . . Oficina Tecnica*: Aline produced three overlapping reports on Liesau and his company: May 15, May 17, and May 18, 1945, located at RG 226, Entry 127, Box 22, NARA.

160 *family owned palaces and estates . . . mining . . . coal*: Huddleston, *Edmundo*, 76.

161 *Actually anti-Nazi . . . What do you expect*: Romanones, *Spy Went Dancing*, 31 (Aline disguising ARGUS's code name as MOZART and Agatha's name as Renata).

162 *Aline, hold it a moment . . . I'm meeting Casilda . . . Pimpinela*: Ibid., 33–34 (Aline disguising Pimpinela von Hohenlohe as Carola Lilienthal).

162 *My pet*: Ibid., 35.

163 *when Gloria had arrived in Portugal*: Gloria's Palacio registration shows that she checked in on August 9, 1944, and checked out on November 20, 1944. See also Pacheco, ed., *Hotel Palácio*, 310–11. The Palacio registrations, which are held by the Arquivo Histórico de Cascais, also reveal Gloria's likely means of support. Prince Almed Falhry, a wealthy Arabian whom Gloria would marry in 1946, checked in to the Palacio on August 25, two weeks after Gloria arrived, and stayed until September 1. See ibid., 294–95.

163 *Thomas had X-2 investigate . . . Dutch passport . . . left town owing*: Gloria's X-2 file is located at RG 226, Entry 124, Box 14, Stack 190, Row 7, Compartment 17, Shelf 4, NARA. See in particular correspondence from X-2's Lisbon officer C. H. van Brink to Charles Grey, September 30, 1944, wherein he states: "Madrid informs me that this woman [Gloria von Fürstenberg] has recently left Spain. . . . She is supposed to live at the Palacio Hotel, Estoril. Complaints from a Spanish firm at Madrid about some unpaid bills put our Legation there on her track. She has never presented herself to the Dutch authorities, either in Spain or in Portugal."

163 *1,500 pesetas . . . Julio Laffittee*: See October 13, 1944, correspondence from Charles Grey to C. H. van Brink, responding to his September 30 inquiry in the note above. RG 226, Entry 124, Box 14, NARA.

163 *two children . . . virtually penniless, Frank Scholtens, no funds*: See the fifteen questions posed to Gloria by Portuguese authorities on October 3, 1944, and her written responses, at RG 226, Entry 124, Box 14, NARA. See also Charles Grey's summary report to C. H. van Brink dated September 30, 1944, as well as Gloria's X-2 file card ("Emphasized that she must join these relatives within the very near future as she is virtually penniless"). RG 226, Entry 124, Box 14, NARA.

164 *Aline . . . Are you serious . . . As Ratibor's husband . . . Every day . . . My dearest*: Romanones, *Spy Wore Red*, 284–86. In her dialogue, Aline replaces Edmundo's real code name, PELOTA, with TOP HAT, and Gregory Thomas's real code name, ARGUS, with MOZART.

Chapter 17: Butch

167 *Edmundo went to a society ball . . . Gloria*: See Edmundo's correspondence to Emilie Lassalle from the Palace Hotel on February 4, 1945. Huddleston, *Edmundo*, 74.

167 *February 5 . . . Evarista Murtra*: BUTCH memorandum to QUERES, February 5, 1945, located at RG 226, Entry 127, Box 22, NARA.

168 *Edmundo . . . illegal financial transactions*: See routing sheet of Thomas's cable to Washington (Madrid P.L. 286), April 27, 1945, at RG 226, Entry 127, Box 17, NARA.

169 *German embassy . . . 50 to 100 million in francs*: QUERES (James MacMillan) memo to ARGUS (Gregory Thomas) and 1006 (a staff assistant; assistants carrying four-digit code numbers), May 1, 1945, citing Washington's April 16, 1945, Safehaven cable. RG 226, Entry 127, Box 17, NARA.

169 *there is a reported flow*: ARGUS (Gregory Thomas) memo to 983 (Larry Mellon) and QUERES (James MacMillan), April 17, 1945, via Pouch Letter 160, at RG 226, Entry 127, Box 17, NARA.

169 *May 12 . . . six reports*: These reports are all located in the BUTCH files at RG 226, Entry 127, Box 22, NARA. The Dollar-Peseta Exchange, Liesau, and Oficina Tecnica reports were prepared for MacMillan, while the Marta Film, Podevils, and Reuss reports were prepared for Mellon.

169 *Spain's official exchange rate*: BUTCH memorandum (Dollar-Peseta Exchange) to QUERES, May 12, 1945. Ibid.

170 *In May 1943 . . . Dr. Liesau . . . has been a dangerous*: BUTCH memorandum (Spanish Decree Ordering Freezing of Assets) to QUERES, May 12, 1945, located at RG 226, Entry 127, Box 22, NARA.

170 *sister memo to MacMillan*: BUTCH memorandum (Oficina Technica Francisco Liesau) to QUERES, May 12, 1945, located at RG 226, Entry 127, Box 22, NARA.

170 *Larry Mellon . . . Marta Film . . . Guillermo Linhoff . . . Hans Schieb*: BUTCH memorandum (Marta Film [Safehaven]) to LEGION, May 12, 1945, located at RG 226, Entry 127, Box 22, NARA.

170 *Countess Hexe Podevils . . . full-fledged Gestapo*: BUTCH memorandum (Countess Hexe Podevils) to LEGION, May 12, 1945, located at RG 226, Entry 127, Box 22, NARA.

171 *Walt Disney Productions . . . Roy Disney . . . Pierre de Beneducci*: BUTCH memorandum (Pierre de Beneducci) to LEGION, May 12, 1945, located at RG 226, Entry 127, Box 22, NARA.

171 *We want you to investigate*: Ibid.

172 *State Department . . . Gloria von Fürstenberg . . . Subject is not actually . . . Ahmed Fakhry*: "Report on Condesa Gloria Rubio de Furstenberg," May 2, 1945, Foreign Service of the United States of America, American Embassy, located at RG 226, Entry 127, Box 22, NARA.

172 *Ambassador Carlton Hayes . . . animosity toward the OSS*: Hayes, *Wartime Mission in Spain*, 20 (regarding his arrival date on May 16, 1942), 77–78 (regarding his attitude about the OSS).

173 *OSS chief historian Kermit Roosevelt . . . Members of the Madrid*: Kermit Roosevelt, *Overseas Targets*, 33.

173 *anathema to effective diplomacy*: Ibid. "The Ambassador considered espionage against a 'friendly' country to be 'un-American,'" wrote OSS historian Kermit Roosevelt, adding: "He stated that OSS activities were jeopardizing his efforts to maintain close bonds between Spain and the United States."

174 *I have become*: Huddleston, *Edmundo*, 80.

174 *he was already married . . . Emilie Dew Sandsten . . . Pepita*: Ibid., 3, 5.

174 *At the time of Germany's . . . 3,000 agents*: Kermit Roosevelt, *Overseas Targets*, 35.

174 *May 19 . . . Barcelona . . . Mariano Calvino*: BUTCH memorandum (Mariano Calvino) to BC-005, May 19, 1945, located at RG 226, Entry 127, Box 22, NARA.

Chapter 18: Pay Dirt

175 *Heinrich Mueller . . . Herbert von Bibra*: BUTCH memo to KATHY (Margaret J. Kasley), June 12, 1945, located at RG 226, Entry 127, Box 22, NARA. Aline's informant was Countess Renata del Monti.

175 *SS man . . . the SD's representative in Spain*: Ladislas Farago, *The Game of Foxes*, 711.

175 *von Hohenlohe's . . . wedding . . . Larry Mellon asked her*: BUTCH memo to QUERES (James MacMillan), June 19, 1945, located at RG 226, Entry 127, Box 22, NARA.

176 *Bienvenida bullfighters . . . Liechtenstein . . . Hayes . . . Franco . . . Hitler*: Ibid.

176 *Chipén . . . Max be followed . . . FLAMENCO*: BUTCH memo to KATHY (Margaet J. Kasley), June 15, 1945, located at RG 226, Entry 127, Box 22, NARA.

177 *Juanito . . . finca in Andalucia . . . HISMA*: BUTCH memo to QUERES, June 25, 1945, located at RG 226, Entry 127, Box 22, NARA.

177 *COLUMN*: BUTCH memo to KATHY (Margaet J. Kasley), June 26, 1945, located at RG 226, Entry 127, Box 22, NARA.

177 *Calle Conde de Aranda . . . I was looking for you*: Romanones, *Spy Went Dancing*, 79–80.

178 *I didn't find . . . His touch*: Ibid., 81–82.

178 *Rastro . . . I'm afraid a dealer*: Ibid., 86.

179 *FRANCISCO*: BUTCH memo to 983 (Larry Mellon), July 2, 1945, located at RG 226, Entry 127, Box 22, NARA.

179 *Beistegui*: BUTCH memo to QUERES (James MacMillan), July 3, 1945, located at RG 226, Entry 127, Box 22, NARA.

179 *memo on the Hohenlohe family*: BUTCH memo to LEGION (Larry Mellon) regarding August Hohenlohe, July 5, 1945, located at RG 226, Entry 127, Box 22, NARA.

179 *Manuel Ávila Camacho . . . plane to bring them to Mexico*: BUTCH memo to QUERES (James MacMillan), July 6, 1945, located at RG 226, Entry 127, Box 22, NARA.

179 *July 9 . . . Monsieur Brois*: BUTCH memo to QUERES (James MacMillan), July 9, 1945, located at RG 226, Entry 127, Box 22, NARA.

180 *If you don't keep*: Romanones, *Spy Went Dancing*, 90.

180 *Villa Rosa . . . pasadoble*: Ibid., 93–94.

181 *I think it's better . . . Casilda's my best*: Ibid., 95.

181 *There are rumors . . . Our jobs*: Ibid., 97.

Chapter 19: Intelligence Goes to Ground

183 *Las Ventas . . . Ritz . . . El Coto . . . Bar Basque*: Romanones, *Spy Went Dancing*, 110. Aline places the date here in September, but as explained two notes below, the month was August.

183 *I still thought*: Ibid.

184 *ARGUS wants to see . . . I have disagreeable . . . Sorry*: Ibid., 110–11. Aline uses her alias for Thomas's code name, calling him MOZART. She also places the date of this meeting in September, which is a month off. Numerous records in Aline's OSS personnel file show that the Madrid office was closed on August 15, 1945, and that this date was her last official day of employment with the agency. RG 226, Entry A1 224, OSS Personnel Files 1941–1945, Box 294, NARA.

185 *Dunev . . . Allied Mission in Spain*: Dunev, *Spy Reminisces*, 63.

185 *supervised the closing of the German embassy*: Memorandum from WIL-LIAMS (Dunev) to LEGION (Larry Mellon), May 9, 1945, located at RG 226, Entry 127, Box 19, NARA.

185 *Foreign Economic Administration . . . Aline being accepted on August 8*: Multiple memoranda in Aline's personnel file record this anticipated transfer, which never panned out. See, e.g., July 24, 1945, file notation: "FEA Madrid wants to hire BUTCH. Embassy approves. Suggest she be employed on 'reimbursable detail'"; memo from QUERES to George, August 8, 1945, sent via diplomatic pouch to Washington ("she is being employed by the F.E.A. . . . as of September 1st, on reimbursable detail"). RG 226, Entry A1 224, OSS Personnel Files 1941–1945, Box 294, NARA.

186 *Dunev was accepted into X-2 on August 9*: See memo from E. W. Andrews to Special Funds, August 9, 1945, requesting the transfer, and memo from B. Homer Hall to Special Funds, July 25, 1946, acknowledging it ("On August 16, 1945, he was transferred from S.I. to X-2. This transfer was approved by Washington in a cable to Madrid dated late July 1945"). RG 226, Entry 224, Box 204, NARA. In his memoir, *A Spy Reminisces* (p. 63), Dunev recalled being transferred to an interim agency, the Strategic Services Unit (bridging the OSS to the CIA), but his first stop, as of August 16, 1945, was with X-2.

186 *FEA decided at the end of August*: See the handwritten memorandum

to Aline's personnel file by Miss Wise, August 29, 1945 ("someone advised FEA that we would not release Miss Griffith on reimbursable basis"). RG 226, Entry A1 224, OSS Personnel Files 1941–1945, Box 294, NARA.

186 *September . . . Friday . . . Señorita . . . I can't believe . . . Are you pleased*: Romanones, *Spy Went Dancing*, 113–14.

187 *OSS is being disbanded . . . You're one of the lucky ones*: Ibid., 115. In all of her accounts about this transition with Frank Ryan, Aline asserts that she was the only one from the Madrid office who had been selected to carry on with espionage. This was untrue; Robert Dunev was the only Madrid staffer selected to carry on with intelligence (see *Dunev accepted into X-2*, above). While the Donovan-Stephenson-Ryan entity *might* have conducted espionage through British American Canadian Corporation (or its successor, World Commerce Corporation), there's no evidence in the record that it did, and Aline provides no verifiable incident where she personally did so. Dunev, on the other hand, continued with X-2, and was then transferred to the SSU, and then the CIA, which sent him to the Philippines. Dunev, *Spy Reminisces*, 70.

188 *And you must convince*: Romanones, *Spy Went Dancing*, 115–16. Aline's recollection of whom she was to persuade is confused. In *The Spy Went Dancing* (p. 115) that person was "Culbertson, who is acting ambassador." In "The OSS in Spain" (p. 126), however, she writes that the person is "Walter Butterworth, the Acting Ambassador." Paul T. Culbertson was indeed the chargé d'affaires and acting ambassador in Madrid, but not until June 1947. With Butterworth, Aline botches the name slightly; William Walton Butterworth was the US embassy counselor in Madrid in 1945, but he was never the acting ambassador. Given that the month in question is September 1945, the person she would have met with was Ambassador Norman Amour, who was in office from December 15, 1944, to December 1, 1945.

188 *36 Wall Street*: See Frank Ryan's personal stationery with this address in his letter of May 26, 1947, to Colonel Knox Pruden. Ryan also gives this address for Bache & Co. in his correspondence to Colonel Pruden on May 20, 1947. Both letters are in Aline's personnel file located at RG 226, Entry A1 224, OSS Personnel Files 1941–1945, Box 294, NARA.

188 *John J. Ryan & Sons . . . Frank's brother*: Continuing with her cover name for Ryan—John Derby—Aline cites the company name as John

J. Derby & Sons in *The Spy Went Dancing* (p. 116). In "The OSS in Spain" (p. 126), however, she gives the correct name. John J. Ryan, Jr. was the eldest of the four Ryan brothers. See the obituary for Frank's brother, Joseph, in the *New York Times*, October 26, 1950.

188 *That very month . . . international trade company*: "World Trade Body Ready to Function," *New York Times*, September 24, 1947. While author Anthony Cave Brown provides an organization date of May 1945 in his excellent work, *Wild Bill Donovan: The Last Hero*, 795, the *Times* article listed a commencement date of September 1945 ("World Commerce Corporation was originally formed in September, 1945, as the British American Canadian Corporation").

188 *formed in Panama*: Brown, *Wild Bill Donovan*, 795.

188 *British American Canadian Corporation*: "World Trade Body Ready to Function," *New York Times*, September 24, 1947. As the *Times* article notes, the company name was subsequently changed to World Commerce Corporation. Aline cites it as "World Commerce, Inc." in *The Spy Wore Silk* (p. 65) and "The OSS in Spain" (p. 127); as "World Commerce" in *The End of an Epoch* (p. 45); but disguises it as "Worldwide Trade, Inc." in *The Spy Went Dancing* (p. 122).

189 *who's who of espionage . . . Donovan . . . Stephenson . . . Hambro*: "World Trade Body Ready to Function," *New York Times*, September 24, 1947, 35; Brown, *Wild Bill Donovan*, 796.

189 *none had any experience in international trade*: While Ryan's father had founded the textile export company John J. Ryan & Sons, Ryan was not active in it. He appears to have been a general partner in Bache & Company, the legendary investment banking firm, before the war and until he joined the OSS in August 1942. After the war Ryan was a general partner at Bache until May 1948, when he changed his status to limited (inactive, nonmanagerial) partner. He also joined his family's firm as a vice president after the war, apparently so that he could use it as his cover business while working with Donovan and Stephenson to establish the BACC. For Ryan's dual role as general partner with Bache and vice president with John J. Ryan & Sons, see "Flies to Europe Today for Business Survey," *New York Times*, November 6, 1945. For his change of status with Bache, see "Changes in Bache & Co. Include a New Partner," *New York Times*, May 17, 1948.

189 *president—Frank T. Ryan*: "World Trade Body Ready to Function," *New York Times*, September 24, 1947; Thomas E. Mullaney, "Anglo-U.S.

Group Called 'Little ECA': World Commerce Corporation Supplies Raw Materials to Non-Satellite Nations," *New York Times*, January 2, 1949; "Brokerage Firm Acquired," *New York Times*, December 12, 1949. Anthony Cave Brown suggests that John Pepper had originally been slated to be the company's president (*Wild Bill Donovan*, 796), but cites no authority for the notion. Indeed, it was Ryan who traveled to Europe on November 6, 1945, to "survey" possibilities for international trade ("Flies to Europe Today to Survey Business," *New York Times*, November 6, 1945).

Chapter 20: Paris

190 *office . . . No. 11 Calle Marqués de Riscal . . . Barcelona . . . manufacturers*: Romanones, *Spy Went Dancing*, 117; "The OSS in Spain," 126.

190 *Robert Dunev . . . married on September 12 . . . Barnaby Conrad*: Dunev, *Spy Reminisces*, 61–63.

192 *rumors of Gestapo agents . . . Hans Lazar*: Romanones, *Spy Went Dancing*, 117.

192 *Edmundo . . . Walt Disney Company*: Huddleston, *Edmundo*, 82–83. On October 28, 1945, Edmundo wrote to his wife, Emilie (who was in Washington), while he was in New York: "I am just waiting around for developments . . . Roy Disney has written to the State Department for my passport." Two days later, he sent an update: "Roy Disney wants me to go with him to Washington next week. I suggest we have him for dinner. . . . He is very sweet and unassuming. You will like him." Ibid.

192 *She has a special aptitude*: Correspondence from James MacMillan to Whitney Shepardson, November 5, 1945, located at RG 226, Entry A1 224, OSS Personnel Files 1941–1945, Box 294, NARA.

192 *following day Ryan boarded the* Clipper: "Flies to Europe Today to Survey Business," *New York Times*, November 6, 1945.

194 *Jockey . . . La Reboite . . . When we danced*: Romanones, *Spy Went Dancing*, 118.

195 *Puerta de Hierro . . . twenty-five holes . . . swimming pool . . . bar*: Walter Smith, *Glimpses of Spain*, 94.

196 *You seem lost . . . Pulpito*: Romanones, *Spy Went Dancing*, 119.

197 *CLOSE MADRID . . . When can I see you . . . I have no idea*: Ibid., 120–21.

199 *Emilie Lassalle . . . Washington . . . second week of November . . . divorcing*:

Huddleston, *Edmundo,* 83–84. See also Edmundo's letter to his wife on December 7, 1945. Ibid., 84.

199 *November 21 Frank Ryan . . . Estoril Palacio*: Pacheco, ed., *Hotel Palácio,* 350–51.

199 *San Régis*: Romanones, *Spy Went Dancing,* 123; *End of an Epoch,* 47. Note that Aline confuses the spelling of the hotel name with a nearby café, calling it the "Hotel St. Regis."

200 *Hôtel Plaza Athénée*: Romanones, *Spy Went Dancing,* 120; *End of an Epoch,* 47.

200 *boss . . . John B. "Jack" Okie . . . Lisbon . . . thirty*: Romanones, "The OSS in Spain," 127; *End of an Epoch,* 44. In both accounts Aline refers to him as "Jack," but his actual name was John B. Okie. See Okie's entry in the OSS personnel directory at RG 126, Entry 224, Box 571, Stack 230, Row 86, Compartment 37, Shelf 07, NARA.

200 *Czechoslovakia, Switzerland, Sweden . . . Germany*: Romanones, *End of an Epoch,* 45; "The OSS in Spain," 127.

200 *Balenciaga . . . Vogue magazine*: Romanones, *End of an Epoch,* 46–47.

201 *Ryan . . . information he wanted*: Ibid., 45–46.

201 *I've been reading . . . What were you doing*: Ibid., 47.

202 *Aline returned to New York*: It is unclear on which date Aline returned to the US. In her OSS file, handwritten notes from Douglas Hartshorne (handing Aline's OSS transportation expense reimbursement) indicate in one place that she arrived on January 12, 1946, and in another place that she arrived on February 9. Correspondence from W. A. Martinez to Hartshorne on May 5, 1947, located at RG 226, Entry A1 224, OSS Personnel Files 1941–1945, Box 294, NARA. See also Aline's correspondence of February 22, 1946—written from her New York home—to Mr. Rehm; her correspondence to R. C. Read on March 29, 1946—also written from New York—indicating that she was now returning to Madrid; and her correspondence to George White on June 3, 1946, stating that she had been in the US in February and March. Ibid.

It is also unclear, what, if anything, Aline did during this six weeks or so in New York. Aline's various writings skip from the period after she is hired by Frank Ryan and leaves for Paris, November 1945, to April 1946 when she is again back in Paris. In her OSS file, there is a peculiar "memo to the file" dated June 13, 1946, and signed by W. Wyllys Andrews, a former OSS Washington staffer. The memo is from "Iberian

Desk, SI," to "Files," and the subject is "Marie Aline Griffith." But in June 1946 there was no Iberian Desk, and there was no OSS. The Iberian Desk had been closed some ten months earlier, and the OSS followed with its own dissolution shortly thereafter.

In his memo to the file (which specifically noted that no copies were made; it went to no one), Andrews writes about Aline: "Upon her return to this country, and apparently at her own behest, large pictures appeared on the front pages of at least a dozen prominent U.S. newspapers under such captions as 'Modern Mata Hari returns from Spain.' These also stated that subject had 'worked as a spy for the Office of Strategic Services in Spain under the U.S. State Department throughout the war.' . . . Subject must under no circumstances ever be considered for undercover or clandestine employment by this organization."

It is possible that Aline could have given such interviews during this six-month stay in the US, but it would have been an egregious violation of OSS's confidentiality commitment. What is curious is that this memo comes just seven months after James MacMillan's recommendation of Aline for further espionage work. In addition, Andrews provides no copies of said newspaper articles, nor does he provide the identity of a single paper where such stories supposedly ran—not even the Mata Hari story he identified. Without such, his entry is hearsay. Additionally, no such story was ever published in the *New York Times*.

202 *delirious with joy . . . dinner at Le Grand Vefour*: Romanones, *Spy Went Dancing*, 122–23.

202 *April 9, 1946*: As with all of her books, Aline's dates in *The Spy Went Dancing* are wholly unreliable, some as far off as a year. In Chapter 16, for example, she records a date of April 1947 (p. 122). She writes that she is twenty-three at the time (p. 124), and that Luis has not yet proposed (p. 130). Aline was born on May 22, 1920, which means that she was twenty-six; she's off on her own age by three years. Similarly, in *The End of an Epoch* (pp. 49–50) she writes that in April 1947 she was twenty-four—two years off from her actual age. And as for Luis, he had proposed no less than four months earlier, as the engagement was announced by United Press on December 12, 1946, and published in the *New York Times* the following day. "Aline Griffith Engaged: Former OSS Madrid Aide Fiancee of Ex-Premier's Grandson," *New York Times*, December 13, 1946.

April 9, 1946, was a Tuesday and is the most likely date for the planned rendezvous.

Chapter 21: *La Tienta*

203 *Hans Czernin*: Romanones, *End of an Epoch*, 48. Aline writes that Czernin was a former OSS agent, although his name does not appear in the OSS personnel directory. It's possible that he could have been an MI6 agent, or simply a source for the OSS.

203 *Eric Erickson*: Erickson was the OSS's most successful agent in Stockholm. See, e.g., George Axelsson, "Swedish 'Pro-Nazi' Duped Foe 3 Years," *New York Times*, June 3, 1945; William Casey, *The Secret War Against Hitler*, 40; Farago, *Game of the Foxes*, 606.

204 *Bauer au Lac—It's obvious to me*: Romanones, *Spy Went Dancing*, 123. Interestingly, the Bauer-au-Lac was the hotel where British double agent Dusko Popov holed up immediately after the war while he was looking for Johnny Jebsen (his best friend and German case officer, who was never heard from again after being abducted from Lisbon and cashiered to Berlin on April 30, 1944).

204 *Helga Nehring ... Benito Llambí ... father*: Romanones, *End of an Epoch*, 70.

205 *They decided she could go in June*: Aline's correspondence (on her personal stationery, showing her address as Marqués del Riscal, 11, Bajo 2, Madrid) to George White on June 3, 1946, confirms the June date. RG 226, Entry A1 224, OSS Personnel Files 1941–1945, Box 294, NARA. On June 26, R. G. Read of the War Department wrote to Aline at the same Madrid address, indicating that she was still in the city. Ibid.

206 *Hendaye ... conditions*: For excellent summaries of the Franco-Hitler meeting at Hendaye, see Dear and Foot, eds., *Oxford Companion to World War II*, 1034; Baudot, et al., eds., *Historical Encyclopedia of World War II*, 431; and Shirer, *Rise and Fall of the Third Reich*, 814.

206 Franco's ploy and actions: For details on Franco's ploy, actions, and true intentions, see Hayes, *Wartime Mission in Spain*, 297–309; and Eccles, *By Safe Hand*, 417–18.

206 *rather have had three or four teeth*: Malcolm Muggeridge, ed., *Ciano's Diplomatic Papers*, 402, cited in Shirer, *Rise and Fall of the Third Reich*, 814.

206 *Spain has refused*: Winston Churchill, *The Second World War*, vol. 3, *The Grand Alliance*, 11–12.

207 *I was wondering . . . That's what you*: Romanones, *Spy Went Dancing*, 126–27.

208 tienta . . . *Count of Mayalde*: Romanones, *History of Pascualete*, 10; *Spy Went Dancing*, 127–28; *End of an Epoch*, 53. For a general background on the *tienta*, see Conrad, *La Fiesta Brava*, 18–19, and Hemingway, *Death in the Afternoon*, 114, 116.

209 *The bravery of the bull*: Hemingway, *Death in the Afternoon*, 113.

209 *size from his father . . . heart from his mother*: Conrad, *La Fiesta Brava*, 18; Conrad, *Fun While It Lasted*, 128.

209 *heifers . . . trickier to fight*: Conrad, *La Fiesta Brava*, 19.

209 *Manolete*: His real name was Manuel Rodríguez: Ibid., 4; Conrad, *Matador*, 229.

210 *undriven nail*: Conrad, *Matador*, 61.

210 *face was long*: Manolete's gaunt face, melancholy eyes, and deep scars are perhaps best seen on Barnaby Conrad's excellent drawing of him in *Fun While It Lasted*, 111.

210 *Would you like*: Romanones, *Spy Went Dancing*, 128. In all cases of Aline's retelling of the story, she wrote that her *tienta* exhibition was with a bull calf (*History of Pascualete*, 10; *Spy Went Dancing*, 129; *End of an Epoch*, 53), but this would not have been the case, as explained in the text (males never saw a cape or man on foot until their fight in the bull ring).

210 *A bullfighter is a dancer*: Conrad, *La Fiesta Brava*, 48–49.

211 Aline, what are you: Romanones, *Spy Went Dancing*, 129.

211 *horn ripped through her jacket . . . airborne*: Ibid.; *End of an Epoch*, 53. In Aline's telling of the story in *The History of Pascualete* (p. 10), she was not thrown by the calf, but trampled. In addition, in this version of the story she had kneeled for the second pass, imitating the *pases de rodilla* that she had seen bullfighters perform.

Chapter 22: The Bookkeeper

212 *What a silly thing . . . You'd better stop*: Romanones, *Spy Went Dancing*, 129–30; *History of Pascualete*, 10; *End of an Epoch*, 53.

213 *A week went by . . . golf*: Romanones, *End of an Epoch*, 53.

213 *next post would be in Prague*: Romanones, "The OSS in Spain," 127; *Spy Went Dancing*, 133 ("Czechoslovakia").

213 *This time my work*: Romanones, *Spy Went Dancing*, 133.

213 *Why is Angustias . . . tonight*: Ibid., 134.

214 *Raimundo Lanza*: Romanones, *End of an Epoch*, 54; *Spy Went Dancing*, 135.

214 *But I thought . . . No, I prefer*: Romanones, *Spy Went Dancing*, 135.

215 *Aline, I would like . . . No, I told him*: Romanones, *End of an Epoch*, 54; *Spy Went Dancing*, 135–36.

216 *My son says . . . I cannot afford*: Romanones, *Spy Went Dancing*, 136.

217 *the home on the Castellana*: In *The Spy Went Dancing* (p. 137) Aline states that the Romanones palace was "along the Castellana . . . number 36." However, the correct address appears to be closer to Calle Rafael Calvo, 39, which sits on the corner of Rafael Calvo and Castellana, and is directly across from the American embassy, as Aline described in *The End of an Epoch* (p. 55). See Chapter 8 and accompanying notes.

217 *Do not be frightened . . . My grandfather is accustomed*: Romanones, *End of an Epoch*, 55–57; *Spy Went Dancing*, 137–38.

218 *Don't worry*: Ibid.

218 Quien es . . . Bueno . . . *Now give me*: Romanones, *Spy Went Dancing*, 139; *End of an Epoch*, 57.

219 *Luis, your marriage . . . I'm getting married . . . he's no kind of*: Romanones, *Spy Went Dancing*, 140–41.

220 *cabled Frank Ryan in New York*: In *The End of an Epoch* (p. 58), Aline recalled cabling Ryan in Washington, but he was running BACC from New York, and his business address during this time was 36 Wall Street.

220 *Forty-eight hours later . . . Ryan*: Romanones, *Spy Went Dancing*, 141; *End of an Epoch*, 58.

Chapter 23: *Cortando la Coleta*

221 *I have come here . . . Here is your ticket*: Romanones, *End of an Epoch*, 59. In Aline's original quote she has Ryan saying that she had served "three years in wartime activities," but apparently this was an oversight. Aline's time with the OSS was from November 1, 1943, to August 15, 1945, or the better part of two years. As such, I have changed her "three" to "two." Ibid.

221 *Prague*: Romanones, "The OSS in Spain," 127.

222 cortando la coleta: Romanones, *Spy Went Dancing*, 148. For background on the saying, see Hemingway, *Death in the Afternoon*, 398; Conrad, *La Fiesta Brava*, 178.

222 *Juanito's father*: Conrad, *La Fiesta Brava*, 27.

222 *You are unaware*: Romanones, *End of an Epoch*, 60.

222 *Think this over*: Romanones, *Spy Went Dancing*, 141.

223 *He and Princess Agatha were getting married*: In *The Spy Went Dancing* (second page of photo section, bottom) Aline records that Edmundo and Maria Agatha were married in October 1945, which is off by some ten months. See "Disney Iberian Agent Marries Princess of Ratibor and Corvey," *New York Times*, August 3, 1946, indicating that. The *Times* article erred, however, in declaring that Edmundo's father had been a foreign minister of Mexico, that Edmundo had received a doctorate, and that he had been an associate professor of history, none of which was true. See Huddleston, *Edmundo*, 86. Inexplicably, Aline also recorded the wrong date for her own wedding on the following page, citing it as "August 1947," when her wedding date was June 26, 1947. See "U.S. Girl Weds Count: War Department Employee Bride of Wealthy Spanish Nobleman," *New York Times*, June 27, 1947.

223 *They wed at the San Jerónimo*: "Disney Iberian Agent Marries Princess of Ratibor and Corvey," *New York Times*, August 3, 1946.

223 *Edmundo*: Huddleston, *Edmundo*, 89.

224 *mother . . . dress . . . tiara . . . mother had died . . . That, you will have*: Romanones, *Spy Went Dancing*, 142; *End of an Epoch*, 61–62.

224 *tradition . . . But Luis . . . I'd like a ring*: Ibid.

224 *Luis, what about the woman's . . . Ahhhh, si*: Romanones, *End of an Epoch*, 62–63; *Spy Went Dancing*, 142–43.

225 *the* New York Times *made it*: "Aline Griffith Engaged: Former OSS Madrid Aide Fiancee of Ex-Premier's Grandson," *New York Times*, December 13, 1946.

226 *Preposterous . . . You, a spy*: Romanones, *Spy Went Dancing*, 146.

227 *Balenciaga's . . . somebody*: Romanones, *End of an Epoch*, 61–62.

227 *We will decide later*: Ibid., 63.

227 *Isabel, the Duchess of Tamames*: Ibid., 66; *Spy Went Dancing*, 146.

227 *My great-grandfather . . . run-of-the-mill*: Romanones, *End of an Epoch*, 64–66.

228 *June 26, 1947 . . . Church of San Fermín*: As reported in the *New York Times* the following day, February 27.

228 *she was trembling . . . Bill, she whispered*: Romanones, *Spy Went Dancing*, 147; *End of an Epoch*, 68–69.

229 *Benito Llambí . . . revolver*: Romanones, *End of an Epoch*, 69.

Chapter 24: Countess Quintanilla

230 *Luis's friends . . . When they spoke to him*: Romanones, *End of an Epoch*, 69–70.

230 *Before we go . . . Aline, I have attended*: Ibid., 70; *Spy Went Dancing*, 147–48.

232 *Eva Perón . . . Querida, take my advice*: Romanones, *Spy Went Dancing*, 148–49; *End of an Epoch*, 71–72.

233 *What a pleasure*: Romanones, *End of an Epoch*, 74.

235 *When we were children*: Ibid., 76–77.

235 *The day the war . . . I loved my grandfather . . . Exactly nineteen*: Ibid., 120–25.

237 *We were too young . . .* chekas: Ibid., 127.

237 *Manolete . . . Linares . . . August 28*: Conrad, *La Fiesta Brava*, 2; Sam Pope Brewer, "Manolete, 30, Dies After Goring by Bull; All Spain Mourns Her Greatest Matador," *New York Times*, August 30, 1947; Romanones, *End of an Epoch*, 77.

238 *Malo—bad . . . Stay away from this one*: Conrad, *La Fiesta Brava*, 11–12.

239 *The bullfight is sometimes . . . bullfight fans go*: Ibid., 29.

240 *What you are saying . . . I will make a*: Romanones, *End of an Epoch*, 78.

241 *world-wide coverage*: "World Trade Body Ready to Function," *New York Times*, September 24, 1947.

241 *Robert Dunev . . . Philippines . . . the CIA's first*: Dunev, *Spy Reminisces*, 71.

Chapter 25: Living the Dream

242 *the* New York Times *article*: See "World Trade Body Ready to Function," *New York Times*, September 24, 1947.

242 *Did WCC conduct any type*: In *Wild Bill Donovan* (p. 799), Anthony Cave Brown concludes that World Commerce Corporation was not conducting espionage, but was "enlightened capitalism's answer to Communist imperialism."

243 *he met with*: Ibid., 797.

243 *In our view the restoration . . . The financial resources*: Correspondence of Frank Ryan to General Lucius Clay, October 16, 1947, cited in Brown, *Wild Bill Donovan*, 865.

244 *November . . . Queen Elizabeth*: Romanones, *End of an Epoch*, 79. See also correspondence from Aline's father, William F. Griffith, to the War Department (which was trying to reach her to finalize Aline's

OSS account) on November 1, 1947, wherein he indicated she would be traveling to New York aboard the *Queen Mary*, arriving on November 9 or 10. RG 226, Entry A1 224, OSS Personnel Files 1941–1945, Box 294, NARA.

244 *Jack Warner*: Romanones, *End of an Epoch*, 81–82. Aline claims that Elsa Maxwell seated Luis next to Grace Kelly, "the most famous movie star of the moment," at this first party on November 12, 1947. The meeting here seems unlikely since November 12 was Kelly's eighteenth birthday, and she would not appear in her first movie, Henry Hathaway's *Fourteen Hours,* until 1951.

244 *Duke and Dutchess of Windsor . . . El Morocco . . . Stork Club*: Ibid., 82.

244 *Americans are always running . . . You really spent*: Ibid., 85–86.

245 *I saw the sign*: Ibid., 84.

245 *Humphrey Bogart, Lauren Bacall . . . June 21*: Ibid., 93–94.

246 Bueno, bueno: Ibid., 99.

246 *father's green eyes and light brown hair*: In Aline's *The Spy Went Dancing* (pp. 52, 160), Luis has green eyes. In *The End of an Epoch* (p. 257), however, he has blue eyes. In all of her books she states that his hair was blond. Color photos of Luis in the Getty Images archives reveals that his eyes were, in fact, green, and that his hair was brown.

247 *Álvaro . . . vegetables*: Romanones, *End of an Epoch*, 163.

248 *Archibald Roosevelt . . . CIA*: Ibid., 503. See also note below regarding what she did for the CIA.

248 *The work she did for the CIA*: In 2019 I requested from the CIA any and all files on Aline Griffith, Robert Dunev, and Frank Ryan through the Freedom of Information Act. Several months later I received a short letter stating that all OSS records had been turned over to the NARA. I had not requested their "OSS records," of course, but that was the response. On a prior request for another operative, I was told that I needed to supply a death certificate for the individual before they would look into the matter, notwithstanding that he would have been 115 years old if he had been alive.

248 *World Commerce Corporation . . . $16.1 million*: Brown, *Wild Bill Donovan*, 799.

249 *1963 article*: Bernadine Morris, "A Well-Dressed Countess Takes Fashion Role Lightly," *New York Times*, October 22, 1963.

249 Life *magazine*: "Madrid's Best-Dressed U.S. Beauty," *Life*, October 9, 1964, 85–86.

249 *I'm so excited . . . I've never been*: Romanones, *Spy Went Dancing*, 195–96; *End of an Epoch*, 268–69.

250 *But she had such*: Romanones, *End of an Epoch*, 208.

251 *May 1970 . . . Marsha Gayle . . . Ryan*: Charlotte Curtis, "Now Even in May, There's Just No Rest for the Partygoer," *New York Times*, May 10, 1970.

Chapter 26: Twin Souls

252 *Casey . . . apartments in Washington*: Romanones, *End of an Epoch*, 504.

252 *honorary doctorate*: Ibid., 407, photo preceding page 439.

252 *diamond bracelet and wrist watch*: Ibid., 514–15.

253 *I felt destroyed*: Ibid., 516–17.

253 *If it is for love*: Fyodor Dostoyevsky, *Notes from the Underground*, 669.

254 *The great sadness . . . grandchildren*: Romanones, *End of an Epoch*, 516, 518.

255 *1992 article*: Romanones, "The OSS in Spain," 122–28.

255 *Hemingway's bullfighters . . . all the way up*: Hemingway, *Sun Also Rises*, 9.

Epilogue: The Rest of the Story

257 *Juanito Belmonte . . . married . . . heart attack*: Romanones, *End of an Epoch*, 43.

257 *It was a sad shock*: Ibid.

257 *Barnaby Conrad . . . It's rather difficult*: Harvey Breit, "Talk with Barnaby Conrad," *New York Times*, July 6, 1952.

258 *Steinbeck . . . Faulkner . . . I'm sending you*: Conrad, *Matador*, 223, back cover.

258 *Noël dahling . . . Gored but never*: Conrad, *Fun While It Lasted*, foreword.

259 *Robert Dunev . . . Manila . . . Madrid . . . Lima . . . Buenos Aires*: Dunev, *Spy Reminisces*, 71, 74, 78–87; interview with Michael Dunev, February 7, 2020.

260 *Gloria von Fürstenberg . . . penniless*: See the questions posed to Gloria by Portuguese authorities on October 3, 1944, and her written responses, at RG 226, Entry 124, Box 14, NARA. See also Charles Grey's summary report to C. H. van Brink dated September 30, 1944, as well as Gloria's X-2 file card ("Emphasized that she must join

these relatives within the very near future as she is virtually penniless"). Ibid.

260 *Ahmed Fakhry . . . checked in to the hotel on August 28*: See Pacheco, ed., *Hotel Palácio*, 294–95.

261 *Gemini . . . $195 million*: See Josh Baumgard, "Tour the $195M Manalapan Mansion That Just Publicly Listed for the First Time," miami.curbed.com, January 25, 2016.

261 *Sotheby's . . . $115 million*: See the listing at https://www.sothebys homes.com/palmbeach/sales/0077253.

261 *the Guinness estate in Epalinges, Switzerland*: The estate is called the Villa Zanroc and is located at Chemin de Ballègue 58.

261 *Prince Max . . . El Quexigal . . . Sotheby's . . . Grupo Eulen*: "Los Propietarios de 'El Quexigal' Quieren Que el Tesoro Permanezca en España," *El País*, May 20, 1979; Jorge Piedrahita, "El Quexigal: Finca de Reyes y Nobles Desde Inmemorial," July 30, 2010, https://jorgepiedrahita .blogia.com/2010/073001-el-quexigal-finca-de-reyes-y-nobles-desde -inmemorial.php; "El Quexigal," nuestroincondecebreros.es/pagina/6 .html.

262 *Edmundo Lassalle . . . dying in London in 1966 . . . CIA . . . KGB*: Romanones, *Spy Went Dancing*, 158, 244, 272–74, 314–15.

262 *August 1, 1974 . . . divorced Emilie . . . Roy Disney*: Huddleston, *Edmundo*, 84, 90, 94, 106. See also Lassalle's obituary in the *New York Times*, August 15, 1974.

263 *Nancy Norman . . . Patricia Rinehart . . . International Fund for Monuments*: Huddleston, *Edmundo*, 102–3, 106.

263 *doctors say my condition*: Ibid., 105.

263 *Edmundo took his own life*: Ibid., 106. See also Lassalle's obituary in the *New York Times*, August 15, 1974.

263 *Mellon . . . cattle ranch . . . Rimrock*: Glenn Fowler, "W. L. Mellon, Humanitarian, Is Dead at 79," *New York Times*, August 5, 1989. See also Mellon's home address on his OSS personnel pay cards at RG 226, Entry 127, Box 1, NARA.

264 *Mellon . . . Haiti . . . Albert Schweitzer Hospital*: Glenn Fowler, "W. L. Mellon, Humanitarian, Is Dead at 79," *New York Times*, August 5, 1989.

264 *1951 . . . ten million units of penicillin*: Romanones, *End of an Epoch*, 164, 167.

264 *Pierre . . . Francois Ferronière . . . 333*: Romanones, *Spy Wore Red*, 294.

265 *The man I call*: Ibid., ix.

265 *Gregory Thomas . . . Chanel . . . Masarkytown*: "H. Gregory Thomas, Chanel Executive, 82," *New York Times*, October 10, 1990.

265 *Ryan . . . Stettinius retired . . . 1950 . . . Alfred V. Du Pont*: "A. V. Du Pont in Post Left by Stettinius," *New York Times*, January 26, 1950.

BIBLIOGRAPHY

Archives and Official Documents

American Historical Association, Washington, DC
Arquivo Municipal de Cascais, Portugal
Arquivo Municipal de Lisboa, Portugal
Câmera Municipal de Cascais, Departmento de Cultura, Portugal
Casas das Historias Paula Rego, Cascais, Portugal
Central Intelligence Agency (OSS) Secret Control Intelligence Reports
Centro Documental de la Memoria Histórica, Madrid, Spain
Ministerio de Asuntos Exteriores, Madrid, Spain
National Archives, Kew, London, England
National Archives and Records Administration (NARA), College Park, Maryland
National Archives and Records Administration (NARA), Kansas City, Missouri
Polícia de Vigilância e Defesa Estado, Serviços de Informação, Biblioteca Nacional, Lisboa, Portugal

Books and Articles

Abramovici, Pierre. *Szkolnikoff: Hitler's Jewish Smuggler*. Barnsley, UK: Pen & Sword, 2016.

Alcorn, Robert Hyden. *No Banners, No Bands: More Tales of the OSS*. New York: David McKay, 1965.

———. *No Bugles for Spies: Tales of the OSS*. New York: David McKay, 1962.

Alford, Kenneth D. *Nazi Plunder: Great Treasure Stories of World War II.* New York: Da Capo Press, 2001.

Allen, Roy. *The Pan Am Clipper: The History of Pan Am's Flying Boats, 1931 to 1946.* New York: Barnes & Noble, 2000.

"Allies in Madrid Gain Ton of German Gold." *New York Times,* December 13, 1945.

Alsop, Stewart, and Thomas Braden. *The O.S.S. and American Espionage.* New York: Reynal & Hitchcock, 1946.

Anjos, Maria Cristina de Carvalho dos. *O Turismo no Eixo Costeiro Estoril-Cascais (1929–1939): Equipamentos, Eventos e Promoção do Destino.* Lisbon: Universidade de Lisboa, Faculdade de Letras, Departmento de História, 2012.

Anthony, Edwin D., ed. *Records of the Office of Inter-American Affairs.* Washington, DC: National Archives and Records Service, 1973.

Atwood, Kathryn J. *Women Heroes of World War II: 26 Stories of Espionage, Sabotage, Resistance, and Rescue.* Chicago: Chicago Review Press, 2011.

Balfour, Michael. *Withstanding Hitler in Germany, 1933–45.* New York: Routledge, 1988.

Bassett, Richard. *Hitler's Spy Chief: The Story of Wilhelm Canaris.* New York: Pegasus, 2012.

Baudot, Marcel, et al., eds. *The Historical Encyclopedia of World War II.* New York: Greenwich House, 1977.

Bayles, William D. "Lisbon: The City of Refuge." *Picture Post,* June 28, 1941.

———. "Lisbon: Europe's Bottleneck." *Life,* April 28, 1941.

Bear, Frederick. "Dusko [007] Popov: Exclusive Interview." *Genesis,* November 1974.

Beesly, Patrick. *Very Special Admiral: The Life of Admiral J. H. Godfrey C. B.* London: Hamish Hamilton, 1980.

Beevor, Anthony. *The Battle for Spain: The Civil War 1936–1939.* London: Weidenfeld & Nicolson, 2006.

Benton, Kenneth. "The ISOS Years: Madrid 1941–3." *Journal of Contemporary History* 30, no. 3 (July 1995).

Bess, Demaree. "American Strategy Pains Portugal." *Saturday Evening Post,* August 30, 1941.

Bloch, Michael. *Operation Willi: The Nazi Plot to Kidnap the Duke of Windsor.* New York: Grove, 1986.

Blume, Lesley M. "Barnaby Conrad: Author, Matador, Bon Vivant, and Thorn in Hemingway's Side." *Paris Review*, March 4, 2013.

Bower, Tom. *Nazi Gold: The Full Story of the Fifty-Year Swiss-Nazi Conspiracy to Steal Billions from Europe's Jews and Holocaust Survivors*. New York: HarperCollins, 1997.

Breitman, Richard. "Research in OSS Records: One Historian's Concerns," *The Secrets War: The Office of Strategic Services in World War II*. Washington, DC: NARA, 1992.

Breuer, William. *Hitler's Undercover War: The Espionage Invasion of the U.S.A.* New York: St. Martin's, 1989.

Brissaud, André. *Canaris: The Biography of Admiral Canaris, Chief of German Military Intelligence*. New York: Grosset & Dunlap, 1974.

Bristow, Desmond. *A Game of Moles: The Deceptions of an MI6 Officer*. London: Little Brown, 1993.

Brown, Anthony Cave. *Bodyguard of Lies*. New York: HarperCollins, 1975.

——. *Wild Bill Donovan: The Last Hero*. New York: Times Books, 1982.

Burdick, Charles and Hans-Adolf Jacobsen, eds. *The Halder War Diary, 1939–1942*. Toronto: Presidio Press, 1988.

Burns, Jimmy. *Papa Spy: Love, Faith, and Betrayal in Wartime Spain*. New York: Walker, 2009.

Busch, Noel F. "Juan Trippe: Pan American Airway's Young Chief Helps Run a Branch of U.S. Defense." *Life*, October 20, 1941.

Carvalho, António, and João Miguel Henriques, eds. *O Estoril e as Origens do Turismo em Portugal 1911–1931*. Cascais, Portugal: Câmara Municipal, 2011.

——and Cristina Pacheco, eds. *Grande Hotel e Hotel Atlântico: Boletins de Alojamento de Estrangeiros: Boletins Individuais e Relação de Hóspedes da Divisão Policial de Cascais, 1939–1944*. Cascais: Câmara Municipal, 2005.

Casey, William. *The Secret War Against Hitler*. Washington, DC: Regnery, 1988.

Chalou, George C., ed. *The Secrets War: The Office of Strategic Services in World War II*. Washington, DC: NARA, 1992.

Chambers, John Whiteclay II. "Office of Secret Services Training During World War II." *Studies in Intelligence* 54, no. 2, 2010.

——. *OSS Training in the National Parks and Service Abroad in World War II*. Washington, DC: US National Park Service, 2008.

Charleston, Beth Duncuff. "Cristobal Balenciaga (1895–1972)." *Heilbrunn*

Timeline of Art History. New York: Metropolitan Museum of Art, October 2004.

Churchill, Peter. *Spirit in the Cage.* 1954. Reprint. London: Elmfield Press, 1974.

———. *Of Their Own Choice.* London: Hodder and Stoughton, 1952.

Churchill, Winston. *The Second World War.* Vol. 2, *Their Finest Hour.* Boston: Houghton Mifflin, 1949.

———. *The Second World War.* Vol. 3, *The Grand Alliance.* Boston: Houghton Mifflin, 1950.

Colby, William E. "The Legacy of the OSS." *The Secrets War: The Office of Strategic Services in World War II.* Washington, DC: NARA, 1992.

Colvin, Ian. *Admiral Canaris: Chief of Intelligence.* London: Colvin Press, 2007.

Conrad, Barnaby, ed. "Bullfighting." universalium.academic.ru (undated).

———. *La Fiesta Brava: The Art of the Bull Ring.* New York: Houghton Mifflin, 1953.

———. *Fun While It Lasted.* New York: Random House, 1969.

———. *Matador.* Cambridge, MA: Riverside Press, 1952.

Conroy, Sarah Booth. "The Spy's New Clothes." *Washington Post*, April 27, 1991.

Costello, John. *Ten Days to Destiny.* New York: HarperCollins, 1991.

Crowdy, Terry. *Deceiving Hitler: Double-Cross and Deception.* Oxford: Osprey, 2008.

Cunningham, Cyril. *Beaulieu: The Finishing School for Secret Agents.* London: Leo Cooper, 1998.

Davison, Phil. "Aline Griffith, American-born spy, Spanish Countess and Author of Espionage Tales, Dies at 94." *Washington Post*, December 13, 2017.

"A Dazzling Flair from Spain: Madrid's Best-Dressed U.S. Beauty." *Life*, October 9, 1964.

Deacon, Richard. *Spyclopedia: The Comprehensive Handbook of Espionage.* New York: William Morrow, 1988.

Dear, I. C. B., and M. R. D. Foot, eds. *The Oxford Companion to World War II.* Oxford: Oxford University Press, 1995.

Delmer, Sefton. *The Counterfeit Spy: The Untold Story of a Phantom Army That Deceived Hitler.* New York: Harper & Row, 1971.

Doerries, Reinhard. *Hitler's Intelligence Chief: Walter Schellenberg.* New York: Enigma, 2009.

————. *Hitler's Last Chief of Foreign Intelligence: Allied Interrogations of Walter Schellenberg.* London: Frank Cass, 2003.

Dulles, Allen W. *Germany's Underground: The Anti-Nazi Resistance.* 1947. Reprint. New York: Da Capo Press, 2000.

Dunev, Robert. *The Spy Reminisces.* Unpublished memoir, 1987.

Eccles, David. *By Safe Hand: The Letters of Sybil and David Eccles, 1939–1942.* London: Bodley Head, 1983.

Fairbairn, W. E. *Defendu: Scientific Self-Defense.* Reprint. East Sussex, England: Naval & Military Press (undated).

————. *Get Tough! How to Win in Hand-to-Hand Fighting, as Taught to the British Commandos and U.S. Armed Forces.* Reprint. East Sussex, England: Naval & Military Press (undated).

Farago, Ladislas. *The Game of the Foxes.* New York: David McKay, 1971.

Foot, M. R. D. *SOE in France.* London: Whitehall History Publishing, 1966.

————. *S.O.E.: The Special Operations Executive, 1940–46.* 1984. Reprint, Mandarin, 1993.

Godfrey, John H. *The Naval Memoirs of Admiral J. H. Godfrey.* Vol. 5, *1939–1942*, Naval Intelligence Division, Part I. Churchill Archives Centre, The Papers of Admiral John Henry Godfrey, GDFY 1/6.

Goebbels, Joseph. *The Goebbels Diaries, 1939–1941.* Trans. Fred Taylor. Reprint. New York: Putnam, 1983.

————. *The Goebbels Diaries, 1942–1942.* Trans. Louis P. Lochner. New York: Doubleday, 1948.

Green, Michelle. "The Countess of Romanones Commands a Dazzling Cast in Her Second Memoir of Espionage, *The Spy Went Dancing*." *People*, May 7, 1990.

Handel, Michael. *Strategic and Operational Deception in the Second World War.* London: Frank Cass, 1987.

Hart, B. H. Liddell, *History of the Second World War.* New York: Putnam, 1971.

Hassell, Augustino von, and Sigrid MacRae. *Alliance of Enemies: The Untold Story of the American and German Collaboration to End World War II.* New York: Thomas Dunne, 2006.

Hayes, Carlton J. H. *Wartime Mission in Spain, 1942–1945.* New York: Macmillan, 1945.

Hemingway, Ernest. "Bullfighting, Sport and Industry." *Fortune*, March 1930.

————. *Death in the Afternoon.* 1932. Reprint. New York: Touchstone, 1996.

————. *The Sun Also Rises.* 1926. Reprint. New York: Scribner, 2016.

Himmler, Katrin, and Michael Wildt. *The Private Heinrich Himmler: Letters of a Mass Murderer.* New York: St. Martin's, 2016.

Hinsley, F. H. *British Intelligence in the Second World War.* Vol. 1, *Its Influence on Strategy and Operations.* London: Her Majesty's Stationery Office, 1979.

————. *British Intelligence in the Second World War.* Vol. 3, Part 2. New York: Cambridge University Press, 1988.

————. *British Intelligence in the Second World War.* Vol. 4, *Security and Counter-Intelligence.* New York: Cambridge University Press, 1990.

Hoare, Samuel J. G. *Ambassador on Special Mission.* London: Collins, 1946.

Hoffman, Peter. *The History of the German Resistance, 1933–1945.* Cambridge, MA: MIT Press, 1977.

Höhne, Heinz. *Canaris: Hitler's Master Spy.* New York: Doubleday, 1979.

————. *The Order of the Death's Head: The Story of Hitler's SS.* Originally published in 1966 in German as *Der Orden unter dem Totenkopf.* Trans. Richard Barry. Reprint, Penguin, 2000.

Holt, Thaddeus. *The Deceivers: Allied Military Deception in the Second World War.* New York: Scribner, 2004.

Höttl, Wilhelm. *The Secret Front: Nazi Political Espionage, 1938–1945.* 1953. Reprint. New York: Enigma Books, 2003.

Howard, Michael. *Strategic Deception in the Second World War.* 1990. Reprint. New York: Norton, 1995.

Hoyt, Edwin. *The Invasion Before Normandy.* New York: Cooper Square, 1999.

Huddleston, Robert. *Edmundo: From Chipas, Mexico to Park Avenue.* College Station, TX: Virtualbookworm, 2007.

Hull, Cordell. "Inter-Allied Declaration Against Acts of Dispossession Committed in Territories Under Enemy Occupation or Control." *Foreign Relations of the United States: Diplomatic Papers, 1943, General,* vol. 1.

Hymoff, Edward. *The OSS in World War II.* New York: Richardson & Steirman, 1986.

Kahn, David. *Hitler's Spies: German Military Intelligence in World War II.* New York: Macmillan, 1978.

Kanfer, Stefan. *Ball of Fire: The Tumultuous Life and Comic Art of Lucille Ball.* New York: Knopf, 2003.

Klemperer, Klemens von. *German Resistance Against Hitler: The Search for Allies Abroad, 1938–1945*. New York: Oxford University Press, 1992.

Knightley, Phillip. *The Second Oldest Profession*. New York: Norton, 1987.

Lacher, Irene. "A Woman of Mystery: Espionage: Countess Aline Romanones." *Los Angeles Times*, March 10, 1991.

Ladd, James, et al. *Clandestine Warfare: Weapons and Equipment of the SOE and OSS*. London: Blandford, 1988.

La Farge, Henry, ed. *Lost Treasures of Europe*. New York: Pantheon Books, 1946.

Langelaan, George. *Knights of the Floating Silk*. London: Hutchinson, 1959.

Lassalle, Edmundo. *The Araucanians*. Pan American Union, with cooperation from the Office of the Coordinator of Inter-American Affairs, 1942.

———. "Argentina." *Higher Education in Latin America*. Pan American Union, 1943.

Leverkeuhn, Paul. *German Military Intelligence*. Trans. R. H. Stevens and Constantine FritzGibbon. New York: Praeger, 1954.

Lochery, Neill. *Lisbon: War in the Shadows of the City of Light, 1939–1945*. New York: Public Affairs, 2011.

Loftis, Larry. *CODE NAME: LISE—The True Story of the Woman Who Became WWII's Most Highly Decorated Spy*. New York: Gallery, 2019.

———. *Into the Lion's Mouth: The True Story of Dusko Popov—World War II Spy, Patriot, and the Real-Life Inspiration for James Bond*. New York: Berkley Caliber, 2016.

Longerich, Peter. *Heinrich Himmler*. Oxford: Oxford University Press, 2012.

Lorain, Pierre. *Clandestine Operations: The Arms and Techniques of the Resistance, 1941–1944*. New York: Macmillan, 1983.

Lorenz-Meyer, Martin. *Safehaven: The Allied Pursuit of Nazi Assets Abroad*. Columbia: University of Missouri Press, 2007.

Marks, Leo. *Between Silk and Cyanide*. New York: HarperCollins, 1998.

Masterman, J. C. *The Double-Cross System in the War of 1939 to 1945*. New Haven: Yale University Press, 1972.

Mateos, Josefina. "El Quexigal," Nuestro Rincón de Cebreros. http://nuestrorincondecebreros.es/pagina/6.html.

Mauch, Christof and Jeremiah Rierner. *The Shadow War Against Hitler: The Covert Operations of America's Wartime Secret Intelligence Service*. New York: Columbia University Press, 2002.

McConville, Mark, and Chris Summers. "The Jewish Crook Who Was Hitler's Top Smuggler for Stolen Loot." *Daily Mail*, June 23, 2016.

McDonald, Lawrence H. "The OSS and Its Records," *The Secrets War: The Office of Strategic Services in World War II*. Washington, DC: NARA, 1992.

McIntosh, Elizabeth P. *Sisterhood of Spies: The Women of the OSS*. Annapolis, MD: Naval Institute Press, 1998.

McLachlan, Donald. *Room 39: A Study in Naval Intelligence*. New York: Atheneum, 1968.

Michel, Henri. *The Shadow War: Resistance in Europe, 1939–1945*, trans. Richard Barry. New York: Harper & Row, 1972.

Miller, Francis Trevelyan. *The Complete History of World War II*. Chicago: Readers' Service Bureau, 1947.

Morgenthau, Henry Jr. "Concern of the United States over Enemy Attempts to Secrete Funds or Other Assets in Neutral Countries; Inception of the Safehaven Program." *Foreign Relations of the United States: Diplomatic Papers, 1944, General: Economic and Social Matters*, vol. 2.

Mosely, Leonard. *Dulles: A Biography of Eleanor, Allen, and John Foster Dulles and Their Family Network*. New York: Random House, 1978.

Mueller, Michael. *Nazi Spymaster: The Life and Death of Admiral Wilhelm Canaris*. New York, Skyhorse, 2017.

Muggeridge, Malcolm, ed. *Ciano's Diplomatic Papers*. London: Odhams Press, 1948.

"Nazi Gold in Spain in Reparations Pot." *New York Times*, December 26, 1945.

Nicholas, Lynn H. *The Rape of Europa: The Fate of Europe's Treasures in the Third Reich and the Second World War*. New York: Knopf, 1995.

O'Donnell, Patrick K. *Operatives, Spies, and Saboteurs: The Unknown Story of the Men and Women of World War II's OSS*. New York: Free Press, 2004.

Oleson, Peter C. "From Axis Surprises to Allied Victories: The Impact of Intelligence in World War II." *Guide to the Study of Intelligence*. Falls Church, VA: Association of Former Intelligence Officers, 2016.

O'Reilly, Bill. *Killing the SS: The Hunt for the Worst War Criminals in History*. New York: Henry Holt, 2018.

"Our Propaganda Gaining in Spain." *New York Times*, January 21, 1944.

Ousby, Ian. *Occupation: The Ordeal of France, 1940–1944*. New York: Cooper Square, 2000.

Pacheco, Cristina, ed. *Grande Hotel e Hotel Atlântico, Boletins de Alojamento de Estrangeiros: Boletins Individuais, 1939–1944.* Cascais: Câmara Municipal, 2005.

———. *Hotel Palácio, Estoril-Portugal: Boletins de Alojamento de Estrangeiros: Boletins Individuais, 1939–1944.* Cascais: Câmara Municipal, 2004.

Padfield, Peter. *Hess: Flight for the Führer.* London: Weidenfeld & Nicolson, 1991.

Paine, Lauran. *German Military Intelligence in World War II: The Abwehr.* New York: Stein and Day, 1984.

Payne, Stanley. *Franco and Hitler: Spain, Germany, and World War II.* New Haven: Yale University Press, 2008.

Pearson, John. *The Life of Ian Fleming.* New York: McGraw-Hill, 1966.

Philby, Kim. *My Silent War.* 1968. Reprint. New York: Modern Library, 2002.

Piedrahita, Jorge. "El Quexigal: Finca de Reyes y Nobles Desde Inmemorial." July 30, 2010. https://jorgepiedrahita.blogia.com/2010/073001-el -quexigal-finca-de-reyes-y-nobles-desde-inmemorial.php.

Plaut, James S. "Loot for the Master Race." *Atlantic*, September 1946.

Popov, Dusko. *Spy Counter-Spy.* New York: Grossett & Dunlap, 1974.

Pujol, Juan. *Operation Garbo.* New York: Pocket Books, 1987.

Reynolds, Michael. *Hemingway: The 1930s Through the Final Years.* New York: Norton, 2012.

Rigden, Denis. *How to Be a Spy: The World War II SOE Training Manual.* Dundurn, 2004.

Roberts, Sam. "Model, Countess, Author, Spy: Aline Griffith is Dead." *New York Times*, December 15, 2017.

Romanones, Aline. *The End of an Epoch.* Fundación Aline Condesa vda. De Romanones, 2015.

———. *The History of Pascualete: The Earth Rests Lightly.* Reprint. New York: Keedick Press, 1964. First published in Spanish as *The Story of Pascualete* by La Condesa de Quintanilla. London: John Murray, 1963.

———. "The OSS in Spain During World War II." *The Secrets War: The Office of Strategic Services in World War II.* Washington, DC: NARA, 1992.

———. *The Spy Went Dancing.* New York: Putnam, 1990.

———. *The Spy Wore Red.* New York: Random House, 1987.

———. *The Spy Wore Silk.* New York: Putnam, 1991.

———. *The Well-Mannered Assassin.* New York: Putnam, 1994.

Roon, Ger van. *German Resistance to Hitler: Count von Moltke and the Kreisau Circle.* New York: Van Nostrand Reinhold, 1971.

Roosevelt, Franklin D. *The Public Papers and Addresses of Franklin D. Roosevelt.* Ann Arbor: University of Michigan, 1950.

Roosevelt, Kermit. *The Overseas Targets: War Report of the Office of Strategic Services.* Vol. 2. New York: Walker, 1976.

———. *War Report of the OSS (Office of Strategic Services).* Vols.1–2. New York: Walker, 1976.

Rothfels, Hans. *The German Opposition to Hitler.* 1947. Reprint. Regnery, 1963.

Rudgers, David F. *Creating the Secret State: The Origins of the Central Intelligence Agency.* Lawrence: University Press of Kansas, 2000.

Rürup, Reinhard, ed. *Topography of Terror: Gestapo, SS and Reichssicherheitshauptamt on the "Prinz-Albrecht-Terrain": A Documentation.* Trans. Werner T. Angress. Berlin: Verlag Willmuth Arenhövel, 2006.

Schellenberg, Walter. *The Memoirs of Hitler's Spymaster.* 1956. Edited and translated by Louis Hagan. Reprint. London: Andre Deutsch, 2006.

"Secret Agents." *People,* June 7, 1982.

Sewell, Dennita. "Hattie Carnegie: 1886–1956." *The Encyclopedia of Jewish Women.* Jewish Women's Archive. https://jwa.org/encyclopedia/article/carnegie-hattie.

Sherry, Norman. *The Life of Graham Greene,* vol. 2. New York: Viking, 1994.

Shirer, William. *The Rise and Fall of the Third Reich.* New York: Simon & Schuster, 1960.

Smith, Bradley F. *The Shadow Warriors: O.S.S. and the Origins of the C.I.A.* New York: Basic Books, 1983.

Smith, R. Harris. *The OSS: The Secret History of America's First Central Intelligence Agency.* Guilford, CT: Lyons Press, 1972.

Smith, Walter. *Glimpses of Spain.* New York: Altamira, 1953.

"Spanish Put Guards at French Embassy." *New York Times,* June 24, 1945.

Speer, Albert. *Inside the Third Reich (Memoirs).* New York: Macmillan, 1970.

Srodes, James. *Allen Dulles: Master of Spies.* Washington, DC: Regnery, 1999.

Stafford, David. *Secret Agent: The True Story of the Covert War Against Hitler.* New York: Overlook Press, 2001.

Stettinius, Edward Jr. "Concern of the United States over Enemy Attempts to Secrete Funds or Other Assets in Neutral Countries; Implementation of the Safehaven Program," *Foreign Relations of the United States: Diplomatic Papers, 1945, General: Political and Economic Matters*, vol. 2.

———. "Concern of the United States over Enemy Attempts to Secrete Funds or Other Assets in Neutral Countries; Inception of the Safehaven Program," *Foreign Relations of the United States: Diplomatic Papers, 1945, General: Political and Economic Matters*, vol. 2.

———. "Interest of the United States in Measures for the Protection and Salvage of Artistic and Historical Monuments in War Areas," *Foreign Relations of the United States: Diplomatic Papers, 1945, General: Political and Economic Matters*, vol. 2.

———. "The Acting Secretary of State to the Ambassador in the United Kingdom" (requesting Safehaven compliance as condition precedent to trade with Spain), *Foreign Relations of the United States: Diplomatic Papers, 1945, General: Political and Economic Matters*, vol. 2.

Steury, Donald P. *The OSS and Project Safehaven: Tracking Nazi "Gold."* Washington, DC: Center for the Study of Intelligence, Central Intelligence Agency, 2007. https://www.cia.gov/library/center-for-the-study-of-intelligence/csi-publications/csi-studies/studies/summer00/art04.html.

Stevens, Donald G. "World War II Economic Warfare: The United States, Britain, and Portuguese Wolfram." *Historian* 61, no. 3, 1999.

Thomas, Gordon, and Greg Lewis. *Shadow Warriors of World War II: The Daring Women of the OSS and SOE*. Chicago: Chicago Review Press, 2017.

Thomas, Hugh. *The Spanish Civil War*. New York: Penguin, 1976.

"Thousand Nazi Agents in Spain, Data Reveal." *New York Times*, November 24, 1945.

Todd, Tank and James Webb. *Military Combat Masters of the 20th Century*. Morrisville, NC: Lulu.com, 2006.

Toland, John. *The Last 100 Days*. New York: Random House, 1966.

Trautman, James. *Pan American Clippers: The Golden Age of Flying Boats*. Erin, ON: Boston Mills Press, 2007.

Trippett, Frank. "Honoring the Loyalists." *Time*, June 9, 1986.

Troy, Thomas F. *Donovan and the CIA: A History of the Establishment of the Central Intelligence Agency*. Washington, DC: Center for the Study of Intelligence, Central Intelligence Agency, 1981. https://www.cia.gov/library/readingroom/document/cia-rdp90–00708r000600120001–0.

———. "Knifing of the OSS." *International Journal of Intelligence and Counterintelligence* 1, no. 3 (1986).

Waller, Douglas. *Wild Bill Donovan: The Spymaster Who Created the OSS and Modern American Espionage*. New York: Free Press, 2011.

Waller, John H. *The Unseen War in Europe: Espionage and Conspiracy in the Second World War*. New York: Random House, 1996.

Warlimont, Walter. *Inside Hitler's Headquarters*. 1962. Translated from German by R. H. Barry. Reprint. Toronto, ON: Presidio Press, 1991.

Warner, Michael. *The Creation of the Central Intelligence Group*. Washington, DC: Center for the Study of Intelligence, Central Intelligence Agency, 2007. https://www.cia.gov/library/center-for-the-study-of-intelligence /kent-csi/vol39no5/html/v39i5a13p.htm.

———. *The Office of Strategic Services: America's First Intelligence Agency*. Washington, DC: Center for the Study of Intelligence, Central Intelligence Agency, 2000. https://www.cia.gov/library/publications/intelli gence-history/oss.

Weber, Bruce. "Barnaby Conrad, Man of Many Hats and a Cape, Dies at 90." *New York Times*, February 16, 2013.

Weber, Ronald. *The Lisbon Route: Entry and Escape in Nazi Europe*. New York: Ivan R. Dee, 2011.

West, Nigel. *The A to Z of British Intelligence*. Plymouth, MA: Scarecrow Press, 2005.

———. *Counterfeit Spies*. New York: Little Brown, 1998.

———. *Historical Dictionary of Sexpionage*. Plymouth, MA: Scarecrow Press, 2009.

———. *Historical Dictionary of World War II Intelligence*. Plymouth, MA: Scarecrow Press, 2008.

———. *MI5: The True Story of the Most Secret Counterespionage Organization in the World*. New York: Stein and Day, 1982.

———. *MI6: British Secret Intelligence Service Operations, 1909–45*. London: Weidenfeld and Nicholson, 1983.

———. *A Thread of Deceit: Espionage Myths of World War II*. New York: Random House, 1985.

Whitney, Craig R. "Riviera Intrigue: With Everyone but Claude Rains." *New York Times*, August 16, 1999.

Wigg, Richard. *Churchill and Spain: The Survival of the Franco Regime, 1940–1945*. Eastbourne, UK: Sussex Academic Press, 2008.

Wighton, Charles, and Günter Peis. *Hitler's Spies and Saboteurs*. New York: Holt, Rinehart & Winston, 1958.

Winks, Robin W. *Cloak & Gown: Scholars in the Secret War, 1939–1961*. New York: HarperCollins, 1987.

———. "Getting the Right Stuff: FDR, Donovan, and the Quest for Professional Intelligence." *The Secrets War: The Office of Strategic Services in World War II*. Washington, DC: NARA, 1992.

Woodward, Sir Llewellyn, ed. *British Foreign Policy in the Second World War*, vols. 1–5. London: HMSO, 1970–1976.

Wylie, Neville, ed. *European Neutrals and Non-Belligerents During the Second World War*. Cambridge: Cambridge University Press, 2002.

Yglesias, Linda. "Elegance and Espionage: Aline, Countess of Romanones, Looks Back at Her Life as a Spy for the OSS in 'The Spy Wore Red.'" *New York Daily News*, May 10, 1987.

INDEX

Page numbers in *italics* refer to photographs.

A

ABC, 233

Ablege Kommandos, 67–68

"Abuelo," El, see Figueroa y Torres-
Sotomayor, Álvaro de

Abwehr, 25–26, 45, 47, 67, 68, 78,
80, 86–88, 99, 100, 121, 149,
156–57, 177, 292n, 307n

Agatha, Princess, *see* Maria Agatha,
Princess of Ratibor and Corvey

Agnelli, Gianni, 24

Air Force Department, 240

Albert Schweitzer Hospital, 264

Alfonso III, King, 46

Alfonso XIII, King, 24, 86

American Oil Control Commission,
33, 35, 44, 45, 51, 55–57, 72,
162, 226

Angustias, 104, 116, 117, 186–87,
206, 207, 213–14

Argentina, 45, 177, 205, 232, 233

Aristotle, 239

Arruza, Carlos, 136n

Arteaga, Casilda, xi, 95–100,
112–14, 162, 174, 178, 180,
181, 183, 194, 196, 197, 207

Arteaga, Nena, 99

art looting, 154, 155, 158, 169, 177,
205

Art Looting Investigation Unit
(ALIU), 155

Avila, Count of, 77

Ávila Camacho, Manuel, 179

B

Bacall, Lauren, 245

Bache & Co., 193, 194, 324n

Balenciaga, Cristóbal, xi, 73–74, 78,
159, 200–201, 225, 227, 233

Bañolas, 110

Barcelona, 72, 79–80, 110, 154,
174

INDEX

Bardot, Brigitte, 249
Beck, Ludwig, 88, 91, 91n, 92n
Beistegui, Carlos, 99–101, 179–80
Belmonte, Juan, 49–50, 119, 136n, 139, 177, *191*, 222
Belmonte, Juanito, xii, 50–54, 66–67, 76, 84–85, 98, 118–26, *120*, *125*, 127–31, 132–33, 139, 142–43, 151–53, 177, 181, 183–84, 197, 208–11, 222, 257, 311n, 315n
  Aline's "suit of lights" from, 50, *53*, 73
  death of, 257
Beneducci, Pierre de, 171
Benton, Kenneth, 45n
Berle, Adolf, 141–42
Bibra, Herbert von, 175
Biltmore Hotel, 9, 14, 36, 275n
blacklist, 160, 161, 164–66, 170
Blomberg, Werner von, 87, 88
Bock, Fedor von, 88, 89
Bogart, Humphrey, 245
Bonin, Bogislaw von, 91n
Botín, 85
Brauchitsch, Walther von, 88–89
Braunsdorf, Julius, 4, 272n
Brazil, 45
Breit, Harvey, 258
Britain, 59
  MI6 in, 17, 45n, 187n, 189, 193
  plot against Hitler thwarted by, 90–91
  Spain and, 44, 45
  Special Operations Executive in, 17, 79, 189, 193, 242, 243
British American Canadian Corporation (BACC), 188–89, 192–94, 199, 201, 204, 240, 266, 322n

British Security Coordination (BSC), 189, 193
Brockdorff-Ahlefeldt, Walter Graf von, 89
Brois, Monsieur, 179–80
Brown, Clarence, 60
Brüning, Heinrich, 87
bullfighting, xiii, 46–48, 54, 73, 84, 118–19, *120*, 137–38, 151, 176, 208–11, 222, 249, 255, 315n
  Aline's experience in the ring, 210–11, 212
  Conrad and, 137–39, 191, *191*, 210–11, 239, 257–59, 315n
  Joselito and, 49n, 119
  Juan Belmonte and, 49–50, 119, 136n, 139, *191*, 222
  Juanito Belmonte and, 50, 52–54, 76, 118–26, *120*, *125*, 127–31, 133, 139, 143, 151–52, 183, 208–11, 222, 257.
  Manolete and, xii, 54n, 119, *120*, 121–23, 139, 209–11, 228, 237–39
  Manolete's death in, 239, 257
  Miura bulls in, 124
Burial of the Count of Orgaz, The (El Greco), 74n, 112n
Burton, Richard, 249
Bussche-Ippenburg, Erich Freiherr von dem, 87
Butler, Richard Austen, 59

C
Cairo Conference, 150
Calviño, Mariano, 174
Cameron, Roberta, 141
Canaris, Constantin, xii, 99–101, 103–4, 309n

Canaris, Wilhelm, xii, 25–26, 86–89, 91, 92, 92n, 99, 121, 307n
Candelas, Luis, 85
Candotti, Bruce, 39
Capri, 234
Caraciollo, Princess, 234
Carlos IV, King, 84
Carnegie, Andrew, 7
Carnegie, Hattie, 6–8, 33, 35, 73, 147, 228
Carral, Magdalena, 252
Casey, William, xvi, 252
Casino Estoril, 41–43, 42
Casino Royale (Fleming), 42n
Catedral de Santa María, 139–40
Cecilia, 116–17, 206, 207, 213
Cervantes, Miguel de, 112
Cézanne, Paul, 177, 178
Chamberlain, Neville, 90
Chanel, Coco, 73n
Charles V, Holy Roman Emperor, 112
Chiang Kai-she, 150n
chicken feed (false, misleading, or late information), 151, 167
Choltitz, Dietrich von, 154
Churchill, Pamela, 234
Churchill, Peter, 107–11
Churchill, Winston, 150n, 173
Church of San Antonio de la Florida, 84
Church of San Fermín de los Navarros, 225, 228–29
CIA (Central Intelligence Agency), 240, 241, 242, 248, 252, 259, 260, 262, 333n
Aline's work for, 247–48
Ciano, Count, 234
Clay, Lucius, 243

coding and decoding, 31, 33, 45n, 63–64, 104, 140–42, 184
Colby, William, xvi
communism, communists, 25, 77, 113, 192, 194, 243
Conrad, Barnaby, xii, 137–42, 191, 191, 210–11, 239, 257–59, 315n
death of, 259
Cordoba, 227
Coward, Noël, 258
Crawford, Joan, 60
Crook, Compton, 21–22
Culbertson, Paul, 229
Czechoslovakia, Sudetenland in, 89, 90
Czernin, Hans, 203

D
Dalí, Salvador, 249
Death in the Afternoon (Hemingway), 137, 209
Defendu, 21
de la Renta, Oscar, 73
de Pombo, Ana, xii, 121, 147–49, 153, 156–57, 172
Dexter, Talbot C., 4
Dietrich, Marlene, 71
Dior, Christian, 73n
Disney, Roy, 66, 171, 263, 324n
Disney Company, 12, 27, 66, 70–72, 71, 79–80, 155, 171, 192, 262–63, 284n, 302n
Dodds-Parker, Douglas, 243
Dominguín, Luis Miguel, 136n, 238
Donovan, William, xi, 18, 32, 56, 187–89, 192, 242–43, 266, 322n
Don Quixote (Cervantes), 112

Dostoyevsky, Fyodor, 253–54
Dulles, Allen, 59, 299n
Dunev, Louise Marie, 156, *157*, 190–91, 259
Dunev, Robert, xi, 57–58, 62, *63*, 64, 68–69, 70n, 79, 86, 104, 117, 132, 149, 156, *157*, 184–86, 190–91, 203, 217, 240, 241, 242, 259–60, 264, 277n, 285n, 286n, 311n, 322n
death of, 260
Du Pont, Alfred V., 266
Du Pont family, 193

E
Eccles, David, 293n
Edelweiss, 74, 99
Eichmann, Adolf, 205
Eisenhower, Dwight D., 79, 169
El Greco, 74, 98, 112
El Quexigal, 95–102, *97*, 175, 176, 179–80, 207, 262
Erickson, Eric, 203
Ernst von Ratibor and Corvey, Prince, 160
Estoril, 40
Casino Estoril, 41–43, *42*
Palacio Hotel, 3–4, *4*, 40–43, *40*, *41*, 163, *163*, 172n, 199, 260, 271n, 272n, 318n
WonderBar, *42*, 43
Eyre, Consuelo, 160

F
Fairbairn, William, xii, 20–21, 104
Fairbairn-Sykes fighting knife, 20
Fakhry, Ahmed, 172, 260
Falange, 24, 58, 61, 174
falcatas, 112

Farm, The (OSS school), xvi, 2, 11–22, 285n
Aline's training at, 16–22, 23–24, 27–31, 35, 47, 78, 93, 188, 275n, 282n, 285n, 287n
models of German soldiers at, 16, *16*
Faulkner, William, 258
FBI (Federal Bureau of Investigation), 141
Fellgiebel, Erich, 92n
Ferrer, Mel, 248, 249
Figueras, 110
Figueroa, Luis, xv
Figueroa y Alonso-Martinez, Luis de (Count of Velayos; father of Aline's husband), xii, 131, 196, 202, 203, 204, 214–17, 233, 235, 236
death of, 250
Figueroa y Griffith, Álvaro (son), 246–47, *247*, 255
Figueroa y Griffith, Luis (son), 246–47, *247*
Figueroa y Griffith, Miguel (son), 246–47, *247*, 252
Figueroa y Perez de Guzman, Luis de (Count of Quintanilla and later of Romanones; husband of Aline), xii, xiv–xv, 99–102, 162, 174, 177–79, 180–81, 183–84, 194–98, 201–2, 203–8, 212–20, 233–37, 239–40, 248, *250, 251*
Aline's marriage to, 212–20, 221–29, 230–33, 254
children of, 246–47, *247*
death of, 253–54
honeymoon of, 228, *231*, 230–34, 244–46

as painter, 250–51, *250*
Pascualete estate of, 249
Pearl River visited by, 244–45
in Spanish Civil War, 235–37, 240, 245
Figueroa y Torres-Sotomayor, Álvaro de (Count of Romanones; grandfather of Aline's husband; "*El Abuelo*"), xii, 86, 217–19, 224, 230–31, 233, 246
death of, 250
fincas, 95
flamenco, 47–48, 249
Fleming, Ian, 4, 42n, 243
Flores, Lola, 47–48
Foreign Economic Administration (FEA), 154, 155, 185–86
Forgan, Russell, 242
Forte, Ralph, 92
Foster, Reginald C., 225n
France, 33, 90, 154
Marseille, 104, 105, 145–47, 150
Normandy landing in, 79, 145
Operation Anvil in, 33
Operation Dragoon in, 111, 145, 146, 150
Paris, *see* Paris
safe houses and escape lines between Spain and, 37, 56, 104, 110, 132, 136, 185
Franco, Francisco, 24–26, 44–45, 49, 55, 75n, 77, 113–14, 121, 129–30, 176, 293n
Hitler and, 206
French Cameroon, 206
Fritsch, Werner Freiherr von, 88
Fromm, Friedrich, 92n
Fürstenberg, Franz Egon Graf von, 60, 83, 172

Fürstenberg, Gloria Rubio von, xii, 60, 81–83, *82*, 85, 96, 99–102, 104, 120–21, 123, 146–49, 153, 155, 156–57, 163–64, 167, 172–74, 260–61
death of, 261
marriage to Fakhry, 172, 260
marriage to Fürstenberg, 60, 83, 164, 172
marriage to Guinness, 172n, 260–61
marriage to Scholtens, 164
at Palacio Hotel, 163, *163*, 260, 318n

G
Gabor, Eva, 258
Garbo, Greta, 60
Gardner, Ava, 73n, 245, 261
Gayle, Marsha, 251, *251*
Germany, 37, 87–92, 192, 243
Ablege Kommandos in, 67–68
Abwehr in, 25–26, 45, 47, 67, 68, 78, 80, 86–88, 99, 100, 121, 149, 156–57, 177, 292n, 307n
art looting and, 154, 155, 158, 169, 177, 205
blacklist for doing business with, 160, 161, 164–66, 170
Gestapo in, 45, 58–60, 67, 78, 86, 88, 89, 160, 161, 171, 173n, 175, 192
Italy and, 234
kidnappings and, 67–69, 123
Kriegsmarine in, 87
Luftwaffe in, 37, 87
postwar control of, 243
Reichswehr in, 87; *see also* Wehrmacht

Germany (*cont.*)
  Safehaven economic warfare
    against, 154, 155, 156–59,
    167–70, 174, 175, 178–80,
    183–85, 205
  Schutzstaffel (SS) in, 80, 87–89,
    91n
  Sicherheitsdienst (SD) in, 26n,
    45, 67, 88, 177
  South American flight of
    criminals from, 175, 177, 192,
    205
  Spain and, 24, 25, 44–45, 55, 67,
    206
  Sturm Abeilung (SA) in, 87,
    88
  surrender of, 169, 173, 174
  tensions between military and
    Nazi Party in, 87–91
  territorial expansion of, 88–90
  Wehrmacht in, 45, 60, 87, 87n,
    88, 91n
  Weimar Republic, 90
  see also Hitler, Adolf
Gestapo, 45, 58–60, 67, 78, 86, 88,
    89, 160, 161, 171, 173n, 175,
    192
Gibraltar, 37, 107, 206
Givenchy, Hubert de, 73
Gloria, *see* Fürstenberg, Gloria Rubio
    von
Godfrey, John, 243
Göring, Hermann, 58–59, 80, 83
Goya, Francisco, 74, 84, 177, 178
Griffith, Aline, *52, 232, 247, 250,*
    251
  apartment as safe house, 111
  arrest and imprisonment of, 134,
    135–37, 143, 314n
  birth of, 4

  books written by, xiv–xvii, 253–55
  in bullfighting ring, 210–11, 212
  BUTCH code name of, xv, 23, 56,
    276n, 282n, 283n
  childhood of, 5
  children of, 246–47, *247*
  CIA work of, 248
  death of, 255
  desire for involvement in war
    effort, 8, 32–33, 184
  engagement to Luis announced
    in *New York Times*, 225, 226,
    226
  first formal field report of, *168*
  honeymoon of, 228, *231*, 230–34,
    244–46
  honorary doctorate of, 252
  letter of recommendation from
    MacMillan, 192, *193*, 326n
  Luis's death and, 253–54
  marriage to Luis, 212–20, 221–29,
    230–33, 254
  microfilm assignment of, 132–34,
    135–36, 139–40, 142, 315n
  modeling of, 6–8, 35, 228
  Mount Saint Vincent attended
    by, 6, 252
  OSS oath of office of, 26–27, *26*,
    281n
  OSS recruitment of, 9–10,
    13–14
  OSS training at The Farm, 16–22,
    23–24, 27–31, 35, 47, 78, 93,
    188, 275n, 282n, 285n, 287n
  Pascualete estate of, 249, 253,
    254
  salaries of, 35, 78
  wedding of, 227–29, 230–31, *231,*
    232
Griffith, Bill, 228, 230

Griffith, Dexter, 6
Griffith, Tom, 6, 228
Gubbens, Colin, 243
Guinness, Gloria, *see* Fürstenberg,
   Gloria Rubio von
Guinness, Thomas Loel, 172n,
   260–61
Guzmán, Felix, 138

H
Halder, Franz, 89–91, 91n
Hambro, Charles, 189, 242, 243, 266
Hamilton, James, 11–13
Hammerstein, Kurt Freiherr von,
   87, 88
Hannibal, 112
Hase, Paul von, 89, 92n
Hay Adams Hotel, 14–15, 40, 277n
Hayes, Carlton, 44, 55n, 65–66,
   85–86, 154, 172–73, 176, 293n
Heinz, Friedrich Wilhelm, 89
Helldorf, Wolf Heinrich Graf von,
   89
Hemingway, Ernest, xiii, 50, 57,
   118–19, 137, 209, 255, 257,
   315n
Hepburn, Audrey, 73n, 245, 248–50
Herfurth, Otto, 92n
Heymann, Ernesto, 149
Himmler, Heinrich, 26, 58–60, 81,
   83, 86, 88, 91n, 121, 309n
HISMA, 177
Hitler, Adolf, 24, 25, 45, 55, 58, 59,
   87–92, 121, 154, 169, 185, 205,
   234
   Chamberlain's meeting with, 90
   Franco and, 206
   plots against, 26, 59, 88–92
   territorial expansion plans of,
      88–90

Hindenburg, Paul, 87
Hoare, Samuel, 59, 75, 76, 100
Hoepner, Erich, 89, 92n
Hohenlohe, Alfonso von, Prince, 96
Hohenlohe, Beatriz von, Princess, 96
Hohenlohe, Christian von, Prince, 96
Hohenlohe, Elizabeth von, Princess,
   96, 119, 120, 122
Hohenlohe, Maria Francisca von,
   Princess ("Pimpinela"), xii,
   95–99, 101, 119–22, 129, 130,
   162, 175–76, 309n
Hohenlohe, Max Emanuel von,
   Prince, 96
Hohenlohe, Maximilian Egon von,
   Prince, xii, 58–60, 95, 96, 99,
   156, 159, 160, 172, 175, 176,
   179, 185, 261–62, 264, 299n
   death of, 261
honor, 118
Horcher, Otto, 80
Horcher's, 80–83, *81,* 147, 162
Hotel Miramar, 142
Hôtel San Régis, 199–200, 202
House, Edward, 32

I
Inönü, Ismet, 150n
Irun, 206–7
Isabel, Duchess of Tamames, 227,
   230, 235
Italy
   Germany and, 234
   Rome, 230, *231,* 232–34

J
Japan, 43
   Pearl Harbor attacked by, 6
Jebsen, Johann "Johnny," 45n, 67–68,
   80n, 327n

Jodl, Alfred, 169
John J. Ryan & Sons, 188, 190, 194, 197, 198, 324n
Joint Chiefs of Staff, 65n
Joselito, 49n, 119
Juan, King, 233

K
Kaltenbrunner, Ernst, 26n
Kanō Jigorō, 21
Keitel, Wilhelm, 169
Kelly, David, 59
Kelly, Grace, 73n
Kennedy, Jacqueline, 73n
Kerr, Deborah, 245
Kesselring, Albert, 91n
Keswick, W. T., 243
kidnappings, 67–69, 123
Kluge, Günther von, 89, 92n
Kriegsmarine, 87

L
Laffittee, Julio, 163, 164
Lamborghini, Ferruccio, 124n
Lane, Jocelyn, 262
Lanza, Raimundo, 214–16, 234
Lassalle, Edmundo, xi, 11–13, 27, 66, 67, 70–77, 71, 79–83, 92, 95, 99, 129, 133, 147, 154, 155, 156–62, 164–66, 167–71, 173–74, 181–82, 185, 192, 199, 254, 262–64, 276n, 284n, 292n, 295n, 300n, 301n, 302n, 324n
  death of, 262, 263, 264
  marriage to Agatha, 199, 223, 223, 262–63, 330n
  marriage to Emilie, 174, 199, 262
Lassalle, Emilie, 174, 199, 262, 324n

Latin America, 12–13
Lazar, Hans, xii, 4, 60–61, 81–83, 82, 96, 99–102, 104, 147, 149, 156, 172, 192
League of Nations, 32
Lequerica, José Félix de, 75, 154
Lerma, Duke and Duchess of, 75, 177
Lhardy, 142–43
Liesau, Francisco, 170
Liesau, Franz, 160
Life, 249
Lindemann, Fritz, 92n
Linhoff, Guillermo, 170
Lisbon, 39–40, 42, 43, 70, 169, 231
List, Wilhelm, 89
Llambí, Benito, 205, 229, 230
Lozado, Enrique de, 13
Luftwaffe, 37, 87
Luis (Aline's husband), see Figueroa y Perez de Guzman, Luis de
Lyons, Leonard, 258

M
MacMillan, James H., xi, 37–41, 43, 48, 56, 159, 167, 168, 169, 170, 176, 177, 179, 185
  Aline recommended by, 192, 193, 326n
  Palacio registration of, 41
Madeleine, 111–12, 115, 116–18
Madrid, 43–48, 49–61, 64–67, 70–71, 77, 78–80, 104–5, 107, 111, 117, 156, 157, 159, 169, 184–86, 198, 205–8, 226, 237, 244
  Botín, 85
  Church of San Fermín de los Navarros, 225, 228–29

Horcher's, 80–83, *81*, 147, 162
Lhardy, 142–43
Palace Hotel, 46–47, 71, 74n, 78, 99, 146, 159
Ritz Hotel, 46, 78, 79
US embassy compound, 85–86
Maffitt, Edward, 229
Mahonesa, La, 54
Málaga, 132–34, 135–37, 139–40, 143
Mamal, Pepe, 173
Manolete, xii, 54n, 119, *120*, 121–23, 139, 209–11, 228, 237–38
death of, 239, 257
Manona Pignatelli, Princess, 234
Manstein, Erich von, 92
Marbella, 248, 261–62
Maria Agatha, Princess of Ratibor and Corvey, xii, 75, 76, 160–61, 164–66, 170, 174, 176, 192, 199, 223
Edmundo's marriage to, 199, 223, *223*, 262–63, 330n
Maria-Piedad de Iturbe, 96
Marks, John, 239
Marseille, 104, 105, 145–47, 150
Marta, 111–12, 115, 116–18
Marta Film, 170
Maxwell, Elsa, 240, 244
Mellon, William Larimer "Larry," Jr., xi, xvii, 37–41, 43, 48, 56, 111, 132, 136, 159, 169–71, 174, 175, 179, 185, 193, 242, 263–64, 266
death of, 264
Palacio registration of, *41*
MGM, 60
MI6, 17, 45n, 187n, 189, 193

Mimosa, Marquesa of Torrejón, 72–77
Montellano, Duke of, 86
Mount Saint Vincent, College of, 6, 252
Mueller, Heinrich, 175
Munich Agreement, 90–91
Munich Conference, 90
Murtra, Evarista, 167–68
Mussolini, Benito, 206n, 234
Mussolini, Eva, 234

N
National Military Establishment, 240
National Security Act, 240
Nehring, Helga, 205
New York Times articles
on Aline's engagement, 225, 226, *226*
on Aline's wedding, 231, *231*
on art exhibition, 251, *251*
on Conrad, 258
on Edmundo's marriage to Princess Agatha, 223, *223*, 330n
interview with Aline, 248–49
on Ryan's trip, 194, *195*
on World Commerce Corporation, 240–41, *241*, 242
Norman, Nancy, 263
Normandy landing, 79, 145
Notes from the Underground (Dostoyevsky), 253–54
Novak, Kim, 262

O
OAS (Organization of American States), 11

Oberkommando der Wehrmacht
(OKW), 88, 91n
see also Wehrmacht
OCIAA (Office for Inter-American
Affairs; formerly Office of
the Coordinator of Inter-
American Affairs, OIAA),
12–13, 275n
Oficina Tecnica, 160, 170
Ogilvy, David, 189
Oil Control Commission, 33, 35,
44, 45, 51, 55–57, 72, 162
Okie, John B. "Jack," 200, 203
Olbricht, Friedrich, 92n
Operation Anvil, 33
Operation Dragoon, 111, 145, 146,
150
Operation Safehaven, 154, 155,
156–59, 167–70, 174, 175,
178–80, 183–85, 205
Operation Willi, 123n
Ortega, Domingo, 136–37
OSS (Office of Strategic Services),
xiv–xvii, 11, 12, 18, 27, 33,
37, 117, 169, 174, 185–87,
189, 190, 192, 193, 199,
200, 221, 225–26, 240, 242,
248, 265–66, 287n, 326n,
333n
Aline recruited by, 9–10, 13–14
Aline's oath of office for, 26–27,
26, 281n
chains of agents and informants,
104–7, 105, 106, 185
escape plans for agents of, 64
Farm, see Farm, The
German invasion preparations for
agents of, 64–65
New York Times's outing of agents
in, 225n, 226

Safehaven and, 154, 155, 156–59,
167–70, 174, 175, 178–80,
183–85, 205
sections of, 18, 24, 32, 279n
State Department and, 173
termination of, 181, 184, 185, 187,
266
training at, 278n; see also Farm,
The
Oster, Hans, 88, 89, 91, 92n

P
Palace Hotel, 46–47, 71, 74n, 78,
99, 146, 159
Palacio Hotel, 3–4, 4, 40–43, 40,
41, 163, 163, 172n, 199, 260,
271n, 272n, 318n
Panama, 188
Pan American Union, 11–12
Pan American Yankee Clipper,
36–39, 38, 70n, 192, 199
Paris, 154, 197–202, 206
Hôtel San Régis, 199–200,
202
Pascualete, 249, 253, 254
Pasolé, 107–11
Pearl Harbor, attack on, 6
Pearl River, NY, 4–6, 52, 244–47,
272n
Pepper, John, 189, 242
Perón, Eva, 232–33
Perón, Juan, 205, 232
Peter II, King, 201–2
Philippines, 241, 242
Pierre, xi, 16, 21, 22, 29–31, 33–34,
94–95, 145–47, 150–51, 153,
155, 156, 167, 264–65
Pimpinela, see Maria Francesca von
Hohenlohe, Princess
Podevils, Hexe, 170–71

INDEX

Popov, Dusko, 42n, 45n, 67n, 80n, 292n, 315n, 327n
Porter, Amy, 7
portero, 78–79, 117
Portugal, 25, 43, 67, 70, 168–69, 265–66
   Estoril, *see* Estoril
   Lisbon, 39–40, 42, 43, 70, 169, *231*
   secret police in, 40
Prado, 46
Primate Cathedral of Saint Mary of Toledo, 112
Primer Plano, 70, *71*
Primo de Rivera, Miguel, 176, 177
pundonor, 118
Pyrenees, 104, 107–11, 132

Q
Queen Elizabeth, RMS, 244
Quintanilla, Count of, *see* Figueroa y Perez de Guzman, Luis de

R
Reagan, Ronald, 252
Reichswehr, 87
   see also Wehrmacht
Resistance, 18, 104, 107, 108, 111, 136
Rinehart, Patricia, 263
Ritz Hotel, 46, 78, 79
Rockefeller, John D., 12
Rockefeller, Nelson, 12, 275n
Röhm, Ernst, 87–88
Romans, 112
Rome, 230, *231*, 232–34
Rommel, Erwin, 91, 92n, 154n
Roosevelt, Archibald, 248
Roosevelt, Kermit, 173n

Roosevelt, Franklin D., 18n, 150n, 154, 173, 181, 275n
Rothschild, Guy de, 249
Rothschild, Marie-Hélène de, 249
Ruiz, Gonzalo, 74n
Rundstedt, Gerd von, 88, 89, 92
Russia, 25, 237, 243
Ryan, Frank T., xi, xv, 3–4, *4*, 13–15, 23–27, 29, 31–32, 35, 36, 64, 72, 169, 185–89, 190, 192–94, 197, 199–202, 203–5, 208, 213, 220, 221–22, 231, 240, 241, 242–43, 248, 251, 254, 264–67, 271n, 274n, 276n, 281n, 282n, 286n, 322n, 324n
   Aline's meeting of, 7–9
   death of, 267
   New York Times announcement of trip of, 194, *195*
Ryan, John, 188
Ryan & Sons, 188, 190, 194, 197, 198, 324n

S
Safehaven, 154, 155, 156–59, 167–70, 174, 175, 178–80, 183–85, 205
Salmini, John, 39
Saludos Amigos, 12n
San Fermín de los Navarros, 225, 228–29
Sangroniz, Señor, 233
Santo Domingo, Paquito, 176
Scheib, Hans, 170
Schellenberg, Walter, 26n, 58, 60, 83, 86, 91, 92, 121, 123, 129, 147, 149
Scholtens, Frank, 60, 164
Schoonmaker, Frank, 65–66
Schubach, Herr, 171

Schulenburg, Fritz-Dietlof Graf von der, 89
Schutzstaffel (SS), 80, 87–89, 91n
Schweitzer, Albert, 263
Schweitzer Hospital, 264
Sciolitti, Max, 147
Second Punic War, 112
Selborne, Lord, 243
Serpa Pinto, SS, 70n
sereno, 78–79, 84
Serrano-Suñer, Ramón, 58, 61
Seville Festival, 249
Shanghai Municipal Police, 20
Shepardson, Whitney, xi, 32–33, 266, 287n
  MacMillan's letter of recommendation of Aline to, 192, *193*, 326n
Sicherheitsdienst (SD), 26n, 45, 67, 88, 177
Sinatra, Frank, 245
Smith, Walter, 55–56, 296n
SOE (Special Operations Executive), 17, 79, 189, 193, 242, 243
South America, 175, 177, 192, 205
Spain, 23–26, 29, 31–33, 39, 44–48, 49–61, 64–67, 70, 79, 92, 206, 219, 249, 265–66
  Aline's transport to, 35–44, *36*, 70n
  Allied Mission in, 185
  American Oil Control Commission in, 33, 35, 44, 45, 51, 55–57, 72, 162, 226
  Barcelona, 72, 79–80, 110, 154, 174
  Britain and, 44, 45
  Civil War in, 24, 25, 60, 73, 113, 235–37, 240, 245

Cordoba, 227
  exchange rate and, 169–70
  Falange in, 24, 58, 61, 174
  Germany and, 24, 25, 44–45, 55, 67, 206
  Madrid, *see* Madrid
  Málaga, 132–34, 135–37, 139–40, 143
  Renaissance in, 73
  safe houses and escape lines between France and, 37, 56, 104, 110, 132, 136, 185
  Toledo, 112–14
spies, xiii–xiv
Spies, Adrian, 137, 138
Stalin, Joseph, 243, 266
Starry Night, The (van Gogh), 112n
State Department, 13, 32, 35, 65, 65n, 140, 155, 170, 172–73, 188, 287n
  OSS and, 173
Steinbeck, John, 131, 258
Stephenson, William, 187n, 189, 192, 242–43, 266, 322n
Stettinius, Edward, 189, 193, 266
Stief, Hellmuth, 92n
Stork Club, 34
Stülpnagel, Karl-Heinrich von, 89, 91n, 92n
Sturm Abeilung (SA), 87, 88
Suárez, Nacho, 137–38
Sudetenland, Czechoslovakia, 89, 90
Sueca, Duchess of, 75, 76
Switzerland, 205

T
Taylor, Elizabeth, 249
Teatro de la Zarzuela, 47, 50
Thiele, Fritz, 92n

Thomas, H. Gregory, xi, xvi, 37,
    55n, 56, 57, 59, 60, 62, 64, 72,
    78, 80, 81, 83–86, 116–17, 132,
    145–47, 149, 150–51, 154–55,
    156–59, 163, 165, 167–69, 184,
    185, 265, 302n, 315n
  death of, 265
Thome, SS, 70
Thuengen, Karl von, 92n
Time, 49
Toledo, 112–14
Tomlinson, Mr., 8–9, 274n
Torlonia, Prince and Princess of, 233
Torrejón, Mimosa, 99
Toulouse, 104
Tresckow, Henning von, 92n
Truman, Harry, 173, 181, 184, 218,
    266
Turpin, Robert, 56–57

U
US Forces in Europe, 243

V
Vanderbilt, William, 277n
van Gogh, Vincent, 112n
Vanity Fair, 248
Vascones, 207
Velázquez, Diego, 73
Versailles Peace Conference, 32
Victoria Eugenia, Queen, 55
View of Toledo (El Greco), 112n
Villa Rosa, 180
Vogue, 200

W
Wagner, Eduard, 92n
Waldorf-Astoria, 39

Wallace, Henry A., 13
Walt Disney Company, 12, 27, 66,
    70–72, *71*, 79–80, 155, 171,
    192, 262–63, 284n, 302n
Warner, Jack, 244, 245
Wehrmacht, 45, 60, 87, 87n, 88, 91n
  Oberkommando der Wehrmacht
    (OKW), 88, 91n
West, Nigel, xv–xvi
Wilson, Woodrow, 32
Windsor, Duchess of, 244, 245, 248,
    252–53
Windsor, Duke of, 123, 244, 248,
    253
Witzleben, Erwin von, 88, 89, 92n
wolframite, 25, 45
WonderBar, *42*, 43
World Commerce Corporation,
    194, 222, 225, 233, 240–41,
    241, 242–43, 248, 254, 266,
    322n
World War I, 32
World War II, 6, 7
  Aline's desire for involvement in,
    8, 32–33, 184
  end of, in Europe, 169, 173,
    174
  Normandy landing, 79, 145
  Pearl Harbor attack, 6

Y
Yankee Clipper, 36–39, *38*, 70n, 192,
    199
Yebes, Count and Countess of, 75,
    99

Z
Zurich, 203–4, 206, 208, 213

THE
PRINCESS
SPY

LARRY LOFTIS

This reading group guide for **THE PRINCESS SPY** includes an introduction, discussion questions, ideas for enhancing your book club, and a Q&A with author **Larry Loftis**. The suggested questions are intended to help your reading group find new and interesting angles and topics for your discussion. We hope that these ideas will enrich your conversation and increase your enjoyment of the book.

Introduction

In 1941, Aline Griffith, born and raised in a quiet New York suburb, is a college graduate desperate to aid in the war effort as World War II rages across Europe. Although she studied Spanish and French, she has hardly left New York and doesn't know where to begin as a bright-eyed young woman whose only career experience is modeling clothes.

Aline's life changes when she meets a man named Frank Ryan and reveals her love of adventure and her desire to do her part for her country. Within a few weeks, he recruits her to join the Office of Strategic Services—the forerunner of the CIA. With a code name and expert training under her belt, she is sent to Spain to be a coder, but is soon given the additional assignment of infiltrating the upper echelons of society, mingling with high-ranking officials, diplomats, and titled Europeans, any of whom could be an enemy agent. Against this glamorous backdrop of galas and dinner parties, she recruits subagents and engages in deep-cover espionage to counter Nazi tactics in Madrid.

Even after falling in love with and marrying the Count of Romanones, one of the wealthiest men in Spain, Aline secretly continues her covert activities, taking special assignments when abroad that would benefit from her impeccable pedigree and social connections. Full of adventure and danger, *The Princess Spy* is the story of a woman who risked everything to serve her country.

Topics & Questions for Discussion

1. When Aline meets Frank Ryan on a blind date at a friend's house, she doesn't know that he works for the Office of Strategic Services, an intelligence operation that served as the forerunner to the CIA. She tells him she wants to get into the war, stating, "I love adventure. I like taking risks. All the men I know are eager to get over there. Why should it seem strange that a woman wants to also?" (8). How does this chance encounter with Ryan influence the rest of her life? What do you believe he saw in her then and later that made him think she had a talent for intelligence work?

2. Discuss the role of Spain during World War II. Why was Spain critical to both Allied and Axis powers during the war, despite its purported neutrality? Why was the Iberian Peninsula (and the cities of Madrid and Lisbon in particular) such a hub for intelligence operations?

3. Aline's flight on the Yankee Clipper reveals how important the OSS felt she was to their operation in Madrid. Why do you think that was the case?

4. The OSS and the American Embassy in Spain had a frosty relationship throughout this period, especially given Ambassador Hayes's disdain for the OSS (65). What reasons did both organizations have for this animosity? Did the lack of cooperation hinder American efforts in Spain? During the time, espionage was a crime in Spain that could carry a sentence of death. What effect did this have on the relationships between the OSS, the American Embassy, and the Spanish authorities?

5. Aline frequently mixes her social life and espionage work, attending parties held by the Marquesa of Torrejón in Madrid, the Count of Avila in Toledo, and the Hohenlohe family in Escorial. How did the qualities that made her a welcome guest also make her a capable spy? What personal advantages might she have had that made her well-suited for the role? And how do these relationships foreshadow her many friendships later on with aristocrats, political figures, and Hollywood stars?

6. Bullfighting and flamenco seem to play a central role in Aline's world of espionage, and she had a close relationship with two bullfighters (Juanito Belmonte and Manolete). She also took a turn in the ring with a young heifer, a dangerous activity for anyone. Discuss the relationship of bullfighting, flamenco, and espionage, and how Aline's exposure to all three affected and reflected her decision-making and bravery.

7. When Aline returns from Toledo she finds Marta, the young woman she had been harboring, killed by a gunshot wound to the head while sleeping in Aline's bed. How does Marta's killing reflect the real dangers of Aline's work?

8. Aline frequently believes she is being followed. Does her enthusiasm for espionage overshadow concerns for her personal safety? Do you think she was well-prepared for her job in Spain?

9. The realization that Ana de Pombo's salon functioned as a letter box is a turning point in Aline's career with the OSS, although it was "still conjecture at this point and she wasn't actually a field agent" (149). Was it Aline's training at The Farm that led her to act and think as a field agent at this point, her personality, or both?

10. Toward the end of the war, Aline works closely with Edmundo, whose intention is to find "an aristocratic wife with an impressive title and bank account" (171). How do Aline and Edmundo's romantic and social lives mix and diverge? How do they compare with the usual expectations of spies?

11. When Aline tells her husband about her espionage work during the war, he replies incredulously with "You, a spy!" (226). Why does he find this unbelievable? Is his disbelief a testament to Aline's training to disguise her work, or perhaps due more to Aline's socialite personality, or her husband's own upbringing and understanding of women's roles?

12. Macmillan notes that Aline had "a special aptitude for intelligence work," including "an unusual sense of the importance of security" (192). How do you think Aline acquired this sense? Or was it something innate?

13. In a book that leaves many mysteries, one of the largest and most personal is the identity of Pierre. Who do you think he was? Which side do you believe he was on? And what about World Commerce Corporation? Do you think it conducted espionage, or was it merely a business organization? Could it have conducted both?

Enhance Your Book Club

1. Get out a map of Spain and plot the places Aline visited or mentioned, including Escorial, Toledo, Malaga, and Irun. Have members of your group research each of these towns and report any interesting discoveries about their history.

2. Read Larry Loftis's previous book *Code Name: Lise* and discuss the similarities and differences between the story of Odette Sansom and Aline Griffith.

For more information and research, visit the
author's website at larryloftis.com.

Author Q&A

Q: What drew you to the story of Aline Griffith? How did you know she would become the focus of your next book?

A: As I note in the preface, a friend mentioned her to me with the caveat that much in her story might be untrue. He was right. Of the nine murders/killings mentioned in her first two espionage memoirs (*The Spy Wore Red* and *The Spy Went Dancing*), eight were untrue. A real turning point for me was the murder of Marta, which—like the other killings Aline wrote about—is not mentioned in the OSS files. However, during my research I met the sons of Aline's code room partner, Robert Dunev, and they gave me a copy of their father's unpublished memoir, *A Spy Reminisces*. In this document (prepared only for the Dunev family) Robert mentions, "the night I removed a body from Aline's apartment." *Bingo!*, I thought at the time. With my background as a lawyer, I knew that this was highly credible evidence since Dunev was an eyewitness and had no potential conflicts of interest (such as making money on a book).

Since I write nonfiction thrillers, I knew that I had at least one frightening event to include in the book, and now had to dig in. A trip to the National Archives to review the OSS files, along with materials from other primary sources, allowed me to include everything you find in the book.

Q: Your previous books, *Into the Lion's Mouth* and *Code Name: Lise*, were also about World War II spies. The former became an international bestseller, and the latter a national bestseller. Why do you think readers are hungry for these World War II espionage stories?

A: I think these stories are popular for a number of reasons. First, World War II was one of the only truly worldwide events in history, and readers never seem to tire of learning more about it. Look at the popularity of movies like *Saving Private Ryan* and *Dunkirk*, and the never-ending supply of books about D-Day. Second, with the creation of James Bond, Ian Fleming (and Sean Connery) made espionage "cool" and exciting, thus spawning countless books and movies in the genre. Third, I only write nonfiction stories that have enough exciting events and suspense to quality as legitimate thrillers, and I think readers are drawn to this unusual combination.

Ironically, the subject of *Into the Lion's Mouth*, Dusko Popov, was Ian Fleming's inspiration for Bond, and Aline Griffith was a real-life female version of Bond. In fact, they were both trained in close combat (including knife fighting) by the same man, the legendary William Fairbairn.

Q: Tell us a little about your research process. Knowing about the embellishments Aline created in her own memoirs, how did you establish the veracity of documents and stories and then weave them into a compelling narrative?

A: With all of my books, I start with any autobiography (Dusko Popov's *Spy/Counter-Spy*, Aline's five books) or biographies

(Russell Miller's of Popov, Jerrard Tickell's of Odette Sansom) of my subject. After that I go to the pertinent archive files (UK and US for Popov, UK for Sansom, US for Aline), which are the most reliable and the most credible under evidentiary rules. For Aline, these were the OSS Madrid files. After pouring through all of the memos, agent reports, and letters in these files I can generally determine the errors contained in the autobiographies or biographies, and in some cases discover what was simply invented. A quick illustration would be the two operations Aline claimed to have worked on: "Operation Bullfight" and "Operation Safehaven." The former Aline invented, but the latter was very much true, and she played a key role in it, second only to Edmundo Lassalle.

In my endnotes, I always explain these discrepancies or embellishments. Popov, for example, had written that MI5 had given him a small banquet in Lisbon "as the bombs of D-Day were falling." His case officer, however, who was at the event, put a memo in the MI5 file at the time showing that the date was actually April 26, 1944. Since Popov was writing thirty years later, the error on dates is understandable.

A more serious error, of course, is when spies simply make up events. In *The Spy Wore Red*, for example, Aline writes that she witnessed the murder of an OSS informant at Casino Estoril (Lisbon, Portugal) on Christmas Day 1943, and that the murderer was her OSS partner, Edmundo Lassalle. The problem with this story is that Aline and Edmundo were both in the US at this time. Aline would not arrive in Lisbon (OSS files and hotel records show) until February 8, 1944, and Edmundo would not arrive until June 1, 1944 (leaving from Philadelphia aboard the *SS Thoma* on May 13). This is why I often include copies of hotel registrations in my books (showing Popov's and Ian Fleming's in *Into the Lion's Mouth*, and Aline's in *The Princess Spy*).

After reviewing archive files I then fill in gaps with details gleaned from primary sources (e.g. memoirs of Robert Dunev, Ambassador Carlton Hayes, Barnaby Conrad, Walter Smith, Edmundo Lassalle's daughter, etc.).

I then weave the story into a compelling narrative by preparing a calendar of what happened on each day throughout the entire time frame, which serves as my outline. I have to follow the calendar in setting out the story, of course, but I get to pick where and how I end chapters (with cliffhangers!).

Q: What was the most intriguing bit of information you uncovered in your research?

A: Without question, World Commerce Corporation. This was the mysterious company that apparently bridged the gap between closure of the OSS on August 15, 1945, and the commencement of the CIA on September 18, 1947.

I was also amazed to discover Barnaby Conrad's background in coding, his rise to a diplomatic post, and his activities as a bullfighter.

Q: There are many mysteries still unanswered by the end of the book—Marta's death, Frank Ryan's postwar business, Pierre's identity. Are there any you wish you had visible trails or conclusions?

A: This is the ongoing problem of investigating historical events: sometimes the evidence is unclear or missing. With some events, such as Marta's murder, you simply have to apply logic. As I point out in the text, Marta had already killed two civil guards and was at risk of being shot upon capture. Aline's cover had not been broken, and even if it had, the Germans would have been more likely to take her prisoner than shoot her. So the only logical explanation is that the killer was Spanish.

In some cases, like Frank Ryan's World Commerce Corporation, there is evidence on both sides. Tax records show that WCC certainly conducted normal business operations, but on the flip side, the entity was founded by and stacked with espionage officers from the OSS, BSC, MI6, and SOE. That's all we really know so my job is to give all of the dots the records provide, and then let the readers decide where and how to connect them.

With Pierre, as I point out at the end of the book, there's simply no traceable evidence without his real name or real code name. So I made a judgment call on each bit of dialogue or each scene Aline claimed to have had with him, deleting some (where it was impossible or highly unlikely) and keeping some.

I would love to see all CIA records, but in my experience that organization will release nothing (even under the FOIA).

Q: Which real-life character in the book do you identify with most and why?

A: Barnaby Conrad, for sure. Like Conrad, I have an unquenchable thirst for knowledge, adventure, new challenges, and a bit of danger now and then. I was a corporate lawyer for many years but never really felt challenged (except in law school) or fulfilled in that career. If you recall from the story, Conrad became a vice-consul because he was bored to tears as a coder in Washington. I could relate.

Recall, too, that Conrad had gone to Mexico for a little adventure, and to learn Spanish. I have gone to Colombia many times for adventure, to brush up on my Spanish as well.

Then the bulls. Conrad, you remember, was a bullfighter. Growing up in Texas, I went to many rodeos and know well the ferocity of these beasts. And just as Conrad (with no prior training) jumped the fence to fight a bull, I (with no prior training) rode a massive, nasty bull in a rodeo in Beaumont. Fortunately, we both escaped our adventures uninjured, but I learned firsthand that a bull can toss you a country mile. And remember that scene with Juanito Belmonte being launched out of his shoes? The same happened to me that night, as my boots were halfway off when I hit the ground.

Q: You write beautifully about bullfighting, a sport little known in the US. Is this a particular interest of yours? What drew you to the subject matter?

A: Thank you. Part of it was my connection to Barnaby Conrad, as explained above. Like Conrad, I had been drawn to bullfighting by reading Ernest Hemingway's *Death in the Afternoon*. And because bullfighting played such an important role in Aline's story, I felt I had to be somewhat of an expert on it. So in addition to Hemingway's book, I read three of Conrad's bullfighting books: *Matador*, *La Fiesta Brava*, and *Fun While it Lasted*. It was his bullfighting books that propelled Conrad's writing career, eventually leading him to found the Santa Barbara Writers Conference.

Q: And, just for fun: Aline's code name was BUTCH. If you were able to choose a code name for yourself, what would it be?

A: Ha! Well, I queried my Facebook (or was it Instagram?) followers about a year ago with that very question (what my code name should be) and two people came up with a name I had thought of as well: BARRISTER. So with a nod to my British legal colleagues, I guess that shoe fits.